TRANSATLANTIC POLICYMAKING IN AN AGE OF AUSTERITY

T0346624

American Governance and Public Policy series

SERIES EDITOR: BARRY RABE, UNIVERSITY OF MICHIGAN

TRANSATLANTIC POLICYMAKING IN AN AGE OF AUSTERITY

DIVERSITY AND DRIFT

MARTIN A. LEVIN AND
MARTIN SHAPIRO

Editors

GEORGETOWN UNIVERSITY PRESS
Washington, D.C.

Georgetown University Press, Washington, D.C.
© 2004 by Georgetown University Press. All rights reserved.
Printed in the United States of America.

10 9 8 7 6 5 4 3 2 1 2004

This book is printed on acid-free paper meeting the requirements of the American
National Standard for Permanence in Paper for Printed Library Materials.

Chapter 6 by David Vogel was previously published as "The Hare and the Tortoise
Revisited: The New Politics of Consumer and Environmental Regulation in Europe," in
the *British Journal of Political Science* 33 (2003):557–80. It is reprinted with permission
of Cambridge University Press.

Library of Congress Cataloging-in-Publication Data

Transatlantic policymaking in an age of austerity : diversity and drift / Martin A. Levin
and Martin Shapiro, editors.
    p. cm. — (American governance and public policy series)
    Includes bibliographical references and index.
    ISBN 1-58901-031-0 (pbk. : alk. paper)
  1. Social policy—Case studies. 2. Economic policy—Case studies. 3. United
States—Social policy—1993– 4. United States—Economic policy—1993–2001.
5. United States—Economic policy—2001– 6. Europe—Social policy. 7. Europe—
Economic policy I. Levin, Martin A. II. Shapiro, Martin M. III. American
governance and public policy.
    HN17.5.T717 2004
    361.6'1'0973—dc22   2004005620

CONTENTS

FIGURES AND TABLES

FIGURES

TABLES

PREFACE

Transatlantic Policymaking in an Age of Austerity compares policymaking across a broad spectrum of regulatory and social welfare policies in several European and North American nations in areas ranging from health care policy to corporate governance, from environmental regulation to management reforms.

Political leaders need to win elections to stay in office. But this often conflicts with choosing the most effective policy solution. Financial, cognitive, and political constraints are especially acute in this new century's age of austerity: On both sides of the Atlantic, parties are weaker, more evenly divided, and more competitive. This results in more frequent alternations in power, with a more active and competitive struggle to win over the marginal voter.

The sometimes-unspoken background of all of this book's policy studies is a prototypical electoral situation: On both sides of the Atlantic in these closely contested elections, parties of the left typically have moved toward the center, especially acknowledging the virtues of free markets. Parties of the right, mindful of the huge number of voters in the middle both wedded to existing entitlements and favorably inclined toward further risk regulation, have also moved to the center and acknowledged the welfare state, albeit a constrained one. This delicate electoral balance is one factor that counsels against bold policy strokes. Less innovative and more moderate policies tend to be the result.

Thus, during this period, policy movement is as often adrift as it is a bold march forward: The public sector moves only very sluggishly and reactively, or not at all rather than by taking major steps forward. Much policymaking moves by default to the private sector. But the drift and undeveloped policy initiatives and reforms in many of the areas we analyze in this book are not the result of incompetent or weak policymakers. Policymakers must deal not only with delicate electoral balancing, but also with complex and difficult policy choices. It's not that policymakers can't get their act together; rather it is that, in addition to facing the financial and political constraints just noted, there are also cognitive ones. Policymakers are not sure which acts are the right ones. Thus, lack of policy action also seems to stem in part from an uncertainty about what to do.

The appeal of markets on the one hand, and welfare and risk reduction on the other, are factors common to the countries studied, as are electoral pressures, severe financial constraints, and the perception that there are few quick and easy policy fixes. The broad contours of policy outcomes are also shared. Those outcomes tend toward incremental change, drift, and very often "reform without change and change without reform." Within these common contours, however, there is significant cross-national variation. This variation results from the mediation of common pressures through national policymaking processes and policy starting points.

Where you end up in policymaking is partially determined by where you begin and how you make your policy choices. Because different countries start in somewhat different places and employ somewhat different modes of policymaking, they follow somewhat diverging paths of policy development. With country-by-country variation, this path dependency is a highly contingent one, with many unanticipated byways and paths not taken—some unfinished, others not attempted. Ultimately, our story is one of varying hesitations and small victories rather than a common march to glory.

Research and writing, like most pursuits, are best done in community. Our participation in several fine research communities has been crucial to the development of *Transatlantic Policymaking*. This book began in the stimulating environment of the Gordon Public Policy Center. The newer community of the project titled "The New Politics of Public Policy" provided an additional layer of collaboration. The authors created an interactive conversation from which we all have learned much. Their creative feedback through the long process of preliminary seminars, drafts, conference papers, and then draft chapters produced an illuminating dialogue that broadened our thinking. Through this process, a series of initially individual works by many authors became a book with coherent themes, arguments, and conclusions. We are grateful to them for making this a rich product and a stimulating journey.

An effort of this type also involves the administrative support of many individuals. We had the fine assistance of the Gordon Center's energetic staff: Gila Ashtor, Brian Schon, Kelly Baker, Linda Boothroyd, and Rosanne Colocouris. Throughout the process, Sarah Orzalli of Brandeis provided excellent editorial aid. Barry Hayes and the staff of the Brandeis Printing Center gave us efficient service time and again. Eve Kitchen provided strong support in moving the project ahead and excellent insights on our writing in this book as she has done so often for our previous projects. Paul Pierson and Peter Hall have been good friends and colleagues; their own work helped and inspired us for this book and earlier ones.

We appreciate the intelligent and well-managed editorial process provided by Georgetown University Press, led by Gail Grella, an understanding and intelligent editor who was particularly helpful in navigating the occasional obstacles that arise in any collaborative project.

We appreciate the material and personal support of Cookie and Malcolm Kates, dedicated members of the Gordon Center board. Of course, the trustees of the Gordon Foundation of Chicago—John Adelsdorf, Sandy Bank, Robert Green, and David Silberberg—deserve special thanks for their intellectual interest and personal support of this project.

INTRODUCTION

Diversity and Drift in an Age of Austerity

LITERARY CRITICS OFTEN ASK TWO QUESTIONS: FIRST, WHAT HAPPENS IN THE STORY; second, and more significantly, what is the story about? As to the first, *Transatlantic Policymaking in an Age of Austerity* compares policymaking across a broad range of social welfare and regulatory policies in several European and North American nations. Individual chapters include analyses of health care policy, pensions, and labor market activation; immigration and disability policy; risk regulation; environmental regulation; corporate governance; and management reforms.

What is *Transatlantic Policymaking in an Age of Austerity* about? Common causes on both sides of the Atlantic that lead to a range of nationally path-dependent effects. But it is a highly contingent path dependency, with many unanticipated byways and paths not taken—some unfinished, others not attempted. Movement down the path is as often drift as it is a bold march forward. Thus, the policy outputs are often characterized by a slow yielding to circumstances and incremental change.

The particular direction of this drift and the paths and byways taken are shaped and determined by the political dynamics at hand. These cluster around the electoral imperative (especially the search for marginal voters in highly competitive party systems) and budgetary austerity pressures. That the movement down the path is often drift reflects the era's austerity and governments' reduced ability to confer benefits on citizens: a time in which policymakers search for alternatives to the heroic state—policies "on the cheap" such as off-budget items like regulations and highly symbolic low-cost ones like management reforms.

Transatlantic Policymaking in an Age of Austerity is about the determinants of public policy. Like our two earlier books—The *New Politics of Public Policy* and *Seeking the Center*—it is explicitly designed to integrate policy and political process studies. Our analysis comparatively describes what happened in several nations' policymaking and explains why it happened by examining the political dynamics of what these governments do. Indeed, one factor facilitating transatlantic analysis is that electoral politics on both sides of the Atlantic typically involve closely contested elections in which parties of the left acknowledge the virtues of free markets and parties of the right acknowledge the virtues of the welfare state. Thus, this book explores the realm of that crucial, though rarely considered, connection between politics and policymaking.

As we suggested in these earlier volumes, it is no mean feat to push political people toward seeing the policy outputs of the institutions, processes, and behaviors they study as key to understanding these institutions. As Shapiro's chapter argues, "In spite of many years of urging by people inside and outside their fields, it is still the rare American Congress specialist who looks at congressional outputs with anything like the care he or she expends on Congressional inputs and throughputs." This book's authors are primarily policy people incorporating political stories. But their concentration on politics is such that they show how analyzing policy outputs illuminates our understanding of political dynamics.

Like our earlier books, this one restores the politics of policymaking to the forefront of the political science agenda. Indeed, separating politics and policy has obscured a pattern found in both this book and its immediate predecessor: competitive elections and even highly partisan ones do not necessarily mean a policy deadlock. *Seeking the Center* found that, in the 1990s, partisan electoral competition in the United States resulted in modest policies rather than stalemate. In *Transatlantic Policymaking*, we found that at the turn of the new century, on both sides of the Atlantic, the policy products of highly competitive elections were policies with relatively little innovation and policy movement.

COMMON CHALLENGES AND DIFFERING POLICYMAKING PROCESSES AND OUTPUTS: PATH DEPENDENCY, DRIFT, AND THE SHIFTING LOCUS OF DECISION MAKING

The transatlantic policymaking analyzed here is characterized by broad common causes and pressures facing both the United States and Western European nations. These include common but differentially felt economic and demographic forces such as declining worker-to-pensioner ratios, external immigration pressures, fiscal austerity pressures from both slower economic growth and political constraints, and international economic competition.

These pressures are mediated simultaneously through three sets of differing factors: national differences in general political structure, national differences in the particular decision-making process of a particular policy area, and the particular differences in the initial substance of each policy before the process of change began. Often there is the persistence of divergence in particular transatlantic policies. Yet at the most general level, the transatlantic politics of policymaking in these chapters is commonly characterized more by drift than dramatic innovation. Finally, the shifting of the locus of decision making—downward and outward, as well as upward—is often in evidence in these chapters.

This mediation through differing national policymaking processes and policy starting points is exemplified in Hacker's chapter. In all the health care systems that he examined, the collision between rising costs and limited resources generated cost-containment outcomes, but differing outcomes depending on differing national health policymaking processes and previous health care practices.

Weaver found a broad commonality of policy agendas for public pension reforms across nations. This is generated by a common set of economic and demographic forces, especially austerity constraints. But national differences in preexisting pension regimes shape all the countries in his broad study and produce major differences in pension retrenchment policies: "Wealthy industrialized countries have all built even their restructuring reforms on the foundations of their current systems."

POLITICAL DYNAMICS: ELECTORAL IMPERATIVES AND BUDGETARY AUSTERITY

These broad common pressures may be necessary for producing these patterns, but they are not sufficient. They are only one element in the policymaking process. If these pressures were determinative, then there would be much larger changes, and they would tend to be much more similar across nations. Because these common pressures typically bring about only small policy changes from dissimilar policy starting points, large national variations continue to exist in the policy outcomes we describe. Moreover, national differences in political institutions and processes mean that even what changes there are often run in different directions and dimensions.

While differing in substance, these political dynamics often cluster around the electoral imperative, especially the search for the marginal voter in highly competitive party systems and sensitivity to blame avoidance in a veto-ridden policymaking process. In a period of budgetary austerity and low trust in government, electoral volatility is on every policymaker's mind. In this context, policymakers find that a low-visibility setting often facilitates passing policies. On both sides of the Atlantic, as freer markets generate particular harms for which politicians will be held electorally responsible, they seek to respond and we experience "freer markets but more rules."

On both sides of the Atlantic, too, a central political issue becomes the appropriate public–private sector mix in the provision of benefits and goods and services, although conclusions about what mix is appropriate tend to vary widely from country to country. In the following sections we turn to more detailed descriptions of these policymaking patterns and the political dynamics that produce this policy variation.

A CONTINGENT PATH DEPENDENCY

Electoral blockages are perhaps the most significant factors leading to "paths not taken." As the Hacker and Cioffi chapters each show, electoral blockages in the United States resulted in the failure to enact both national health insurance in the 1990s and national corporations law for over 100 years until the corporate scandals of the new century. European policymaking also has often failed to move down crucial paths as much as might have been expected because of electoral blockages that seem to be behind the general European failure to enact much needed structural economic reforms aimed at reducing unemployment.

THE PERSISTENCE OF DIVERGENCE

When change does occur, complex patterns of convergence and divergence emerge. Policies remain distinctive across nations as often as they are similar. For instance, in all three countries analyzed by Cioffi, there has been a broad wave of reform, and all three tended to converge along the lines of the American model of securities market regulation. Nevertheless, each retained substantially distinctive regulatory policies as well as corporate structures. These divergent patterns, according to Cioffi, reflect "the institutionalization of interests within broader institutional structure and politics" that differ country by country.

U.S. policy choices recapitulate the nation's fragmented political power. During this period, the United States did not undertake fundamental policy reform of corporate governance and financial market regulation. Rather, it buttressed its well-established regulatory institutions and, with some qualifications, continued along familiar paths. That is, it sought to regulate stock transactions rather than regulate corporate managers directly.

By contrast, Germany and France maintained their traditional relatively high degree of direct central government intervention in corporate management while supplementing that control with new layers of more or less American-style securities regulation.

Weaver shows that the convergence of pension policy regimes in the wealthy nations has been limited by path dependence: these countries have all built their restructuring reforms on the foundations of their current systems. Thus, Weaver concluded that in developing reforms,

> different policy regimes pose distinctive policy problems and opportunities. . . . Countries where a large income related pension system is already in place are likely to develop both substrata clientele support for such programs and have limited tax room for a mandatory system of individual accounts.

POLICY DRIFT

The transatlantic policymaking in these chapters is characterized more by drift than dramatic innovation—by what Hacker labels "reform without change, change without reform." Indeed, as Shapiro argues, almost every policy story here "records more fits and starts than real innovations." One of the most striking of these stories is that told by Hacker about the United States' continued failure to enact national health insurance.

Perhaps an even larger instance of drift was the failure for over 100 years of the U.S. federal government to enact a general national corporations law. As Cioffi shows, despite their national and even international reach, U.S. corporations were subject to state rather than national law until the corporate scandals of the new century. He found that the United States drifted on both securities regulation and corporate governance in the 1990s. But in 2002 these scandals precipitated modest but significant change in these areas with the passage of the Sarbanes–Oxley law. While creating neither a complete national corporations law nor full national control over corporate governance, these reforms limited the previously all-encompassing state authority over corporations. Somewhat similarly, both Vogel and Kelemen's chapters show that the United States has recently created little new environmental regulation, compared with Europe, which has been more active.

But there has been just as significant a policy drift on the other side of the Atlantic in several other key areas. Hacker shows how European nations generally have not been able to successfully execute cost-control measures in health care. Even more significant, all across the continent, Europe has failed to reduce its chronically high unemployment. The inability to enact structural economic reforms seems to be key to this failure.

Guiraudon suggests that immigration policy on both sides of the Atlantic has been less restrictive than popular and political needs would predict. But in absolute terms, on both sides, recent immigration policy has been a mix of incremental restrictive and expansionary measures that hardly can be described as innovative or dramatic.

We noted that Weaver found pension reform efforts constrained by their being built on current systems that have substantial clientele support for current programs and limited tax room for changes. Thus, this path dependence of these reform efforts "contributed to the failure of the European Union to harmonize pension regimes in member countries."

The significant resistance to retrenchment in health care indicates another face of both "drift" and path dependency. The failure in the United States to expand health care in the 1990s through the enactment of national health care frustrated many policymakers and citizens. Unsuccessful efforts to reduce the federal health care programs and spending by cutting the Medicare programs frustrated others. As Hacker points out, "the same institutional fragmentation and multiple veto points that once hindered the passage of large-scale social programs now present an effective barrier to conservative attempts at retrenchment."

Policymaking in health care at the new century in the Organization for Economic Cooperation and Development (OECD) countries that Hacker analyzed has been characterized, on the whole, more by drift than innovation. However, as in almost all policy sectors analyzed in this book, there was significant variation across these countries in health policy outcomes. Again, the variations in their political systems help explain these differing outcomes. Hacker, for example, contrasts the experience of Germany and the United States. Through the 1990s Germany had experienced decades of what was called "Reformblockade." But then in the 1990s, Germany achieved two major health policy breakthroughs. These passed because a new coalition of payers formed against providers' interests. This new coalition managed to work its way through an institutional setting of dense, fragmented corporate health insurance interests entrenched in Germany's federal institutions and bicameral parliament. Hacker concluded, "on the one hand this structure thwarted swift or radical change. . . . [But it also] created the opportunities for openings for potential new and ultimately successful alliances."

Policy drift thus has its purposive side. These failures to retrench, for example, need not necessarily be seen as failures of the political process. As Shapiro suggests, they may instead be "signs that the political process is highly responsive to the popular desire to achieve a certain mix of values different from maximum gross national product or maximum personal income." The policy studies in this book do not provide definitive answers about differences between continental Europeans and Anglo-Saxons in preferences for different mixes of personal income, leisure, and public goods. But they do seem to indicate significant transatlantic differences in attitudes on the appropriate public–private sector mixes in the provision of benefits and goods and services. In the United States, the private sector tends to be more valued than the public sector and in turn is stronger than the public sector. In Europe, especially on the continent, the public sector tends to be more highly valued.

More specifically, there are significant transatlantic differences in attitudes about the most appropriate way to handle risk in the form of pensions and medical costs: in the United States, the inclination is to rely on the private provision of medical insurance and pensions, while in Europe, the tendency is to rely more on their public provision. And there are parallel transatlantic differences in the amount of trust in government, with Europeans putting more trust in government and the Americans putting more trust in the private sector. Most Americans, for example, prefer to have their health care and medical cost insurance provided privately. Europeans prefer to have theirs provided by government, even when this public provision has significant problems, as it did recently in several European countries.

THE SHIFTING OF THE LOCUS OF DECISION MAKING

The shifting of the locus of decision making—downward, outward, and upward—often appears in these chapters. Shifts in the locus of decision making upward to the supranational level are well known. In addition to the European Union (EU), international lending agencies shape individual nations' policies. Weaver found that the International Monetary Fund (IMF) and World Bank influence countries' pension policy choices in several distinct ways.

But we also found patterns in which there has been devolution of power downward to regional or local governments in many nations that is comparable to such shifts in the United States that we encountered in *Seeking the Center*. There we found Clinton's positive small-government policies being devolved from the federal to the state and local levels. More significantly, the 1995 Welfare Reform Act involved major policy devolution to the states. And even in the highly centralized French government there was a shift downward. Sheingate's analysis of management reforms found that, beginning in the early 1980s, local and regional governments gained greater autonomy and responsibility over a host of policy areas.

Even more striking than these upward and downward shifts has been the movement of power outward to nongovernmental agencies and actors through privatization and increasing incorporation of the "social partners" into regulatory and welfare decision making by government agencies. The movement toward more privatization of health care in the United States during this period shows this shifting outward. This was policymaking independent of the initiative or control of public policymakers through what Hacker calls the "semi-sovereign role of employers." There was a shifting of the risk of medical costs from insurers and employers to workers through cost increases paid by individuals (premiums and copayments) and decreases in coverage and accessibility.

Hacker also analyzes this erosion of the boundaries between public and private decision making, which is sometimes labeled "governance," in the privatization of health care. He also finds that increased private participation in public policy making through privatization may be accompanied by increased and more centralized government authority: "Market oriented reform . . . everywhere . . . is highly regulatory." More governance does not necessarily mean less government.

Cioffi's chapter is another instance of this. Here, the locus is shifting in two directions simultaneously—upward and outward. When corporate governance undergoes centralized regulation, it moves upward. But it also moves outward when nongovernmental actors play a role as they inherently do in corporate governance. Indeed, these reform plans are designed to strengthen these particular nongovernmental actors—the new corporate players.

In Guiraudon's chapter on immigration, there are policies that shift the locus of decision making outward. For example, "remote control" policies try to constrain migrants from even reaching the territory of the receiving countries through various tactics including increased cooperation from sending and transit countries, visa requirements, and carrier sanctions.

POLITICAL DYNAMICS

PLURALIST POLITICS AND DRIFT

What factors might explain these policymaking patterns of drift, contingent path dependency, and mixed convergence and divergence? As suggested, political dynamics including the electoral imperative, the context of budgetary austerity, low-visibility policymaking settings, and the others briefly noted above seem to be behind these patterns and their variations across countries and policy sectors.

Let us start this more detailed picture of the impact of these dynamics by analyzing policy drift. Perhaps the beginning of wisdom here is the fundamental nature of that bundle of political dynamics that we refer to as pluralistic politics: decision processes with multiple veto points, sensitive to many constituencies with competing interests, are unlikely to produce heroic policies. Indeed, in this context of budgetary austerity, low trust in government, and electoral volatility, the search is for policies on the cheap and for low-visibility, incremental responses that do not engender the mobilization of contending forces. For instance, Guiraudon tracks a swing in general public sentiment in Europe toward more restrictive immigration policies. At the same time, however, actual policies moved in a slightly more expansive direction. This is because these policies were composed of the sum of low-visibility, case-by-case decisions favorable to immigrants made by judges and immigration officials.

LOW-VISIBILITY POLICYMAKING

In this context of austerity and low trust, policymakers find that a low-visibility setting facilitates policymaking. In addition to the case of immigration policy just noted, there were several other instances of policymaking facilitated by these settings. A low-visibility arena is frequently sought for policies that tend to lack a high level of public support and can be done on the cheap in terms of explicit budgetary outlays. The low-visibility policymaking for expansionist immigration policy fit these criteria. The management reform and labor activation policies analyzed by Sheingate and Levy, respectively, also fit them. None of these policies were popular or strongly demanded by any influential group. Indeed, elements of both were unpopular. (Both were initially pushed by academic experts.) Their passage was largely facilitated by what Guiraudon refers to as being shaped "in the shadows" and by the fact that they did not have major impacts on public budgets.

Much of the drive behind these management reforms was an effort not to have high-visibility confrontations with the civil service. One of the civil service unions' several strengths is that dealings with them tend to become high visibility, which is their preferred setting. So management reform is a way of indirectly dealing with them in a low-visibility context because there is little general interest in such policies.

The Swedish, Danish, and Dutch labor activation policies analyzed by Levy are in many ways parallel efforts to avoid high-visibility confrontations. These policies reflect the "new social liberal" goal of increasing the quality of employment. Their premises are that the government ought to focus not only on lowering unemployment but also on "maximizing employment" and that people ought to earn their wages rather than receive subsidies. These policies involved closing pathways to early retirement in Sweden, increasing part-time and temporary employment in The Netherlands, and moving people from transfer payments to work in Denmark, Sweden, and The Netherlands.

These labor activation policies are instances of positive small government consisting of marginal adjustments pursued because these governments were not able to achieve fundamental restructuring of labor rules. Such restructuring would involve high-visibility and thus major election risks. This parallels *Seeking the Center*'s findings: during the Clinton administration, when larger and more significant policies were impossible to adopt, there was a successful effort to develop policies of positive small government.

Some aspects of pension reform also depended on a low-visibility setting. Pension retrenchment bumped into the opposition of clientele groups and others. Weaver found, therefore, that low-visibility approaches to policymaking were often favored to get retrenching done: "The governments of all the rich countries used delay, obfuscation, and other blame-avoiding techniques to reduce the visibility and immediate effects of retrenchment, refinancing, and restructuring initiatives."

IDEAS AND DRIFT

Policy pulls in different directions that result in intermediate outcomes are not, however, entirely the result of the contending political pressures. As we saw in *The New Politics of Policymaking*, ideas matter—even when held ambivalently. A significant portion of irresolute policy is a function of policymakers being unable to make up their minds fully as to the direction and degree in which they wish to go.

This policymaking of "two minds" parallels *Seeking the Center*'s theme of the dualistic acceptance of a "constrained" welfare state and a "regulated" free market that shaped so much of the policymaking described there. Here, Hacker's chapter indicates similar tension in several instances. He notes, for example, that the United States is slouching not toward national health insurance, but perhaps toward a new compromise between market and state. And while the European states are more oriented toward public provision of health care, Hacker also charts their pulling in other directions. He describes, for example, the incremental moves of several of these states to control government health expenditures and alter the mix of public and private provision of health insurance and services.

Modest outcomes often are also the product of genuine puzzlement about what to do in the face of seemingly insoluble problems. The rapidly escalating medical costs of aging populations or the migration of industrial jobs to low-wage locales are some instances of this pattern.

PARTY COMPETITION AND MODEST POLICIES

Perhaps the most significant political dynamic linked to this noninnovative policymaking is party competition in close elections. *Seeking the Center* found that in the 1990s, partisan electoral competition in the United States resulted in modest policies rather than stalemate. Here we similarly found that on both sides of the Atlantic, the policy product of this period's highly competitive elections was moderate policies. And, as in our earlier volume, this modesty means less policy movement and innovation.

Thus, for example, Guiraudon suggests that in the United States, as the competitive search for the marginal voter became more pronounced in recent years, even the Republicans, who for years had flirted with more restrictive immigration policies, began wooing Hispanic voters with at least modestly expansionary policy proposals. In Europe, pressing needs for pension and labor market reforms run up against electoral realities and often result in minor or cosmetic changes such as those being undertaken now by the German socialist government.

BUDGETARY AUSTERITY AND POLICIES ON THE CHEAP: NEW REGULATIONS, ROLES, AND RIGHTS

The constraints of policymaking at the new century limit political leaders' search for ways to win and ways to compete. The severe financial constraints of this period of budget austerity in particular lead policymakers and institutions to search for policies on the cheap and new, enhanced roles for themselves as alternatives to the heroic state. New regulations are a prime example of policies produced by this cost-driven orientation. For policymakers, these regulations are ostensibly costless because they are not "on budget"—their costs are shifted to the private sector.

Both Vogel and Kelemen's chapters show EU policymakers pursuing new and, in comparison to the United States, surprisingly stringent (more legalistic and enforcement oriented) regulatory policies. Both suggest that these policymakers have a political and institutional stake in these regulations. Such policies enhance the EU's role as a regulatory regime in face of its legitimacy deficit. Many suggest that the EU needs a mission to justify its existence and its costs—financial and political—to member states and individual citizens. The EU wants to be seen not simply as greasing the wheels of commerce. The small budgetary impact of regulatory policies makes them an especially strategic choice for EU policymakers now. They both fit the era's general austerity constraints and the EU's particular legitimacy needs.

Burke's chapter on disability policy parallels the patterns found by Vogel and Kelemen. Burke shows another way in which the EU is developing a new role as a regulatory regime. He found that disability became redefined in Europe as a rights issue through the efforts of a small group with seemingly few political resources: a network of no more than a few dozen academics and activists successfully lobbied for a new law that Burke suggests could become a "Europeans with Disabilities Act."

How did such a small group, without much political influence, gain so much? Burke's primary answers go to the issue of the EU's lesser influence over social policy in Europe. He suggests that the redefinition of disability as a rights issue served the institutional interests of the EU. As long as disability was a matter for welfare policy, it was the province of the member states and beyond the "competence" of the EU. But once disability became defined as a rights issue—a matter of "exclusion" from the market—it was in line with the EU's founding goals of dealing with member state restrictions on the European free market. Here, this meant dealing with barriers to commerce. Thus it enhanced the EU's role as a regulatory regime. Redefining disability as a right was also attractive because it was costless to EU staff members. They can create mandates and regulations for member states, but they do not have to pay for them. Finally, Burke suggests that the rise of the EU as protector of civil rights seems to help it deal with its "legitimating needs."

AUSTERITY AND STRUCTURAL REFORMS

Pursuing polices in which structural reforms play a key role also fits well in this context of budgetary austerity. Structural reforms are key in both Sheingate's chapter on management reforms and Hacker's on health care reform. When policymakers are constrained in conferring benefits on citizens, structural reforms are an attractive alternative. Such policies are perceived by policymakers as giving citizens the feeling of something being acted on by government, even though it is small and to a significant degree symbolic. Moreover, structural reforms also tend not to be costly. Indeed, in both health care reform and management reforms, one of the key policy dynamics is constraining cost.

The management reforms analyzed in Sheingate's chapter are a striking reflection of this context of austerity and declining trust. When policymakers cannot afford to pursue major policies and there is low trust in government, management reforms have several advantages: they allow policymakers to appear to be doing something, and they do not require much spending or faith. And like many of the structural reforms in health care that Hacker analyzes, management reforms tend to produce a pattern of reform without much change. This allows policymakers to take actions that ultimately arouse minimal competing interests.

SOME FINAL THOUGHTS

Observers of transatlantic policymaking at the new century, especially journalists, are wont to complain about the inability of policymakers to get their act together about pressing social and economic problems. But the tendency toward policy drift and unfulfilled policy initiatives and reforms in many areas analyzed here is not the result of incompetent or weak policymakers. It is not so much that they cannot get their act together. Rather, it is that they are not sure which acts are the right ones. More generally, this policy drift seems to be a product of the constraints that policymakers operate under—financial, cognitive, and political. This is an age of austerity with pressures from both slower economic growth and deficits.

The second constraint is one of policy knowledge. The problems that these nations face are complex and difficult. For many of the most significant of them, we are not sure about the best policy solution. We are not, for example, certain about how to reduce increasing health care costs. To the extent that we have some plausible hypotheses, there tends to be disagreement about how to resolve the tensions between keeping down rising health care costs and achieving or maintaining a satisfactory degree of access to health care services.

These cognitive complexities were perhaps best captured by Hacker:

> Rising longevity, rising expectations, and, above all, rising costs—all have magnified the pressures that medical industrial complexes face. Leaders find themselves caught between fiscal constraints and public demands, besieged with competing evaluations and prescriptions, and embroiled in bitter struggles in which questions of equality, justice, professional sovereignty, the role of markets, and indeed life and death are never far beneath the surface.

The third constraint is political. Even when we know or think we know enough about what to do about a policy problem, political leaders have difficulty getting enough of the interests involved to agree on this course of action. By the new century, so many interest groups have grown up around benefits programs that it is increasingly difficult to get this agreement. It is probably no accident that corporate governance reform in the United States—a modest change, yet one of the most significant analyzed here—was associated with an outside force: it was only the atypical pressure of scandal that broke through the usual political constraints maintaining stasis in this long-unreformed policy area.

Political leaders need to win elections to stay in office. But this often conflicts with choosing the most effective policy solution. Both of these constraints are especially acute in this period. On both side of the Atlantic, parties are weaker, more evenly divided, and more competitive. This results in more frequent alternations in power, with a more active and competitive struggle for the marginal voter. Because many voters tend to be centrist, appeals to them are moderate rather than extreme or demagogic. Less innovative and more moderate policies tend to result.

These financial, cognitive, and political constraints tend to interact. One of the reasons that many voters are marginal is that no party seems able to come up with policy proposals that are distinctly its own, feasible, capable of enactment, and potentially effective. Recent U.S. partisan compromises over Medicare reform are a clear example of the dual uncertainties of voters and political elites, as are the very tentative moves toward structural economic reforms in France and Germany and the whole EU muddle over national deficits.

Thus the sometimes unspoken background of all the policy studies that follow is a prototypical electoral situation: major political parties of the left have, while engaging in internal debates over the move, nonetheless moved toward the center. Parties of the right, mindful of the huge numbers of voters in the middle both wedded to existing entitlements and favorably inclined toward further risk regulation, seek to create a distinct but still middle position attractive to voters that is not too far to the right. Delicate electoral balances, combined with uncertainties about what will work affordably, counsel against bold policy strokes.

REFORM WITHOUT CHANGE, CHANGE WITHOUT REFORM

The Politics of U.S. Health Policy Reform in Cross-National Perspective

JACOB S. HACKER

GOVERNMENT-SPONSORED HEALTH INSURANCE IS A CENTRAL PILLAR OF THE MODERN welfare state. In wealthy democracies, public medical spending accounts for an average of 6 percent of gross domestic product (GDP), making it the largest category of government spending after retirement pensions. Yet, the enormous resources at stake are not the only reason why health policy dominates contemporary debate. Rising longevity, rising expectations, and, above all, rising costs—all have magnified the pressures that medical–industrial complexes face. Leaders find themselves caught between fiscal constraints and public demands, besieged with competing evaluations and prescriptions, and embroiled in bitter struggles in which questions of equality, justice, professional sovereignty, the role of markets, and, indeed, life and death are never far beneath the surface. Little wonder, then, that governments have risen and fallen, leaders prospered and suffered, and political fortunes swelled and vanished in the ubiquitous but elusive quest for health care reform.

The fierceness of the clashes cannot be overstated. In the late 1990s, doctors' strikes over pay, personnel, and working conditions wracked Canada's provinces. In Germany during the same period, tens of thousands of protesters took to the streets at the instigation of medical professionals to denounce proposed health care reforms. In Britain in 2002, the growing rift between union leaders and Prime Minister Tony Blair over the use of private contractors within the National Health Service (NHS) threatened to erupt into a wave of strikes. And in the United States, of course, the failure of the Clinton health plan in 1994 opened the door to the Republicans' capture of Congress after forty years in the wilderness—and in turn set the stage for the fierce battles over Medicare, the federal health program for the elderly, that eventually sank the health reform goals of the GOP and revitalized the Clinton presidency.

The conflict is unmistakable. What it has reaped in terms of concrete change is far less clear. Among students of comparative health policy, the conventional wisdom is that the 1990s were the age of fundamental reform. "An epidemic of health reform is sweeping across Western industrialized countries," proclaims a recent report.[1] Other respected analysts tell a similar story: after the stalemate of the 1980s, a large number of nations enacted major structural changes embodying a shared model of market-based reform.[2] In this now-familiar tale of global gravitation toward the North Star of market-driven medicine, "the common effects of demographic changes and technological advances seem in large part to overwhelm unique historical and structural patterns."[3]

And yet, turn to another source of wisdom, and the tale is entirely the reverse. For more than a decade, students of the welfare state have examined how national systems of social provision have weathered the challenges of the post-1970s order. Their overwhelming conclusion: the changes have been surprisingly modest given the strains welfare states have faced. As Paul Pierson argues in one of the more influential accounts,

> Economic, political, and social pressures have fostered an image of welfare states under siege. Yet, if one turns from abstract discussions of social transformation to an examination of actual policy, it becomes difficult to sustain the proposition that these strains have generated fundamental shifts.[4]

These are arguments for continuity, not change—for ingrained "path dependence" as countries continue to follow entrenched and divergent historical tracks, not common reform trajectories.

It would be easy to dismiss this clash of perspectives as reflecting the myopia of one or the other side, either health policy analysts for taking the rhetoric of leaders too seriously or welfare state researchers for ignoring recent health reforms. Although both charges have more than a grain of truth, both miss the broader reality: these starkly different diagnoses are, in fact, two sides of the same paradoxical coin. Major health policy changes have indeed occurred, and they have indeed borne important surface similarities, particularly in the area of cost control. Yet, as welfare state scholars argue, these changes cannot be classified as retrenchment of the public sector. In a number of nations, cost control has actually gone hand in hand with significant expansions of public coverage, and no affluent nation has seen a major decline in statutory protection. Nor have these changes pushed in a common neoliberal direction. The pull of market-oriented ideas has varied greatly; the ability to implement them, even more so. Similar strains, and even relatively similar rhetoric, have coexisted with fundamental and enduring differences in how governments regulate, finance, and deliver medical care.

Change without retrenchment, convergence of rhetoric but not of action—these are summaries of tendencies, not explanations of them. What are the sources of these dual movements? To answer this question, we must first observe a second paradox: what might be called "the irony of procompetitive reform."[5] The irony is this: nations with the most centralized and dirigiste health policy regimes—nations where prior commitments and demonstrated success in controlling costs while providing broad access would seem to counsel cautious incrementalism—have most eagerly embraced the tenets of market reform. At the same time, however, the effect of these ideas when implemented has been surprisingly modest and, on the whole, augmented state authority rather than unleashed market forces. Creating markets, it turns out, rests on the extensive application of coercive power, and the incentives and signals that market-style interventions engender further encourage micromanagement from the center. It is almost as if the politics of market reform were characterized by a perverse law of negative affinity: *Procompetitive reform ideas are attractive precisely where they are least capable of being realized.*

If the irony of procompetitive reform has escaped attention, another oversight is even more glaring. Neither the literature on health reform nor scholarship on the welfare state has taken seriously enough the public–private and pluralist structure of modern health systems. From both perspectives, reform is essentially a process of intervention from above, an exercise of coercive authority within the dictates of democratic politics. Yet, as I will show, change without choice has been the order of the day in the medical arenas of affluent democracies. On the whole, the most consequential structural shifts have resulted not from legislatively engineered reforms, but from the long-term working out of cost containment within the context of established public–private frameworks—a process that has created privatization at the margins in universal public systems but significant regress in the United States, where private coverage sponsored by employers has sharply contracted in spite of efforts to broaden protection. These changes in policy effects without changes in formal policies I term policy "conversion and drift," and we shall see that they are at the heart of the contradictory processes that are subtly but surely changing the role of the welfare state in the lives of citizens—particularly in the United States.[6]

First, however, the stage must be set. How can we understand the diversity across national health systems? Why have these systems come under strain? And what are the links between these strains and the reforms that leaders have considered? These are the questions that animate the next two sections of this chapter. I then turn to the reform process and its outcomes, tracing the politics of policy change in two areas—cost containment and structural reform—in advanced industrial states in general, and in Britain, Canada, Germany, The Netherlands, and the United States in particular.

As the analysis will show, four critical factors lie at the heart of the politics of reform: political incentives for action, politically appealing policy ideas, political–institutional constraints, and preexisting policy structures. In an environment of austerity, leaders have found themselves pressed to act not simply to cope with fiscal pressures or rising spending, but to avoid blame for the perceived deterioration of strained medical complexes. Rather than counseling the cautious step-by-step changes that welfare-state scholars highlight, the fear of incurring political blame from a disgruntled public has instead frequently encouraged politicians to pursue major reforms. Under these circumstances, the ideology of market reform has proved extremely seductive, not only because it holds out the hope of improving services within constrained budgets, but also because it has the potential to deflect blame to newly empowered private or quasiprivate actors, while allowing politicians to temporarily elide deeply contested value and resource conflicts.[7]

These forces set the agenda for reform. They do not dictate a unique response. Nor do they determine the degree to which change occurs, either in formal policies or on the ground. Instead, the direction and impact of reform are profoundly conditioned by the interaction of two broad sets of factors. The first is the framework of political institutions that shapes electoral incentives and the governing latitude of leaders. The second is the distinctive opportunities and risks that medical structures create for politicians, patients, and private and subnational actors with independent policy authority. I argue that this interaction can be captured with a simple framework emphasizing government structure and the character of the medical sector, and I suggest that this perspective casts in fresh light the dilemmas faced by America's leaders as they struggle with embedded medical structure that they have inherited.

DISTINCTIVE SYSTEMS, SIMILAR GOALS

Discussions of comparative health policy usually bog down quickly in the sheer complexity of the terrain. A recent text, for example, identifies "11 structural 'parameters' or 'dimensions' along which the systems of various countries differ."[8] The Organization of Economic Cooperation and Development (OECD) adopts a comparatively parsimonious scheme that involves just two key dimensions and eight distinct types, although these categories are then further divided across three more continua. As Joseph White argues, however, this baffling diversity masks substantial underlying similarity across rich democracies, virtually all of which have adopted programs that share two key characteristics: they cover all or nearly all citizens through some sort of shared-financing system, and they employ some variety of measures to contain costs at a high level of aggregation.[9] Against this "international standard," only the United States looks like a conspicuous outlier, its public programs covering less than half the population, its overall spending largely unconstrained.

Among nations that uphold the international standard, the standard distinction is between a "national health service" and "national health insurance." But this division is much less pure than supposed. The British NHS and Canadian national health insurance (known as "Medicare") are in key ways more alike than different, and both are quite distinct from Germany's system of nonprofit sickness funds, which is also classified as national health insurance. To capture the similarities, it is helpful to note that both are *single-payer systems*—that is, systems in which the government (in the Canadian case, the provincial governments) pays for services directly. Germany and most other continental European nations, by contrast, have *multipayer systems* based on insurance funds that pay for care

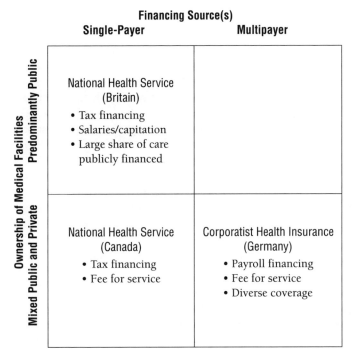

Figure 1.1. Major Types of Medical Systems

within a public regulatory framework. What distinguishes the British and Canadian systems is not so much financing arrangements as the ownership of medical facilities, which are mostly public in Britain and mostly private in Canada.

As figure 1.1 shows, then, national health programs divide fairly neatly across two axes: the number of payers and ownership of facilities. Three of the four resulting combinations capture the most common system types: a prototypical *national health service* (single payer/public ownership), Canadian-style *national health insurance* (single payer/mixed ownership), and German-style *corporatist health insurance* (multiple payer/mixed ownership).[10] Several other distinctions are closely associated with these two axes. Single-payer systems tend to rely heavily on general tax revenues, whereas multipayer systems generally employ payroll-tax financing. Systems with public ownership of medical facilities usually pay doctors at least partly on a salaried or per-patient basis, whereas fee-for-service payment is the norm when ownership is mixed. In public-ownership systems, too, a significantly larger share of spending is generally governmental than in mixed-ownership systems. Finally, multipayer systems, because they entail different sources of insurance for different portions of the population, usually provide the greatest diversity of coverage and, in some cases, even exclude from statutory protection wealthier citizens, who are expected to buy into the public system or insure themselves.

Why do the structures, if not the goals, of national health policies differ so starkly? One obvious reason is that political parties have differed historically on the proper role of government in medical finance. In cross-national research on welfare states, a well-supported finding is that rule by parties of the left, particularly during the formative years of welfare state development, is associated with more expansive and generous public social programs.[11] Leftist rule is certainly not a necessary condition for universal health programs, as they have been adopted under governments of varying partisan stripes, but it does appear strongly associated with the establishment of national health services and, more generally, with a diminished role for private insurance and direct consumer payments, which the left has long viewed as inegalitarian.[12]

The scope for political leaders to achieve their favored goals is heavily constrained, however, by the structure of political institutions, particularly the opportunities for blocking activity that institutions create for powerful opponents of national health programs, such as the medical profession. As Ellen Immergut has convincingly argued, opponents of large-scale government entry into the health field have generally been advantaged when a polity has a large number of potential "veto points," such as federalism, a bicameral legislature, an independent judiciary, popular referenda, and a separation of powers between the executive and legislature.[13] This no doubt helps explain why no federal state has adopted a national health service; why across nations the share of medical spending financed by government is strongly correlated with the number of institutional veto points; and why Switzerland, with its strong federalism and tradition of the use of popular referenda by organized groups, has long been characterized by the most anemic government role in health policy of all European nations. It is also consistent with the fact that the United States, which has the most veto-point–ridden polity of any rich democracy, remains the only advanced industrial state that does not have a broad framework of public coverage or cost containment and the only one that relies principally on voluntary employment-based coverage.

Still, with the exception of the United States, all advanced industrial democracies have adopted some version of the international standard. This suggests that institutional barriers are better at slowing than halting government's entry into the health insurance field. Nonetheless, the timing and sequence of policy interventions may be highly consequential for the *form* that such policies ultimately take. Most countries began to intrude into the doctor–patient relationship by subsidizing nongovernmental insurers, rather than directly financing services. These policies created important vested interests in a pluralist financing structure (patients, providers, insurers) and reinforced doctors' preferences for fee-for-service payment. How extensive and long-lived these arrangements were thus had crucial effects on the types of systems countries ended up with.[14] Countries in which authoritative government action to consolidate or supplant nongovernmental insurance took longer to achieve generally ended up with more decentralized and costly health-financing systems in which private insurance and finance played a more pivotal role—in part because delay allowed the formation and enrichment of a formidable collection of private stakeholders, in part because sophisticated private care represents such a massive burden for government budgets to assume.

This is a paradigm example of *path dependence*, temporal processes in which early choices create self-reinforcing effects that are inherently difficult to reverse.[15] The United States, again, represents an extreme case: private insurance has, in effect, come to play the role in the United States that public programs do elsewhere, and this role has proved as difficult to dislodge as the public foundations of mature welfare states.[16]

The path-dependent effects of public and private health policies are an important reason why analysis of the contemporary politics of health reform must take seriously the constraints created by existing structures of medical finance. Even when facing similar strains, governments differ greatly in the challenges and demands that they confront and the policy tools they have at their disposal, quite apart from the institutional constraints that electoral and decision-making systems create.

STRAINS FACING MATURE MEDICAL COMPLEXES

The 1980s marked the arrival of an era of austerity in welfare-state politics.[17] The reasons for this shift were both economic and political. In the economic realm, the 1970s ushered in a seemingly permanent decline in underlying rates of economic growth. In the political arena, the period saw the emergence of political movements hostile to the welfare state, symbolized by the ascendance of Prime Minister Margaret Thatcher in Britain and President Ronald Reagan in the United States. The effect of these linked developments was exacerbated by demographic trends—notably, population aging and the rise in single-parent families—and by strains emerging out of welfare states themselves. In many nations, core social programs had grown to the point where avenues for further expansion were limited and the opportunity cost of pursuing them was high. Caught between enduring support for the welfare state and the fiscal demands posed by these new realities, politicians everywhere faced hard choices, and many countries ran large budget deficits in a temporary effort to elide tough trade-offs.

As the second most expensive area of the welfare state, health care was scarcely immune from these pressures. Indeed, whereas public pensions often presented the greater long-term fiscal threat, the rapid inflation of health care spending was usually the largest and most immediate source of budgetary strain for countries facing up to the new fiscal order. In one sense, this was nothing new, and it had more to do with the distinctive economics of medical care than with the particularities of welfare state programs. For as long as health spending has been recorded, it has tended to grow at a faster rate than general price inflation.[18] But the persistent problem of "excess" medical inflation caused by technological change and weakly checked demand suddenly took on new and pressing urgency in the straitened fiscal circumstances of the period.

Moreover, nearly all nations (again, with the conspicuous exception of the United States) entered this harsh new era with public programs in place covering all or most citizens. Not only, then, was access no longer the central rallying cry, but the cost of medicine had in most nations been effectively socialized. This is evident in the remarkably high average share of total medical spending borne by OECD governments in 1980—some 80 percent, excluding the United States. Although health costs are ultimately borne by society regardless of the source of financing, it makes a profound political difference whether they are financed by government or the private sector. An old adage of health policy is that every dollar spent on medical care is a dollar of somebody's income. In the 1980s, leaders came to face another unpleasant truth: every dollar spent by government on medical care is a dollar that cannot be spent on other ends (or, in systems financed by mandatory employer and employee contributions, a dollar that crowds out other possible uses of payroll taxes and that risks distorting labor markets.)

To this straightforward, if daunting, challenge, shifting public expectations added a treacherous and volatile political dimension. In the immediate postwar years, government programs of health insurance had been laid down on the hierarchical and paternalistic structures of doctor–patient interaction that traditionally characterized the medical sector. The 1970s, however, witnessed a broad decline in trust in traditional sources of authority, including doctors. At roughly the same time, critics of medical paternalism articulated new conceptions of patient rights and autonomy that gained widespread credence. Like the imperative of cost containment, these demands challenged the authority of the medical profession. Yet, they also bestowed on elected leaders the vexing dilemma of trying to rein in costs without seeming to limit too heavily the access to sophisticated, high-quality care that well-off citizens increasingly expected.

Many commentators have argued that "globalization" created an additional heavy burden on welfare states during the 1980s and 1990s. As capital and goods flowed ever more quickly across borders, these analysts prophesized, organized labor and the left would lose their ability to offer a credible alternative to market-conforming policies, and nations would find themselves increasingly forced to adopt lowest-common-denominator social interventions that prevented business from fleeing high taxes and public protections. As a wave of studies has demonstrated, however, the effects of increasing financial and trade integration pale in comparison to the internal strains that welfare states have faced, and even these effects have themselves been highly mediated by domestic political and economic institutions.[19] All this seems particularly true in the health care sector, where fiscal strains are largely caused by persistently high medical inflation. Employers' need to compete abroad may well have provided a rationale for assaults on national health programs. But the distinctive sources of cost pressure in health care and the internally generated fiscal strains that all social programs faced are sufficient to explain why control of health spending became a paramount issue in the 1980s.

The empowerment of supranational institutions is another form of globalization that is often seen as consequential in social policymaking. Indeed, as other chapters in this volume show, it is impossible to discuss transatlantic public policy without noting the remarkable rise of the European Union (EU), a true supranational political institution, with substantial bureaucratic powers, a supreme judicial authority, and significant policy capacities. For all this, however, the direct role of the European Union in shaping major programs of domestic social policy remains profoundly limited—by EU directive, by the general weakness of EU fiscal capacities, and by the strong role of member states in EU decision making.[20] This does not mean, of course, that the European Union is without effect. The Maastricht criteria for monetary union have undoubtedly prompted cuts in government budgets to bring debt in line. In addition, and less noticed, EU rules governing private insurance and medical services have made it harder for EU member states to regulate health care and insurance, while encouraging the formation of large EU-wide insurance companies operating in many countries. These developments have encouraged competition between public and private insurance within more decentralized systems, allowing some lower-risk and wealthier citizens to opt out of statutory schemes or to purchase private coverage to jump queues. In all, however, the effect of the European Union on core state programs of health insurance to date still seems relatively modest.

If economic integration and supranational institutions do not appear pivotal, however, the same cannot be said so easily about another form of increasing global interdependence: the cross-national diffusion of policy ideas. The "globalization of commentary in the world of medical care" is impossible to deny.[21] Information about national episodes of reform travels nearly instantaneously across borders; international institutions constantly gather evidence and dispense advice; and a new breed of self-described health policy experts, many of them trained in the relatively young discipline of health economics, stands ready to offer their pet solutions to idea-hungry officials. And yet, despite this feverish cross-national exchange of ideas, it remains an open question how new—or how consequential—the cross-border flow of information truly is. The building of national health programs, after all, saw similar processes of diffusion, with Germany's pioneering establishment of a compulsory insurance program in 1883, for example, profoundly influencing developments in continental Europe and Britain, and even inspiring proposals forwarded in Progressive-Era America.[22]

Viewed against this historical backdrop, what seems distinctive about the present is not the fact of cross-national policy diffusion, or even its velocity, but rather the direction of transmission and the kind of ideas that are diffusing. In previous rounds of global reformist ferment, the United States was the laggard, attempting to adopt and adapt models that other nations had long ago pioneered. Yet, perhaps the most striking feature of the global reform debate of recent years is the extent to which, rhetorically at least, central aspects of the American model—the rise of "managed care," the emphasis on health outcomes research, the heavy reliance on private benefits and competitive forces—have become a prominent part of discussion within countries that have already achieved what the United States plainly has not—namely, universal health care at a reasonable price. As

Michael Moran colorfully puts it, "Taking advice from Americans about health care cost containment is like having lessons in seamanship from the crew of the Titanic. Yet, many of the key policy entrepreneurs in the reform wave. . .were American; and many of the key policy innovations were American-inspired."[23]

Moran raises a pivotal question: What explains the apparent appeal of the American model in nations that have rejected its underlying foundations? Yet, he prejudges the answer in his phrasing of the issue. Whether leaders in other nations are taking "lessons in seamanship" or simply adapting aspects of the U.S. boat to their own fundamentally intact watercraft is precisely what needs to be investigated. The analysis to come will show that movement in the direction of the American model has, in fact, been extremely limited, halting, and uneven. This is so for a simple reason: the very pressures that impel politicians to reach out for American-style solutions—the confluence of cost constraints and public dissatisfaction—also mitigate against their true adoption. Furthermore, the introduction of market-based instruments within the fundamentally politicized and well-established context of mature health programs has effects quite different from those that advocates often expect. If there has been drift toward America's beckoning policy shores—and the growing role of private benefits in many nations suggests some movement—it has so far stemmed more from the decentralized response of major health care players to the strains imposed by cost containment than from the imposition of market reforms by leaders caught in the thrall of America's example.

THE WEAKNESSES OF EXISTING ACCOUNTS

As the preceding quote from Moran suggests, the conventional story told by health policy experts is one of convergence, as embattled policymakers turn to U.S. innovations to square the policy circle of providing low-cost, high-quality care. According to this view, health care reform is widespread, fundamental in its effects, and similar across nations in its goal and character.[24] But while these accounts have rightly emphasized the global character of health policy discourse and the increased prominence of market rhetoric, they have also frequently generalized from atypical cases, confused rhetoric and planning with true legislative change, and failed to investigate gaps between legislative aspirations and policy results—errors that have seriously undercut their portrayal of common movement toward market-oriented medicine.

WHY HEALTH POLICY EXPERTS OVERSTATE CHANGE

Generalization from extreme cases is the simplest problem to illustrate. In nearly all recent research, the focus is on captivating but arguably atypical cases of allegedly market-based reform. Typically, a few such cases are compared and dis-

cussed, and little or no attention is paid to the large universe of cases where legislative change is more modest or incremental.[25] Moreover, even when a wide range
of nations enter into the analysis, health policy experts are still prone to overstate
the extent of change and the similarity of response. This seems to reflect a temptation to equate rhetorical change with legislative change and legislative change, in
turn, with policy change.[26] On close inspection, however, politicians who invoke
the rhetoric of the market mean different things by words such as "competition"
and "efficiency," and they vary greatly in their commitment to the goal.[27] Even the
ubiquitous label "market-based" turns out to be less revealing than it might at first
seem. The two major models to which the label is usually applied are "internal
markets," in which some element of competitive purchasing is introduced into
health care delivery, and "managed competition," in which consumers are encouraged to choose among high-quality insurance products. Though allied in their aim
of encouraging micro-efficiencies and consumer responsiveness, these ideas differ
sharply and invoke contrasting policy mechanisms. It may well be appropriate to
treat them as united under the common rubric of market reform, but the differences must be kept in mind.

By far, however, the most important reason that rhetoric is a poor guide to
change is that even politicians who wholeheartedly embrace procompetitive proposals face serious barriers to their ambitions, from the standard institutional obstacles to legislative victory, to the specific constraints created by existing policy
frameworks, to latent public concerns about competition in health care.[28] Market-
based ideas are thus a double-edged sword for politicians. They offer promises, but
also threats—threats to established arrangements, and threats to underlying conceptions of solidarity, which might well erode if competition were to spread too
widely or deeply. This makes it a priori implausible that it is simply the sheer per-
suasiveness of market-based ideas that accounts for their influence. Instead, their
appeal must be understood as rooted in their *political* attractiveness as well as their
technical suitability. Reformers may sincerely believe that market-based ideas will,
in the words of one health policy text, "increase consumers' satisfaction and the efficiency of services, while keeping the principle of free and equal access." But there
are also potent political reasons for the ascendance of procompetitive ideas, and
understanding is critical for grasping both the rhetorical appeal and the real-world
limits of the vision.[29]

Two sources of appeal deserve the greatest emphasis. First, by creating competitive relations where none previously existed, market reform has the potential
to deflect blame to newly empowered private or quasiprivate actors, shifting responsibility away from embattled leaders. In practice, as we shall see, such blame
shifting has proved exceedingly difficult to realize. But hope springs eternal that
market means will defuse and "depoliticize" endemic resource and value conflicts.

The second key feature of market rhetoric may be even more seductive: its essential ambiguity, as crystallized in the popular reform cry of the 1990s ("managed
competition") and its similarly ambiguous spin-offs ("planned markets," "internal
markets," "public competition," "quasimarkets"). Surveys suggest that these terms

leave the public utterly confused—and that may be why politicians like them.[30] Reform requires the reconciliation of conflicting objectives and the navigation of deep ideological differences. Managed competition or quasimarkets cannot be everything to everyone, but they can be many things to many people: fiscal probity and better services, enhanced regulatory control and augmented market forces, expanded state responsiveness and increased personal responsibility. Bridging these antinomies may be unrealistic as a policy goal, but it has irresistible qualities as a political goal. And it is as a response to the *political* dilemmas created by cost containment that procompetitive ideas must first and foremost be understood. To be sure, market-based ideas are not simply a political smokescreen thrown up to mask inaction. Nonetheless, contrary to much policy commentary, the turn to market has been as rhetorical as it has been real, a contradictory as it has been clear eyed, and as political as it has been principled. Partly for these reasons, its policy effects to date have been more modest than—and often quite different from—those that market advocates desired or foresaw.

WHY WELFARE STATE SCHOLARS UNDERSTATE CHANGE

It would be natural to assume, based on this bill of particulars, that students of the welfare state offer a persuasive alternative account. Social policy research, after all, has concentrated like a laser beam on legislative change, and it has been highly skeptical of the facile conclusion that strains on the welfare state have precipitated neoliberal reform. And yet, welfare state scholars have been extremely slow to exploit the comparative advantages they enjoy. In the first place, welfare state studies have long given extremely short shrift to health policy, despite its fiscal prominence. No less important, the dominant conceptual trope of welfare state scholarship—"blame avoidance"—becomes brittle in its assumptions and ambiguous in its predictions when applied to health policy.

Blame avoidance is the theoretical core of the new scholarship on the welfare state.[31] Whereas leaders once vied to "claim credit" for social policies, this argument goes, retrenching existing programs requires instead that they "avoid blame" for electorally risky decisions. Cuts in programs thus require either safe electoral margins or strategies that obfuscate, offset, or blur responsibility for unpopular choices. More often than not, the blame-avoidance imperative is too great. The welfare status quo reigns.

In the areas of the welfare state on which most attention has focused, the blame-avoidance account is indeed frequently compelling. When specific and predictable benefits that citizens like are pitted against the diffuse and uncertain gains that cuts might yield, it is no surprise that democratic politicians recoil. The "irresistible forces" of fiscal strain meet the "immovable objects" of public resistance.[32]

Notice, however, that this line of argument hinges crucially on public satisfaction with the status quo. If, by contrast, citizens have deep concerns about existing programs, then the model's implications are ambiguous. Politicians' desire to "claim credit" for fixing perceived problems with existing programs may well outweigh the imperative of blame avoidance. Indeed, the motive of blame avoidance may actually impel them to *pursue* reform to avoid being punished at the polls for failing to take decisive action.

This is, in fact, a common pattern in health policy. Over the past two decades, as rising public expectations and provider resistance have bumped up against increasingly strict cost-containment efforts, politicians in many nations have come under significant electoral pressure to champion ameliorative reforms. Blame avoidance, rather than counseling "stand-pattism" to avoid electoral retribution for tampering with popular benefits, has instead encouraged political bidding wars in which parties and candidates pronounce ever more insistently that they are committed to improving strained medical complexes. This suggests that the line between blame avoidance and credit claiming is less pure than analysts of retrenchment often suppose. Although visibly reducing widely expected benefits is indeed the most perilous of social policy ventures, the fact that even relatively stable health systems can produce mounting public discontent indicates that politicians must often seek to *claim credit* for reform precisely in order to *avoid blame* for perceived deteriorations in existing programs' performance.

This is in part because legislative reforms are not the only source of policy change. Health policy experts and students of retrenchment have tended to view reform as a process of government-directed change, in which political decision makers impose outcomes from above. As a result, both have tended to miss cumulatively important, but often individually subtle, changes in policy purposes or outcomes that occur without changes in policy rules—what I call *drift and conversion* within the bounds of existing policies.

A SHARED OVERSIGHT: POLICY DRIFT

Policy drift occurs when stable policies change in their effects because of shifts in their context, their interaction with it, or both. Increasing evidence suggests, for example, that welfare states are characterized by a growing mismatch between traditional structures of social provision and the new types of social risks that citizens face.[33] As Gøsta Esping-Andersen puts it, "The real 'crisis' of contemporary welfare regimes lies in the disjuncture between the existing institutional configuration and exogenous change. Contemporary welfare states . . . have their origins in, and mirror, a society that no longer obtains."[34] In this view, public social programs have weathered the storms of recent decades, but major changes in the employment sector and family relations have significantly altered the effects (and effectiveness) of longstanding policy strategies.

Esping-Andersen and others who discuss this type of externally induced drift imply that it is largely an apolitical process, driven by exogenous social shifts over which politicians have little or no control. To the extent that arguments in this vein concern the *politics* of reform, their ambition is limited to explaining welfare state responses to the disjunction between risks and benefits *once* it has arisen. Yet, the emergence of this mismatch should itself be seen as a process that is highly mediated by politics. In an environment of new or worsening social risks, opponents of expanded state responsibility do not have to enact major policy reforms to move policy toward their favored ends. Merely by delegitimizing and blocking compensatory interventions designed to ameliorate intensified risks, they can gradually transform the orientation of existing programs. Although externally induced policy drift may sometimes be wholly inadvertent, much of it is probably mediated by political struggle, a result not of failures of foresight or perception, but of deliberate efforts by political actors to prevent the recalibration of social programs.

This "second face" of political influence over policy exposes an important soft spot in retrenchment scholarship.[35] Retrenchment studies have made the clever argument that the same institutional fragmentation and multiple veto points that once hindered the passage of large-scale social programs now present an effective barrier to conservative attempts at retrenchment.[36] This argument does not go far enough, however, in acknowledging the conditional character of institutional effects. Advocates of welfare state cutbacks have had two central projects—restricting existing policies and preventing new initiatives or the updating of existing ones— and while institutional fragmentation has indeed hindered the former project, it has facilitated the blocking activities that are central to the latter. Paradoxically, in fact, policy drift is likely to be most pervasive and consequential precisely where the formal legislative process is most prone to stalemate.

Nonetheless, externally induced policy drift (whether politically mediated or inadvertent) is not the only means by which policies may change without formal revision. In addition, what Kathleen Thelen calls *conversion* may also cause ground-level change.[37] When we envision the welfare state, we are inclined to think of programs of social spending and provision with explicit and often intricate formulas governing eligibility, benefits, and the like. Public pensions are the quintessential example. In these areas, it makes sense to focus on changes in formal policies when judging whether reform has occurred and what its effects are likely to be. Yet, there are important realms of social provision in which the link between policies and effects is much less tight. Many social policies, for instance, entail decentralized administration, dividing authority between units of government or between government and private actors, such as service providers, insurers, unions, and employers. And even programs that are run entirely by government may allow significant "street-level bureaucracy," making problematic the assumption that what a policy dictates is what is actually carried out.[38]

Of the major components of the welfare state, health policy arguably provides the strongest illustration. As a service rather than cash benefit, government insurance has always required the state to enter into a negotiated settlement with providers. Most national programs also rest substantially on private hospitals, as well as on commercial insurers or quasipublic insurance funds. And most grant key responsibilities to employers, labor unions, and subnational political units. The U.S.

health system stands out in all these areas, featuring an extensive private medical sector and employment-based benefit system, both of which are extensively buttressed and shaped by government policy.[39] In this respect, as in so many others regarding social policy, the United States is clearly exceptional. Nonetheless, subsidiary frameworks in which nongovernmental insurers and providers play a substantial role alongside the public sector are common in European health systems, too, and there are signs that such arrangements are becoming more prevalent and extensive.[40] If this is so, it may become increasingly difficult to judge the effect of health policies by simply reading the statute books or examining disputes over policy rules. We will need to look at what really happens on the ground.

What is happening on the ground—and, more important, why—is the subject of the next two sections. In them, I trace the pattern and progress of reform in relation to the two major policy challenges of the day: cost containment and structural reform. *Cost containment* refers to efforts to control spending without changing the fundamental scope or structure of insurance protections. By *structural reform*, I mean major changes in that scope or structure, which often have as their goal cost containment but almost always entail additional goals, such as microefficiency and responsiveness. The imperative of cost containment has been universal, and the instruments adopted similar. In contrast, the emergence and fate of structural reforms, and their character and effects, have varied greatly. Making sense of these similarities and differences is the task ahead.

COST CONTAINMENT

By the early 1980s, health care cost containment was a leading item on the political agenda of all advanced industrial democracies. High rates of economic growth had facilitated a generous framework of accommodation with medical providers, in which tight control over fees was traded off against decreased professional resistance to the socialization of finance. In the 1970s and 1980s, this bargain came under universal strain. Rather than "states and interests" in uneasy cooperation, the pattern became "states versus interests" in the struggle to control costs.[41] The first question, then, is how successful governments were in this new policy context.

As table 1.1 suggests, if the standard is whether countries reduced health spending, the overall story is one of remarkable success, and it carries few clear messages about the effectiveness of different types of medical systems (or political systems, for that matter). Indeed, the most striking feature of the comparison between 1960 and 1980 levels of spending growth and 1980 to 2000 levels is the universality of decline. Only Canada comes close to bucking the trend. Among OECD nations as a whole, the average increase in health spending as a share of GDP is roughly a fourth as large in the second period as the first. Sweden and Denmark actually experienced a decline in health spending as a share of GDP between 1980 and 1998, and a number of countries saw extremely modest

Table 1.1. Health Spending in Selected OECD Countries, 1960–2000

Country	Total Health Spending as Share of GDP, 2000 (%)	Percentage Change in Share of GDP Devoted to Health Spending, 1960–1980 (%)	Percentage Change in Share of GDP Devoted to Health Spending, 1980–2000 (%)	Public Medical Spending as Share of Total Health Spending, 1980 (%)	Public Medical Spending as Share of Total Health Spending, 2000 (%)	Percentage-Point Change in Public Share, 1980–2000
Australia	8.9	70.7	27.1	63	68.9	+5.9
Austria	7.7	76.7	1.3	68.8	69.4	+0.6
Belgium	8.6		34.4		72.1	
Canada	9.2	31.5	29.6	75.6	70.9	−4.7
Denmark	8.3		−8.8	87.8	82.5	−5.3
Finland	6.7	68.4	4.7	79	75.1	−3.9
France	9.3				75.8	
Germany	10.6		21.8	78.7	75	−3.7
Iceland	9.3	106.7	50.0	88.2	83.7	−4.5
Italy	8.2				73.4	
Japan	7.7	113.3	20.3	71.3	77.7	+6.4
The Netherlands	8.6		14.7	69.4	63.4	−6
New Zealand	8		35.6	88	78	−10
Norway	7.6	137.9	10.1	85.1	85.2	+0.1
Spain	7.5	260.0	38.9	79.9	71.7	−8.2
Sweden	8.4		−4.5	92.5	85	−7.5
Switzerland	10.7	55.1	40.8		55.6	
United Kingdom	7.3	43.6	30.4	89.4	80.9	−8.5
United States	13.1	74.0	50.6	41.5	44.2	+2.7
Mean[a]	8.7	94.4	23.3	77.2	73.1	−4.1

Source: Organization for Economic Cooperation and Development, *OECD Health Data 2003* (Paris: OECD, 2003).
[a]Excluding Turkey, Ireland, Portugal, Greece, and Luxembourg, as well as the five most recent additions to the OECD: Poland, Hungary, Korea, Mexico, and the Czech Republic.

increases. In light of past trends, as well as the general impression that health costs are inherently "uncontrollable," the unambiguous and sustained response of most nations to the new fiscal realities of the 1980s and 1990s bears emphasis.

Nonetheless, this aggregate comparison does not reveal the strategies that governments used or the reasons for their effectiveness, or how it is that countries once deemed incapable of overcoming perennial institutional blockages suddenly found vast new reservoirs of power. Undertaking these more fine-grained inquiries requires looking more deeply at particular national experiences. Besides the United States, the countries examined here are Britain, Canada, Germany, and The Netherlands—which exemplify the three key models of health care finance and delivery introduced earlier: a national health service (Britain), national health insurance (Canada), and corporatist health insurance (Germany and The Netherlands).[42] In examining these four nations, three common themes emerge: a decline in professional power, a shift toward budgeting, and a record of real, though variable, success in containing expenditures—all of which have been achieved largely without legislated cuts in public benefits or explicit cost shifting. The main contrast requiring explanation is the United States' uniquely high health spending and medical inflation, despite public and private attempts at cost containment.

If one were to cast the development of national health programs as an epic drama, the key actors would be the medical profession and the state. In all industrialized nations, including the United States, doctors ultimately lost the war—government insurance of some sort came into being—but in all, professional self-regulation and generous payment were the price paid to ensure doctors' submission to state power. By the 1980s, however, political and business leaders had almost universally come to see the cost of this concord as too high. Stewards of public and private benefits increasingly conceived of themselves as "payers," rather than guarantors; and, as payers, their goal was to control what was paid. Although national embodiments of this shift were distinctive, its general direction was consistent and its cumulative results were profound. In Britain, Thatcher waged a relentless assault on the British Medical Association's traditional consultative role. In Germany, successive legislative changes strengthened the sickness funds vis-à-vis providers and forced doctors to work within increasingly tight limits. Similar changes occurred in The Netherlands. In Canada, where the collegial model of professional self-regulation had reigned supreme, the provinces moved to cap total spending on physician services. Even amid the antigovernment fervor of the 1980s, the U.S. Medicare program adopted new controls on hospital and physician spending. And, of course, U.S. physicians saw their power wane even further in the 1990s, as health plans contracted selectively with providers, micromanaged doctors' decisions, and bargained down fees.

To be sure, providers remain powerful and watchful players in health care politics. Their main influence in the contemporary era, however, is felt less through their direct political muscle than their ability to shape public perceptions. Providers have found it extremely difficult and risky to withhold their services to protest fee cuts, in part because "doctors' strikes" are extremely unpopular. But they have had considerable success in convincing patients that national health programs are underfunded, even as their immediate power over legislative outcomes has declined substantially, and control over costs has shifted to the state, employers, and insurers.

The decline of professional influence is, however, only one manifestation of a broader move by public authorities to slow the growth of medical spending via new regulatory and budgetary controls. Even a cursory review of the legislative changes listed in table 1.2 conveys both the frequency and increasing stringency of these measures. Medical cost control has followed a ratchetlike pattern quite different from the zigzag of change and reversal seen in some other areas of health policy. New state capacities for cost control, once in place, tend to remain in place and, indeed, grow tighter and more comprehensive over time. Thus authorities in Canada, Germany, and The Netherlands introduced or strengthened fee controls for physician services, set or tightened budget ceilings for hospitals, and attempted to put in place relatively fixed budgets for specific sectors or areas of health spending. The British NHS, financed as it is by general tax revenues, has long worked within an overall budget constraint, but the NHS budget was tightened in the early 1980s and new fiscal procedures established in the early 1990s heightened the visibility of trade-offs across policy priorities and between taxes and spending. In the United States, not only the two largest public health insurance programs—Medicare and Medicaid—but also private health plans moved to rein in provider fees. For reasons to be discussed, however, U.S. gravitation toward the "international standard" in cost containment yielded decidedly mixed results, and more global restrictions on spending proved impossible. Still, the overarching movement across the five nations was toward increasingly stringent controls.

There is no need to postulate some independent "reason of state" for this tendency, although the strong autonomy of states in the face of provider resistance is certainly worth remarking on. Rather, cost-containment efforts followed an eminently political logic in their genesis and character. The underlying imperative was to restrain health spending so as to minimize restrictions on other prized areas of public finance and avoid politically explosive tax increases. Notable here are the German and Dutch experiences, where rapidly rising payroll taxes became the key focal point of cost-control efforts. Given widespread cries by employers that payroll taxes stunted job growth and abetted structural unemployment, it was at least as politically risky for leaders in these countries to avoid tackling medical inflation as it was for them to take on providers.

The specific character of cost-containment efforts also had roots in political incentives. It is striking, when one reviews the catalog of diverse cost-control measures employed within public programs, how few directly imposed new costs or explicitly reduced the scope of benefits. This is not to say that consumer spending on private insurance and services has not increased, nor is it to deny that there are increasingly important areas of care that fall outside the scope of public protections. As the next section emphasizes, these forms of policy drift are crucial. Yet, these

Table 1.2. Significant Legislative Changes in Health Policy in Five Nations, 1980–2003

Britain

- Series of modest reorganizations accompany a tightened National Health Service budget (1980–1989).
- 1990 NHS and Community Care Act emerges from 1989 White Paper; it envisions the creation of new purchasing agents to contract with hospitals and the authorization of general practitioner (GP) "fundholding" under which GPs would be given budgets to purchase secondary services.
- 1997 White Paper of Labour government proposes the abolition of "internal market," but the proposed changes retain purchaser–provider split and expand GP fundholding, key elements of 1990 reform.
- Labour leadership commits itself to reaching spending parity with continental Europe.

Canada

- Canada Health Act (1984) tightens federal standards for provincial programs, limiting role of private finance. Reaffirmed through federal actions in mid-1990s.
- Dramatic long-term decline of federal transfers to support provincial programs under Progressive Conservatives (1983–1993).
- 1997 Report of National Forum on Health Care, a creation of federal Liberal government, endorses existing structure and calls for some expansions, to date largely unimplemented.
- Ongoing provincial efforts at hospital restructuring yield change mainly at the margins. A few provinces consider but do not enact more ambitious reforms.

Germany

- Series of cost-containment acts expand copayments and tighten budgeting and rate-setting.
- 1988 Health Care Reform Act extends preventive check-ups and home care and increases copayments, particularly for pharmaceuticals. Only increased copayments survive implementation.
- 1993 Health Care Structural Reform Act makes substantial change to hospital budgeting (further reformed in 1995 and 1996), creates scheme for equalizing contribution levels across sickness funds, and allows patients greater choice of funds while further expanding copayments for pharmaceuticals.
- 1995 Statutory Nursing Care Insurance expands long-term care coverage.
- 1997 Health Care Reorganization Act lifts some budgetary restrictions imposed in 1992, maintains and expands patient choice of funds, places new cost-containment responsibilities on the sickness funds, and imposes greater cost-sharing, though not all cost-sharing provisions are fully implemented.
- New Social Democratic leadership repeals some of the market-based elements of previous reforms and promises but postpones further structural reforms.

Table 1.2. Significant Legislative Changes in Health Policy in Five Nations, 1980–2003

The Netherlands

- Series of cost-containment acts strengthen central budgeting, introduce prospective budgets for hospitals and other medical institutions, and create price control system for prescription drugs.

- 1987 Dekker Report, supported by center-right government, outlines a major reorganization to encourage competition among insurers and providers and to change the premium structure, separating basic from supplementary coverage and eroding firewall between sickness funds and private insurance.

- Labor government elected in 1989 revises plan, stressing need for broader uniform social insurance. Series of subsequent revisions foster conflict, leaving many reforms unimplemented.

- During the 1990s, policymakers, following a more cautious course, manage to increase scope for and freedom of private insurance while creating scheme to compensate insurers that cover high risks.

United States

- Medicaid spending is significantly cut in first Reagan budget (1981).

- Passage of two cost-control measures for Medicare: prospective payment in the hospital sector (1982) and fee schedule for the physician sector (1989).

- Series of coverage expansions under Medicaid through federal mandates on states (1984–1989).

- Medicare Catastrophic Coverage Act expanding Medicare is passed, then repealed (1988–89).

- Kassebaum–Kennedy (1996) regulations encouraging health insurance portability pass in wake of failure of Clinton health plan (1994) and aggressive Republican drive to cut social spending (1995).

- 1997 budget aims to foster Medicare contracts with private health plans while also cutting payments; it also funds new state plans for low-income children.

- New Republican administration enacts prescription drug benefit for elderly beneficiaries of Medicare in 2003; it includes measures designed to increase role of private health plans within the program.

changes are for the most part *not* the result of explicit attempts at cost shifting. To date, the use of cost sharing has not increased dramatically in Britain, Canada, Germany, or The Netherlands, or within the U.S. Medicare program, and the increases that have occurred have been unpopular, riddled with exceptions, and vulnerable to reversal. "Delisting" of benefits once covered by public programs is quite rare, and the explicit exclusion of previously covered populations is essentially nonexistent. Instead, cost containment has focused overwhelmingly on controlling fees or overall spending. The motive is no secret: imposing controls on providers and then leaving them to cope has proved a far more politically attractive strategy than imposing direct costs or restrictions on patients. The medical maxim "do no harm" has its counterpart in the political sphere: "never be seen to impose highly visible and traceable costs on large numbers of voters." Here the dictates of blame avoidance have offered clear counsel, which politicians have largely followed.

Health policy experts continue to disagree about how well alternative cost-control strategies have worked. Part of the analytic problem is that reducing medical inflation is only a limited measure of success in cost control. The word "control," after all, implies not any particular outcome, but simply that it is in the hands of policymakers to decide. Judged by this standard, Britain has long had the most control, and the United States the least, with Canada, Germany, and The Netherlands in between. In terms of spending growth, however, the striking fact is the substantial cross-national similarity in overall pattern. After rising steeply over the postwar period, the curve of spending growth leveled off in the 1980s and became flat or actually turned down in a number of nations in the 1990s. Between 1993 and 1998, for example, the share of GDP devoted to health spending fell in every one of the five cases but Germany. Even accounting for the strong economic growth of this period, this is a notable development.

Despite the moderation of medical inflation in the mid-1990s, however, the United States continues to stand out as an outlier. Why has the American way of financing medical care proved so distinctly incapable of reining in medical costs? The strongest hypothesis is that the fragmentation and opacity of major financing sources and the limited scope of collective insurance pools have simultaneously muted concern about costs and prevented public and private authorities from exercising decisive control. For all the differences in their financing systems, Britain, Canada, Germany, and The Netherlands all route a large proportion of health spending through highly visible and encompassing financing pipelines—principally, the general tax system (Britain and Canada) and the payroll tax system (Germany and The Netherlands). Of necessity, then, the costs of health care are highly transparent, and few obvious avenues exist for public authorities or employers to shift or obscure these costs. In the United States, by contrast, financing not only comes from a huge multiplicity of sources, but much of it is hidden in the form of tax subsidies for private health benefits (which cost $88 billion in 1998) and reductions in workers' take-home pay.[43] And even when payers undertake concerted attempts to clamp down, as did Medicare in the 1980s and employers in the 1990s, their universe of control is strictly circumscribed, and their efforts are likely to be dissipated by broader health-sector trends and cost shifting. Moreover, as the next section discusses, private efforts to control spending have over time resulted in significant shifts of risk and costs from collective risk pools to workers. Such risk and cost shifting is much more difficult in frameworks in which all or nearly all citizens have coverage guarantees that must be altered through democratic processes.

The barriers to cost containment posed by the fragmentation of American financing would seem to imply that fiscal concentration is a precondition for cost control, and, indeed, monopsonistic financing, in which governments pay for most care, have proved quite effective at controlling spending. The German and Dutch experiences suggest, however, that more pluralistic systems can nonetheless achieve similar levels of budgetary control through the creation of hard sectoral budgets within which insurers and providers negotiate—a functional equivalent to monopsonistic financing. (The success, albeit temporary, of U.S. managed care to control costs also rested largely on sharp reductions in fees paid to providers.) Furthermore, because monopsonistic financing makes it easier to hold politicians responsible for cost control's negative effects, governments face a trade-off between control and accountability, which may help explain why centralized systems do not demonstrate a greater cross-national advantage. Despite these caveats, it is the case that levels of spending are typically lower in tax-financed national health services, which appear to create the greatest capacity for—although not necessarily the greatest political interest in—restraint on spending growth. The recent Canadian reversal of inflationary spending trends suggests that declining national contributions in fiscally decentralized systems can also be a powerful tool for spending reductions. (Although not one of the five cases, a similar process lies behind Sweden's impressive cost restraint.) Here the mechanism would seem to be the capacity of central governments to minimize direct blame for subnational cost-containment efforts precipitated by declining contributions from the center.[44]

If blame-avoidance imperatives explain key features of cost-containment policies, a natural question is whether cost control creates political fallout. The answer would seem to be yes, but without any one-to-one relationship between spending trends and levels of public support. In 1990, public satisfaction with national health systems correlated with overall per capita health spending relatively closely—except in the case of the United States, which spent more than any other nation but showed little public satisfaction for it.[45] But because public satisfaction is related to public expectations, which are likely to vary across nations as well as across individuals, the more relevant indicator is changes in public satisfaction over time.[46] On this measure, the striking feature of the scattered available evidence presented in table 1.3 is the very sharp decline in public enthusiasm that occurred in Canada in the decade after 1988. A smaller but still notable decrease occurred in Germany between 1988 and 1994, whereas public views in the United Kingdom remained relatively stable. The United States presents a mixed picture that hints at increased opinion polarization: growing support for only minor changes alongside growing support for completely rebuilding the system.

Looking at events in individual countries, the conclusion that cost containment has prompted political backlash is considerably strengthened. In Britain in the late 1980s, for example, public dissatisfaction fueled by media stories, provider appeals, and mounting waiting lists forced the NHS to the top of Thatcher's political agenda. In the United States, increasing micromanagement of clinical decisions by private health plans prompted a wave of public revulsion against "managed care." In Canada, the decline of federal funds set off an orgy of recrimination between doctors and provincial governments that fed Canadians' growing sense of

Table 1.3. Public Satisfaction and Health Spending in Four Nations, 1990–2001

Country	Responds Minor Changes Needed (%)	Increase/ Decrease	Responds Fundamental Changes Needed (%)	Increase/ Decrease	Favors a Complete Rebuilding of the System (%)	Increase/ Decrease	Health Spending as Share of GDP (%)	Increase/ Decrease
Canada								
1990	56		38		5		9.0	
1994	29	−27	59	+21	12	+7	9.5	+0.5
1998	20	−9	56	−3	23	+11	9.1	−0.4
2001	21	+1	59	+3	18	−5	9.7	+0.6
Germany								
1990	41		35		13		8.5	
1994	30	−11	55	20	11	−2	9.9	1.5
United Kingdom								
1990	27		52		17		6	
1998	35	+8	58	+6	14	−3	6.9	−0.2
2001	21	−14	60	+2	18	+4	7.6	+0.7
United States								
1990	10		60		29		11.9	
1994	18	+8	53	−7	28	−1	13.2	+1.3
1998	17	−1	46	−7	33	+5	13	−0.3
2001	18	+1	51	+5	28	−5	13.9	+0.9

Sources: Robert J. Blendon et al., "Satisfaction with Health Systems in Ten Nations," *Health Affairs* 9, no. 2 (1990):185–92; "Who Has the Best Health Care System? A Second Look," *Health Affairs* 14, no. 4 (1995):220–30; and "Inequities in Health Care: A Five-Country Survey," *Health Affairs* 21, no. 3 (2002):182–91. Spending from Organization for Economic Cooperation and Development, *OECD Health Data 2003* (Paris: OECD, 2003).

unease. Public perceptions, however, are mediated by provider strategies and the dynamics of political competition. Government cost control seems most likely to become a topic of public concern when competition between contending parties centers on the ruling government's health care stewardship, when payment disputes are highly frequent and visible, and when providers feel sufficiently aggrieved to adopt an "outside" strategy of stoking public fears, rather than working through established mechanisms of state–professional bargaining.[47]

The most straightforward conclusion, however, is that the politics of blame avoidance cuts both ways. Leaders who fail to act as health care consumes ever larger shares of public and private budgets risk the wrath of employers and the clienteles of nonhealth programs. But cost-containment efforts create their own potent political risks, raising the specter of waiting lists and outmoded facilities, and creating highly public conflict with providers. In this environment, the appeal of competition is its twin promise to foster more effective utilization of existing resources (thus eliding the potential cost–quality trade-off) while shifting responsibility away from embattled political leaders and onto newly sovereign quasi-market actors. As we shall see, that promise has been exceedingly difficult to realize. Unlike cost containment, structural-reform campaigns have been marked by substantial diversity across nations, in their emergence as well as their character and effects. To explain this variation requires exploring the contradictions of market-based reform, the interaction between political and medical systems, and the subtle but fundamental shifts that have occurred without legislative change, as the effects of cost containment have played out within distinctive medical complexes.

THE POLITICS OF STRUCTURAL REFORM

In one form or another, structural reform initiatives have emerged on the decision-making agenda of Britain, Canada, Germany, and the United States over the past two decades, with Canada only recently moving toward consideration of the issue. The most ambitious of these proposals was President Bill Clinton's plan for universal health insurance via managed competition, but this initiative failed to even come up in Congress for a vote. The next most sweeping proposal was arguably the so-called Dekker reforms pursued in The Netherlands since the late 1980s, which have proved exceedingly difficult to implement, followed by Thatcher's internal market reforms of 1989, which were enacted and in large part realized.[48] German leaders have charted a more cautious course, with structural reforms that were significantly less comprehensive and radical than the Dekker reforms but also more fully realized. The overall Canadian policy framework remained extremely stable throughout this period.

From the foregoing, it should already be clear that interest in reform is not confined to any single type of medical or political system. The conditions under which structural reform rises to prominence, however, do seem to differ between more centralized and more fragmented political structures. In the former, the commitment of the ruling government to major structural reform seems to be the necessary and sufficient condition for raising reform to the top of the agenda. The question thus becomes why parties in power seek the goal. In more fragmented political settings, the conditions for the emergence of reform are less clear cut. Economic downturns appear quite helpful. Serious momentum toward reform also seems to require cross-party interest, perhaps because leaders anticipate the need for oversized coalitions to achieve legislative results. Thus, while major structural reforms seem favored in centralized political settings when ruling parties enjoy a strong position, close divisions between the parties may actually facilitate the rise of the issue in more fragmented systems.

To begin the analysis, therefore, we need a more systematic classification of political and medical systems. At the risk of papering over subtle variations, the framework I present here reduces the complexities of the empirical terrain to two key dimensions. In the case of political systems, I emphasize the presence or absence of formal institutional veto points, which shapes the incentives and opportunities of policymakers. In the case of medical systems, I emphasize the centrality of the state in financing and regulating medical care, which shapes the kinds of challenges policymakers confront and their ability to implement legislative aims. Figure 1.2 maps out the fourfold division that results. Political systems

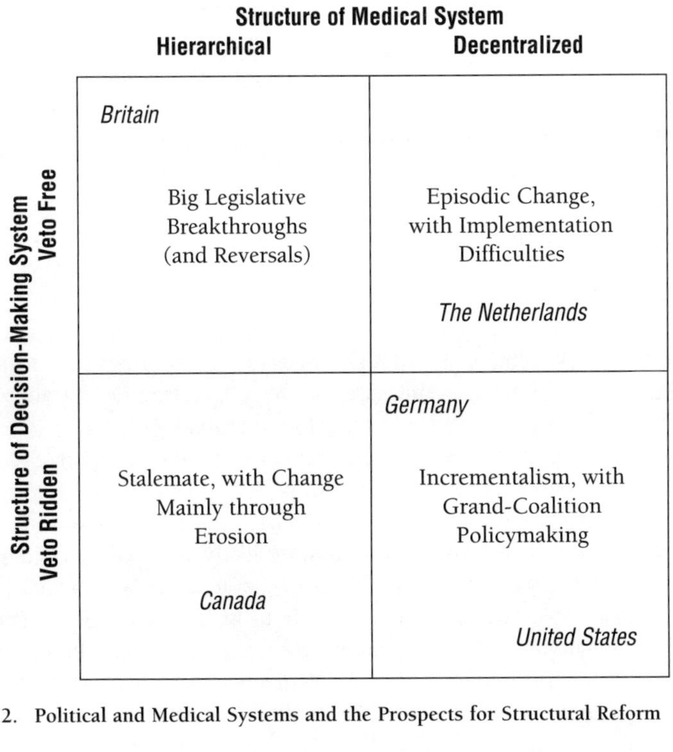

Figure 1.2. **Political and Medical Systems and the Prospects for Structural Reform**

may be either *veto free* or *veto ridden*; medical systems may be either *hierarchical* or *decentralized*. I have placed the five cases at different points within the cells to indicate their relative location on these axes. For the purposes of classification, however, the divisions are binary and mutually exclusive. To have a veto-free decision-making structure, a nation must have a parliamentary government and be a unitary, rather than federal, state. To have a decentralized medical system, it must rely significantly on multiple payers, such as sickness funds, commercial insurers, and private employers. Of the five nations under consideration, therefore, Britain exemplifies the veto-free/hierarchical quadrant, The Netherlands the veto-free/decentralized category, the United States and Germany the veto-ridden/decentralized cell, and Canada the veto-ridden/hierarchical type.[49]

Inevitably, some countries fit into this framework less well than others.[50] In addition, the framework does not perfectly capture two common distinctions in comparative politics: between "consensual" and "majoritarian" party systems, and "pluralist" and "corporatist" interest representation. Although it cannot be doubted that unitary parliamentary governments with single-member districts (in this dataset, Britain and New Zealand) differ from the larger class of parliamentary systems that use proportional representation (PR), it is difficult to determine the extent to which the distinctive partisan dynamics of the former (such as two-partyism and oversized parliamentary majorities) are the result of formal institutions rather than societal factors or public opinion. For this reason, I prefer to treat these dynamics as an intervening variable and focus on the crucial uniting characteristic of Westminster and PR systems—namely, the absence of formal veto points for blocking legislative change, which allows committed majorities or stable coalitions to pursue their goals without interference from second chambers, subnational governments, judicial decree, or popular referenda.

As for "corporatism"—stable, recurrent bargaining between the state and key policy stakeholders—it is indeed a distinctive feature of many continental and northern European polities. Yet, it, too, is not a formal veto point. In the present framework, corporatism enters in via the characterization of medical systems. This obviously raises concerns about the classification of the American medical system, which is arguably so distinctive it needs a category of its own. But, again, a virtue of the present scheme is that it allows us to see important similarities across otherwise diverse nations—in this case, between America's decentralized financing and the corporatist financing systems found abroad.

How, then, should we expect the different configurations of political and medical authority to shape the politics of health policy reform? Figure 1.2 again maps out the basic expectations. Veto-free/hierarchical regimes are the settings in which structural reforms, once proposed, are most likely to be enacted and implemented. In veto-free/decentralized regimes, the political system facilitates legislative change, but the medical system is likely to become a serious barrier at the stage of implementation. In veto-ridden/decentralized regimes, by contrast, it is highly difficult to consolidate authority for major policy change. Yet, the pluralism of the system may actually facilitate smaller scale reform by leaving room for shifting coalitions of interest. Legislative change can occur when broad coalitions form to overcome veto points and diffuse potential blame. Finally, veto-ridden/hierarchical regimes—of which, admittedly, Canada is the only OECD example—may actually be more prone to policy stalemate than veto-ridden/pluralist–corporatist regimes. This is not only because the political system makes change inherently difficult, but also because the hierarchical structure of medical authority leaves limited room for coalitional reshuffling among key stakeholders—and, in particular, limits the ability of business firms to become key political players or to alter benefits independently of government action.

The remainder of this section examines the dynamics and effects of structural reform within this framework of expectations, focusing on the five key cases but drawing on the experience of other nations when necessary to amplify or test key claims. As will become clear, market-oriented reforms are, surprisingly, almost entirely clustered in the veto-free/hierarchical regimes, all of which have seen a decline in the government share of health spending. Yet, the effects of market-oriented reforms have been relatively modest and, on the whole, tended to enhance state authority rather than augment market forces. In the fragmented and decentralized regimes, by contrast, large-scale structural reforms have fared poorly. Nonetheless, these systems saw an overall shift toward an expanded public share of spending in the 1980s and 1990s. Finally, in all five nations, many of the largest changes in ground-level outcomes were the result not of structural reforms, but of the long-term and mostly unintended effects of cost-containment policies, which have increased dramatically the private share of spending in many nations while enabling significant retrenchment of the public–private framework of protection in the United States despite overall stability in public policy.

THE VETO-FREE CASES: BRITAIN AND THE NETHERLANDS

When health policy experts speak of a sweeping trend toward market-oriented reform, they typically cite a few familiar examples. Britain, Sweden, and The Netherlands are on everyone's list, with Denmark, Finland, and New Zealand often mentioned, too.[51] Taking just the six agreed-on exemplars, fully five of them are located in the veto-free/hierarchical quadrant, and all are characterized by relatively centralized political systems. Indeed, given the extreme difficulties that Dutch policymakers have faced in transforming the Dekker vision into actual policy change, it is arguable that the only true cases of realized market reform fall into the veto-free/hierarchical category. As figure 1.3 shows, moreover, all but one of the nations in this veto-free/hierarchical quadrant display a notable decline in the share of medical spending funded by government. On average, the public share of spending in these nations dropped 5.4 percentage points between 1980 and 2000. By contrast, the public share of spending remained essentially stable in the veto-free/decentralized quadrant and rose by an average of 1.6 percentage points in the veto-ridden/decentralized quadrant. (Canada, the lone veto-ridden/hierarchical

Structure of Medical System

Hierarchical	Decentralized

Structure of Decision-Making System

Veto-Free

Public Share of Total Health Spending

Country	1980 (%)	2000 (%)	Pct. Pt. Change	Total* (%)
Denmark	87.8	82.5	–5.3	8.3
Finland	79.0	75.1	–3.9	6.7
Iceland	88.2	83.7	–4.5	9.3
Italy	79.3[a]	73.4	–5.9	8.2
Norway	85.1	85.2	0.1	7.6
NZ	88.0	78.0	–10	8.0
Sweden	92.5	85	–7.5	8.4
UK	89.4	80.9	–9.5	7.3
Mean	86.2	80.5	–5.4**	8.0

*2000 total expenditure on health, share GDP.
**Weighted by years between observations.
[a]1990

Public Share of Total Health Spending

Country	1980 (%)	2000 (%)	Pct. Pt. Change	Total* (%)
Austria	68.8	69.4	0.6	8.9
Belgium	70.5[b]	72.2	1.7	8.6
France	76.6[a]	75.8	–0.8	9.3
Japan	71.3	77.7	+6.4	7.7
Netherlands	69.4	63.4	–6	8.6
Mean	71.3[c]	71.7[c]	+0.2**[c]	8.62[c]

*2000 total expenditure on health, share GDP.
**Weighted by years between observations.
[a]1990
[b]1995
[c]Different from veto-free/hierarchical mean at 95 percent confidence level.

Veto-Ridden

Public Share of Total Health Spending

Country	1980 (%)	2000 (%)	Change	Total* (%)
Canada	75.6[c]	70.9[c]	–4.7[c]	9.2[c]

*2000 total expenditure on health, share GDP.
[c]Different from veto-free/hierarchical mean at 95 percent confidence level.

Public Share of Total Health Spending

Country	1980 (%)	2000 (%)	Change	Total* (%)
Australia	63	68.9	+5.9	8.9
Germany	78.7	75	–3.7	10.6
Switzerland	52.4[a]	55.6	+3.2	10.7
United States	41.5	44.2	+2.7	13.1
Mean	58.9[c]	60.9[c]	1.6**[c]	10.8[c]

*2000 total expenditure on health, share GDP.
**Weighted by years between observations.
[a]1990
[c]Different from veto-free/hierarchical mean at 95 percent confidence level.

Figure 1.3. Political and Medical Systems and the Public Share of Health Spending

regime, saw a 4.7-point drop.) Within the OECD, therefore, a significant con-vergence of the public share of spending has occurred since 1980, much of it driven by the universal decline in the public fiscal role in the veto-free/hierarchical regimes.[52]

At first glance, the concentration of market reforms in the veto-free/hierarchical regimes is at odds with conventional expectations. These are nations, after all, that have demonstrated the greatest commitment to an expansive government role in health care, and they have generally been the most successful in restraining both the overall level of health spending and its growth. Countries with national health services, moreover, have progressed farthest toward the social-democratic ideal of a universal right to publicly funded and provided medical care, free at the time of treatment. These are precisely the countries, it might be thought, where new challenges would promote an energetic reaffirmation of founding principles, rather than efforts to introduce markets.

The paradox evaporates, however, once one considers the policy capacities and definition of reform goals that the existing policy frameworks in these nations engendered, the political opportunities that governments in these countries had, and the actual character and effect of the reforms that were put in place. First, and most obvious, the idea of introducing highly limited forms of market freedom simply made intuitive sense in nations where medical care had previously been governed through extremely hierarchical mechanisms. Whereas other nations came under acute fiscal strain at a point when their means for controlling spending were often quite underdeveloped, the veto-free/hierarchical regimes had in place financing systems and forms of payment that already embodied substantial capacities for cost control. For example, fee-for-service reimbursement of physicians, which abets medical inflation in the absence of strict limits on payments and service volume, was much less prevalent in these nations than it was elsewhere. To the extent that these nations faced a common challenge, it was less how to develop the means for cost control than how to exercise these means without public backlash or serious sectoral distortions. In this environment, it was natural for politicians to gravitate toward efficiency-promoting interventions, however unproven.

Second, and far more important, leaders in these nations worked within formal political institutions that gave them the *opportunity* to exercise decisive authority. To be sure, the more consensual style of policymaking in the PR systems of the Scandinavian states differs markedly from the seesaw pattern of majority-party dominance in Britain and New Zealand. In both settings, however, ruling governments did not have to cope with the veto points introduced by federalism, a powerful judiciary, the separation of powers, or popular referenda—all features evident individually or in combination in the more veto-ridden systems. This proved crucial in Britain and New Zealand in particular, where all evidence suggests that proposed reforms were initially quite unpopular. Leaders in veto-free systems did not always have the inclination or maneuvering room to pursue structural reforms, but they had the means to do so more often than elsewhere, and, particularly when faced with a debilitated opposition, they were typically more willing to adopt the longer time horizons that structural reform requires.[53] In fragmented settings, by contrast, leaders instead generally followed a path of preemptive accommodation and incrementalism—"tiptoeing in" rather than "crashing through." On this point, it is revealing that the two major attempts to use the high-risk strategy of one-shot reform within veto-ridden polities—the Dekker reforms and the Clinton health plan—were distinguished mainly by the glaring gap between aspirations and accomplishments.

Third, and perhaps least recognized, there was an important *policy* logic to reformers' strategies in the veto-free/hierarchical regimes, a logic that is often obscured in the literature on market-based reform. Health policy experts in the United States typically contrast regulation and competition. Though few are naïve enough to think that health care competition requires *no* government role, they usually see that role as limited to policing and enabling autonomous market processes. The experience of international market reform shows that this perspective grossly understates the extent of central power needed for, and indeed encouraged by, market-oriented reforms. The ability of countries such as Britain, New Zealand, and Sweden to pursue market reforms was not at odds with the hierarchical structure of their systems but deeply dependent on it, and the surest effect of market-oriented reforms was to strengthen the state's regulatory role quite fundamentally. Moreover, these reforms carried with them the seeds of further state intervention. Although one motive for pursuing reform was to shift responsibility to other actors, the result was usually the opposite. Introduced into hierarchical systems, market mechanisms entailed strong government claims for system improvement, the deployment of highly visible levers of state power, and new performance measures to encourage responsive resource allocation. With these conditions in place, it proved nearly impossible for governments to let go of the new instruments they had deployed. Technically, true marketization may have been feasible. Politically, it was not.

As the nation where market reforms went furthest, Britain presents the hardest test for the argument. On close inspection, however, it is a veritable showcase of the limited and contradictory effects of market reforms. As already discussed, Thatcher turned to internal market reform not as part of an ideological crusade against the welfare state—even at the height of her power she had carefully avoided attacking public health provision—but as an attempt to head off a mounting crisis over NHS funding. Once audit and reform of the NHS had been promised, however, Thatcher and her aides were "loathe" merely to sink more money into the system and instead presented a comprehensive blueprint for structural reform, the centerpiece of which was a new internal market in which regionally based public managers would be given the authority to contract selectively with hospitals (both public and private) for the provision of services.[54] In a third term in power at the time of the reform campaign, the conservatives were nearly brought down by public furor over the proposal, and Thatcher's chastened successor, John Major, did not fully implement the envisioned changes. Nor were more radical reforms, such as the infusion of large amounts of private finance or a shift toward national health insurance, ever considered feasible. Nonetheless, the internal market reforms still marked a dramatic break with previous patterns of NHS adjustment.

What they did not mark, however, was a dramatic shift toward markets. If anything, in fact, the opposite was true. Political scientist Susan Giaimo concludes, for example, that "the managerial reforms worked in the opposite direction of devolution to strengthen both the legal authority and institutional capacity of policymakers for centralized intervention in the NHS."[55] Rudolf Klein, a distinguished scholar of British health politics, observes:

> Far from leading to the devolution of decision making—the ultimate logic of a market system—the Conservative reforms led to increasing centralization. From the start ministers insisted that the internal market should not cause disruption. . . . In short, competition was hobbled by central regulation and direction; the logic of market competition and the logic of NHS politics pulled in opposite directions.[56]

As Klein's commentary suggests, it is tempting to see the limits of competition as a result of political constraints on implementation. As economist Julian Le Grand puts it, "The British quasi-market in health care neither succeeded nor failed, simply because it was never tried."[57] It is worth emphasizing, however, that the key innovation of the internal market—the creation of regional purchasers—was inherently centralizing in its emphasis on greater managerial power to bargain with providers, and this power in turn flowed directly from, and was directly accountable to, the central government. Conservatives no doubt correctly saw this as the most effective means of managing initial resource deployment and of crippling the only other real center of power within a hierarchical medical system—namely, doctors. But it had the effect of creating levers and accountability measures that were inherently centralizing. In turn, by selling reform on the basis of responsiveness and improved outcomes, politicians set themselves up to be judged on these results. Each new performance indicator was an invitation to intervention—the "bedpan . . . dropped on a hospital floor" that the creator of the NHS, Aneurin Bevan, predicted would henceforth "resound in the Palace of Westminster."[58] Implementation, in this sense, conformed to the logic of market-oriented ideas as Thatcher adapted them to a hierarchical system, rather than repudiated that logic.

As might be expected from the foregoing, moreover, the ground-level changes introduced by the internal market reforms were underwhelming, especially if judged against the grandiose rhetoric of reform's promoters. Giaimo writes that the fears of critics of the internal market have not been borne out "precisely because competition has been so limited."[59] Political scientist Carolyn Tuohy notes that "arguably little change occurred in the broad balance among state actors, the medical profession, and private finance."[60] In a comprehensive survey of the relevant microlevel evidence, Le Grand concludes that "[p]erhaps the most striking conclusion to arise from the evidence is how little overall measurable change there seems to have been."[61] That the internal market seems to have had little effect on ground-level policy outcomes does not mean that no such changes have occurred. The increasing role of private finance is an important shift that will be taken up in a moment. But on all the available evidence, this shift has relatively little to do with the NHS reforms around which so much controversy has swirled. Perhaps the strongest indication of the reforms' relative lack of impact is the decision of the post-1997 Labour government not to alter fundamentally arrangements it had long criticized.

The story of the Dekker reforms bears important similarities to the British saga. Here the reform ideal, although also dressed in market garb, was actually markedly different: greater competition among sickness funds within a framework of expanded basic risk protection. And more so than in Britain, the Dutch reform proposal had to adopt preemptive concessions, both to accommodate the coalition partners in power at the time and to head off the plethora of potential opponents—sickness funds, insurers, employer, doctors—thrown up by The Netherlands' pluralist–corporatist financing structure. All the same, the reforms eventually passed were in many respects *more* ambitious than the British reforms, and many health policy experts writing in the early 1990s saw them as the surest sign of a global trend toward market-based innovation.

That judgment, however, proved wildly premature, as the reform train ground to a halt in the implementation stage, blocked by the corporatist medical system that it aimed to remodel. As political scientist Alan Jacobs observes, "Dutch governments have been unable to bring the Dekker vision to life, leaving the old system largely intact."[62] Two Dutch policy insiders conclude: "[T]he restructuring process generated growing opposition and, despite a seemingly realistic time-table of five years for implementation, it was subsequently abandoned. In many ways, decision-making . . . lies in limbo."[63] Instead of decentralizing power to consumers, another insider writes, the Dutch reform process "provoked a largely unplanned process of creeping etatization."[64] Although one clear effect of the reforms has been to increase the autonomy of insurers in negotiating fees with providers, other key elements of the enacted reforms—notably, efforts to level the playing field between funds and private insurers and the shift of some fund-provided benefits to a state-run catastrophic insurance program—were in the direction of enhanced state power.

What, then, are we to make of the notable decline in the public share of spending seen in all of the veto-free/hierarchical regimes, as well as a few other nations? Is this not evidence of significant diminution in the role of the state caused by market-oriented changes? The fall in the public share of spending suggests that the role of the welfare state is changing. But this change is almost certainly not caused by market reforms. The British experience is instructive. The overall level of private spending and the reliance of Britons on private health insurance rose most precipitously in the 1980s, *before* the 1989 reforms, and have been relatively stable since. Despite dire stories about the flight of the rich from the NHS, popular support for the system remains overwhelming, and the reach of private health insurance is still minimal. All signs are that the rise of private spending, in Britain as in the other veto-free/hierarchical cases, has principally been a byproduct of austerity in public spending and only secondarily a result of affirmative policy changes, such as increased cost sharing or the shift of services outside the universe of covered benefits. The British experience thus strongly suggests that what I have termed "policy drift and conversion"—that is, change within established policy parameters, either through decentralized adaptation (conversion) or failure to adjust policies to changing circumstances (drift)—has been more consequential than politically initiated reforms.

So far, too, the feared effects of private spending on equity and solidarity have largely failed to materialize. This is not because private finance cannot have such effects; the U.S. case strongly supports the contrary view. Nor is it meant to gainsay the real hardships that have been imposed. But despite the drop in the public share of spending in veto-free/hierarchical regimes, private finance remains on the margins. The exception is New Zealand, where private insurance has historically played a much larger role than in Britain (covering roughly half of New Zealanders, versus less than a seventh of Britons) and where the welfare state has been under broad and successful assault for over a decade. New Zealand, however, is atypical. In most of the nations that have seen a drop in the public share, the strains of austerity have been broadly distributed. Cost sharing has increased. Affluent patients are sometimes buying their way off waiting lists. But the fundamental role of public finance remains.

THE VETO-RIDDEN CASES: CANADA, GERMANY, AND THE UNITED STATES

In contrast with the across-the-board reduction in the public share of spending in veto-free/hierarchical regimes, more fragmented political systems have demonstrated much greater diversity of policy response. And despite the possible affinity between the more heavily privatized structure of the medical systems in these nations and market-based reforms, procompetitive reform legislation has faced a rough road. In the United States, the Clinton proposal for managed competition met an inglorious legislative fate, and the main legislative achievements of the period were increased regulatory requirements on health plans to encourage portability of coverage across jobs and an expansion of public coverage for low-income children and their parents. In Germany, reforms allowed greater choice of sickness funds and moved to equalize contribution levels across funds, but this package was a "rather tame strategic contrivance" justified by a sprinkling of market rhetoric and "so far . . . unspectacular" in its effects.[65]

Judged against the veto-free/hierarchical regimes, the clearest pattern that unites the fragmented decentralized regimes is the fairly consistent, and often striking, expansion of the public share of spending. The only country in this cell where the public share dropped is Germany, whereas Australia saw an increase of roughly 6 percentage points in the public share, and Switzerland and the United States saw a roughly 3-point increase (in the Swiss case, in just the last decade). Indeed, if we expand our field of inquiry to all the decentralized medical systems, what stands out is the degree to which these systems appear to have been catching up with the more hierarchical regimes during the 1980s and 1990s. One obvious reason for this is the weaker control over expenditures that public programs in these nations exercised. Population aging may also play a role, for even in countries with significant private financing, the elderly almost always rely principally on public programs.

Yet, even when actual legislative changes are considered, one cannot avoid the conclusion that a major reason for the shift is the expansion of public programs. This is most obviously the case in Australia and Switzerland, both nations in which universal statutory coverage was achieved only after 1980. In Japan, public long-term care insurance for the elderly was expanded in the 1990s, and the same was true in Germany. In the United States, public coverage for the poor under Medicaid expanded significantly in the 1980s and 1990s, although not enough to offset declining private protections. The U.S. public share of spending rose to 46 percent in the 1990s. And if the cost of tax breaks for private health benefits are included, the share now exceeds half of total spending.[66] Given recent challenges to the welfare state, the continued expansion of public health insurance in the decentralized systems is a noteworthy development.

Explicit alterations in public policy are not, however, the only source of change within mature medical complexes. In two nations in particular, Canada and the United States, policy drift has been pervasive and important. In each, legislative stalemate has plagued the debate over structural reform, and, in each, legislative stalemate has opened the door to transformation of policy through the erosion of public programs and the decentralized adjustment of private and subnational policy actors. In the United States, however, these changes have been far more rapid and fundamental, reflecting the primary role of private employers in the American financing structure. Canada and the United States, in turn, are both distinct from Germany in that inclusive political coalitions have not formed behind structural reform as they have across the Atlantic.

Canada is the appropriate place to begin, because its experience is in key respects idiosyncratic. The defining feature of the Canadian Medicare program is the prominent role that federalism played in its development and continues to play in its operation.[67] Indeed, recent developments in Canada cannot be understood independently of the growing decentralization of Canadian federal relations. Consolidated in the early 1970s, and codified in the Canada Health Act of 1984, the Canadian health policy framework relies on the provinces and territories to insure their citizens via public programs that meet tight federal guidelines. Between 1984 and the late 1990s, a period marked by deep provincial–federal conflicts (most notably over the separatist movement in Quebec) and by a dire fiscal situation at the federal level, the federal government took a hands-off policy toward Medicare in general but slashed federal contributions to provincial programs while demanding that provinces continue to adhere to the terms of the 1984 settlement. The result, understandably, was political acrimony, worsened by fierce disputes at the provincial level between cash-strapped provinces and medical providers. Amid this stalemate and dispute, the formal legislative changes introduced into Medicare have been modest and concentrated at the provincial level.

The acrimony and stalemate that have marked recent Canadian health politics can be understood as an outgrowth of the peculiar fragmented-hierarchical regime created during the formative years of Medicare's creation. Canada bears very close comparison with the United States, where the federal Medicare program essentially adopted the Blue Cross/Blue Shield model then prevalent among the working population. In Canada, provincial experimentation, beginning as early as 1948, and a parliamentary form of government facilitated the creation of a similar program not for the elderly alone but for the entire population. In transporting the existing private coverage model into the public sector, however, Canada departed sharply from the corporatist regimes of Germany and The Netherlands, which continued to rely on preexisting organizations of nongovernmental finance. The Canadian path thus institutionalized a relationship of bilateral monopoly between the state and providers, which was inherently stable and difficult to dislodge, and then overlaid it on a highly decentralized political structure that was actually becoming more fragmented and acrimonious. The resulting constellation of political forces was highly inimical to large-scale legislative reform. The provinces had exclusive jurisdiction over health policy but were constrained by the strict terms of federal transfers under the Canada Health Act. The federal government, meanwhile, could shift responsibility and blame for cost control downward by cutting funds but had strong incentives to retain ultimate control over basic policy parameters through federal mandates. And given the stability of the professional–provincial divide and the lack of an integral employer role, there was no obvious new coalition of interests that might appeal for alternative arrangements.

The exact effects of the resulting two decades of stalemate and infighting are difficult to pin down, but two are unmistakable. The first is a massive decline in public confidence in the system. The second is a fairly dramatic drop in the share of health spending provided by public sources, all the more notable because it runs sharply against the grain of the near-universal trend toward expanded public spending in other veto-ridden polities. The stability of the Canadian policy framework makes it implausible that this shift is a result of legislative reforms, and indeed no province has had the policy latitude or political will to enact substantial changes. Instead, the decline in the public share of spending is in large part a reflection of government austerity. As in the veto-free/hierarchical regimes, the private medical sector in Canada is not governed by systemwide price controls and thus has grown faster than public payments. But another major cause of rising private spending has been what Tuohy felicitously terms "passive privatization"—a process of policy drift evident in many countries and thus usefully parsed.[68] First, there has been rapid growth in spending areas not traditionally covered by Medicare.[69] Second, the shift of many services onto an outpatient basis has effectively decreased the public role, because under the Canada Health Act, some goods and services that must be covered in the hospital, such as long-term care and pharmaceuticals, do not have to be covered outside it.[70] Although the exact distributional effects of these changes are unknown, it can only be assumed that their main effect is to drive up costs for those who utilize uncovered services intensively: namely, the elderly and chronically ill. Thus, the highly segmented structure of Canadian coverage—which is shared with the U.S. Medicare program—probably means that the burdens of policy drift are more concentrated on the sick than in more expansive systems of public provision, where the main divide is between the vast bulk of the population and the small minority of people who can buy their way off waiting lists.

The distinctiveness of the Canadian experience is easier to appreciate in comparison with developments in Germany and the United States, two other nations where federalism has impinged on health policy. The German case is the less dramatic of the two, but also the more hopeful for those who believe governments can cope with the fiscal and political strains of the post–1980s order. After more than a decade of political immobilization, two major legislative breakthroughs occurred under Helmut Kohl's government. Although introducing some elements of competition, neither initiative can be described as market oriented. Instead, in keeping with the inclusive coalitional bases on which they rested, the reforms can best be seen as a sometimes uneasy combination of the reform interests of the right (higher cost sharing), center (increased reliance on the principle of subsidiarity as embodied in the sickness funds), and left (greater equality across workers). Practically the only group truly abandoned in the process was medical professionals, who nonetheless managed to obstruct some reforms at the implementation stage. In keeping with the pattern elsewhere, the single truly procompetitive element of the German reforms—greater choice of sickness funds in the context of increased risk sharing across the funds—was inherently centralizing, because it gave the state the authority to redistribute finances across funds to equalize contribution rates, which had once varied greatly according to the health and earnings of participants. Since the reforms, contribution rates have indeed come into greater harmony, and the number of sickness funds has actually dropped by more than half.

If the German reforms were scarcely revolutionary in their character or impact, it still remains to ask how they happened at all. After all, close observers of German health politics had coined the phrase "Reformblockade" to describe the paralysis of the German health policy framework in the 1980s.[71] What allowed reformers in the 1990s to do what reformers in the 1980s could not? The short answer is that the shifting and overlapping goals of the payers—specifically, employers, unions, and the *Länder* (states)—made reform possible by allowing a new coalition to form against provider interests and by catalyzing cooperation among disparate factions. Employers and unions were the key players, and hence their shared interests were most important. As in the United States, employers were acutely worried about the cost of health benefits. But as Giaimo argues, because all employers were forced to bear this burden, they faced strong incentives to organize for the collective good of lower overall spending, rather than to try to achieve savings through individualized cost-control efforts.[72] Employers, however, did desire to shift costs onto patients, and their demands were one reason the reforms included new copayments. (Many of these were reversed by the Social Democrats in the late 1990s.) But employers were constrained in their cost-shifting goals by the unions, which jointly managed the system and wanted greater equality of payroll contribution across sickness funds. Finally, strained by the cost of reunification, the *Länder* sought greater federal contributions for long-term care, then principally a state responsibility.[73]

The importance of reunification in catalyzing the 1992 reforms may make the German experience appear wholly unique. But other aspects of Germany's successful reform drive—which, it should be remembered, continued into the late 1990s—seem highly useful for grasping the dynamics of reform in fragmented/decentralized regimes. For one, Germany's cautious but productive path suggests that a decentralized medical system may well give reformers some advantages in a fragmented political setting, or at least temper their ambitions to the point that they are not tempted to pass legislation that cannot be implemented, as did overeager Dutch politicians. The dense and fragmented overlay of corporatist health insurance, on the one hand, and Germany's federal institutions and bicameral parliament, on the other, have clearly thwarted swift or radical change. Yet, these have also given potential opponents of reform strong institutional guarantees that their interests will be accommodated in any changes made and created the potential for new alliances of interests—alliances that were plainly not possible in the bilateral framework of interest representation in Canada.

For another, the relatively limited changes that have occurred at the ground level in German health policy, particularly in comparison with the United States, indicate that residualization through policy drift is not inevitable in pluralist–corporatist systems. Indeed, Germany's policy of equalizing contribution levels across the sickness funds reflected a conscious effort to undo past policy drift caused by the gradual concentration over time of higher-risk workers in specific funds. Although copayments have shifted some risk and costs to patients, elaborate protections for lower-income and higher-risk patients have mitigated their effects. Moreover, the extremely broad scope of German coverage has limited the sort of passive privatization seen in Canada.

The main concern voiced by those who fear that the German commitment to solidarity is eroding is that increased choice of insurer will encourage healthier and wealthier citizens to opt out of higher-cost funds or even buy out of the statutory system altogether. Only Germans with incomes below a set threshold are required to join the statutory system, but more than half of the roughly 25 percent of Germans who are exempt from compulsory membership voluntarily join a statutory fund. Thanks in part to the liberalization of cross-border insurance activities under EU law, private insurers have aggressively competed for subscribers in the German market. There is some movement of "younger and healthier members to the company funds (or to private insurance, if their incomes are high enough to allow such a move)," which has prompted new efforts to improve the mechanisms for risk equalization across the funds.[74] Nonetheless, the potential for risk fragmentation and privatization in the present German framework is inherently constrained.

A sense of the differential effect of drift and conversion in these nations can be gleaned from comparative data on out-of-pocket health spending. As table 1.4

Table 1.4. Out-of-Pocket (OOP) Health Spending in Selected Nations, 1980–2000

Nation/Type	OOP Spending as a Share of Total Health Spending, 1980 (%)	OOP Spending as a Share of Total Health Spending, 2000 (%)	Percentage-Point Change in OOP Share
Veto-Free/Hierarchical			
Denmark	11.4	16.4	+5
Finland	18.4	20.6	+2.2
Iceland	11.8	15.2[a]	+3.4
Italy	15.7[b]	22.9	+7.2
New Zealand	10.4	15.4	+5
Norway	14.6[c]	14.3	−0.3
United Kingdom	8.6	11[d]	+2.4
Mean (weighted by years between observations)			+3.1
Veto-Free/Decentralized			
Austria	14.6[e]	18.6	+4
France	11.5[c]	10.2	−1.3
Japan	17.7[f]	17.1[a]	−0.6
Mean (1990–2000, weighted)	+0.3		
Veto-Ridden/Decentralized			
Australia	16.1	18.4[f]	+2.3
Germany	10.3	10.6	+0.3
United States	24.2	15.3	−8.9
Mean (weighted)			−2.2
Veto-Ridden/Hierarchical			
Canada	14.7[b]	16.1[a]	+1.4
Mean for all fourteen nations (weighted)			+1.1

Source: Organization for Economic Cooperation and Development, *OECD Health Data 2003* (Paris: OECD, 2003). Data are unavailable for Belgium, The Netherlands, Sweden, and Switzerland.
[a]1999
[b]1988
[c]1990
[d]1996
[e]1995
[f]1998

shows, the first simple conclusion is that citizens in most advanced industrial democracies were paying a larger share of national health spending out of pocket at
the end of the 1980–2000 period than at the beginning. Although some of the rise
may well have been due to introduction of copayments and other forms of explicit
cost sharing, the evident paucity of such legislated changes and the large magnitude of the increase witnessed in a number of nations suggest that most of the shift
is an indirect result of patients buying out of public programs or purchasing services that are only modestly covered by public programs, such as pharmaceuticals.

The second conclusion, however, is that the average increase obscures substantial variation across different nations and regime types in the degree to which
cost control has precipitated increases in out-of-pocket spending. At the extremes,
for example, the share of health care financed by direct consumer payments increased by more than 7 percentage points in Italy while it fell by almost 9 points in
the United States, as the share of the population covered by Medicaid and
Medicare expanded. It is not surprising, given the large decline in the public share
of spending in the veto-free/hierarchical nations, that the role of out-of-pocket
spending increased the most in these regimes (3.1 percentage points, on average).
It rose more modestly in the veto-free/decentralized regimes and Canada and actually declined in the veto-ridden/decentralized regimes—although the decline is
entirely due to the United States and data are unavailable for Switzerland. Germany, for its part, saw only a modest increase in out-of-pocket spending (0.3 percentage points), suggesting, again, that German reforms have produced little of
the dislocations seen in Canada or the United States.

At first glance, the United States might be thought to represent a polar opposite to the German case—the breakdown lane of health reform versus the German
Autobahn. But, in fact, the institutional context and reform process, and even
some of the legislative achievements, were similar across the two countries. In
both nations, comprehensive reform emerged onto the political agenda in the
early 1990s in response to concerns about economic decline, intensified fiscal
pressures, and the global competitiveness of firms. In both, employers and state
governments, fearful of rising medical inflation, were key instigators of reform.
And in both, reform was eventually taken up by a moderate conservative leader—
Kohl in Germany, George H. W. Bush in the United States—who faced strong
pressures from the left. Had Bush returned to office in 1993, there is reason to believe he would have pursued a cautious reform course similar in conception to
that of Kohl's (but, of course, vastly different in content) and reason to believe that
modest but meaningful reforms would have passed, just as they did in Germany.

Indeed, such reforms *did* pass in the United States. The spectacular implosion
of the Clinton health plan has obscured the substantial track record of smaller-
scale legislative achievements that marked the 1980s and 1990s, including a
stealth expansion of the state–federal Medicaid program for the poor through the
budget process and the creation of a new Children's Health Insurance Program
(CHIP) in 1997. Medicaid, in fact, stands out as a remarkable oasis of spending
and coverage growth amid a parched desert of political support for antipoverty

programs. The number of Medicaid beneficiaries, for example, increased from 21.6 million in 1980 to 50.7 million in 2003, while spending increased from 2.3 to 7.4 percent of the federal budget.[75] These expansions gained support from a broad alliance of conservatives and liberals, and in the case of CHIP, from state leaders eager for greater flexibility under Medicaid. In comparative perspective, the Medicaid expansions are of a piece with a larger pattern of compensatory intervention in nations that have slashed assistance for poor families: free or low-cost health insurance facilitates the movement of former clients of public assistance into low-wage employment, where private health coverage is rare. As in Germany, therefore, cost containment was coupled with modest expansions in coverage.

There, however, the similarities end. For what stands out in the American experience are the profound constraints on expansive policy reform imposed by America's fragmented political institutions and heavily privatized social welfare framework. Exhibit A here is the stunning defeat of the Clinton health plan—arguably the most dissected legislative failure in modern history. Rather than rehash the saga, I wish simply to emphasize three key aspects of the debate. First, although business concerns about rising costs helped push structural reform onto the agenda, as it did in Germany and The Netherlands, American employers were deeply split along multiple lines by the highly uneven incidence of health insurance costs in America's voluntary employment-based system. Firms with older, unionized workforces or large benefit costs, for example, were willing to support fairly expansive proposals.[76] Other large firms that provided insurance, however, preferred to encourage firms to adopt innovative private purchasing strategies. In smaller firms, private coverage was rare, while in larger firms, the overwhelming majority of workers had direct coverage.[77] These divisions plagued the Clinton administration's efforts and ultimately doomed any chance for employers to play a constructive and relatively united role of the sort seen in Germany and The Netherlands.

Second, like other procompetitive proposals, the Clinton health plan turned out to be highly regulatory and complex once the theoretical ideal of managed competition had been translated into legislative details. Although it is customary for advocates of managed competition in the United States to dismiss the Clinton plan with the same charges used by free-market conservatives to attack the British and Dutch experiments—all the talk of competition was a rhetorical subterfuge; the Clinton plan was a big-government wolf in competitive sheep's clothing—careful study of the plan's genesis and development shows that among Clinton's key advisers, the commitment to aspects of procompetitive reform was in fact genuine and strong.[78] The problem was not insincerity, but inherent barriers to translating the procompetitive ideal into workable policy results.

Third, the failure of the Clinton plan suggests that the inherited path of health policy in the United States represents an even more substantial barrier to government-led structural reform than do the well-known institutional barriers posed by America's fragmented political–institutional framework. Indeed, the stark difference between U.S. policy reversals and the more consensual and expansionary pattern in other veto-ridden/decentralized regimes cannot be explained without an appreciation of the deep political divisions and enduring political barriers created by America's distinctive reliance on private employment-based insurance. In the end, the Clinton plan was brought down by much the same political dynamic that stymied efforts to scale back *public* programs abroad: the easily ignited fears of citizens that reform would compromise the health protections on which they relied—in this case, employment-based insurance.[79]

Although the Clinton plan died, however, health care reform did not—which brings us to the final and most striking feature of U.S. policy developments: the extent to which policy change occurred independently of the initiative or control of public policymakers. The scope of private control over health benefits is the key reason why policy drift was so much more consequential and inequality producing in the United States than it was elsewhere. Because policies encouraging private benefits allow considerable discretion on the part of private actors, they allow substantial changes *within* the confines of existing policy. Furthermore, nongovernmental actors working within these often loose constraints do not have to engage in collective political action to achieve their ends. If they are able to overcome internal resistance, they can adopt changes unilaterally.[80]

And thanks to these largely unilateral efforts, the private foundation of the American health system has undergone what can only be described as a radical contraction. From a peak of more than 80 percent of Americans, private insurance coverage (both employment based and individually purchased) fell during the 1980s and early 1990s to less than 70 percent, before rebounding slightly in the strong economy of the late 1990s.[81] Employment-based protection was the biggest casualty: between 1979 and 1998, the share of workers who received health insurance coverage from their own employers fell from 66 percent to 54 percent.[82] At the same time, employers have grown less willing to cover workers' dependents, and they have required that workers pay a larger share of the cost of their coverage, which has discouraged some from taking coverage even when it is offered. The result has been a marked rise in the proportion of Americans who are without health insurance. For more than a decade, the number of uninsured Americans has been rising at the rate of about 1 million per year and now hovers around 44 million. A stunning 75 million Americans, a third of the nonelderly population, are without insurance at some point during the year, and spells without insurance have been growing longer.[83]

The gravest effects have been felt by those most disadvantaged by the economic trends of recent decades. The share of workers in the lowest 20 percent of the wage spectrum receiving insurance from their employers fell from almost 42 percent to just over 26 percent between 1979 and 1998.[84] Workers lacking a high school degree have seen a 35 percent drop in the probability of employment-based coverage since the mid-1970s. African Americans and Hispanics have been hit particularly hard: the share of the nonelderly with job-based coverage contracted by 18 percent among African Americans between 1977 and 1996, and by

28 percent among Hispanics—to 47.9 percent and 42.1 percent, respectively, versus 71 percent for whites.[85] These trends reflect multiple factors, including falling rates of unionization and changing patterns of employment. But above all, they mirror the simple reality that medical costs have risen much faster than most workers' wages, increasingly outstripping the ability of workers (and their employers) to finance protection.[86] With American employers free to drop coverage (unlike their counterparts in Germany and The Netherlands), and workers under financial pressure to decline it even when it is offered, the risk of medical costs is being shifted from insurers and employers back onto workers and their families. For foreign policymakers who wish to increase the role of private health insurance in their medical systems, the continued erosion of American health insurance sounds a distinctly cautionary note.

CONCLUSION

At the dawn of a new century, many of the rallying cries of the last seem no longer to inspire citizens. Faith in government has plummeted. Public budgets have stabilized, even fallen. New social programs have all but disappeared from the political agenda. Yet, this era of austerity has been accompanied by anxiety about evolving economic conditions that have produced both greater prosperity and greater inequality, both new wealth and new risks. For political leaders, this has been a volatile and confusing environment, equally threatening to those who would cling to the ideas of the past and to those who would deny their continued relevance.

The reform of medical systems has been an important aspect of this brave new world. As constrained public budgets have sagged under the weight of rising medical costs, leaders in every affluent democracy have found themselves spurred to action, despite the potent risks of challenging established stakeholders or threatening cherished benefits. Yet, once we look past the feverish talk of reform on which health policy experts have fixated, the legislative changes that nations have undertaken appear at once more modest and more variable than commonly recognized. As welfare state scholars have emphasized in other policy contexts, the dominant pattern of reform over the past two decades is not radical retrenchment. Containing costs rather than cutting benefits has been the major aim, and there is little evidence that these changes have done anything more than restrict public programs at the margins. No country has seen a contraction of the share of the population entitled to statutory protection, and in fact many nations in which coverage was less than universal or where public programs left out important benefits have seen expansions of protection in the last two decades.

Nonetheless, cost containment has imposed visible and unpopular strains in many nations—from waiting lists and eroding facilities to copayments and increasingly transparent gaps in coverage. These strains have been magnified in popular perception by the persistent acrimony of relations between the state (and, in decentralized systems, insurers and employers) and medical professionals, who have responded to their declining influence within the corridors of power by appealing ever more stridently to public sympathies. In this environment, political leaders have found themselves forced to take action not to cope with fiscal constraints or rising medical spending, but to avoid blame for perceived deterioration in the performance of strained medical complexes. The imperative of blame avoidance, rather than counseling the cautious step-by-step changes that scholars of the welfare state have highlighted, has sometimes impelled politicians to instead pursue major structural reforms. And these reforms, in many cases, have been justified by the notion of "managed competition" or "quasimarkets"—Janus-faced ideals that momentarily allow politicians to elide endemic value conflicts and claim that they can improve quality and responsiveness even while keeping costs in check.

And yet, as my detailed review of reform politics in Britain, Canada, Germany, The Netherlands, and the United States indicates, the reality of market-oriented reform has been at odds with the rhetoric. Moreover, the distribution of structural reforms within the advanced industrial world has been at odds with the expectations of comparative welfare state scholarship. First, it is in nations with the most statist and expansive medical systems that procompetitive reform ideals have been most likely to take root, rather than the decentralized systems where the idea of competition would seem most congenial. Second, in nearly every case of alleged procompetitive reform, the largest and most enduring change introduced was a substantial increase in the power of the state. This paradox can be unraveled, I have shown, by considering the political and policy capacities that leaders in these nations enjoyed and the problem definitions that existing policy frameworks encouraged.

More important, once we recognize that the turn toward the market is a response to a distinctive constellation of political conditions, rather than an invariant expression of underlying ideological commitments, then we can see more clearly why marketization has produced centralization and why the very political appeal of managed competition contains the seeds of its surprisingly statist effects. By holding out the lure of protective restraints on competition's potentially destabilizing effects, procompetitive proposals have managed to find a comfortable home at many points on the political spectrum. At the same time, they have established policy capacities and signals that have pulled politicians toward interventionism. As much scholarship has shown, market reform requires reregulation, not deregulation.[87] Yet, more so than in other sectors, the net effect of this reregulation has been centralization. This is not merely because the state is the only plausible manager of competition in a world of decreased professional influence, but also because procompetitive proposals hinge on the development and deployment of performance measures that further encourage intervention from above.

If structural reform has not had the consequences expected, however, it has also not proved to be the most important source of change in the nations considered. Instead, explaining the most critical shifts within these nations' medical systems—the rise in the private share of spending, the real hardships at the margins of coverage, and, above all, the ongoing privatization of risk in the United

States—requires attention to powerful sources of change that neither health policy experts nor students of the welfare state have given sufficient emphasis. These are policy drift and conversion, changes in the context of decentralized operation of policies that alter program purposes or effects without alterations in formal policy. In a climate of austerity characterized by formidable barriers to expansionary reforms, the scope and effect of welfare states are crucially evolving despite (and in important respects because of) the hurdles to large-scale legislative change. New risks are arising with which public programs are poorly equipped to grapple. Gaps in coverage that once seemed tolerable are increasingly hard to close. Strains on public programs are creating cracks in networks of solidarity that once united rich and poor, healthy and sick. Because of the semisovereign role of employers in the American framework and the huge barriers to legislative change uniquely created by the collision of fragmented institutions and uniquely decentralized financing, the effects of conversion and drift have been most pronounced—and most inegalitarian—there. But reform without change and change without reform has been the dominant policy dynamic in most advanced industrial states.

In short, the politics of structural reform is not an "it" but a "they"—a set of related but distinct constellations of political and policy outcomes in contrasting medical and political systems. Two divisions, I have argued, are crucial for understanding which constellation will be realized in any particular nation: whether political systems are veto free or veto ridden, and whether medical systems are hierarchical or decentralized. Countries on the same sides of these twin divides have followed surprisingly similar paths. If the veto-free/hierarchical regimes have seen a decline in the state's financing role, the veto-free/decentralized regimes and especially the veto-ridden/decentralized regimes have actually witnessed a significant overall increase. Equally important, reform efforts in veto-ridden/pluralist–corporatist regimes have not, as of yet, produced the balkanization and retrenchment that doomsayers have prophesied. New coalitions have formed to navigate the shoals of reform, and their efforts have been tempered and sometimes facilitated by the pluralism of interests in these nations. Even in the United States, significant expansions of public coverage have come about through this route. Yet, the United States is also the only nation in which private employers have had the latitude to remake American social protection along the lines they prefer. The most pronounced effect of this freedom has been a marked privatization of risk in health policy, as coverage has eroded and costs and responsibility have been shifted from broad collective pools onto firms, families, and workers themselves.

The picture that emerges, in sum, is one of widespread strains that, at times, have produced major shifts but usually without legislative direction. The character of this nonlegislated adjustment is not, however, identical across nations. To the contrary, four distinct patterns emerge from the analysis, each associated with a distinctive financing structure: "buying out," "passive privatization," "cost sharing," and "risk privatization." In hierarchical financing systems, the most prominent form of drift has been buying out in response to (comparatively effective) restraints on public spending, which have threatened the timely availability of

high-quality care. The Canadian experience is an exception in the world of hierarchical systems (though it is paralleled by the trajectory of the U.S. Medicare program). There, the limited public role at the beginning of the 1980s—which
focused on physician and hospital services to the exclusion of drugs and other services—has allowed passive privatization, as spending on services poorly covered
by the public sector has increased.

In more decentralized financing regimes, by contrast, policy drift and conversion have not generally produced either buying out or passive privatization. Indeed,
the trend has been toward an *expanded* role for public coverage. Rather, to the extent that cost control has produced strains, it has resulted mainly in higher consumer cost-sharing. Here, the United States, as the only nation in which employers
have had the latitude to remake health benefits along the lines they prefer, is the
great exception. Only in the United States have the strains of recent decades produced a true dismantling of key areas of risk protection. The effect, I have argued,
has been a marked privatization of risk, as private coverage has eroded and responsibility has shifted from collective risk pools onto families and workers themselves.

Although I have grouped these diverse trends under the common labels of
conversion and *drift*, their distributional effects are likely to vary greatly. Buying
out, to the extent that it is limited to the very well off, is likely to exacerbate inequities in access relatively little—and in fact, if anything, reflects the special dissatisfaction of affluent citizens. (In the United Kingdom, for example, quality is
actually perceived much more favorably among *lower-income* citizens than among
the well-off.)[88] Modest cost-sharing, too, especially when focused on the wealthy,
is also likely to have relatively limited consequences.[89] The same cannot be said,
however, of passive privatization and risk privatization, which impose the greatest
burden on those with limited resources. It is notable that among the nations for
which adequate opinion data exist, only in Canada and the United States do
lower-income citizens have substantially less favorable perceptions of the quality
of care than do higher-income citizens—in the U.S. case, dramatically so.

Those troubled by these shifts may find solace in the growing role of public financing in the United States. And they may see hope in the success of expansionary reforms in other nations with veto-ridden polities, such as Germany. Yet, the
United States still stands alone. For more than two decades, the American welfare
state has been running to stay still—doing more merely to secure past gains. In the
years after World War II, the rise of private health insurance made state action
seem unnecessary. Now, when it is recognized by many as necessary and indeed
essential, American government is stalemated by the very private protections in
which so much faith was once invested.

NOTES

This chapter has benefited greatly from the guidance of the editors, as well as of other
authors in this volume. I also received valuable comments from participants in workshops

at Yale University and the University of Chicago; advice and support from Oona Hathaway, Alan Jacobs, and Ted Marmor; and indefatigable research assistance from Nelson Gerew and Nicole Kazee. Financial support came from the William Milton Fund of the Harvard Medical School, the Peter Strauss Family Fund, and the Yale Institution for Social and Policy Studies. Portions of this chapter appeared previously as "Dismantling the Health Care State? Political Institutions, Public Policies, and the Comparative Politics of Health Reform," in *British Journal of Political Science* 33, no. 4 (October 2004). They are reprinted here with the kind permission of Cambridge University Press.

1. David P. Chinitz, "Hiding in the Market Place: Technocracy and Politics in Israeli Health Policy," in *Health Policy Reform, National Variations, and Globalization*, ed. Christa Altenstetter and James Warner Bjorkman (London: MacMillan, 1997), 236.

2. Organization for Economic Cooperation and Development, *The Reform of Health Systems: A Review of Seventeen OECD Countries* (Paris: OECD, 1994), 3, 45, 50.

3. Francis D. Powell and Albert F. Wessen, eds., *Health Care Systems in Transition: An International Perspective* (Thousand Oaks, CA: Sage Publications, 1999), 388.

4. Paul Pierson, "The New Politics of the Welfare State," *World Politics* 48, no. 2: 143–79.

5. For a similar formulation, see James A. Morone, "The Ironic Flaw in Health Care Competition: The Politics of Markets," in *Competitive Approaches to Health Care Reform*, ed. Richard J. Arnould, Robert F. Rich, and William D. White (Washington, DC: The Urban Institute, 1993).

6. Jacob S. Hacker, "Privatizing Risk without Privatizing the Welfare State: Hidden Realities of Social Policy Retrenchment in the United States," *American Political Science Review* 98, no. 2 (May 2004). See also the discussion of "utility drift" in Douglas Rae, "The Limits of Consensual Decision," in *American Political Science Review* 69, no. 4 (1975):1270–94. Although rarely acknowledged in current welfare state scholarship, policy drift was clearly recognized by Hugh Heclo in his classic *Modern Social Politics in Britain and Sweden* (New Haven, CT: Yale University Press, 1974). Heclo writes of the Swedish Pension Act of 1913 (211): "In large part, it was precisely because this basic framework remained unaltered in the midst of changing circumstances that the framers' intentions were unconsciously subverted. As noted throughout this volume, one of the easiest ways to change a policy is to fail to change a program to accord with the movement of events." I am grateful to Kent Weaver for this citation.

7. R. Kent Weaver, "The Politics of Blame Avoidance," in *Journal of Public Policy* 6 (1986):371–98.

8. Powell and Wessen, *Health Care Systems in Transition*, 12.

9. Joseph White, *Competing Solutions: American Health Care Proposals and International Experience* (Washington, DC: Brookings, 1995).

10. The fourth logical combination—multiple payer/public ownership—has no clear exemplars, although some corporatist systems rely more heavily on public ownership than others.

11. See Evelyne Huber and John Stephens, *Development and Crisis of the Welfare State: Parties and Politics in Global Markets* (Chicago: University of Chicago Press, 2001). Using Huber and Stephens's dataset (www.lisproject.org/publications/welfaredata) and OECD expenditure data, the correlation between 1945–75 cumulative left-party governance and the 1975 private share of health spending is −0.58.

12. In the OECD, only Italy's national health service was not enacted under social-democratic rule.

13. Ellen Immergut, *Health Politics: Interests and Institutions in Western Europe* (New York: Cambridge University Press, 1992).

14. Jacob S. Hacker, "The Historical Logic of National Health Insurance: Structure and Sequence in the Development of British, Canadian, and U.S. Medical Policy," in *Studies in American Political Development* 12, no. 2 (spring 1998):57–130.

15. Paul Pierson, "Increasing Returns, Path Dependence, and the Study of Politics," in *American Political Science Review* 94 (2000):251–67.

16. Jacob S. Hacker, *The Divided Welfare State: The Battle over Public and Private Social Benefits in the United States* (New York: Cambridge University Press, 2002).

17. Paul Pierson, "Coping with Permanent Austerity: Welfare State Restructuring in Affluent Democracies," in *The New Politics of the Welfare State*, Paul Pierson, ed. (New York: Oxford University Press, 2000).

18. This is so for least three reasons. First, in some highly labor-intensive and low-technology areas (such as nursing), medical care presents a classic example of William Baumol's "cost disease of personal services," wherein low-productivity growth leads to rapidly rising costs relative to high-productivity sectors of the economy. In many areas of health care, however, a second cause of high inflation dominates: increasing technological sophistication. Third, and finally, key features of the medical market—particularly uncertainty and risk aversion—empower agents with an interest in higher spending (that is, doctors) and encourage the reliance on third-party insurance, which blunts the price signals that, in other sectors, help restrain inflation.

19. See, for example, Geoffrey Garret, *Partisan Politics in the Global Economy* (New York: Cambridge University Press, 1998); Duane Swank, *Global Capital, Political Institutions, and Policy Change in Developed Welfare States* (New York: Cambridge University Press, 2002); and Paul Pierson, ed., *The New Politics of the Welfare State* (New York: Oxford University Press, 2001).

20. A telling example is the main EU directive governing private health insurance. The preamble declares that citizens of member states should have "complete freedom to avail themselves of the widest possible insurance market." This freedom, however, is limited to "policyholders who, by virtue of their status, their size or the nature of the risks to be insured, do not require special protection in the Member State in which a risk is situated"—which turns out to mean that no provision of the directive should interfere with the right of a member state to regulate insurers whose products "serve as a partial or complete alternative to health cover provided by the statutory social security system." Council Directive 92/49/EEC, June 18,1992, preamble and Article 54.

21. Theodore R. Marmor, "Global Health Policy Reform: Misleading Mythology or Learning Opportunity?" in *Health Policy Reform, National Variations and Globalization*, 357.

22. Indeed, the story of U.S. health policy can be told largely as a tale of failed diffusion, as foreign-inspired ideas for compulsory insurance repeatedly ran headlong into America's fragmented political institutions, private vested interests, and fierce ideological attacks on the sinister imports of "Bolshevism," "socialized medicine," and "government-run health care."

23. Michael Moran, *Governing the Health Care State: A Comparative Study of the United States and Germany* (Manchester, UK: Manchester University Press, 1999), 172.

24. As a recent book puts the point, "Various countries not only have similar problems; they appear to be addressing them in similar ways." Marshall Raffel, ed., *Health Care and Reform in Industrialized Countries* (University Park, PA: Pennsylvania State University Press, 1997), xii.

25. Colleen Flood's recent *International Health Care Reform* provides a case in point. The book looks at four countries, all of which "have either proposed or implemented internal market and managed competition models." Far from constituting a representative sample, these four nations were chosen, says Flood, because of "the radical nature of the reforms proposed." Flood, *International Health Care Reform: A Legal, Economic, and Political Analysis* (New York: Routledge, 2000), 9.

26. Howard Glennerster and his colleagues, for example, contend that Thatcher's NHS reforms reflected a "much wider move towards contracting and competition in health and social service . . . internationally." Although the word "move" suggests actual policy change, they in fact have examples of only two countries outside Britain—Sweden and Finland—that are "beginning" to implement contracting. Howard Glennerster, Manos Matsaganis, and Patrick Owens, *Implementing GP Fundholding: Wild Card or Winning Hand?* (Bristol, PA: Open University Press, 1994), 1–4.

27. Susan Giaimo reports, for example, a revealing exchange with a high official in the German Federal Ministry of Health, who insisted that the only viable goal of market reform was "social competition, socially connected competition. This . . . is something different than free competition." Giaimo, *Markets and Medicine: The Politics of Health Care Reform in Britain, Germany, and the United States* (Ann Arbor: University of Michigan Press, 2002), 141.

28. Even in the United States, the tenets of procompetitive reform run afoul of deeply held public values. See, for example, Robert J. Blendon, Tracey Stelzer Hyams, and John M. Benson, "Bridging the Gap between Expert and Public Views on Health Care Reform," in *Journal of the American Medical Association* 269 (May 19, 1993):2573–78. For a general discussion of the disjuncture between rhetoric and outcomes in health care market reform, see Alan Jacobs, "Seeing Difference: Market Health Reform in Europe," in *Journal of Health Politics, Policy, and Law* 23, no. 1 (1998):15.

29. Glennerster, Matsaganis, and Owens, *Implementing GP Fundholding*, 3.

30. Blendon, Hyams, and Benson, "Bridging the Gap."

31. See, in particular, Weaver, "The Politics of Blame Avoidance"; and Paul Pierson, *Dismantling the Welfare State? Reagan, Thatcher, and the Politics of Retrenchment* (New York: Cambridge University Press, 1994).

32. Paul Pierson, "Irresistable Forces, Immovable Objects: Post-Industrial Welfare States Confront Permanent Austerity," in *Journal of European Public Policy* 5, no. 4 (1998): 539–60.

33. For a review of such evidence, see Hacker, "Privatizing Risk without Privatizing the Welfare State."

34. Gøsta Esping-Andersen, *Social Foundations of Postindustrial Economies* (New York: Oxford University Press, 1999), 5.

35. Peter S. Bachrach and Morton S. Baratz, "The Two Faces of Power," in *American Political Science Review* 56, no. 3 (1962):942.

36. Huber and Stephens, *Development and Crisis of the Welfare State*; Pierson, *Dismantling the Welfare State?*; Duane Swank, "Political Institutions and Welfare State Restructuring: The Impact of Institutions on Social Policy Change in Developed Democracies," in *The New Politics of the Welfare State*.

37. Kathleen Thelen, "How Institutions Evolve: Insights from Comparative-Historical Analysis," *Comparative Historical Analysis in the Social Sciences*, ed. James Mahoney and Dietrich Rueschemeyer (Cambridge: Cambridge University Press, 2003).

38. Michael Lipsky, *Street-Level Bureaucracy: Dilemmas of the Individual in Public Services* (New York: Russell Sage Foundation, 1980).

39. Jacob S. Hacker, *The Divided Welfare State*, Part 3.

40. Willem Adema and Marcel Einerhand, "The Growing Role of Private Social Benefits," in *Labour Market and Social Policy: Occasional Papers*, no. 32 (Paris: Organization for Economic Cooperation and Development, 1998).

41. David Wilsford, "States Facing Interests: Struggles over Health Care Policy in Advanced Industrial Democracies," in *Journal of Health Politics, Policy, and Law* 20, no. 3 (1995):571–613.

42. The experience of The Netherlands deserves special attention because it is often cited as a key example of market-oriented reform. All four nations are at relatively similar levels of economic development, three (Britain, Canada, and the United States) share a common cultural heritage, and three (Canada, Germany, and the United States) led the global pack in terms of spending at the beginning of the 1990s.

43. John Sheils and Paul Hogan, "Cost of Tax-Exempt Health Benefits in 2004," *Health Affairs*, Web Exclusive (25 February 2004).

44. Or, in the case of Sweden, by central government limits on local taxation.

45. Robert G. Evans, "Going for the Gold: The Redistributive Agenda Behind Market-Based Health Care Reform," in *Journal of Health Politics, Policy, and Law* 22, no. 2 (1997):436.

46. On the general problem of comparing survey results across nations (and other cultural groupings), see Gary King, "Enhancing the Validity and Cross-Cultural Comparability of Survey Research," paper presented at the Politics of Public Policy Seminar, Yale University, Nov. 7, 2002.

47. For this reason, the decline of professional influence over policy, which has encouraged popular appeals, may well be an indirect cause of the increased dissatisfaction voiced in many nations.

48. The Dutch reforms were named after the head of the committee that formulated them.

49. Canada is the only OECD example of a veto-ridden/hierarchical system, indicating a strong elective affinity between political centralization and hierarchical organization of the medical sector.

50. Most problematic are Belgium (which has seen the development of federal institutions in the past thirty years but not in the area of social policy and is thus classified as centralized) and Australia (which has, since the creation of Medibank in 1984, had a hierarchical system of public medical finance but which, unlike Canada, has witnessed successive government efforts to encourage private health insurance and is thus characterized as corporatist–pluralist). With regard to political structure, France might be seen as ambiguous, because it has an independently elected president. The president, however, shares power with the prime minister, who can be defeated by a no-confidence vote—the hallmarks of a parliamentary system.

51. Germany is occasionally included in the roster, although the extremely limited move toward competition among sickness funds—which one respected observer acerbically terms "manacled competition"—does not even begin to compare to the bolder aspirations in evidence elsewhere. Lawrence D. Brown and Volker E. Amelung, "Manacled Competition: Market Reforms in German Health Care," in *Health Affairs* 18, no. 3 (1999): 761–91.

52. A revealing indication of this convergence is that the mean public shares of spending in veto-free/hierarchical regimes, on the one hand, and in veto-free/decentralized and veto-ridden/decentralized regimes, on the other, were statistically distinct in 1980 ($p = 0.005$ and 0.028) but not in 1998 ($p = 0.232$ and 0.072).

53. Geoffrey Garrett, "The Politics of Structural Change: Swedish Social Democracy and Thatcherism in Comparative Perspective," in *Comparative Political Studies* 25 (1993):521–47.

54. Jacobs, "Seeing Difference," 19. A second key element was primary care physician "fundholding," under which doctors would be given new latitude to purchase services.

55. Susan Giaimo, *Markets and Medicine*, 72.

56. Klein, "Why Britain Is Reorganizing Its National Health Service—Yet, Again," in *Health Affairs* (July/August 1998):117.

57. Julian Le Grand, "Competition, Cooperation, or Control? Tales from the British National Health Service," in *Health Affairs* (May/June 1999):37.

58. Klein, "Why Britain Is Reorganizing Its National Health Service," 117.

59. Giaimo, Markets and Medicine, 221.

60. Carolyn Tuohy, Accidental Logics: *The Dynamics of the Health Care Arena in the United States, Britain, and Canada* (New York: Oxford University Press, 1999), 198.

61. Le Grand, "Competition, Cooperation, or Control?" 31.

62. Jacobs, "Seeing Difference," 15.

63. James Warner Björkman and Kieke G. H. Okma, "Restructuring Health Care Systems in The Netherlands: The Institutional Heritage of Dutch Health Policy Reforms," in *Health Policy Reform, National Variations and Globalization*, 106.

64. Frederick T. Schut, "Health Care Reform in The Netherlands: Balancing Corporatism, Etatism, and Market Mechanisms," in *Journal of Health Politics, Policy, and Law* 20, no. 3 (1995):649.

65. Brown and Amelung, "Manacled Competition," 84.

66. Steffie Woolhandler and David Himmelstein, "Paying for National Health Insurance—And Not Getting It," in *Health Affairs* 22, no. 4 (2002):88–98.

67. Hacker, "The Historical Logic of National Health Insurance," 96–106.

68. Tuohy, *Accidental Logics*, 235.

69. These are "notably pharmaceuticals, nonmedical professional services, and 'other' expenditures such as home care and various prosthetic devices including eyeglasses and hearing aids." Ibid.

70. Some provinces have covered these benefits nevertheless, suggesting the importance of subnational policy decisions in determining the extent of drift.

71. Christina Altenstetter, "Health Policy-Making in Germany: Stability and Dynamics," in *Health Policy Reform, National Variations and Globalization*, 136.

72. Susan Giaimo, "Who Pays for Health Care Reform?" in *The New Politics of the Welfare State*.

73. In addition, the *Länder* had significant influence because of their control over the territorially based second chamber, which at the time was dominated by the Social Democratic Party—a key reason for the opposition's bargaining power. On German politics during this period, see Andrea Campbell and Kimberly Morgan, "The Political Mechanisms of Social Solidarity: Long-Term Care Policymaking in Germany and the United States," paper presented at the Health Policy Seminar, Yale University, April 1, 2002.

74. Giaimo, *Markets and Medicine*, 137.

75. Data on enrollment are from Center for Medicare and Medicaid Services (www .cms.gov/researchers/); spending data are calculated from Office of Management and Budget historical data. www.whitehouse.gov/omb/budget/ fy2003/pdf/hist.pdf.

76. These large corporations were the backbone of the National Leadership Coalition for Health Care Reform, a coalition of employers and unions that included Bethlehem Steel, Chrysler, and GE.

77. *Employee Benefits Research Institute*, Databook on Employee Benefits (Washington, DC: EBRI, 1992), table 6.23.

78. Jacob S. Hacker, *The Road to Nowhere: The Genesis of President Clinton's Plan for Health Security* (Princeton: Princeton University Press, 1997).

79. Hacker, *The Divided Welfare State*, 286–92, chaps. 4–5.

80. On this general point, see Stewart Wood, "Labour Market Regimes under Threat? Sources of Continuity in Germany, Britain, and Sweden," in *The New Politics of the Welfare State*, 374.

81. Health Insurance Association of America (HIAA), *Source Book of Health Insurance Data* (New York: Health Insurance Association of America, 1996); Kaiser Commission on Medicaid and the Uninsured, *The Uninsured: A Primer* (Washington, DC: Kaiser Family Foundation, 2002).

82. James L. Medoff and Michael Calabrese, "The Impact of Labor Market Trends of Health and Pension Benefit Coverage and Inequality," final report (Washington, DC: Center for National Policy, February 2001).

83. Families USA, *Going without Health Insurance: Nearly One in Three Non-Elderly Americans* (Washington, DC: Families USA, March 2003). www.familiesusa.org.

84. Medoff and Calabrese, "The Impact of Labor Market Trends."

85. Calculated from Jon R. Gabel, "Job-Based Health Insurance, 1977–1998: The Accidental System under Scrutiny," *Health Affairs* 18, no. 6 (1999):62–74.

86. Richard Kronick and Todd Gilmer, "Explaining the Decline in Health Insurance Coverage, 1979–1995," *Health Affairs* 18, no. 2 (1999):30–47.

87. Steven Vogel, *Freer Markets, More Rules: Regulatory Reform in Advanced Industrial Countries* (Ithaca, NY: Cornell University Press, 1998).

88. Robert J. Blendon et al., "Inequities in Health Care: A Five-Country Survey," *Health Affairs* 21, no. 3 (2002):182–91.

89. The available evidence suggests, however, that it also does relatively little to encourage the allocation of services to those who most need them. Cf. Joseph P. Newhouse, *Free for All?: Lessons from the Rand Health Insurance Experiment* (Cambridge, MA: Harvard University Press, 1996); and Robert G. Evans, Morris L. Barer, and Greg L. Stoddart, "Charging Peter to Pay Paul: Accounting for the Financial Effects of User Charges" (Toronto: Ontario Premier's Council on Health, Well-Being, and Social Justice, 1994).

PUBLIC PENSION REGIMES IN AN AGE OF AUSTERITY

R. KENT WEAVER

PUBLIC OLD-AGE PENSION PROGRAMS ARE THE LARGEST SINGLE ITEM OF PUBLIC EXPEN-ditures in most advanced industrial countries. These pension systems have been buffeted by a number of pressures for change in recent years, however—notably an aging population and uneven economic growth. Thus, it is hardly surprising that pensions have received much attention from policymakers, both in the United States and abroad.

Policymakers have three very broad sets of options for responding to the increased funding demands of their pension systems. First, they can cut back on the generosity of specific provisions of their pension programs through what will be referred to here as *retrenchment* in benefits and/or eligibility. Retrenchment options may include increases in the retirement age, cuts in indexation of benefits for inflation, and targeted reductions in benefits to upper-income recipients. Second, governments can *refinance* their pension programs by, for example, increasing contribution rates, broadening the contribution base (e.g., by requiring contributions above ceilings for which no pension rights are accrued), adding more general revenues to finance the pension system, or devoting other dedicated taxes to the financing of pensions. Third, they can attempt to *restructure* their pension programs in fundamental ways. For example, governments may phase out a universal flat-rate pension financed by general revenues. They may also add a "defined contribution" pension tier, in which workers each have their own individual pension account, with final benefits depending on contributions made to that account over the entire course of their working lives as well as the return on investments accrued on that account's funds.

While the advanced industrial countries draw on a common repertoire of reform options, very significant differences are visible in individual countries' *policy agendas* (the subset of options they actively consider) and in the *policy changes* they actually adopt.

Broadly speaking, pension policy *agendas* across the OECD—the range of options that individual countries seriously consider—can be described as *overlapping but distinctive*. Some options, such as changes in retirement ages and changes in benefit formulas, have been considered in almost all countries, while others, such as increases in payroll taxes and a partial shift to a system of "defined contribution" individual accounts, have been considered in some countries but not others.

Patterns of policy *change* across the rich industrial countries show five interesting patterns. First, and not surprisingly, there are substantial commonalities in sequencing: most countries have initially responded to austerity pressures primarily with refinancing measures, followed by a mixture of retrenchment and refinancing, and only then turning to more fundamental restructuring. Second, there have been great differences across countries in the amount of policy change; some advanced industrial countries have restructured their pension systems quite substantially over the past two decades, while others have mostly tinkered at the edges and still others have made very few changes. Third, virtually all of the advanced industrial countries have built on their current pension systems when making changes rather than—as in some developing and transitional economies—discarding their old pension systems and starting fresh with a new set of programs.[1] In short, continuity in pension policy is a strong theme as countries institute policy change. Fourth, there has been movement in many (but by no means all) wealthy countries toward an increased role for individual accounts on defined contribution principles. But this movement has taken many different forms, ranging from increased tax concessions for voluntary accounts to several types of mandatory accounts. This movement should not be overstated, moreover: a fifth characteristic of pension system change is that overall "convergence" in the pension systems of the advanced industrial countries has been very limited.

The United States shows some distinctive traits on each of these dimensions of pension policymaking. Some aspects of the United States pension reform agenda have been surprisingly broad in recent years. For example, the United States has considered both proposals for collective investment of Social Security funds in equity markets (under the Clinton administration) and individual "defined contribution" pension accounts. But in other respects—notably the virtual absence of payroll tax increases from serious debate by policymakers—the pension policy agenda in the United States has been quite limited. The United States is also distinctive in the virtual absence of major policy changes since passage of a major Social Security reform package in 1983.

This chapter tries to make sense of cross-national patterns of pension policymaking in the advanced industrial countries, notably overlapping but distinctive agendas and variability in the amount of policy change but a high overall level of policy continuity in most countries. It also attempts to explain how and why U.S. patterns have been distinctive.

In examining these patterns, the chapter will make use of three models of pension policymaking. These models are not alternatives to one another, but rather additive. Each subsequent model brings more variables to bear in understanding the politics of pension reform and is therefore better equipped to explain its complexity. The first model, which can be called the *economic–demographic* model, emphasizes broad social changes, notably an aging population and slower and uneven economic growth, that have caused a shift over the past thirty years from what can be called "enrichment politics" to what Paul Pierson has labeled "the politics of permanent austerity."[2] A second, *politically mediated* model recognizes the importance of the forces in the first model but suggests that the impact of demographic and economic forces is heavily influenced by political calculations by politicians and by political actors such as labor unions and senior citizen organizations as well as by the structure of pension programs and by political institutions and policy ideas.

A third, *"beyond-austerity,"* model builds on the first two models but recognizes that pension politics in recent years has not just been about managing a shift from enrichment to austerity. At least three additional issues that cut across the enrichment-to-austerity pattern have also appeared regularly in the Organization of Economic and Cooperative Development (OECD), although to varying degrees across countries: *investment politics* concerns how pension savings (in either collective or individual accounts) are invested, *labor market politics* concerns how pension policies are used to affect the supply of labor, and *gender politics* concerns issues of pension access, entitlement, and adequacy for women.[3] Each of these issues has the potential to mobilize a distinctive set of constituencies that might otherwise be only tangentially involved in pension politics and to raise a set of issues that may make resolution of conflicts over pension policy more or less difficult.

The first section of the chapter briefly outlines different types of pension systems that are found in the advanced industrial countries. It then reviews overall patterns of pension policy change in those countries, with a special emphasis on major programmatic restructuring. The second section of the chapter outlines the increased pressures for austerity encapsulated in the economic–demographic model and points out the shortcomings of that model in explaining patterns of change. The third section discusses how the politically mediated and beyond-austerity models can improve explanations of pension policy choices in the complex, democratic political systems of the wealthy industrial countries. The concluding section of the chapter assesses the arguments suggested by the three models of pension politics, with a focus on explaining why United States pension policy is distinctive in some aspects of its pension policy and politics and less distinctive in others.

Overall, I argue that although austerity pressures have been a critical force in pension politics, there has been no single politics of public pension reform.[4] Countries follow distinctive and path-dependent policy trajectories that reflect past choices and coalitions that build up around them. But it would be equally misleading to view pension politics purely as "lock-in" to a specific path: groups of countries do shift over time to new policy regimes in response to shortcomings and challenges in their existing set of pension policies, and some types of pension regimes are more likely than others to be abandoned or heavily modified.

CROSS-NATIONAL PATTERNS OF PENSION REFORM

There are virtually endless permutations of pension programs. But national pension systems have traditionally been categorized into a small number of systems, or "pension regimes," that share broadly similar patterns of provision. The classic formulation of pension regimes contrasts countries with essentially flat-rate universal, or "citizenship," pensions (e.g., New Zealand and, until the 1960s, Canada) with those in which pension benefits are linked to earnings and contributions (also known as social insurance, or "Bismarckian," pension systems, such as those of Germany and Italy) and with "residual" pension systems that rely exclusively on income- or means-tested pensions (Australia).[5] However, most countries now feature a mixture of systems. Both Canada and, until recently, Sweden, for example, have had an earnings-related tier on top of a universal pension and a significant income-tested tier as well. Moreover, the Bismarckian category includes both a number of countries, mostly in western Europe, where replacement rates are quite high, and the United States and Canada, which will here be considered as a distinct "Bismarckian Lite" category because of their modest replacement rates and contribution rates.

Table 2.1 shows the evolution of pension regimes in a number of wealthy countries at four points—around 1950, 1974, 1995, and 2003. As the table suggests, there is significant movement among pension regimes over time, but in specific directions. Reliance primarily on universal flat-rate pensions, quite common in the 1950s, became less common in later years as a number of countries responded to pressure for more generous, and income-related, pensions.

The dominant trend in most public pension systems throughout most of the first thirty years after the end of World War II was toward enrichment. Benefit levels were frequently raised in real terms. Expansion frequently involved restructuring: countries such as Canada and Sweden added contributory earnings-related tiers to flat-rate and means-tested pension systems. New benefits, such as early retirement and disability benefits, were added to existing programs. And when contributory pension systems were created or enriched, current or soon-to-retire seniors who had contributed little or nothing toward enriched benefits were often given those benefits anyway. Those countries that made the move to earnings-related pensions prior to the 1970s, such as Sweden and Canada, tended to add public earning–related tiers, moving to the Bismarckian or Bismarckian Lite categories. Those that added mandatory earnings-related tiers later, such as Australia and Denmark, tended to do so through some type of individual accounts, creating a sort of "mixed" pension regime.[6] More recent restructuring trends that reflect pressures for austerity will be discussed below.

PENSION RETRENCHMENT

Cutbacks in public pension eligibility and benefits have clearly been on the agenda in many countries in all types of pension regimes in recent years. Moreover, the range of retrenchment options that has been considered in the United States is generally similar to those that have been considered in other OECD countries with a variety of pension regimes. These options include temporary cuts in indexation, restrictions on early retirement, and a lengthening of years of employment used in calculating initial benefits.

U.S. Experiences

The first major cutbacks in the U.S. Social Security program were prompted by an impending trust fund crisis (that is, insufficient reserves from present and past contributions to finance payment obligations) in 1977. This crisis resulted from a combination of stagflation that lowered revenue inflow to the fund and a faulty indexation mechanism that gave newly retiring workers benefits higher than had been predicted. Change was widely perceived as necessary, but neither the administration nor the Congress was willing to impose substantial short-term losses on persons already receiving benefits. Policymakers relied almost exclusively on injecting new revenues into the system through increases in payroll taxes and the wage base (the amount of wages subject to the Social Security tax) to produce short-term improvements in the program's financial status. These tax increases were phased in after the next (1978) congressional election to reduce political blame.[7] Long-term savings were produced largely by reducing the initial benefit of most future beneficiaries. Rather than attempt to retroactively lower the real purchasing power of workers who had already retired or those who were about to become eligible to retire, policymakers phased in a new initial benefit formula for future retirees.

More dramatic changes occurred during the Reagan administration. President Reagan had promised in the 1980 presidential campaign that Social Security would be exempt from budget cuts, and the new administration initially proposed only minor changes in Social Security when it came into office in 1981. But a deteriorating budget outlook led the president to agree to a Social Security reform package proposed by his advisors that contained a large dose of immediate political pain.[8] After a huge political uproar, the Reagan administration backed away from the proposals and settled for relatively modest program cuts in 1981. But another impending trust fund crisis led the White House and congressional Democratic leaders to agree on a bipartisan commission to address Social Security's financial problems. After a long stalemate, the commission did provide a political cover that allowed negotiators for the president and congressional Democrats to come to an agreement that was eventually approved, with some additions, by Congress.[9]

The 1983 Social Security rescue legislation made major changes in the program on both the tax and benefit sides. In the short term, there was a six-month "delay" in inflation adjustments for benefits that really amounted to a permanent benefit cut for current recipients. In the longer term, the legislation imposed a gradual increase in the standard retirement age (the age at which full Social Security retirement benefits are received) from 65 to 67. This increase was phased in gradually, beginning in the year 2000 and ending in the year 2021. Workers can continue to retire at age 62, with a greater actuarial reduction in their benefits. However, the long delay between 1983 passage of the Social Security rescue package and the initial "bite" of its retirement age increase, along with its gradual phase-in, lessened near-term blame associated with the cuts. And while Republicans accepted an acceleration of previously scheduled payroll taxes as part of the rescue package, they adamantly opposed further increases in payroll tax rates.

The 1983 Social Security rescue package dramatically altered the short- and medium-term financial condition of old-age survivors insurance (OASI). The trust funds are currently generating surpluses, which has made it politically very difficult to either raise Social Security taxes or cut benefits over the last twenty years. Continued concern over the budget deficit and the recognition that large expenditure reductions were unlikely without a contribution from Social Security led Republican politicians to propose pension cutbacks on several occasions in the final years of the Reagan and George H. W. Bush administrations, but in the absence of a trust fund crisis, each attempt fizzled.[10] Indeed, these retrenchment initiatives suggest that efforts to use cuts in Social Security benefits and eligibility in the battle to shrink the federal deficit in the absence of a looming trust fund crisis are almost certain to fail. Increasingly, as Martha Derthick has noted, "central to deficit politics was a ritual of declaring Social Security to be off the table."[11]

Foreign Experiences

The repertoire of incremental retrenchment instruments that has been considered and adopted in other wealthy countries is generally similar to that in the United States. In particular, cutting postretirement indexation provisions for pension benefits has been a staple of pension retrenchment.[12] Many countries have changed their indexation mechanisms by, for example, shifting from gross to net (postpayroll tax) earnings, or from wages to prices. Temporary ad hoc indexation cutbacks have been used as well. Sweden, for example, put in place a mechanism to lower pension indexation when budget deficits exceeded a target level and did not adjust benefits fully for the effects of a devaluation of the krona. Governments have rarely attempted deindexation or even partial deindexation of existing pension programs on a permanent basis, however.

Several wealthy countries have also joined the United States in revisiting—and raising—standard retirement ages. Raising standard retirement ages for women where they had been lower than those for men has been especially common, propelled in part by a directive from the European Union on gender equality that required equalization of retirement ages by gender. Unlike the United States, however, none of the other countries has moved to increase their standard retirement age higher than 65 (two OECD countries already had a retirement age of 67). A number of wealthy countries have also increased the number of years over which earnings for benefits are calculated.

In designing and implementing these reforms, policymakers have been heavily influenced by a desire to minimize blame from constituents, especially retirees and near retirees. Thus, cutbacks have usually had long phase-in periods. Use of highly technical changes in formulas for years included in calculation of benefits and in indexation procedures also help to minimize the visibility of policy changes.

Countertrends Abroad

There have also been some important exceptions in the general trend toward incremental retrenchment of pension policy commitments in other wealthy countries. First, as noted above, a number of countries have moved to include explicit recognition of years spent in care giving. The United States has not joined in this trend, however.[13]

Trends in provisions for early retirement and retirement under disability have also been somewhat ambiguous in direction. Many OECD countries have relatively generous early retirement policies. Several also have more generous unemployment provisions for older workers; indeed, in twelve OECD countries, it was possible in 1995 to receive unemployment benefits from age 55 until the standard retirement age.[14] Countries also differ dramatically in the extent to which disability pensions are available: in the early 1990s, for example, less than 10 percent of U.S. and Canadian males aged fifty-five to sixty-four were receiving disability pensions, compared with 27 percent in The Netherlands, 40 percent in Finland, and 58 percent in Austria.[15] In recent years, early retirement provisions of pension programs have been expanded in some countries and contracted in others. This pattern reflects conflicting pressures on governments. Continued high unemployment in many parts of Western Europe leads governments to try to open up work opportunities for younger workers. Opposition from both unions and employers to cutbacks in early retirement has also inhibited policy change. However, budget deficits and competitiveness concerns cause governments to try to cut back on social commitments and encourage increased labor supply among older workers.[16]

A third countertrend to the overall trend toward retrenchment in pension policy concerns the movement of a number of countries toward liberalizing income and means-tested minimum pension programs to adapt them more effectively to the needs of low-income citizens. In Sweden, for example, the transformation of the former flat-rate *folkpension* into an income-tested (or, more accurately, "public pension-tested") benefit will also provide a more generous benefit to those with modest rights to an income-related pension. Germany also adopted a minimum pension independent of the social assistance for the first time as part of its recent pension overhaul. The United Kingdom has converted its Minimum Income Guarantee for seniors into a Pension Credit that both increases the minimum guarantee and rewards pension savings by seniors.

In the United States, however, Supplemental Security Income (SSI) has not been modernized to make it into a more effective income floor for the low-income elderly. Both benefit levels and take-up rates remain extremely low. Conversion of SSI into a more adequate retirement income source for the low-income elderly has been inhibited by the fact that the program serves two relatively unpopular clienteles—the low-income disabled and elderly immigrants. Indeed, the major legislative change in SSI over the past two decades was the restriction included in 1996 welfare reform legislation restricting its receipt by noncitizens. Moreover, the sidelining of Social Security from the governmental agenda after 1983 meant that there was no detailed legislative consideration of safety-net income support for the elderly, in which more generous income provision for low-income seniors could be enacted as partial compensation for cutbacks in a larger reform package. Discussions of income support for the aged over the past two decades outside government were almost monopolized by discussions of individual accounts and investment practices of the Social Security trust funds (discussed below).

REFINANCING REFORMS

Increasing demographic pressures have led a number of advanced industrial countries to consider both increasing contribution rates for pension-related payroll tax rates and alternative revenue sources. As noted above, increases and/or accelerations in previously scheduled payroll tax increases were included in the 1977 and 1983 Social Security reform packages. But the United States is very unusual among advanced industrial countries in that significant payroll tax increases have essentially been off the agenda since 1983. The only substantial (and still relatively modest) change made since that time is an increase in the taxation of Social Security benefits of upper-income recipients in 1993—which is probably better seen as a cut in benefits for those recipients rather than as a tax increase.

Financing arrangements in other countries vary widely. Australia and New Zealand, for example, have no earmarked pension revenue source. In the United Kingdom, the social insurance contribution covers a number of programs and is only very loosely linked to expenditures. In Germany, social insurance contributions pay a defined share of pension program costs. In Canada, the Canada Pension Plan (CPP) and Quebec Pension Plan (QPP) expenditures are, as in the United States, expected to cover all program costs, but unlike in the United States, the CPP/QPP operate on top of an essentially flat-rate benefit financed out of general revenues.

These different financing mechanisms make generalization about refinancing very difficult, but a few conclusions can be drawn. First, most countries have experienced strong upward pressures on pension contribution rates over the past thirty years. Blöndal and Scarpetta, in a survey of eighteen OECD countries, found that pension contribution rates rose from an average of 9.3 percent in 1967 to 16.5 percent in 1995; in 1995, the average contribution rate was 1.88 times its 1967 level.[17]

A second trend is that many countries have in recent years tried to stabilize contribution rates through a variety of mechanisms. In Canada, projections that the current legislated contribution rate will be inadequate to finance benefits within a specified projection period will automatically trigger a combination of benefit cuts and contribution rate increases.[18] Sweden's adoption of a combined pay-as-you-go (PAYG) "notional defined contribution" account and individual account system for future retirees (discussed further below) is perhaps the most dramatic of these changes—in the future, contribution rates are expected to remain fixed at 18.5 percent of earnings, and benefits will be adjusted to meet this target. Germany, where pension contribution rates peaked at over 20 percent of earnings in recent years, has also acted to try to stabilize contribution rates at no more than 20 percent through the year 2020.[19]

RESTRUCTURING REFORMS

Restructuring can be defined loosely as the addition, deletion, or fundamental change in the relative roles of one or more pension tiers. Restructuring of a single pension tier may or may not alter the overall "pension regime" (combined effects of multiple pension tiers) that characterizes a country.

U.S. Experiences

The United States has not adopted any fundamental restructuring reforms in its public pension tiers over the past thirty years (the last major innovation was the federalization of the means-tested SSI in 1972). The United States continues to rely heavily on a contributory earnings-related program (Old Age and Survivors Insurance, commonly known as Social Security) and tax incentives to employers and individuals and employers for provision of adequate pensions. Calls for fundamental reform of Social Security have grown over the past decade, however, spurred by critiques from conservative policy intellectuals such as Martin Feldstein and think tanks such as the Heritage Foundation and Cato Institute, as well as by declining public confidence in the long-term ability of the current system to make good on its promises. A general perception on the part of political elites (especially Republican elites) that controlling entitlement spending is essential to controlling deficits and limiting government more generally has also helped to generate more interest in Social Security reform.[20]

Debates on Social Security restructuring have focused largely on two alternative sets of proposals. Democrats have generally been more sympathetic to broadening the range of investment options for the Social Security trust fund, including investing in equities, to increase trust fund returns, while Republicans and conservative critics have called for varying degrees of "privatization" of Social Security through mandatory or optional contributions to personal pensions.[21] Privatizers have in particular focused on the lower returns to contributions by younger workers, arguing that Social Security is a bad deal for this group. Critics of individual accounts, however, have argued that because of stock market volatility, individuals who retire a few years apart after contributing over their working lives to a broad stock index fund could end up with dramatically different earnings replacement rates—and those who pulled out their funds in a stock market trough would end up with very inadequate benefits.[22]

The last two presidential administrations in the United States have taken very different approaches to restructuring Social Security. Bill Clinton proposed broadening the range of allowable Social Security trust fund investments, while using anticipated federal budget surpluses to subsidize supplementary retirement savings accounts as complements to Social Security. But the sense of urgency weakened with the strong economy of the late 1990s as the projected date of Social Security insolvency moved further away—from 2029 estimated in 1997 to 2034 in 1999 and 2041 in 2002. Strong opposition from congressional Republicans and from Federal Reserve Board chairman Alan Greenspan has stymied investment of Social Security trust funds in the stock market.[23]

In the 2000 presidential election campaign, George W. Bush proposed allowing workers to divert part of their Social Security payroll taxes to individual accounts. After the election, President Bush decided to appoint a commission on how best to implement an opt-out plan.[24] Unlike the 1981–83 Social Security reform commission, however, President Bush appointed all of the (bipartisan) members of the commission. All appointees also had to agree in advance to support a set of principles established by the White House, including no increase in Social Security payroll taxes, voluntary individual accounts, and no erosion of benefits for current retirees and near retirees. The commission eventually decided to present a menu of policy options rather than a single plan, in part to shield the administration from criticism over the benefit cuts that would be required to fund a Social Security opt-out.[25] Stock market declines in 2001 and 2002 also appear to have dampened, at least temporarily, support for partial privatization of Social Security, while the quick post–September 11 disappearance of federal budget surpluses made financing a transition to opt out of advance-funded individual accounts more difficult.[26]

Indeed, Republican candidates in the 2002 congressional election were encouraged by the party to distance themselves from the notion of "privatization" because of its perceived political risks.[27] The overall pattern in the United States, in short, is that while Social Security privatization is clearly now on the public agenda, it is likely far from enactment, even with George W. Bush as an advocate and Republican control of both chambers of Congress.

While the United States has not created a mandatory individual accounts tier, it has substantially expanded the role for individual-defined contribution pensions in two ways. First, there has been a major increase in the role played by noncompulsory employer-sponsored 401(k) pension plans. Second, federal policy has facilitated change by not intervening to prevent what Jacob Hacker has called "policy drift" among occupational pensions away from defined-benefit plans toward defined-contribution plans.[28]

Foreign Experiences

A variety of fundamental pension-restructuring reforms have been considered in recent years across the world. As noted earlier, restructuring reforms have generally taken place after a series of refinancing and retrenchment reforms have already been undertaken and have proven insufficient to address countries' financing problems in the short or long term.

Restructuring reforms have taken different reforms in different regions, however. For example, there has been significant growth in the number of countries that have adopted systems of mandatory individual accounts, featuring varying degrees of state, employer, and individual management and control. A complete substitution of mandatory individual accounts for a state system has been adopted in a number of Latin American countries, whereas mixed systems (individual accounts on top of a state system) are more common in Eastern Europe.

The wealthy industrialized countries have mostly undertaken less-fundamental restructuring reforms. For example, New Zealand and Canada have added collective investment "buffer" funds to their PAYG pension systems. These reforms have more frequently taken the form of the addition of new tiers and the diminution rather than abolition of others, but the latter is not completely unknown. Universal flat-rate pensions have been especially vulnerable to abolition (Sweden and Finland). They have also been subjected to income tests at the upper end (Canada and, temporarily, New Zealand).[29] But there has also been substantial resilience. For example, the Chrétien government in Canada proposed but ultimately backed away from a proposal to merge the quasiuniversal and income-tested tiers of Canada's pension system when Canada started running budget surpluses.[30]

Three important trends in restructuring have emerged in pension-regime restructuring among the wealthy countries in recent years. First, large mandatory individual account tiers have been adopted in several wealthy countries with no prior public earnings–related pensions, such as Australia and Denmark. Only one OECD country, the United Kingdom, has allowed an opt-out from the public earnings–related pension system in a fashion roughly comparable to that suggested by the Bush administration. It is in these "mixed" systems that never developed a large public earnings–related tier, but instead added a mandatory occupational tier in the post–World War II era, that private pensions are expected to provide the highest percentage of total pensions once privatized tiers are fully mature.

A second trend has begun to emerge in the past decade, however: movement in countries with very expensive Bismarckian pension systems to add individual-defined contribution account tiers on top of a large state system. In the case of Sweden, these individual accounts are mandatory, whereas in Germany they are quasimandatory. In both countries, these individual account tiers are designed to replace benefits as the state system is cut back, but the state system will remain dominant in both countries. Estelle James and Sarah Brooks estimate that mandatory private pensions will produce 57 percent of the public/mandatory private pension total in Australia and 56 percent in Denmark, 50 percent in The Netherlands and Switzerland, and 49 percent in the United Kingdom, but only 21 percent in Sweden, for example. All of these figures are far less than projections for many Latin American countries, where privatized pension tiers have frequently supplanted rather than added on to public pension tiers.[31]

Third and most recently, Sweden has pioneered an important shift in principle from a defined-benefit pension to what is called a "notional defined contribution" (NDC) pension. Italy, Poland, Latvia, and several other countries have followed the Swedish example. Although many variations are possible, NDC pensions in principle (1) base initial benefits on earnings over the entire course of a worker's earning life, inhibiting redistribution within age cohorts; (2) make future pensions contingent on future changes in life expectancy and economic growth both pre-and postretirement to limit redistribution across cohorts; and (3) make a stable contribution rate possible indefinitely, because automatic adjustments are made on the benefit side. They thus mimic defined-contribution individual account pensions in transferring the risk of longer life spans and poor economic performance to future recipients, but they operate on a PAYG rather than advanced-funding basis. NDC pensions thus have the potential to put in place a mechanism that makes future pension cutbacks automatically while minimizing blame for politicians, because they are gradual and because it is impossible to predict when the mechanism is put in place exactly how big (if at all) cutbacks will be. Because NDC pensions are so new, however, it is too early to say either how broadly NDC pensions will be adopted or whether politicians will in fact allow themselves to be "lashed to the mast" and allow automatic pension cutbacks to go into effect and remain in place over time.[32]

Overall, the picture on pension restructuring is therefore a mixed one. There has been substantial restructuring of individual pension tiers and significant shifts in pension regimes in recent years. In particular, there has been an emptying out of the residual and universal categories in table 2.1, as well as a growth in the number of countries with mixed systems, the emergence of notional defined contribution systems, and increased experimentation with supplemental individual accounts in some Bismarckian countries. But there has also been substantial stability in most categories, especially the small (U.S. and Canada) "Bismarckian Lite" category. Changes in public pension programs still more often take the form of incremental retrenchment and refinancing rather than fundamental restructuring in most

OECD countries, and countries with different pension-regime types exhibit both differing central challenges (the right-hand column in table 2.1) and different trajectories when they do change regime types. There is little evidence that "convergence" around a single pension regime is taking place.

FROM ENRICHMENT TO AUSTERITY IN PENSION POLITICS

How can we understand these complex patterns of ubiquitous policy change combined with substantial stability of pension regime types in most countries and continued diversity of pension regimes? A good starting point is to begin by examining pressures for regime change and how they are felt differentially across countries, and then turn to forces that mediate those pressures.

Three economic and demographic forces have stimulated the push from enrichment to retrenchment, refinancing, and restructuring in pension politics that are outlined above (see the three boxes with slanted lines in the upper left-hand corner of figure 2.1). A first source of pressure for change in pension schemes in the advanced industrial countries is an aging population. Most OECD countries operate their pension systems on a PAYG basis, even where there is a dedicated payroll tax for pensions and (as in the United States) some form of "trust fund" that links revenues and expenditures. When birthrates decline or life expectancy increases—and both have been ubiquitous in the industrialized countries in the postwar era—the ratio of retirees to workers increases, and existing policy commitments become financially unsustainable unless new revenues are committed. Currently, both the percentage of population over retirement age and the ratio of the elderly to those of working age are increasing dramatically throughout the developed (and developing) world. Increased life expectancy, and falling fertility rates throughout the industrialized world after the postwar baby boom, have left fewer workers to support the elderly population—with even fewer expected in the future. Particularly large rates of increase are occurring among the very elderly (those over age 75).

Demographic challenges vary significantly across the industrialized countries, however. The United States is expected to have only modest near-term increases in its elderly support ratio (i.e., the population aged 65 and over as a percentage of the population aged 20 to 64) in the year 2000. That figure will rise to 25 by the year 2020 and to 37 by the year 2030. Germany, on the other hand, faces a much more immediate and severe demographic crisis. Its elderly support ratio is expected to increase from 26 in 2000 to 33 in 2020 and 46 in 2050.[33]

A second source of pressure for austerity in public pension systems is increased *fiscal concerns*. Government deficits were common and debt/gross domestic product (GDP) ratios increased throughout the advanced industrial countries from the 1970s through the end of the century.[34] Pension and health care costs for the elderly were a major contributor to these trends, and the pension drain on government budgets is expected to grow in the future in most countries. The European Union recently estimated that the costs of Germany's pension scheme were expected to rise from an already high 11.8 percent of GDP in 2000 to 16.9 percent of GDP by 2050, whereas Italy's pension scheme was expected to peak at 15.7 percent of GDP around 2040 before declining.[35] In Europe, prolonged high unemployment in the 1990s further strained social insurance systems both by inflating the number of claims made against the system and by lowering the flow of contributions into the system.

Governments can respond to budgetary pressures by raising taxes as well as cutting expenditures. That they have been reluctant to do so is due in part to a third, and related, source of pressure for austerity: *concerns about economic competitiveness*. Many business leaders and conservative politicians argue that the high payroll taxes associated with generous pension and other welfare state programs make firms in the countries providing those benefits unable to compete with firms in lower-cost countries. Labor leaders and politicians on the left, however, worry about second-order effects of competitiveness concerns, notably the possibility of migration of jobs to low-cost countries and/or a "race to the bottom" in social benefits.[36] Academic observers and commentators remain quite divided on how much autonomy nation-states retain in the generosity of their welfare states in the face of economic globalization,[37] but at a minimum, concern among politicians about tax rates is very real. Once again, however, the United States is in the lower half of OECD countries in terms of its overall payroll tax rates as a percentage of payroll and payroll tax revenue as a share of GDP.

The shift from enrichment to austerity politics is clearly a central force in pension policymaking in the advanced industrial countries, and the economic–demographic model is useful in explaining many of the patterns of recent pension politics outlined in the previous section of this chapter. First, the model is helpful in explaining the ubiquity of pension reform issues on governmental agendas among the advanced industrial countries over the past quarter century. Second, the timing of fiscal crises is useful in helping to explain the timing of pension reform initiatives in some countries. And third, the relative weakness of demographic, fiscal, and competitiveness pressures in the United States helps to explain why there has not been major change in Social Security over the past two decades, whereas awareness of a looming long-term Social Security funding problem helps to explain why Social Security reform remains on the government agenda despite the absence of an immediate funding crisis.

The economic–demographic model is clearly insufficient as an explanation of patterns of policy change, however. First, as Giuliano Bonoli has noted, there is no one-to-one correspondence between the degree of fiscal and demographic pressure in a country and the degree of welfare state policy change that has been adopted.[38] Indeed, Sarah Brooks argues in a quantitative study of fifty-seven developed and developing countries that countries with a high public debt to GDP ratio are *less* likely to privatize their pension programs (at least when pension liabilities are low or moderate), because they cannot afford the transitional costs associated with moving from a public PAYG to fully funded individual accounts.[39]

Second, the economic–demographic model does not do a good job of explaining either the strong continuity of pension regimes in most OECD countries or the specific patterns of restructuring where it has occurred. Third, the economic–demographic model does not explain countertrends toward selective expansions of pension programs, notably in relation to child-care credits. Nor does it do a good job of explaining the resistance of early retirement provisions to cutbacks.

SUPPLEMENTING ECONOMIC–DEMOGRAPHIC EXPLANATIONS

The demographic–economic model's stress on population aging, budgetary stringency, and economic competition needs to be supplemented with additional variables to provide an adequate explanation of pension policy agendas and changes in the advanced industrial countries. Two types of variables, which will here be called politically mediating variables and "beyond-austerity" variables, are especially useful.

A POLITICALLY MEDIATED APPROACH

Several kinds of politically mediating variables affect pension politics. First, there are two additional forces—ideology and supranational institutions—that strengthen pressures for pension austerity but are felt differentially across countries. Second, there are political processes, incentives, and feedbacks from established programs that mediate pressures for pension austerity.[40] Third, there is a potential for cross-national learning, especially from countries that national policy elites consider to be among their "peer countries" most likely to offer applicable policy lessons. This expanded set of causal variables is shown by the light shaded boxes in the lower left and upper center of figure 2.1.

Ideology

Ideologically based critiques of current pension systems have been important in moving the debate on pension reform away from simply making incremental cuts in pension programs toward more fundamental restructuring. Conservative policy intellectuals in many nations argue that relying on public PAYG pensions rather than advanced funding in individual accounts reduces national savings and investment (and thus economic growth), because households no longer see savings as necessary to obtain a viable retirement income stream. Public pension programs may also be susceptible to politicians' desire to win elections by pledging more generous benefits rather than being governed by what is sustainable in the long run. The tendency of governments to rely on state pension funds as sources of borrowing at below-market rates may also reduce the amount of money available

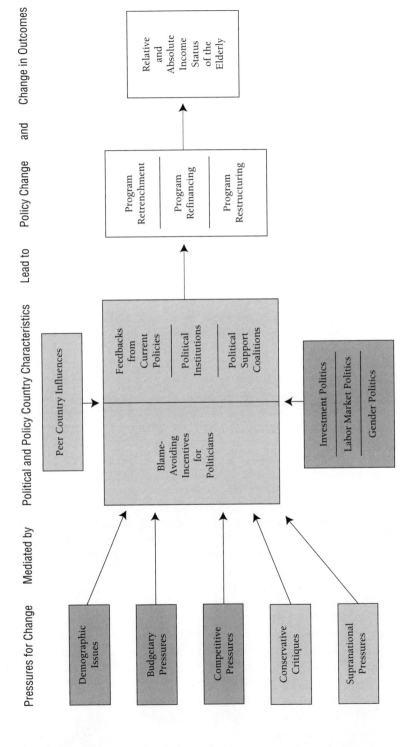

Figure 2.1. A Model of Pension Politics

to pay pension benefits. These critiques suggest an increased role for personal and occupational pensions that are managed by private fund managers.

Ideologically grounded critiques of public PAYG pensions and calls for an increased role for pension privatization have been heard almost everywhere, but whether they have advanced to serious consideration, let alone adoption, depends heavily on (1) a fertile ideological climate in the host country and (2) a policy "window of opportunity," usually furnished by the combination of having sympathetic politicians in office and the apparent exhaustion of incremental retrenchment and refinancing options. Thus, a focus on the role of ideology can help to explain why privatization remains on U.S. discussion agendas despite the absence of an immediate pension crisis, because proponents of pension privatization are well financed and institutionalized and have close ties to the Republican Party. The adamant opposition of Republican policymakers and conservative policy intellectuals and activists to putting any more money into the Social Security system also helps to explain why payroll tax increases have been off the agenda in this country. Having sympathetic politicians in office was also clearly important both to the expansion of the role of personal pensions in Great Britain under Margaret Thatcher and the planning process that led to an individual account tier in Sweden.[41]

Supranational Pressures

Pressures for pension austerity may also result from what can be called "supranational pressures"—pressures from institutions such as the European Union (for member countries) as well as from international lending agencies such as the World Bank and International Monetary Fund (IMF). Recent work by Sarah Brooks suggests that supranational institutions may influence a country's pension policy choice in several distinct ways.[42] First is conditionality: a country may have to adopt certain reforms in order to get loan approval from the IMF, for example. Second is anticipated reaction: a country may adopt reforms that it thinks will win favorable action from the supranational institution even without direct negotiations with that institution. Third, national policy elites may engage in a "two-level game," utilizing perceived threats of negative actions by the supranational institution to win support from reluctant domestic actors and weaken veto points for actions that they would like to take anyway.[43] Fourth, supranational institutions may act simply as agents of knowledge transfer for "best practices" from other countries. A fifth potential channel is what can be called harmonization, where a supranational institution tries to get member countries to develop common practices to lower regulatory barriers to labor and capital mobility.

Several of these channels can be seen in the pension austerity measures taken in EU member countries. Perhaps most important, in countries such as Italy, pension retrenchment was seen as necessary to meet the target of 3 percent of GDP set for government deficit as a condition for entry into the European Monetary Union.[44] However, these actions by national policymakers largely took the form of "anticipated reactions" and strategic choices designed to win the acquiescence of domestic opponents of painful pension reforms. The European Union has also set other requirements (e.g., requiring gender neutrality in retirement ages) that have an impact on austerity policy choices and led indirectly to modest policy harmonization. But the European Union has not even attempted to harmonize most aspects of the disparate pension systems of its member countries, and where it has tried to harmonize policies directly, notably in the area of supplemental pensions, it has had little success. The weakness of broad harmonization pressures within the European Union helps to explain the absence of overall policy convergence.

The economic–demographic pressures for pension austerity, reinforced by ideological critiques and supranational institutions, might be expected to produce massive changes in public pension systems. But change has, as noted above, mostly been incremental, because pressures for austerity are mediated in critical ways by political and policy characteristics of countries. As Paul Pierson put it, austerity politics is different from enrichment politics not just because resources are constrained while there are more elderly to be served, but also because "austerity creates a quite distinct set of political problems, empowers different actors, and dictates new strategies."[45] Most generally, politicians have sought to respond to austerity pressures in a way that minimizes the blame and electoral retribution that they encounter from organized groups and individual voters. Both the strategies and policy choices that they make to avoid blame and the opportunities that their political opponents have to generate blame are in turn influenced by feedbacks from current policies, political institutions, and political support coalitions.

Blame-Avoiding Incentives

Austerity pressures on public pensions pose a common set of challenges for politicians, notably pressures to avoid or diffuse blame and the limited opportunities for claiming credit. Politicians who are interested in seeking reelection must be particularly sensitive to avoiding blame because voters are generally more sensitive to losses that are imposed on them (e.g., cuts in pension benefits) than to equivalent gains that they have made.[46] Pension cutbacks are especially risky because losses are perceived as particularly salient by the target group and because in many countries the elderly are disproportionately likely to vote.

Each of the three broad options that politicians have for responding to austerity pressures—retrenchment, refinancing, and restructuring—poses distinctive opportunities and strategies for policymakers concerned with avoiding blame. And the universality of politicians' seeking to avoid blame for unpopular actions is helpful in explaining some aspects of the national and cross-national patterns in pension policy change that we observe. For example, policymakers frequently attempt to reduce the blame-generating potential of retrenchment by delaying the initial onset of changes for several years into the future, phasing them in gradually, or targeting them on politically weak clientele (e.g., noncitizens). Existing beneficiaries are often "grandfathered," that is, protected from any cutbacks. Similarly, in choosing refinancing options, increases in payroll tax rates and tax bases are often delayed and phased in. Policymakers may also increase use of general revenue or create new sources of dedicated revenue that diffuse costs broadly and are less visible. In restructuring pensions, policymakers generally phase out the universal flat-rate pensions that some countries make available to all citizens over time, or make them subject to a gradually escalating income test. Similar strategies can be used to replace a publicly defined benefit pension with a "defined-contribution" pension based on individual accounts.

The universal pressures for avoiding blame and generating blame in democratic politics are not felt equally in all political systems, however. Instead, they are interwoven with features of specific features of national political systems: policy feedbacks from existing program structures, political institutions, and the structure of political support coalitions. Together, these national contexts affect the types of retrenchment initiatives that are attempted, the strategies used to sell those initiatives and avoid blame, and the eventual timing and scope of pension reform.[47]

Policy Feedbacks

Perhaps the most important influence on prospects for pension retrenchment and restructuring initiatives is the heritage of past pension policy choices, which Pierson refers to as policy feedbacks and "path dependence."[48] Both the overall "pension regime" and what can be called the "microrules" of individual programs can shape later pension policy choices. For example, Karl Hinrichs and Myles and Pierson have noted (and table 2.1 in this chapter confirms) that clear policy feedback or "path dependence" effects are visible in comparing countries that had large public earnings–related systems at the beginning of the 1970s and those that did not.[49] Countries that did not develop a large public earnings–related pension tier prior to the 1970s, notably Australia, Denmark, New Zealand, and the United Kingdom, faced continuing pressures to develop an earnings-related pension. But in the long absence of a state-mandated system, each of these countries developed a substantial occupational pension sector. Proposals for an expanded public pension system had to adapt to these developments, either by creating an opt-out from the state pension system when the latter was created (as in the United Kingdom), or by mandating universal coverage and increased standardization of private occupational pensions rather than an expanded state system (as in Denmark and Australia). Slower economic growth and higher unemployment after the first oil shock also made governments that did not already have a public earnings–related pension tier extremely reluctant to undertake the huge new spending commitments involved in adding one.[50] These "mixed" pension systems can be considered a distinctive new form of pension regime.

As shown in the right hand column of table 2.1, these different pension regimes are likely to respond to current pressures for austerity in pension policy in rather different ways. In Bismarckian countries with a very large public earnings–related pension tier, pressures to reduce pension costs and reduce rather than just stabilize pension contribution rates have been especially severe. Bismarckian countries are likely to begin with incremental retrenchment and refinancing measures, but once these have been exhausted, they may turn toward more fundamental restructuring reforms to reduce current and future costs. Because the public PAYG tier was already so large, however, proposals for a mandatory occupational or personal pension individual account tier had to adapt or be crowded out by the double payment problem. When expanded mandatory or quasi-mandatory individual account tiers have been adopted in these countries, notably in Sweden and Germany, it has been as a relatively small supplement to a still very large public pension tier that faces severe affordability problems. In both countries, the new individual account tier is intended to preserve overall pension replacement rates at or near the levels previously promised while stabilizing contribution rates in the public system.

The Bismarckian Lite countries, Canada and the United States, with lesser pension burdens, are likely to be able to maintain their current pension structures with incremental measures somewhat longer. But the emergence of large supplemental pension sectors in the Bismarckian Lite countries—in part a reflection of their own modest replacement rates—means that policymakers may face pressures to expand a parallel tax-subsidized private pension system whose costs may not be as visible as those in the public system. Countries relying primarily on universalistic pensions—a disappearing category by the 1990s—were likely to continue to confront pressures for earnings-related pensions but equally strong demographic and budgetary counterpressures against adopting them, at least as a public system. Moreover, although Esping-Andersen has argued that universal pensions are most likely to be resistant to austerity pressures because of their broad beneficiary base, universal pensions are also poorly targeted. In an era of huge pension expenditures and fiscal stress, pressures for some form of income testing at the upper end are likely to be strong, both in the few countries such as New Zealand that rely on them exclusively and in countries where they are one tier of a multitier system.

The age of the current pension system in a country can also affect its susceptibility to change. As Pierson has noted, people develop expectations about the level of benefits that they should receive when a pension system has been in place for many years.[51] These expectations are especially powerful in contributory systems, where a sense of entitlement to a given level of "earned benefits" is likely to arise, even if the ratio of benefits to past contributions is extremely high. Thus the prospects for pension restructuring are likely to be greatest in "immature" contributory systems, where few people have begun to draw benefits, and thus political mobilization against those initiatives is likely to be relatively weak. This is most clearly evident in New Zealand, where a new National government in 1975 quickly abolished an earnings-related pension tier put in place by its Labour predecessor the year before, and in the United Kingdom, where the Thatcher government

Table 2.1. Pension Regime Types and Challenges In Industrialized Countries

Pension Regime Types	Country Examples, ca. 1950	Country Examples, ca. 1974	Country Examples, ca. 1995	Country Examples, ca. 2003	Modal Challenges in Period of Pension Austerity
Notional Defined Contribution: lifetime contribution-related pension operated on PAYG basis				Italy Sweden[a]	• Keep pension payroll taxes stable • Avoid lengthening of phase-ins and imputing of credits when no contributions were made
Bismarckian: earnings-related social insurance tier (alone or on top of flat-rate pension) with high replacement rates, is dominant	Austria France Italy Germany	Austria France Italy Germany Sweden	Austria France Italy Germany Sweden	Austria France Germany[a]	• Keep pension payroll taxes at politically sustainable levels (under ca. 20% of payroll) through combination of retrenchment and refinancing • Consider restructuring public tiers and adding mandatory private tiers when those options are exhausted
Bismarckian Lite: earnings-related social insurance tier (alone or on top of flat-rate pension) with low replacement rates is dominant	United States	Canada United States	Canada United States	Canada United States	• Keep pension payroll taxes at politically sustainable levels (under 10%–15% of payroll) through combination of retrenchment and refinancing • Adapt to emerging supplementary occupational and personal pension sectors

Table 2.1. Continued

Pension Regime Types	Country Examples, ca. 1950	Country Examples, ca. 1974	Country Examples, ca. 1995	Country Examples, ca. 2003	Modal Challenges in Period of Pension Austerity
Universal: flat-rate pension financed by general revenues and/or payroll tax is dominant	Canada Denmark New Zealand Sweden Switzerland United Kingdom	Denmark New Zealand Switzerland United Kingdom	New Zealand	New Zealand	• Respond to public pressures for earnings-related pensions • Adapt to rising costs through retrenchment (including income testing at upper end) and refinancing • Adapt to supplementary occupational and personal pension sectors where they emerge
Residual: income or means-tested pension is dominant	Australia	Australia			• Respond to public pressures for earnings-related pensions • Avoid perverse savings and work incentive effects associated with income and asset tests • Adapt to emerging supplementary occupational and personal pension sectors
Mixed: mandatory or opt-out private tier is integrated with residual or universal pension tier	Netherlands	Netherlands	Australia Denmark Netherlands Switzerland United Kingdom	Australia Denmark Netherlands Switzerland United Kingdom	• Integrate public and private tiers and provide transparency, equity, and universal coverage • Control administrative costs in private tiers

aIndicates countries where a mandatory or quasimandatory individual savings tier has been added to a dominant defined benefit or notional defined contribution pension tier.

dramatically reduced the scope of the State Earnings-Related Pension Scheme established by the prior Labour government.

Finally, the prospects for pension policy changes can also be affected by the presence or absence of program microrules such as whether a program has "action-forcing" financing mechanisms. If a pension program relies exclusively on a dedicated revenue source (usually a payroll tax), as in the United States and Canada, pension reform will come to the top of politicians' agenda when fund outflow is about to exceed contributions inflow (or when accumulated funds are about to run out, in partially funded systems). Indeed, the timing of past Social Security reform rounds and the distinctive absence of Social Security refinancing since 1983 can clearly be traced in large part to the way the trust fund operates: payroll tax increases enacted as part of the 1983 Social Security rescue package have proven sufficient to pay out current benefits and accumulate a surplus as well, so payroll tax increases would be almost impossible to sell to the public. If, however, a pension program's governing statutes permit, or even require (as with most universal or means-tested pensions), general revenue financing, retrenchment and restructuring initiatives are likely to be delayed until a government faces a general budget crisis.

Organized Interests

The relative power of political support coalitions, especially labor unions and left political parties, has been widely recognized as an important factor influencing both the way that welfare states develop and their susceptibility to austerity initiatives.[52] Interests are organized in different ways, however. In a number of countries in Europe, centralized bargaining between employers and trade unions, with government as a concerned (and sometimes guiding) third partner, is an important feature of the policymaking process.[53] Myles and Quadagno have suggested that because leaders of these "social partners" can reach binding agreements and allocate costs among their members, such arrangements may facilitate pension retrenchment and restructuring.[54] Pierson has argued that unions may be less influential in periods of pension austerity than they were during the construction of the welfare state. Unions clearly remain important players in many countries, however. For example, Karen Anderson has argued that where labor unions perceive pension policy reform to be part of a broader effort at economic stabilization, and see themselves as essential partners in achieving that stability in collaboration with social democratic governments, they may be willing to make greater compromises than unions that are more marginalized in policymaking.[55] In other countries, unions may have an institutionalized role in administration of the pension system that gives them added leverage to resist changes that they find unacceptable.[56]

The organization of seniors themselves can also affect governments' willingness to undertake and capacity to carry out austerity initiatives. In the United

States and some other countries, seniors groups are a powerful independent political force. In most other countries, seniors organizations are much weaker.[57] In many countries, trade unions and union confederations quite consciously view public pensions as a form of deferred wage and themselves as the major defenders of the public pension system. However, trade unions have more complicated agendas than seniors organizations; faced with a fiscal crisis in which they are forced to choose between cuts in pensions and cuts in health care or unemployment insurance, seniors groups are probably less likely to choose the former than trade unions. Thus, powerful seniors organizations are probably a stronger bulwark against pension retrenchment than powerful trade unions. But senior organizational strength is not an exogenous variable—it is likely to reflect at least in part past austerity initiatives that have mobilized senior opposition.

Overall, organized interests play an ambiguous role in pension reform. Failure to secure the approval of social partners can derail proposed pension reforms of all types (notably in France and in several rounds in Italy). But it is not clear that countries with more organized interest group participation in policymaking have produced more sweeping reforms. Moreover, countries that have instituted major reforms (e.g., Germany, Italy, and Sweden) often did so by affording employers and unions a relatively limited consultative role—and less veto power—compared to what they are normally have.

Political Institutions

The literature on welfare state retrenchment suggests several arguments about how political institutions structure opportunities for pension policy change. Perhaps the most obvious argument is that systems that concentrate power in the executive, with few and relatively weak veto points where retrenchment initiatives can be blocked—single-chamber legislatures with cohesive, executive-dominated single-party majorities and no requirement for a supermajority, for example—are more likely to enact pension retrenchment and restructuring initiatives than those that lack these institutions. Several authors have framed this argument more generally in terms of veto points and veto players and the degree of party fragmentation as influences on governmental capacity for imposing policy change.[58]

As Pierson and Weaver noted in their study of pension retrenchment in Canada, the United Kingdom, and the United States, however, the advantages of concentrated power and minimal veto points are at least partially offset by concentration of accountability in political systems. Voters know that it is the governing party that is imposing losses, and those in power know that they know it, and may therefore be reluctant to undertake initiatives that are very likely to incur retribution at the next election.[59] Moreover, even governing parties with extraordinarily strong formal powers may face pressures not to use them to maximize their own preferences: the financial stakes in pensions are so high for employers, unions, pension providers, and others that they are likely to view stability and predictability over time as supremely important. Thus, even pension policy changes that serve a group's short-term interests may not be desirable if they are seen as posing a high risk of reversal (with the attendant transition costs) by a later government.

Other aspects of political institutions may also affect capacity for policy change, however. For example, countries that have relatively short electoral cycles may find it particularly difficult to make changes that impose visible losses on retirees and those approaching retirement. In this regard, multiple electoral cycles (e.g., the differing electoral cycles for the president and legislature in France, or for federal and provincial legislatures in Canada and Germany) may also inhibit governmental willingness and capacity to retrench, refinance, or restructure their pension systems.[60]

Overall, the role of political institutions in pension reform has been complex, and its contribution to explaining cross-national patterns of pension policy change appears fairly modest. Short electoral cycles have complicated pension reform initiatives in a number of countries that have them (notably Sweden prior to 1994, and New Zealand). Weak governments (Italy) and multiple veto points (the United States) also appear to be associated with unusually long phase-in periods for some austerity-driven pension reforms. And the role of political institutions in contributing to the paucity of Social Security policy change in the United States over the past two decades seems clear: the lack of change is not just the result of short-term economic–demographic pressures and the absence of an immediate funding crisis in the Social Security system. It must also be attributed in part to the combination of multiple veto points and the almost continuous divided government that has kept U.S. presidents from actively pursuing reform agendas that would likely fail to make it through Congress. Alternation of the Democrats and Republicans in the White House and almost perpetual divided government help to explain why the agenda for fundamental reforms has been broad: both parties have been able to put ideas broadly consistent with their political philosophies onto the agenda. And the fact that Republicans have controlled veto points in the federal government almost continually has helped to block broadening investment of the Social Security trust fund in the last decade, while their current hegemony in Washington means that this policy alternative is off the agenda in the near term.

Institutional explanations should not be carried too far, however. Concentration of power is a necessary but not sufficient explanation of the major pension changes instituted by Margaret Thatcher in the United Kingdom, for example. And major retrenchment and restructuring reforms occurred—and did not occur—both in countries that concentrate power in a single party and in those where coalitions—even minority coalitions—held power. It appears that a variety of ad hoc mechanisms ranging from technocratic governments with decree powers in Italy to informal cross-party agreements in Germany and formal multiparty working groups in Sweden may act as functional substitutes for concentrated power.[61]

Peer Country Influences

In addition to cross-national lesson drawing or more direct pressures for harmonization that occur through supranational institutions, such learning may also occur directly through informal networks of specialized policy elites.[62] Policymaking elites are more likely to engage in lesson drawing from specific other countries when (1) the lesson-offering and lesson-drawing countries face similar problems in the short and medium term because they have similar overall policy regimes and specific program microrules, (2) elites in the lesson-drawing country perceive potential lesson-offering countries to be "like us" in terms of their demographic situation, party makeup of government, etc., and (3) policy elites interact on a regular basis through regional organizations such as the European Union. All of these factors suggest that lesson drawing is likely to be heavily regionalized. Thus, it is not too surprising that Latin Americans have looked more to the Chilean model of more radical privatization than pension reformers in other regions. Some similar patterns can also be seen in Western Europe, for example, with substantial copying of the Swedish NDC pension system in both Italy and Latvia. The tendency of the United States to view itself as unique rather than looking reflexively at "peer" countries may also contribute to the absence of policy change in the United States.

BEYOND-AUSTERITY POLITICS

Political mediating factors play an important role in explaining how and why countries respond to pressures for pension austerity in ways that show strong similarities in some attributes but great differences in others. Policy feedbacks play a particularly important role in explaining these patterns. But even taking these variables into account, a number of attributes of pension policy remain poorly explained, notably (1) uneven trends in early retirement programs and the continued decline in labor force participation of older workers in most OECD countries; (2) the widespread expansion of some pension policies, notably child care credits; and (3) differing national choices on collective investment funds. In part, these patterns result from the fact that pension politics is not made in a vacuum. Other policies, ideas, and constituencies can also impinge on pension politics, even when their main focus is elsewhere. In the current era of pension austerity, three such forces are crucial, sometimes reinforcing and sometimes inhibiting austerity pressures (see the dark-shaded box in the lower center of figure 2.1).

Investment Politics

Closely related to the move from enrichment to austerity in public pension systems in recent years is what can be called investment politics. The most basic investment politics question is whether dedicated funding sources that are not currently needed to pay benefits should be accumulated in individual-defined contribution accounts or in collective public funds. This issue clearly mobilizes ideologically oriented constituencies. Developing large public investment funds is also likely to provoke strong opposition among business interests, who may fear that it will lead to increased government influence over corporate decisionmaking and even "backdoor" nationalizations. Mutual funds and other financial sector players may also become involved in investment politics disputes, seeking to increase business opportunities while limiting intrusive government regulation and requirements that they provide accounts to low-wage, low–fund-balance workers on terms that do not allow them to make a profit. Trade unions may also become involved in investment politics, seeing union-administered individual accounts as a way to build member loyalty and organizational capacity. Strong interest in individual accounts within the U.S. financial services industry helped to get the issue on the policy agenda in this country but was not sufficient to enact it.

Labor Market Politics

Many aspects of pension policy have implications for the labor market, notably the standard retirement age, the minimum age at which retirement benefits can be taken and penalty for taking benefits early, and the penalty paid in terms of lost benefits for continuing to work past the standard retirement age. The more generous the conditions under which workers may retire early, the younger the standard retirement age, and the greater the financial penalties for working past that age, the greater the restrictions on labor supply. In most countries, work effort among older workers has fallen substantially in recent decades.[63] In the slow economic growth era that followed the 1970s oil shocks, a number of countries adopted policies that encouraged workers to retire, or partially retire, early, opening jobs for younger workers. Both employers and unions may resist cutbacks in early retirement provisions of public pension systems, despite strong pressures for pension austerity. Resistance to early retirement retrenchment has been especially strong in many of the high-unemployment countries of continental western Europe.

Gender Politics

Gender is relevant to pension policymaking in many ways. Women tend to live longer than men, and thus are more likely to outlive any private retirement savings. They also are likely to spend fewer years as full-time workers in the paid labor market, devoting more of their working years to caregiving for children and parents and as homemakers. And when they are in the paid labor market, their earnings are usually lower than those of men. Thus, they may be particularly vulnerable in pension systems that base retirement pensions on contributions. Because widows are likely to have limited contributions histories, they are likely to be particularly dependent on the earnings history of their spouses—and particularly vulnerable if they divorce or outlive their husbands.

For all of these reasons, elderly women in many OECD countries have higher rates of poverty than do elderly men. And pension policy in many countries has become "gendered"—discussed in terms of differential gender impact and the focus of interest and lobbying by organizations representing women. Three issues have been at the center of the intersection between pension policymaking and gender politics: differential retirement ages for men and women, pension credits for years spent in caregiving, and splitting of pension credits when marriages break down. The way that these issues intersect with austerity pressures differs significantly, however. A number of countries have historically maintained lower retirement ages for women than for men, reflecting both attitudes toward the "fragility" of women and the fact that women tend to marry men who are several years older than themselves. These differentials have come under attack on grounds of both equality before the law and fairness (since women live longer than men). Thus harmonizing retirement ages at the higher level previously applied to men has provided an opportunity to accommodate austerity pressures in pension systems.

There has been more conflict between austerity pressures and pressures to provide additional pension credits for caregiving. In general, pressures for pension austerity have led to movement in pension policy toward a closer linkage of benefits to contributions—for example, by increasing the number of working years that are taken into account in calculating pension replacement rates. Introducing pension credits to caregivers weakens the linkage between labor market income and pension credits; it also weakens the linkage between actual contributions and pension credits unless the state makes contributions on caregivers' behalf (as has been done in Sweden). And in earnings-related pension schemes, caregiving credits also require putting a value based on the caregiving contribution. Should that contribution be based on a parent's previous wage, which is likely to give more money to middle-class families who are already likely to have higher retirement incomes than working class families? Or should it instead be paid at a flat rate? Regardless of the specific approach taken, increasing credits for caregivers is likely to increase the cost of a public pension system in both the short and long terms. Thus, it has frequently been enacted as a "sweetener" in a broader retrenchment-focused pension reform package. The absence of such packages helps to explain why child care credits have not been on the U.S. agenda.

The various beyond-austerity issues intersect with each other and with austerity concerns in a number of ways. Cuts in early retirement provisions and increases in the retirement age for women (where it was previously lower than that for men), for example, can be used to lower the costs of public pension systems. But other issues also cut against austerity concerns. For example, worries about high unemployment rates may lead to an expansion of early retirement pensions, even in the face of strong overall pressures for retrenchment. And successful retrenchment may facilitate increased use of public pension funds for savings and investment.

CONCLUSIONS

Pension policy in the advanced industrial countries over the past quarter century exhibit substantial commonalities as well as continued—in some cases, enhanced—diversity. The most commonality is found in pension retrenchment and refinancing agendas. This commonality stems largely from a common (but differentially felt) set of economic–demographic forces: the demographic shock of a shrinking ratio of workers to pensioners as life expectancy rose and fertility declined, fiscal pressures resulting in part from slower economic growth, and competitive pressures to restrain payroll taxes and other nonwage-labor costs that finance public pensions. As a result, the wealthy industrialized countries have considered very similar sorts of incremental retrenchment mechanisms and payroll tax increases. Of course, these pressures are felt to varying degrees across countries. The United States, for example, faces both weaker demographic and fiscal pressures than many other wealthy countries, meaning that pressures for immediate reductions in Social Security spending have not been strong in the United States. The absence of strong pressure for immediate policy change in Social Security has in turn meant that there has not been a legislative vehicle that would facilitate changes in provisions involving care giving and other beyond-austerity concerns that have become more important over this period in other countries or improvements in the United States' very weak income guarantee for the elderly.

Other, politically mediated pressures for policy change continue to be felt both in the United States and abroad. Common incentives for politicians to minimize blame clearly play an important role in explaining why governments in all of the rich countries use delay, obfuscation, and other blame-avoiding techniques to reduce the visibility and immediate effects of retrenchment, refinancing, and restructuring initiatives.

There is great diversity across countries, however, in the pension-restructuring options that are considered and adopted. Unlike some Latin American countries and transitional economies in Eastern Europe, the wealthy industrialized countries in Western Europe and North America have all built their restructuring reforms heavily on the foundations of their current systems. Differences in the role played by private pensions in these systems can in large part be explained by whether a country already had a robust public earnings-related pension prior to the early 1970s. But as table 2.1 shows, the degree of restructuring that has occurred in these regimes over time is quite striking. The most important restructuring trends include the virtual emptying out of the universalist and residual categories after 1974, the enormous growth in the "mixed" category, and, very recently, both the emergence of a new notional defined contribution category and the addition of mandatory and quasimandatory tiers to a few Bismarckian and NDC-based systems. Further extension of these recent tends is very likely.

As noted above, the patterns of regime transition that are considered and adopted in individual countries are heavily influenced by policy feedback from those countries' existing pension regimes. Well-established pension regimes are unlikely to deviate from the modal transition patterns outlined in table 2.1. Indeed, the analysis in this chapter makes clear that policy feedback is not just about lock-in of the current policy regime; policy feedbacks can introduce pressures for pension regime change as well as rigidity.[64] And the balance between rigidity-inducing and change-inducing characteristics clearly differs across pension regimes and over time. Pressures for regime transition are felt early in universal and residual regimes, for example. Pressures for regime change are felt later in Bismarckian regimes, and those pressures are heavily counterbalanced by rigidities: countries where a large income-related pension system is already in place are likely to develop both substantial clientele support for such programs and have limited tax room for a mandatory system of individual accounts. Therefore, transitions in these regimes thus far have taken the form either of a shift to an NDC system—which to a nonexpert looks very much like a traditional Bismarckian system—and/or a relatively modest "add-on" individual account tier. Bismarckian Lite regimes appear to be among the most sustainable pension regimes, although they are subject to strong policy drift toward the expansion of supplemental individual account pensions on defined contribution principles. The robust character of the United States has helped to prevent adoption not only of individual accounts but also of more modest changes that might be incorporated as "sweeteners" in a big pension reform package, notably a more generous income floor for seniors.

The path-dependent nature of pension policy regime change in the wealthy countries is also critical in explaining why convergence among these regimes has been very limited. Different pension regimes face both distinctive challenges and distinctive (and limited) options for change. Differing policy trajectories also have contributed to the failure of the European Union to try to harmonize pension regimes in member countries. Thus, while supranational integration in Europe has sometimes stimulated retrenchment in individual countries, it has not had a substantial effect on policy convergence.

NOTES

The research reported herein was partially funded pursuant to a grant from the U.S. Social Security Administration (SSA) funded as part of the Retirement Research Consortium at Boston College. The opinions and conclusions are solely those of the author and should not be construed as representing the opinions or policy of SSA or any agency of the federal government. The author would like to thank Sarah Brooks, Jacob Hacker, Martin Hering, and Alan Jacobs for their many helpful comments on earlier drafts of this chapter.

1. For a comparative analysis of countries making more fundamental reforms, see Katharina Müller, *Privatising Old-Age Security: Latin America and Eastern Europe Compared* (Cheltenham, Gloustershire: Edward Elgar, 2003).

2. Paul Pierson, ed., "Coping with Permanent Austerity: Welfare State Restructuring in Affluent Democracies," in *The New Politics of the Welfare State* (Oxford: Oxford University Press, 2001), 410–56. See also Paul Pierson, "Irresistible Forces, Immovable Objects: Post-Industrial Welfare States Confronting Permanent Austerity," *Journal of European Public Policy* 5, no. 4 (1998):539–60.

3. This list of cross-cutting issues is not exhaustive. For example, immigration politics involves debates over the degree to which persons who have moved to a country during or after their working lives (and hence do not have a complete history of contributions to a public pension system) should be eligible for universal and means-tested benefits.

4. For a more general argument about multiple patterns of reform within different welfare state regimes, see Pierson, "Coping with Permanent Austerity."

5. Esping-Andersen originally formulated this tripartite distinction in terms of overall welfare state regimes. See Gøsta Esping-Andersen, *The Three Worlds of Welfare Capitalism* (Cambridge, UK: Polity, 1999). However, Hinrichs and others have pointed out that pension regimes are often quite distinct in their orientations from other welfare state programs. Most notably, the United States, characterized by Esping-Andersen as a residual welfare state, has a primarily social insurance–focused pension system. See Karl Hinrichs, "Elephants on the Move: Patterns of Public Pension Reform in OECD Countries," *European Review* 8, no. 3 (2000):353–78.

6. For cross-national overviews of recent pension reforms, see R. Kent Weaver, "The Politics of Pension Reform: Lessons from Abroad," in *Framing the Social Security Debate: Values, Politics and Economics*, ed. R. Douglas Arnold, Michael Graetz, and Alicia Munnell (Washington, DC: Brookings Institution Press, 1998), 183–229; Hinrichs, "Elephants on the Move"; and Klaus-Jürgen Gern, "Recent Developments in Old Age Pension Systems: An International Overview," in *Social Security Pension Reform in Europe*, ed. Martin Feldstein and Horst Siebert (Chicago: University of Chicago Press, 2002), 439–78. On the continental European systems, see especially Martin Schludi, *The Reform of Bismarckian Pension Systems* (Ph.D. diss., Berlin: Humboldt University, 2002).

7. For a detailed description of the 1977 legislation, see John Snee and Mary Ross, "Social Security Amendments of 1977: Legislative History and Summary of Provisions," *Social Security Bulletin* 41 (March 1978).

8. Proposed cuts include a three-month delay in cost-of-living adjustments, a change in calculating future retirees' initial benefits that would eventually significantly lower the percentage of a retiree's prior earnings replaced by Social Security benefits, and a severe and almost immediate cut in benefits for future early retirees. On this period, see Paul Light, *Still Artful Work: The Continuing Politics of Social Security Reform* (New York: McGraw-Hill, 1995).

9. See Light, *Still Artful Work*.

10. For a description of these episodes, see Paul D. Pierson and R. Kent Weaver, "Imposing Losses in Pension Policy," in *Do Institutions Matter? Government Capabilities in the U.S. and Abroad*, ed. R. Kent Weaver and Bert A. Rockman (Washington, DC: Brookings Institution Press, 1993), 110–50.

11. Martha Derthick, "The Evolving Old Politics of Social Security," in *Seeking the Center: Politics and Policymaking at the New Century*, ed. Martin A. Levin, Marc K. Landy, and Martin Shapiro (Washington, DC: Georgetown University Press, 2001), 193–214.

12. See Daniel Wartonick and Michael Packard, "Slowing Down Pension Indexing: The Foreign Experience." *Social Security Bulletin* 44 (1983):9–15; Henk Vording and Kees Goudswaard, "Indexation of Public Pension Benefits on a Legal Basis: Some Experiences in European Countries," *Social Security Bulletin* 50, no. 3 (1997):31–44.

13. See Heidi Hartmann and Catherine Hill, "Strengthening Social Security for Women," report from the Working Conference on Women and Social Security (Warrenton, VA, July 19–22, 1999), 15–16.

14. Sveinbjörn Blöndal and Stefano Scarpetta, "Early Retirement in OECD Countries: The Role of Social Security Systems, *OECD Economic Studies* 29 (1997):7–53; and Sveinbjörn Blöndal and Stefano Scarpetta, "The Early Retirement Decision in OECD Countries," in *OECD Economics Department Working Papers*, no. 202 (Paris: OECD, February 1999), chapter 4. On the interaction between the German unemployment and pension systems, see Alex Börsch-Supan, "The German Retirement Insurance System," in *Pension Reform in Six Countries: What Can We Learn from Each Other*, ed. Börsch-Supan and Meinhard Meigel (Berlin: Springer, 2001), 13–38.

15. Blöndal and Scarpetta, "The Early Retirement Decision in OECD Countries," 66.

16. For a comprehensive review of early retirement policies in rich nations, see Berhard Ebbinghaus, *Exit from Labor: Reforming Early Retirement and Social Partnership in Europe, Japan and the USA* (Köln: University of Köln Habilitationschrift, October 2002).

17. See Blöndal and Scarpetta, "Early Retirement in OECD Countries," 17–18.

18. A finding of a future deficit in the CPP's triennial review process sets in motion a process under which ministers from Ottawa and the provinces are supposed to agree on any needed changes to keep the plan viable; if they do not agree, contribution rates will increase automatically to meet half of the anticipated deficiency (phased in over three years), and indexation of the CPP will be frozen for the next three years unless cabinet ministers agree to override these procedures. See David W. Slater and William B. P. Robson, *Building a Stronger Pillar: The Changing Shape of the Canada Pension Plan* (Toronto: C.D. Howe Research Institute, March 1999), 6–7.

19. Gern, "Recent Developments in Old-Age Pension Systems," 457.

20. On this period, see Martha Derthick, "The Evolving Old Politics of Social Security."

21. For an outline of major alternatives, see *Report: 1. Findings and Recommendations*, 1994–96 Advisory Council on Social Security (Washington, DC: Advisory Council on Social Security, 1997).

22. See Gary Burtless, *How Would Financial Risk Affect Retirement Income under Individual Accounts?* Issue Brief no. 5, Center for Retirement Research at Boston College, October 2000.

23. Greenspan argues that no mechanisms to insulate investment managers from political pressures would be adequate. For Greenspan's views, see Richard W. Stevenson, "Fed Chief Warns of Painful Choices on Social Security," *New York Times*, January 29, 1999.

24. For a discussion, see Amy Goldstein, "Bush Plans Panel to Study Overhaul of Social Security," *Washington Post*, February 27, 2001; and Sara Fritz, "Proof of Bush's Social Security Intentions Will Be in the Panel," *St. Petersburg Times*, April 2, 2001.

25. President's Commission to Strengthen Social Security, *Strengthening Social Security and Creating Wealth for All Americans* (Washington, DC: President's Commission to Strengthen Social Security, December 2001).

26. Richard Morin and Claudia Deane, "Poll Shows New Doubts on Economy; President's Tax Cut, Policy Are Questioned," *Washington Post*, March 27, 2001.

27. Jim Vanderhei and Juliet Eilperin, "Bush's Plan for Social Security Loses Favor," *Washington Post*, August 13, 2002; Amy Goldstein, "Action on Social Security Debated," *Washington Post*, November 15, 2002.

28. See Jacob Hacker, "Privatizing Risk without Privatizing Benefits: U.S. Welfare State Reform in Comparative Perspective," paper presented at the 2002 annual meeting of the American Political Science Association, Boston, MA, August 29–September 1, 2002; and Hacker, *The Divided Welfare State* (Princeton: Princeton University Press, 2002).

29. On the abolition of basic pension tiers, see Hinrichs, "Elephants on the Move."

30. See Edward Greenspon and Anthony Wilson-Smith, *Double Vision: The Inside Story of the Liberals in Power* (Toronto: Doubleday Canada, 1996), especially chapter 16; and R. Kent Weaver, "Pensions," in *The Government Taketh Away: The Politics of Pain in the United States and Canada*, ed. Leslie Pal and R. Kent Weaver (Washington, DC: Georgetown University Press, 2003).

31. See Brooks, "Social Protection and Economic Integration"; and Estelle James and Sarah Brooks, "The Political Economy of Structural Pension Reform," in *New Ideas about Old Age Security*, ed. Robert Holzmann and Joseph E. Stiglitz (Washington, DC: The World Bank, 2001), 133–70. Individual account systems have problems of their own, moreover. Where administration of individual accounts is decentralized to employers and individuals, high administrative costs—especially for low-earners—have been a particular problem. See, for example, Estelle James, James Smalhout, and Dmitri Vittas, "Administrative Costs and the Organization of Individual Account Systems: A Comparative Perspective," in *New Ideas about Old Age Security*, ed. Holzmann and Stiglitz, 254–307.

32. On notional defined contribution pension systems in general, see in particular Sarah M. Brooks and R. Kent Weaver, "Lashed to the Mast? The Politics of Notional Defined Contribution Pension Systems," paper prepared for World Bank and Riksforsäkringsverket conference on NDC Pension Schemes, Sandhamn, Sweden, September 28–30, 2003. On the Swedish reform, see Sweden, Ministry of Health and Social Affairs, *The Pension Reform: Final Report, June 1998*, Stockholm: Ministry of Health and Social Affairs, 1998; Edward Palmer, "Swedish Pension Reform: How Did It Evolve, and What Does It Mean for the Future?" in *Social Security Pension Reform in Europe*, Martin Feldstein and Horst Siebert, eds. (Chicago and London: University of Chicago Press, 2002), 171–205; Annika Sundén, *How Will Sweden's New Pension System Work?* (Chestnut Hill, MA: Boston College Center for Retirement Research Issue Brief No. 3, March 2000); and Urban Lundberg, *Juvelen I kronan: Social demokraterna och den allmänna pensionen* (Stockholm: Hjalmarson and Högberg, 2003). On the Italian NDC reform, see Daniele Franco, "Italy: The Search for a Sustainable PAYG Pension System," in *Searching for Better Pension Provisions in Developed Countries*, ed. N. Takayama (Tokyo: Maruzen, 2003).

33. Kevin Kinsella and Victor A. Velkoff, U.S. Census Bureau, Series P95/01-1, *An Aging World: 2001* (Washington, DC: U.S. Government Printing Office, 2001).

34. Government debt was a less serious issue in the United States than in many other OECD member countries at the dawn of the twenty-first century, although federal budget surpluses in the late 1990s were very short lived and deficits became an increasing concern with the tax cuts and increased national security expenditures of the George W.

Bush administration. In 1997, the United States was very close to the OECD average in gross general government liabilities as a share of GDP and slightly above the average in net liabilities, but both OECD averages had increased substantially in the 1990s. See Organization for Economic Cooperation and Development, *Reforms for an Ageing Society* (Paris: OECD, 2000), chapter 3.

35. European Union, Economic Policy Committee, *Budgetary Challenges Posed by Ageing Populations* (Brussels, EPC/ECFIN/655-EN-fin, October 24, 2001).

36. See the discussions in Paul D. Pierson, "The New Politics of the Welfare State," *World Politics* 48 (January 1996):143–79; and Leibfried and Pierson, "Semisovereign Welfare States."

37. On the impact of globalization, see for example Joseph Stiglitz, *Globalization and Its Discontents* (New York: W. W. Norton, 2002); Elmar Rieger and Stephan Liebfried, *Limits to Globalization* (Oxford: Polity Press, 2003); Paul Pierson, "Post-Industrial Pressures on the Mature Welfare States," in *The New Politics of the Welfare State,* ed. Pierson, 80–104; and Sven Steinmo, "Globalization and Taxation: Challenges to the Swedish Welfare State," *Comparative Political Studies* 35, no. 7 (September 2002):839–62. See also the review in Gøsta Esping-Andersen, *Welfare States in Transitions: National Adaptations in Global Economies* (London: Sage, 1997).

38. Giuliano Bonoli, *The Politics of Pension Reform* (Cambridge: Cambridge University Press, 2000), 33.

39. Sarah Brooks, "Social Protection and Economic Integration: The Politics of Pension Reform in an Era of Capital Mobility," *Comparative Political Studies* 35, no. 5 (June 2002):491–523.

40. For an earlier and more extensive treatment of some of the themes in this section, see Weaver, "The Politics of Pension Reform."

41. On the United Kingdom, see, for example, Pierson, *Dismantling the Welfare State?* and Bonoli, *The Politics of Pension Reform.* On Sweden, see, for example, Lundberg, *Juvelen I kronan,* and Anders Lindbom, "De borgerliga partierna och pensionsreformen," in *Hur blev den stora kompromissn mojlig: Politiken bakom den svenska pensionsreformen,* ed. Joakim Palme (Stockholm: Pensionsforum, 2001), 50–87.

42. Sarah M. Brooks, "What Was the Role of International Financial Institutions in the Diffusion of Social Security Reform in Latin America?" in *Learning from Foreign Models in Latin American Policy Reform,* ed. Kurt Weyland (Washington, DC: Woodrow Wilson Center Press, and Johns Hopkins University Press, 2004). See also Raúl L. Madrid, *Retiring the State: The Politics of Pension Privatization in Latin America and Beyond* (Stanford, CA: Stanford University Press, 2003).

43. See Robert D. Putnam, "Diplomacy and Domestic Politics: The Logic of Two-Level Games," *International Organization* 42, no. 3 (summer 1988):427–60. See also Andrew Moravsik, "Integrating International and Domestic Theories of International Bargaining," in *Double-Edged Diplomacy: International Bargaining and Domestic Politics,* Robert Putnam, ed. (Berkeley: University of California Press, 1993), 3–42.

44. On Italy and the EMU, see for example Schludi, *The Reform of Bismarckian Pension Systems,* ch. 5. For a detailed discussion of European Union fiscal institutions and their impact on Germany, see Martin Hering, *Major Institutional Change in a Frozen Welfare State: The Politics of Privatizing Public Pensions in Germany* (Ph.D diss., Johns Hopkins University, in progress).

45. Pierson, "Investigating the Welfare State at Century's End," in *The New Politics of the Welfare State,* 2.

46. This does not mean that politicians do not pursue other objectives at the same time. They may for example have "good policy motives" as well as electoral objectives, and seek election and reelection through claiming credit and by generating blame against political opponents as well as through avoiding blame. But avoiding blame is likely to be a particularly important concern. See R. Kent Weaver, *Ending Welfare As We Know It* (Washington, DC: Brookings Institution Press, 2000), ch. 2.

47. As Pierson puts it, "there is no simple 'politics of pensions.' Rather, each country faces the distinctive politics of distinctively constituted systems." Pierson, "The Politics of Pension Reform," 274.

48. See Pierson, *Dismantling the Welfare State*, and Pierson, "Increasing Returns, Path Dependence, and the Study of Politics," *American Political Science Review* 94, no. 2 (2000):251–67.

49. Hinrichs, "Elephants on the Move"; Myles and Pierson, "The Comparative Political Economy of Pension Reform," in *The New Politics of the Welfare State*, 305–33. See also the comparison of Denmark and Sweden in Christoffer Green-Pederson and Anders Lindbom, "Politics within Paths: The Trajectories of Danish and Swedish Pension Systems," paper delivered at the European Consortium on Political Research Workshop on the Politics of Ageing, Turin, March 22–26, 2002.

50. See, for example, Green-Pedersen and Lindbom, "Politics within Paths," 12.

51. Indeed, Pierson has argued that "the likelihood of privatization declines in direct relation to the scope and maturity of a pay-as-you-go scheme." Pierson, "The Politics of Pension Reform," 286.

52. Pierson, "The New Politics of the Welfare State," *World Politics* 48, no. 2 (1996):143–79.

53. On the varieties of relationships between government and social partners and their implications for European social policy, see Bernhard Ebbinghaus, "Reforming the Welfare State through 'Old' or 'New' Social Partnerships?" in *From Collective Bargaining to Social Partnerships: New Roles of the Social Partners in Europe*, ed. Carsten Kjærgaard and Åge Westphalen (Copenhagen: The Copenhagen Centre, June 2001), 103–20.

54. John Myles and Jill Quadagno, "Recent Trends in Public Pension Reform: A Comparative View," in *Reform of Retirement Income Policy: International and Canadian Perspectives*, ed. Keith G. Banting and Robin Boadway (Kingston, ON: Queens University School of Policy Studies, 1997), 247–71.

55. See Karen M. Anderson, "The Politics of Retrenchment in a Social Democratic Welfare State: Retrenchment of Swedish Pensions and Unemployment Insurance," *Comparative Political Studies* 34 (November 2001):1063–91.

56. Daniel Béland, "Does Labor Matter Institutions, Labor Unions and Pension Reform in France and the United States," *Journal of Public Policy* 21, no. 2 (2001):153–72.

57. On seniors groups, see for example Alan Walker and Gerhard Naegele, *The Politics of Old Age in Europe* (Buckingham and Philadelphia: Open University Press, 1999); David Feltenius, "Pensioners' Organizations in the Swedish Policymaking Process: From Lobbying to Corporatism," paper presented at the 30th Joint Session of the European Consortium for Political Research, Turin, March 22–27, 2002; and Andrea Louise Campbell and Julia Lynch, "Whose 'Gray Power'? Elderly Voters, Elderly Lobbies, and Welfare Reform in Italy and the United States," *Italian Politics and Society* 53 (summer 2000); Andrea Louise Campbell, *How Policies Make Citizens: Senior Political Activism and the American Welfare State* (Princeton: Princeton University Press, 2003); and Henry J. Pratt, *Gray Agendas:*

Interest Groups and Public Pensions in Canada, Britain, and the United States (Ann Arbor: University of Michigan Press, 1997).

58. See, for example, Ellen Immergut, "The Rules of the Game: The Logic of Health Policymaking in France, Switzerland and Sweden," in *Structuring Politics: Historical Institutionalism in Comparative Perspective*, ed. Kathleen Thelen and Sven Steinmo (New York: Cambridge University Press, 1992). Brooks argues that fragmentation of legislative power makes pension privatization less likely, but it is statistically significant only in some of her statistical models. See Brooks, "Social Protection and Economic Integration," 515.

59. Paul D. Pierson and R. Kent Weaver, "Imposing Losses in Pension Policy," in *Do Institutions Matter?: Government Capabilities in the U.S. and Abroad*, R. Kent Weaver and Bert A. Rockman, eds. (Washington, DC: Brookings Institution Press, 1993), 110–50.

60. See, for example, Leslie Pal and R. Kent Weaver, *The Government Taketh Away: The Politics of Pain in the United States and Canada* (Washington, DC: Georgetown University Press, 2003); and Bonoli, *The Politics of Pension Reform*.

61. See especially Schludi, *The Reform of Bismarckian Pension Systems*, ch. 9.

62. See Colin J. Bennett, "What Is Policy Convergence and What Causes It?" *British Journal of Political Science* 21 (1991):215–33.

63. Organization for Economic Cooperation and Development, *Reforms for an Ageing Society* (Paris: OECD, 2000), chapter 8.

64. For this point and several others in this concluding section, I am indebted to Alan Jacobs.

ACTIVATION THROUGH THICK AND THIN

Progressive Strategies for Increasing Labor Force Participation

JONAH D. LEVY

IN THE LITERATURE OF COMPARATIVE POLITICS, POLITICAL ECONOMY, AND GLOBALIZA-tion, progressive policy is portrayed typically as an *alternative* to economic liberalization: Social Democratic corporatism as an alternative to neoliberalism,[1] a social investment strategy as an alternative to neoliberal austerity,[2] and a coordinated market economy as an alternative to a liberal market economy.[3] Progressive approaches enable governments to *avoid* economic liberalization. It is by avoiding liberalization that progressive governments are able to project sovereignty and give expression to their political values.[4]

I believe that this dichotomous vision rests on a narrow, impoverished conception of economic liberalization. My central claim is that there is more than one way to liberalize. Economic liberalization need not be synonymous with the harsh, neoliberal methods of Ronald Reagan and Margaret Thatcher. It is possible to reconcile liberalization with concerns about equity and the disadvantaged, depending on how liberalizing reforms are constructed. Such progressive liberalizing reforms are not simply abstract possibilities, but the very real practice of a number of European governments.

I call the progressive, European approach to economic and social reform a "new social liberalism." What is "new" about the new social liberalism is that it does not simply accept a liberal market order while compensating the losers (as under the German "social market economy" or arguments about trade openness and welfare state development). Rather, the social helps define the content of liberalism itself, the character of the more marketized economic order. Under the new social liberalism, the character of the market economy—of the smaller government, lower taxes, and more flexible and active labor markets—is itself defined by social principles and concerns for the disadvantaged.

The new social liberal approach to economic and social reform has marked the actions of European governments, particularly left-led governments, in a variety of areas, including budget cutting, tax relief, and competition in public services. This paper focuses on one strand of the new social liberalism, labor market activation. The term "labor market activation" derives from the distinction between so-called passive labor market expenditures that pay people not to work (unemployment insurance, early retirement, etc.) and so-called active labor market expenditures that help people find jobs.

Labor market activation conveys two main ideas. The first is that people should derive their income primarily from paid employment, as opposed to government transfers. The second notion is that the goal of policy is not simply to minimize unemployment, but also to maximize total employment. In other words, in addition to reducing *formal* unemployment, the goal of activation is to move people *outside* the labor force—stay-at-home mothers, disabled workers, early retirees, discouraged workers—into the labor force.

Within the umbrella category of "labor market activation," my chapter examines three kinds of reforms: (1) closing pathways to early retirement; (2) increasing part-time and temporary employment; and (3) moving people from transfer payments to paid employment (from welfare to work, in the U.S. lexicon). Each of these objectives is associated with economic liberalism and raises serious concerns about equity and distributional outcomes. This chapter analyzes how European governments, often led by or closely cooperating with parties of the left, have addressed these risks—how they have pursued liberal activating measures while striving to uphold principles of fairness and concern for the disadvantaged.

The progressive, new social liberal approach to labor market activation is defined by two main features. The first is a concern for the *quality* of employment, for improving the situation of activated workers, not just for the *quantity* of employment. Whereas the neoliberal approach favors more jobs, the new social liberal approach favors more *and better* jobs, jobs that provide better living circumstances and life chances.

The second feature of the new social liberal approach to labor market activation is a much more extensive, positive role for public policy. The neoliberal strategy consists primarily of withdrawing state protections so as to increase work incentives and employment opportunities. It is largely a negative approach, rolling back state interventions that are seen to be at the heart of labor market dysfunctions. The neoliberal strategy is also a "thin" strategy. It rests on a relatively limited, or "thin," set of policy instruments.

The new social liberal strategy may include some thin measures, but it goes much further. It entails positive as well as negative reforms; it reregulates and deregulates labor markets; and it demands much more of the state and of the individual—a plethora of public policies to support workers as they reenter the labor force. As a result, "thick" labor market policies are often as expensive, or even more expensive, than the passive labor market programs that they replace. The schematic differences between thin, neoliberal activation and thick, progressive activation are summarized in table 3.1.

Table 3.1. Thick versus Thin Labor Market Activation

NOTE: In many cases, thick strategies are a supplement to thin strategies, rather than an alternative.

I. Closing Pathways to Early Retirement

Thin	Thick
1. Reduce early retirement benefits	1. Protect employment of older workers (LIFO)
2. Tighten eligibility for early retirement	2. Provide public employment to older workers
3. Privatize early retirement programs	3. Expand educational opportunities for youths
4. Make older workers compete for jobs	4. Expand social assistance for youths

II. Promoting Part-Time and Temporary Employment

Thin	Thick
1. Remove restrictions on part-time employment	1. Align hourly wages, benefits of part-time workers on hourly wages, benefits of full-time workers
2. Remove restrictions on temporary employment	2. Align wages, benefits of temporary workers on wages, benefits of full-time workers
3. Weaken protections of "insiders"	3. A little less protection for insiders in return for a little more protection for outsiders

III. Moving People From Welfare to Work

Thin	Thick
1. Reduce benefits	1. Allow activated workers to combine government transfers with earnings from employment
2. Tighten job-search requirements	2. Reduce taper rates of public programs; reduce tax rates on labor income
3. Increase coercion, control	3. Substitute universal benefits for means-tested benefits
4. Scale back publicly sponsored alternatives to paid employment (training, education)	4. Increase opportunities for education and training
5. Treat work–family tensions as a "private" matter to be handled by individual, not government	5. Expand services for activated workers, especially childcare

This chapter is divided into five sections. The first section analyzes the strategic choices confronting progressive parties in an age of economic liberalization. The second through fourth sections turn to concrete cases, providing examples of new social liberal reform in the area of labor market activation: respectively, the scaling back of early retirement in Sweden, the expansion of part-time employment in The Netherlands, and the reform of unemployment and social assistance benefits in a number of countries. The last section offers brief concluding remarks.

THE POLITICS OF THE NEW SOCIAL LIBERALISM

The "new social liberalism" has generally been the product of *a constrained or corrective European left*. For parties of the right—even if the continental European right is different from the Anglo-American right—policies that expand the play of market forces fit well with their basic policy orientation, and the upward redistribution of wealth that accompanies such reforms benefits their electoral base. For parties of the left, by contrast, economic liberalization challenges fundamental beliefs, whereas an upward redistribution of wealth harms their supporters. Consequently, the European left has tended to embark on liberalization with great reluctance, usually as a result of some kind of constraint.

Some constraints are economic, such as Maastricht budget deficit targets, whereas others are political, such as the need to govern in coalition with center-right parties. New social liberal reforms have generally been a response by left-led governments to constraints, an effort to pursue liberalization on terms acceptable to the left, in particular, protecting the interests of disadvantaged and low-income citizens. New social liberal reforms have also emerged as a corrective to prior neoliberal reforms by center-right governments, accepting a degree of economic liberalization, but trying to harmonize the more liberal economic context with left values and constituent interests.

There is nothing inevitable about the left's turn toward the new social liberalism. Two alternative approaches have also been widely pursued. The first is to defend the status quo, opposing any and all liberalization. The second strategy is to pursue an essentially neoliberal agenda (perhaps leavened with "postmaterialist," lifestyle themes) under the guise of "modernization" and activism. Both of these approaches have serious drawbacks, however.

The traditional leftist response to economic liberalization has been to resist it. To be progressive is to combat the extension of market forces, not to cultivate the market. From this perspective, left-led governments that engage in liberalizing reforms, such as labor market activation, are guilty of the worst kind of betrayal. In the introduction to his book, *In the Name of Liberalism*, Desmond King explicitly compares the welfare-to-work initiatives of the Clinton and Blair governments to compulsory sterilization because in both instances the state is using coercion to impose its view of how people should behave.[5] More prosaically, progressives argue that unemployment benefits have been "earned" on the basis of past social security/payroll tax contributions, therefore subjecting the receipt of these benefits to behavioral tests is tantamount to expropriation.[6] Others defend unconditional unemployment or welfare benefits on the grounds that they are a right of citizenship, not a privilege extended or retracted at the government's pleasure.[7]

A strategy of resistance to liberalization, while appealing to the leftist rank and file, is not without risks. The recent experience of the center-left Jospin, which governed France from 1997 to 2002, offers a cautionary tale. In the name of progressive principles, Prime Minister Jospin refused to introduce any kind of job search requirements into France's unemployment insurance system and guaranteed minimum income (RMI). Yet, a strong majority of French voters, including leftist voters, supported some kind of reasonable job-search requirement. Thus, the government found itself defending an unpopular status quo. Moreover, Jospin's resistance to reform lent credibility to conservative critiques that he was avoiding hard choices, that he was placating interest groups rather than modernizing the country—a charge that damaged Jospin badly in the 2002 presidential election. Finally and most important, Jospin's refusal to reform the French unemployment system did not mean that liberalizing reform did not happen; rather, it meant that reform was spearheaded by actors other than a government of the left.

In June 2000, the French employer association, the *Mouvement des Entreprises de France* (MEDEF), using a combination of blandishments, threats, and divide-and-conquer techniques, rammed through a collective bargaining agreement with several trade unions that overhauled the unemployment insurance system. The reform contained a job-search requirement, which was softened subsequently under government prodding. Still, the contours of the reform had been crafted by MEDEF, not the left. In addition, although described as a "labor market activation measure," the reform provided no money for job training, placement, or employment and wage subsidies. The absence of carrots to go along with the stick of job-search requirements was all the more remarkable given that France's unemployment insurance system was running a substantial surplus at the time. As part of the employer-drafted reform, however, the entire surplus was channeled to reductions in payroll taxes, leaving no money for measures to help the unemployed locate and become qualified for jobs. *In the end, then, the Jospin government did not "do nothing" on unemployment insurance; rather, it allowed the French employer association to do something in its place.* With the election of a conservative government in 2002, the left has ceded the terrain of unemployment reform for at least the next five years.

If the traditional leftist strategy has been to resist economic liberalization at every turn, self-styled "modernizers" have frequently gone to the opposite extreme, pursuing an essentially neoliberal agenda under the guise of "modernization" and activism. The phrase "Nixon goes to China" is often invoked to describe this strategy,[8] of which German Social Democratic Chancellor Gerhard Schroeder is perhaps the leading exemplar. Just as only a fierce anticommunist like Richard Nixon could recognize Communist China, only a Social Democratic leader like Schroeder can slash social spending, loosen labor market regulations, and lower taxes. Schroeder has appealed to German voters on two counts: first, as an economic modernizer, introducing badly needed liberal reforms into Germany's stagnant economy; second, as a social modernizer, making Germany a more tolerant and cosmopolitan country through a number of postmaterialist, lifestyle reforms (liberalization of citizenship rules, gay rights, restrictions on nuclear power, etc.).

The principal drawback of Schroeder's Nixon-goes-to-China approach is that many of the leftist faithful have been hurt by his reforms. Both Schroeder's pension and tax reforms had regressive consequences and, in a reversal of roles, it was the center-right Christian Democrats who were calling for a fairer sharing of costs and benefits. The electoral risk, of course, is that a demobilized leftist faithful will either stay home or punish the government at the polls. Although Schroeder managed to secure reelection in 2002, pundits are widely agreed that the victory occurred *in spite* of his economic and social record—thanks to a combination of fortune (historic floods that cast Schroeder in a heroic role), an unappealing Christian Democratic Union candidate, and cynical pandering to anti-American sentiment on Iraq—rather than *because* of Schroeder's economic and social record.

The Nixon-goes-to-China metaphor misses an important dimension of Nixon's behavior. Although Nixon recognized Communist China, he continued to sell weapons to Taiwan. In a similar vein, when governments of the left accept economic liberalization, it is still possible for them to protect their traditional allies and pursue traditional priorities. Not all liberalizing reforms need be neoliberal reforms. In between the no reforms of leftist traditionalists and the neoliberal reforms of the self-styled modernizers, there is a third option—new social liberal reforms.

The next three sections describe the new social liberal approach to labor market activation in three areas. The new social liberalism has yielded real change, but change that is distinct from neoliberalism—in particular, change that is more protective of the interests of the weak and disadvantaged. My analysis draws on the experience of a number of European countries, while privileging two, Holland and Sweden. These cases were selected for three main reasons.

The first reason is that Holland and Sweden have experienced dramatic improvements in labor market performance. Unemployment in Holland has dropped from nearly 15 percent in the early 1980s to around 2 percent today, and diagnoses of the "Dutch disease" have given way to paeans to the "Dutch miracle."[9] In Sweden, the turnaround has been more recent, with unemployment falling from 13 percent in the early 1990s to around 3.5 percent today. The "Swedish model," which was supposedly dead and buried, appears to be coming back to life.[10] Part of the reason why phrases such as "miracle" and "model" are bandied about, however loosely, is that these improvements in labor market performance have been achieved without the kind of increase in inequality and poverty that have marked the U.S. and British neoliberal approach.

The second reason for choosing Holland and Sweden is that governments in both countries have been strongly committed to labor market activation. Once unemployment began to decline, Dutch and Swedish authorities moved to tackle nonemployment, that is, to induce people outside the labor force—stay-at-home mothers, disabled workers, early retirees, discouraged workers—to reenter the labor market. This shift in goals was reflected in changes in the instruments for gauging labor market performance. In Sweden, after an initial goal of reducing formal unemployment from 8 percent in 1996 to 4 percent by 2000, the government set a new target of increasing the labor force participation rate to 80 percent by the year 2004.[11] In Holland, the government conditioned increases in the minimum wage and social benefits on a low "dependency ratio" or "I/A ratio," that is, a low proportion of inactive adults to employed adults. The I/A ratio can be reduced by lowering unemployment, but also by scaling back passive labor market measures, such as early retirement and the disability scheme, and by encouraging entry into the labor market among the inactive population.[12] In other words, beyond keeping the unemployment rate down, the I/A ratio, like the Swedish 80-percent participation target, creates strong incentives to push the employment/activity rate up. Whereas adults outside the labor market are not counted in unemployment statistics, they are counted against the Swedish and Dutch targets.

The third reason for selecting Holland and Sweden is that left governments have played a central role in the labor market reforms, albeit left governments that were constrained in important ways. In The Netherlands, the constraints were primarily coalitional.[13] The initial Dutch reforms were conducted under a center-right coalition from 1982 to 1989. Labor then entered the government as a junior partner in 1989, before leading a so-called "Purple Coalition" with the Liberals from 1994 to 2002 (red of Labor + blue of the Liberals = purple). Thus, for Labor to have any influence, it needed to reach an agreement and make important concessions to center-right allies.

In Sweden, the constraints on the left were primarily fiscal. While the Social Democrats, in power since 1994, have lacked an absolute majority in parliament, they needed to enlist the support of only one of the six other mainstream parties in order to govern. The main constraints on the Social Democrats stemmed from a horrendous economic context. When the Social Democrats took office in 1994, the Swedish budget deficit was some 13 percent of gross domestic product (GDP), roughly three times the peak U.S. figure during the Reagan years and over four times the Maastricht budget targets. Sweden and Holland tell a tale, then, of constrained left governments that have raised labor market participation rates significantly, while seeking to safeguard progressive principles and the interests of vulnerable groups. They represent the new social liberalism in action.

CLOSING PATHWAYS TO EARLY RETIREMENT: SWEDEN

In the 1970s and early 1980s, slow growth and massive industrial restructuring drastically reduced demand for labor among Organization for Economic Cooperation and Development (OECD) nations. Across Western Europe, governments and social partners turned to early retirement measures as a way to enable companies to reorganize their workforces without triggering massive social unrest.[14] In mining and heavy industry, workers were generally able to leave the workforce as early as age 50 while receiving upward of 80 percent of their previous wages.

Early retirement operated through different mechanisms in different countries. France set up specific early retirement programs. Denmark provided generous unemployment benefits with no time limits; Danes could stay on unemployment indefinitely. In Holland, the disability system functioned as a vehicle for early retirement. The legal definition of disability was expanded to include labor market considerations, that is, a person was considered disabled if s/he could not find a comparable job, at the same wage, and in the same geographic area.

In Sweden, we see something similar to the Dutch case. Sweden used a combination of unemployment and disability benefits to retire workers early.[15] Although the formal retirement age in Sweden was 65, under the so-called "58.3 rule" employers would routinely lay off workers at the age of 58 years and 3 months. The workers would then receive unemployment benefits for 21 months (the maximum allowable period), which would bring them to age 60. At age 60, they would move onto disability, which would last until age 65, when the workers would formally retire.

Initially, early retirement seemed to work for everyone. Employers were satisfied because they could get rid of expensive, older workers at little or no cost. Employees were satisfied because they could leave oppressive, smelly, dirty, authoritarian jobs at near full salary. It was also argued that by pensioning off older workers, it would be possible to open up jobs for young people. Finally, governments were satisfied because early retirement held down electorally sensitive unemployment figures. Formally, older workers who lost their jobs were not "unemployed," but rather retired and outside the labor force. Early retirement seemed to offer, then, a more humane alternative to U.S. methods, to dumping displaced industrial workers like so much rusting steel.

If early retirement helped maintain social peace while permitting firms to reorganize, the approach has also generated major problems. Early retirement was conceived of in the mid-1970s and 1980s as a kind of one-off measure, to help countries adjust to the OPEC oil shocks or to permit a one-time reorganization of the industrial workforce. Instead, governments and the social partners have become addicted, and the number of people in early retirement has grown to enormous proportions. Today, millions of working-age Europeans are paid not to work. In Holland, one adult in seven is currently classified as "disabled," and roughly one-half of this "disabled" population is actually early retirees.[16] In France, Holland, and Germany, barely one in three males aged 55 to 64 is still employed.[17] To make matters worse, the additional payroll taxes needed to finance early retirement raise Europe's already high labor costs, further dampening job creation.[18]

The thin neoliberal solution to the problem of early retirement is to roll back the protections of older workers. There are four main strands to this approach.

The first is to make early retirement less attractive by reducing benefits: lowering income replacement rates or aligning early retirement benefits with benefits of all other insurance programs, which are usually less generous. The second strand is to tighten eligibility rules, making it harder to qualify for early retirement programs. Narrower definitions of disability or regular medical reexaminations have figured prominently in this strategy. The third strand of reform has been to privatize early retirement programs and introduce experience rating. The idea is that by making company social insurance premiums vary with incidence of early retirement, employers will have a financial incentive to retain older workers. The fourth strand of the neoliberal project is to eliminate labor market restrictions (on firing, part-time and temporary employment, and wages) that are said to hinder job creation for workers young and old.

The problems of the thin, neoliberal strategy are twofold. The first concerns social justice. Under the neoliberal strategy, the lion's share of the costs of economic adjustment are imposed on older workers, a relatively vulnerable group that is not well positioned to embark on new careers. The second problem is one of political feasibility. Older workers are a sympathetic constituency, and firing them unceremoniously after decades of loyal service to the firm offends European sensibilities. Older workers are also a powerful group, enjoying strong backing from unions and political parties. In practice, no European government has been able to simply dismantle early retirement. Instead, the most successful country, Sweden, has pursued a thick strategy of reform, combining a curbing of early retirement with other measures to safeguard the interests of older workers.

In the 1970s and 1980s, Sweden boasted an unemployment rate of 1 percent to 2 percent along with the highest labor force participation rates in the world. But in the early 1990s, the Swedish economy fell into a deep recession, experiencing negative real growth for several years. Open unemployment quadrupled to over 8 percent, with an additional 5 percent to 6 percent hidden unemployment through early retirement and training programs. This terrible recession coincided with a rare period of governance by a non-Socialist coalition from 1991 to 1994. The non-Socialist government used early retirement through the 58.3 rule to hold down official unemployment figures. It also reduced unemployment and other social benefits, although more for fiscal reasons than as a labor market strategy.

When the Swedish Social Democrats returned to power in 1994, they moved immediately to close off early retirement. The Social Democrats followed many of the thin neoliberal prescriptions.[19] The government reduced the replacement rate of disability insurance to the same level as other social insurance programs, making it a less attractive option. The Social Democrats also prohibited the social partners from topping up disability benefits through collective bargaining agreements. Most important, the government restored disability insurance to its original vocation, that of providing financial assistance to people with a medical disability. A 1996 reform barred the use of nonmedical criteria in the attribution of disability pensions. As a result, the use of disability pensions dropped overnight by some two-thirds.[20]

Social Democratic policy did not stop at cracking down on early retirement. The government also deployed a thick array of policies to deal with the early retirement problem. Specifically, the government adopted a two-pronged approach, preserving the employment of older workers, while protecting and retraining younger workers.[21] Both of these initiatives were at odds with the thin, neoliberal approach and were criticized by employers, economists, and parties of the right.[22] Yet these interventions were critical to the progressive goal of reducing wasteful early retirement, while protecting vulnerable groups.

The Social Democrats established programs in both the public sector and the private sector to promote the employment of older workers.[23] In the public sector, they created some 40,000 positions specifically reserved for workers over the age of 55. In the private sector, the government offered subsidies of up to 75 percent of wages, lasting two years, for companies hiring older employees. Even more significant (not to mention controversial) was the government's approach to the seniority principle.

Under Swedish law, the so-called "last in, first out" principle (LIFO), employers must dismiss workers in reverse order of seniority. LIFO was heavily criticized by business groups and the right, who argued that employers should be free to make their own staffing decisions and to bring in younger workers with badly needed skills and energy not possessed by older employees. Furthermore, many older workers would have been more than willing to cede their job to a younger person, provided that some kind of early retirement package were made available.

The government and unions refused to budge on LIFO, however. Indeed, the Social Democrats shut down pathways to early retirement through the disability and sickness insurance programs. Moreover, whereas the non-Socialist government had introduced the possibility for employers to exempt two workers from LIFO, the Social Democrats immediately reversed the reform when they returned to office. As table 3.2 reveals, the effect of these policies was to concentrate the growth of unemployment in the 1990s on younger workers, rather than older workers. Labor force participation rates declined by less than 4 percent for workers aged 55 to 64 (as against an average decline of 7.3 percent for all age groups), but by almost 20 percent for youths aged 16 to 24.

Swedish policy toward younger workers was also at odds with neoliberal tenets. Two sets of measures reduced the incentives for younger workers to take a job but also cushioned the blow of mass unemployment. The first was a massive investment in education for unemployed youths, the idea being to upgrade their

Table 3.2. Change in Labor Market Participation in Sweden, 1990–2000, by Age Group

16–19	20–24	25–34	35–44	45–54	55–59	60–64	Total
−21.2	−18.6	−7.1	−6.3	−4.3	−1.4	−7.3	−7.3

Source: OECD, *Economic Survey: Sweden*, 2001, 98.

Table 3.3. Share of Population in Selected Age Groups Undertaking Full-Time Education, 1998

Country	15–19	20–29	30–39	≥40
Denmark	80.1	27.9	5.5	0.7
France	87.8	19.1	1.9	NA
Germany	88.3	21.7	3.0	0.2
Ireland	80.7	15.5	2.2	NA
The Netherlands	86.0	22.0	3.5	1.4
SWEDEN	**86.1**	**30.4**	**13.3**	**2.7**
United Kingdom	69.5	18.1	8.8	3.2
United States	74.2	21.4	5.6	1.6
OECD average	**76.3**	**20.4**	**4.4**	**1.2**

Source: OECD, Economic Survey: Sweden, 2001.

skills while they waited for the job market to recover. As part of a plan announced in 1996 to reduce open unemployment to 4 percent by the year 2000, the government created 100,000 new places in adult education, a huge increase in a country with a total population of only 8.5 million.[24] The positions were intended primarily for people with low educational levels, especially those with fewer than three years of secondary school. Under the terms of the "Adult Education Initiative," unemployed workers between the ages of 25 and 55 could study for a year at the compulsory or upper secondary level while continuing to receive their unemployment benefits. The combination of mass unemployment and massive educational subsidies led to a doubling of the number of Swedish university students during the 1990s. As table 3.3 relates, by the late 1990s, Sweden had the highest rate of participation in full-time education of any OECD nation.

The second set of measures to cushion the blow of unemployment to young workers was an expansion of social assistance programs. Young people in Sweden replaced the sick and elderly as the primary recipients of means-tested aid, since most jobless youths had not worked long enough to qualify for unemployment benefits.[25] Some 40 percent of Swedish citizens born after 1965 received public assistance by the age of 24. Informal family assistance also expanded: from 1990 to 1997, the proportion of young people between the ages of 20 and 24 who were living with their parents increased from 30 percent to 35 percent.[26] Although unemployed youths were clearly the losers of Swedish adjustment in the 1990s, the expansion of social assistance programs at least attenuated the hardship.

Sweden is one of the few European countries to have sustained high levels of employment among older workers. The labor force participation rate for men aged 55 to 64 is 68 percent in Sweden, more than 20 percentage points higher than the European Union (EU) average.[27] For women workers aged 55 to 64, the gap between Sweden and the European Union is over 35 percentage points.

The preservation of LIFO has been essential for combating early retirement, as even the OECD, no fan of government intervention in labor markets, concedes:

> A noteworthy feature is that—unlike the trend in many other countries—the reduction in employment and participation rates for older workers has not been particularly pronounced in Sweden. This may in part be attributable to strict EPL [Employment Protection Legislation], in particular the last-in/first-out principle, which has tended to favour older workers relative to other groups.[28]

LIFO has perpetuated the jobs of older workers, of course, but equally important, it made the closing down of the 58.3 rule politically feasible. Older workers and their unions would have resisted, blocked, and/or subverted reforms of the early retirement system had they not been assured that the alternative to early retirement was employment, rather than unemployment. In other words, a thin, neoliberal strategy of cutting back labor market regulations, such as LIFO, would have made it politically impossible to overhaul early retirement.

The Social Democrats' decision to favor the employment of the old over the young had a further benefit, that of preventing hysteresis in the labor market. Hysteresis is the failure of the labor market that has experienced a shock to return to its precrisis equilibrium.[29] The Social Democrats reasoned that if older workers left their jobs or were shunted into early retirement, they would never return to the labor market.[30] The damage to labor force participation would be irreversible. Conversely, if young workers were unable to find employment during the recession, they could be expected to return to the labor market once the economy recovered.

The Social Democrats' antihysteresis policy worked very much as intended. During the 1990s, as noted above, Sweden was a complete outlier in that the labor force participation rates of workers aged 55 to 65 did not decline significantly.[31] By contrast, the number of persons aged 20 to 25 outside the labor market doubled between 1990 and 1997, the worst record by far of any age cohort. Fortunately, by the second half of the 1990s, the Swedish economy was recovering and creating jobs anew. Young people are returning to the labor market with enhanced skills, and because older workers never exited, a return to traditionally high levels of participation has been possible. In retrospect, then, the strategy of retaining the old and retraining the young may not have been popular, but it prevented the kind of hysteresis that would have resulted from reliance on early retirement.

The thick, Swedish response to the problem of early retirement has been both humane and economically effective. From a social standpoint, older workers were not forced to choose between losing their jobs and taking a substantial pay cut. Although youth employment suffered from the LIFO system, the expansion of social assistance and educational opportunities limited the pain and permitted young people to upgrade their skills and future earning potential. Economically, Sweden's reforms created a different kind of labor market from either the passive (conservative continental) approach or the thin (neoliberal) approach—with higher rates of participation among older workers, higher skill levels among younger workers, and less long-term labor market and social exclusion.

MAKING ATYPICAL EMPLOYMENT TYPICAL: THE NETHERLANDS

Traditionally, most European countries have placed heavy restrictions on part-time and temporary employment. Unions and the left, in particular, have been wary of part-time and temporary employment for three reasons. The first is that, even under the best of circumstances, such jobs are unlikely to be sufficient to sustain a family. Given that most European societies were long organized according to the so-called male breadwinner model, male workers needed to be able to earn enough to support a nonemployed wife and children. A second reason why progressives have been wary about part-time and temporary employment is that companies have often sought to use these jobs to pay substandard wages and benefits. Left unchecked, the spread of "atypical employment" risks fostering a vulnerable, exploited "reserve army," forced to toil without the protections afforded full-time, core, unionized workers. The third and related concern of progressives is that atypical employment will place downward pressure on the wages, benefits, and rights of core workers. Full-time workers will be forced to either make hefty concessions to employers or see their jobs migrate to the atypical sector.

Part-time and temporary employment may have a legitimate place in contemporary society, however. In an era of mass unemployment, it can be argued that part-time or temporary jobs are better than no jobs, and many jobs can exist only on a part-time or temporary basis. A significant segment of the economy is seasonal in nature, for example. In sectors such as agriculture, construction, and retail trade, there is a lot of demand for workers at certain times of the year, but that demand would dry up if the workers had to be retained permanently.

Changes in the economy have spawned a number of legitimate business needs for part-time or temporary employment. Intensified international competition and shorter product cycles make it harder for employers to forecast their labor needs. To compete in fast-changing markets, companies often seek to employ a portion of their workforce on fixed-term contracts, so that they can reduce costs when demand drops. Another economic change, the shift from manufacturing to services, has expanded the need for part-time employment. The consumption of many services is concentrated at a few times in the day (noon, after work), so companies need to be able to hire part-time workers to meet these moments of peak demand.

Business is not the only potential beneficiary of part-time and temporary employment. With the mass entry of women into the labor market, many employees have substantial caring responsibilities.[32] Mothers with young children, single mothers, and daughters caring for elderly parents often cannot work a full-time job. For them, the choice is a part-time job or no job.

Part-time employment can also be an important vehicle for combating poverty. Dual-income households constitute a form of risk spreading. Even if the male breadwinner loses his job, his wife is still bringing home a paycheck (and may be able to increase her hours to limit the family income loss). Dual-income households are at less risk of poverty, therefore, than single-earner households, even if the second income is from a part-time job. Moreover, as wages at the bottom of the pay spectrum have stagnated or declined in the post-OPEC period, a second (part-time) income has often prevented families from sinking into poverty. Finally, part-time jobs can help preserve the skills and job contacts of mothers with young children. As a result, mothers are less at risk of being unable to find a job when their children are older and they wish to return to paid employment. Perhaps even more important, they possess an independent earning capacity in the event that separation, divorce, or death deprives them of a partner's income.

Temporary and part-time employment offers a number of potential benefits, then: more jobs, jobs that are often better suited to the needs of working mothers, and protections against household poverty. From a progressive standpoint, the problem is not part-time or temporary employment per se, but rather the way in which such employment is generally promoted. The thin, neoliberal approach has been to remove restrictions on part-time and temporary jobs. The argument is that temporary and part-time jobs are better than no jobs and may even enable the employees to secure full-time jobs at some point in the future.[33]

Neoliberals are not too concerned that employers might use part-time and temporary workers to undercut the wages and working conditions of core, full-time workers. Indeed, from a neoliberal perspective, if part-time and temporary employment threaten the status of full-time workers, this is a good thing. Full-time workers are privileged "insiders"; their high wages and job protections come at the expense of "outsiders," who are unable to obtain jobs on these terms.[34] Weakening the privileges of insiders attenuates the "insider-outsider problem," making labor markets more flexible and better able to create jobs for all.

The thin, neoliberal approach is not the only way to promote part-time and temporary employment. The Netherlands has become the world champion of atypical employment, in particular part-time employment, but has done so in a very different manner from the neoliberal approach.[35] Holland has greatly increased part-time employment over the past twenty years. From 1979 to 1996, part-time employment increased from 16.6 percent to 37.4 percent of total employment, far and away the highest figure of any OECD nation.

Part-time employment has not been synonymous with worker exploitation, however. While relaxing prohibitions on part-time employment, Dutch authorities and social partners have simultaneously upgraded the (hourly) wages and benefits of part-time and temporary workers to the levels enjoyed by their full-time counterparts. In this way, Dutch employers are now able to hire part-time and temporary workers in response to genuine needs for flexibility, not as a means of evading wage rates and benefits paid to full-time workers.

The equalization of working conditions has occurred through a combination of collective bargaining and legislation. Over 80 percent of collective bargaining agreements mandate pro rata wages and fringe benefits for part-time work, and the gap between part-time and full-time (hourly) wages has narrowed to only 5 percent. In 1993, the government put an end to the provision exempting jobs of less than one-third the normal working week from the application of the legal minimum wage and related social security benefits. Most recently, the 1995–1996 "flexibility and security" agreements guaranteed pension and social security benefits to all part-time and temporary employees. With few exceptions, these changes have improved the conditions surrounding part-time and temporary employment, as opposed to undercutting the position of full-time employees. In other words, harmonization has occurred as much through a race to the top as to the bottom.

Part-time employment in The Netherlands has been largely female employment (although the rate of male part-time employment in Holland is also the highest in the world, more than double the OECD average). Roughly three-quarters of part-time jobs are held by women, as a generation of Dutch housewives has entered the labor force on a part-time basis. Whether this situation is transitional, with younger Dutch women gravitating toward full-time jobs, or whether the Dutch one-and-one-half earner model constitutes a stable alternative to the Swedish dual-earner model, is an open question. What is not in question is that the expansion of part-time employment in The Netherlands has been conducted in such a way as to protect the interest of both established, full-time workers and new part-time workers.[36]

ACTIVATING THE UNEMPLOYED

Traditionally, progressives have resisted state initiatives to move claimants of unemployment or welfare benefits into paid employment.[37] Welfare-to-work initiatives have been seen as bad for both the welfare recipients and for labor market participants in general. For those pushed into the labor market, "activation" entails the transformation of an unconditional right of citizenship into a privilege that depends on the goodwill of the caseworker.[38] Activated workers are at risk of being coerced, humiliated, and deprived of personal dignity and rights.[39] They can be forced to take substandard jobs at substandard wages, on pain of losing their benefits. In addition to hurting themselves, these substandard jobs undercut the wages and working conditions of those already in the labor market. In short, activation transforms Marshallian citizens into a reserve army of the unemployed, mobilized on behalf of capital and against the rest of the workforce.

The progressive criticisms point to real risks associated with activation. That said, activation also holds potential benefits to both society and the activated individual. From a societal perspective, paying people not to work is incredibly wasteful, especially when the recipients of passive benefits are capable of holding jobs.

Moreover, the legitimacy of the welfare state can be jeopardized when programs are perceived as rife with abuses or encouraging behavior at odds with social norms. When one-seventh of the adult population in Holland is receiving a disability pension, for example, it is only a small step to conclude, in the words of a center-right prime minister, that "the Dutch welfare state is sick."[40] Finally, social expectations about work have changed over the years, and it could be argued that the welfare state should evolve with the times. If in the 1950s, a "good mother" was someone who stayed at home full time with her children, rather than pursuing "selfish" career interests, today, the vast majority of mothers are employed, and it seems unfair for mothers on welfare not to have to go to work like everyone else.[41]

It is not just society that stands to benefit from welfare-to-work initiatives, but also the activated themselves. A job often brings an increased sense of self-worth and pride. Reliance on earnings, as opposed to social transfers, reduces personal dependence of the activated individual on the whims of policymakers and caseworkers (although it substitutes a dependence on employers). From a political perspective, people who are employed are a much more sympathetic constituency, making it easier to upgrade benefits subsequently. Activation neutralizes a wedge issue, transforming "them" (the nonworking poor) into "us" (hard-working people who are struggling to get by).[42] When people who are not working are poor, opponents of government intervention can always argue that the solution to their problem is to get a job; when people who *are* working are poor (or lack health insurance), the case for government support becomes much stronger.

The judgment about the merits of welfare-to-work initiatives depends to a considerable extent, then, on how the measures are conceived and implemented. Are recipients abused, forced into lousy jobs? Do they benefit financially from working? Do they receive support and services that they need? Are the expectations for balancing job and family duties realistic?

The thin, neoliberal strategy attributes unemployment to personal failings or excessively generous benefits, rather than broader social and economic factors. For this reason, workfare initiatives can be launched at any time, independent of the economic context. The most extreme example was provided by the Thatcher government in the early 1980s. Even as Britain suffered its worst recession since the 1930s and unemployment more than doubled to 12 percent, the government eliminated earnings-related unemployment benefits and made other cuts that would reduce the effective replacement rate to pre–World War II levels.[43] The presumption behind these cuts was that high unemployment was due primarily to excessively generous welfare benefits, rather than the collapse of British manufacturing. Unemployed, unskilled, middle-aged steel workers, living in communities where the unemployment rate reached 20 percent or even 30 percent, would find new jobs if the welfare system would only stop coddling them.

Relatedly, the thin, neoliberal strategy emphasizes cutting benefits and training opportunities. This approach is guided by the English Poor Law principle of "less eligibility": welfare benefits should be (considerably) less attractive than the worst paid employment. Typically, benefit levels are lowered, as under the Thatcher government, so that claimants will have more incentive to accept a job. In addition, neoliberals advocate scaling back alternatives to employment, such as training programs and higher education, which are seen as undermining job search and parking the unemployed temporarily in useless programs.

Coercion and control also figure prominently in the neoliberal approach. Eligibility rules are tightened in an effort to move people off the public rolls. Claimants are forced to meet with caseworkers more regularly (meetings that can be quite unpleasant) and can lose their benefits as punishment for missing meetings or declining job offerings.

The neoliberal approach emphasizes moving people into jobs, with little regard for the quality of those jobs. The main metric of "success," under this approach, is the reduction in welfare caseloads, as opposed to improvements in the living standards of welfare leavers. A second measure of success is the reduction in government spending, made possible by shrunken welfare rolls. Relatedly, the work-family tensions arising from paid employment, such as child care and elderly care, are seen largely as a "private" matter to be handled by the individual rather than the government. To the extent that the government may have a role to play in family matters, it is by discouraging teenage and out-of-wedlock births that are said to deepen dependency.

The thin, neoliberal approach is most closely approximated by the Thatcher reforms of the early 1980s and especially by the 1996 welfare reform in the United States.[44] The title of the U.S. legislation, the Personal Responsibility and Work Reconciliation Act of 1996 (PRWORA), reflects the emphasis on personal failings as the root cause of poverty and unemployment. The law tightened work requirements and imposed time limits on the receipt of benefits—a maximum of two years for any individual episode and five years lifetime.

The central objective of the 1996 reform was to move people off welfare. Again, the language is revealing: Aid to Families with Dependent Children (AFDC), the welfare program dating to the 1930s, was replaced by *Temporary* Aid to Needy Families (TANF). The fifty states administering welfare were required to cut their caseloads by 50 percent by the year 2002 or else face steep penalties. By contrast, no targets were set for the earnings and living standards of welfare leavers. Indeed, states were not even required to collect data on the plight of former beneficiaries. Thus, caseload reduction was the central metric of success, the standard by which the fifty states would be punished and rewarded.

The 1996 welfare reform was also supposed to save money—an estimated $52 billion over a five-year period, principally from denying benefits to legal immigrants, reducing spending on food stamps, and tightening eligibility for Supplemental Security Income.[45] Moreover, the legislation capped the federal government's financial commitment to welfare. PRWORA replaced AFDC's open-ended federal commitment to match state spending on welfare recipients with a block grant: if welfare rolls surged, it would be the states, rather than the federal government, that would foot the bill. Moreover, since the federal grant is not indexed to inflation, it has declined in real terms by nearly 15 percent since 1996.

Although greatly increasing the obligations on welfare mothers, the 1996 legislation provided little in the way of support services. In moving from welfare to work, claimants often fall between two health insurance pools, earning too much to qualify for Medicaid but holding low-end jobs that do not provide health insurance. Because single mothers, by definition, have children, they also confront increased outlays for child care. Transportation to and from work represents a further need. Yet, the 1996 legislation offered scant help with these challenges. As two scholars wryly note, "Expanded access to assistance for working families was in no way mandated by TANF."[46]

The 1996 reform was not altogether silent on family matters. The legislation sought to promote marriage and discourage teenage and out-of-wedlock births. States were authorized to deny benefits to new children of teen welfare mothers, the so-called "family caps" provision. In addition, the federal government offered bonuses of up to $20 million per year to the states that made the most progress in reducing illegitimacy rates.

Despite the punitive orientation of PRWORA, the U.S. experiment has yielded quite good outcomes, as even center-left think tanks like the Brookings Institution and the Urban Institute have acknowledged.[47] According to the Brookings evaluation, welfare caseloads have dropped 60 percent since their peak in 1994.[48] The labor force participation rate of single mothers surged from 58 percent in 1993 to 74 percent in 2000—above the 68.5 percent figure for married mothers. Perhaps of greatest importance, welfare leavers are significantly better off financially, with posttax and posttransfer incomes rising over 20 percent for those in the bottom two quintiles. Relatedly, child poverty has dropped to the lowest levels since the 1970s.

Several factors have helped welfare leavers improve their living standards. The most important, of course, was the robust economy of the late 1990s. In a context of full employment and even labor shortages, it was relatively easy to find jobs for welfare leavers, and these jobs paid increasingly well. Low-wage workers have also benefited from a number of supportive public policies. At the state level, the combination of rapidly decreasing welfare rolls and a fixed block grant from the federal government created a fiscal windfall that allowed states to boost spending on transitional and work-related services. The share of program spending consumed by cash assistance fell from 76 percent in 1996 to 38 percent in 2001, freeing up substantial resources for in-work benefits.[49] Common expenditures include child-care subsidies, health insurance, transportation allowances, and more generous treatment of earnings (higher income and asset disregards, lower benefit withdrawal rates).

Federal policy has also helped welfare leavers. The Earned Income Tax Credit (EITC) was more than doubled during the initial years of the Clinton presidency. The EITC pays a 40 percent cash supplement for every dollar of earnings up to $10,000 and can be worth as much as $4,000 to a household with two or more children. The increase in the EITC predated PRWORA, but the passage of welfare reform created a more favorable political climate for other measures to make work pay, notwithstanding Republican control of Congress. In 1996, the minimum wage was increased from $4.25 per hour to $4.75, then increased again the following year to $5.15. The Balanced Budget Act of 1997 established the State Children's Health Insurance Program (SCHIP), which provides federal funds to states that offer health insurance to children of low-income families.

The reformed U.S. welfare system is not without problems. Even in the best of times, there remains a core of hard-to-employ claimants, who cumulate multiple disadvantages (lack of education, drug or chemical dependency, abusive family situations, etc.). For this group, welfare reform has meant a reduction in benefits that were not very generous to begin with. Another problem is that despite increased spending by the states, support services are still inadequate for welfare leavers. SCHIP may provide health insurance to some children, but it generally leaves the parents uncovered, at a time when employer-provided insurance continues to contract. Child care is also a concern. Fewer than one-half of welfare leavers receive help with child care, and this aid is generally confined to a transitional period. Aggravating matters, many welfare leavers have lost Medicaid and food stamp benefits, to which they remain entitled, because of confusing eligibility rules and dissuasive bureaucratic hurdles.

The greatest concern, no doubt, is the solidity of the U.S. welfare system in a recession. The gains of low-income families have been the product of a fortuitous economic climate and a fiscal windfall for the states, rather than any generous intentions on the part of the framers of the 1996 legislation. Today, all of the states are grappling with massive budget deficits, making cuts in "discretionary" work-related services unavoidable. Historically, welfare rolls have increased by 9 percent to 17 percent for every 1 percent increase in unemployment.[50] Although the 1996 reform has dampened welfare take-up, it is clear that even a mild recession can provoke a significant spike in welfare rolls. Equally troubling, many welfare recipients are bumping up against federal time limits, as the recession lingers. Employed recipients are also exhausting eligibility because, perversely, periods of in-work benefits count against the federal time limits in the same way as periods spent on passive TANF assistance. What will happen to America's poor and vulnerable families should the recession persist or deepen is the great unanswered question of the 1996 reform.

Despite the uncertainties surrounding the future of TANF, the U.S. case demonstrates that welfare-to-work programs can have a positive effect on the lives of welfare leavers if conducted in a context of rapid growth and job creation. Moreover, these positive results were obtained almost in spite of the intentions of the framers of welfare reform. Yet, welfare-to-work programs need not be conducted in the harsh U.S. manner.

Although the 1996 welfare reform in the United States has received the most attention, a number of European countries have also acted aggressively to move recipients of income support into the labor force.[51] These initiatives go by a variety of monikers: "New Deals" in Britain, an "activity guarantee" in Sweden, and the "activation" or the "comprehensive approach" in Denmark and Holland. All entail increased surveillance and coercion of claimants to try to induce them to take jobs. That said, there are very significant differences between the U.S. and European approaches.

The "thick," European welfare-to-work strategy increases the obligations and duties on the nonemployed, in the manner of a thin, American strategy, and the risk of unjust coercion and harassment is real. How claimants are treated on a human level is obviously a key dimension in distinguishing between progressive and regressive reform. No less important, though, is the set of obligations and duties imposed on society. *Whereas the thin strategy seeks to scale back public commitments and protections, the hallmark of a thick, progressive strategy is that it imposes significant obligations and expenditures on society as well as the activated individual.* A thick welfare-to-work strategy seeks to increase human capital and skills, so that claimants can obtain better jobs; to provide quality jobs, not just a quantity of jobs; to guarantee the services necessary for people with limited financial resources to be able to balance work and family responsibilities; and to make work pay, to improve the living standards of those who leave the welfare rolls.

Danish social scientist Jacob Torfing distinguishes between "offensive" (Social Democratic) and "defensive" (neoliberal) approaches to labor market activation.[52] The "offensive" approach does not just push people into the labor market—it also strives to improve their labor market position through training and education. Torfing is right to point to the positive or affirmative role of government in a progressive activation strategy. That said, the range of relevant policies should be drawn more broadly. Other policies critical to progressive activation include tax reform, high-quality social services (notably child care), generous treatment of wage earnings, and universal (as opposed to means-tested) benefits.

In a sense, the hallmark of a progressive activation strategy is that it involves much more than labor market policy. A progressive activation strategy is thick; it buttresses the well-being of activated workers with an array of other government programs. Indeed, a thick, progressive activation strategy may be more expensive than the passive policies that it replaces.

Recent reforms in Britain illustrate the possibilities for progressive activation, even within a "liberal welfare world," like that of the United States. Shortly after assuming office in 1997, the New Labour government of Tony Blair launched the first of a series of "New Deals," designed to move benefit claimants into the labor force.[53] The first New Deal centered on youths under the age of 25. Subsequently, New Deals have been established for workers over 25, older workers, lone parents, partners of the unemployed, and the disabled.

The New Deals were inspired by U.S. welfare reform: they include increased surveillance, mandatory meetings with caseworkers to design a program for securing a job, and, in some cases, benefit loss as punishment for noncooperation. To take the most developed program, under the New Deal for Youths, young people are allowed to receive unemployment benefits for six months, before entering the so-called "Gateway period," which lasts four more months. During the Gateway, the employment service and its partners work with the unemployed youth to improve his/her employability and find an unsubsidized job. At the end of the Gateway period, if the claimant is still unemployed, s/he is given four options: (1) a period of subsidized employment lasting six months; (2) a course of full-time education and training; (3) a job with an environmental task force; or (4) a job in the voluntary sector. "There is no fifth option," in the words of British officials, meaning that claimants may not remain at home, passively receiving benefits. This activity requirement marks a departure from the traditional passive orientation of British welfare benefits.

Despite the broad affinity with U.S. welfare reform, the New Deal initiative differs in several important ways. The first is that it allows for a period of full-time training and other alternatives to paid employment in the private sector. Although the training period is brief by Scandinavian standards,[54] it still provides an opportunity for upgrading skills that is generally unavailable to U.S. welfare leavers.

The second difference is in the degree of coercion applied to the target population. None of the New Deals contains the kinds of invasive, degrading provisions permitted under the U.S. legislation, such as "family caps" or requirements that teen mothers live at home. In addition, the job-search requirements vary from one New Deal to the next. Young people under 25 face the tightest restrictions because the government fears that prolonged unemployment will create a "lost generation" of unintegrated youths and because young people tend to be unburdened by family and caring responsibilities. At the other extreme, lone parents are required only to meet with a caseworker to discuss options. In contrast to the U.S. treatment of single mothers, participation in an activation program remains voluntary.

A third difference between the British and U.S. activation strategies concerns in-work services. Because Britain has a universal, public health-care system, welfare leavers do not risk losing their health coverage, as happens so often in the United States. A formidable barrier to activation is thereby eliminated. British authorities are working to attenuate another barrier to employment, the lack of affordable child care. Britain's activation strategy views child care not as a "private matter" to be managed by the individual, but as a public good, a prerequisite for a well-functioning labor market. The government has channeled considerable resources to making child care more widely available and affordable. Public spending on child care is slated to triple between 2001 and 2003/2004, leading to the creation of 1.6 million places.[55] Much of the spending takes the form of a tax credit to offset the costs of child care. The means-tested tax credit can cover as much as 70 percent of child-care expenses up to £135 per week ($203) for one child and £200 per week ($300) for more than one.[56]

Perhaps the most significant difference between the British and American approaches is that the former is part of a comprehensive antipoverty program. In 1999, Prime Minister Blair announced the goal of eliminating all child poverty within a generation. Subsequently, the British treasury translated this goal into quantitative targets: a 25 percent reduction of childhood poverty (measured as 60 percent of median income) by 2004; 50 percent by 2010; and 100 percent by 2020.[57] Because of these targets, the government's activation strategies are being judged less by their impact on employment levels than by their impact on child poverty. Activation is a means to an end, rather than the end itself.

The British government has deployed two main instruments to combat child poverty. The first is the minimum wage, which had been abolished under the Conservatives. The national minimum wage was reestablished in April 1999, at a level of £3.60 per hour ($5.40). It was raised to £4.20 ($6.30) in October 2002, and is scheduled to reach £4.85 ($7.27) in October 2004.[58] The British minimum wage is considerably higher than the U.S. minimum wage of $5.15 per hour, and the impact on poverty is very significant. According to estimates, if the U.S. figure were raised by $1 per hour (still below the British figure), some one million people would be lifted out of poverty.[59]

The second strand of the British government's antipoverty policies is an array of tax cuts and credits. In contrast to recent U.S. practice, British authorities targeted tax cuts at *low* earners, slashing the bottom tax rate from 20 percent to 10 percent, while keeping the top rate unchanged at 40 percent. The Labour government has emulated the U.S. tactic of using tax credits to make work pay, but in line with the emphasis on combating child poverty, the tax credit system is heavily titled toward working *families*. The system has been reformed several times and is extremely complicated (one of the major criticisms). The central thrust, though, is to boost the income of low-wage workers, especially low-wage workers with children. According to the treasury, changes in the tax and benefit system since 1997 have increased the income of the average family with two children by £1,200 per year ($1,800) and of the poorest quintile of families by £2,500 per year ($3,750).[60] Some 500,000 children have been lifted out of poverty by these policies.[61]

In April 2003, the Labour government combined the various tax credits, family allowances, and other forms of aid that have arisen over the years into a single program, the Integrated Child Credit (ICC).[62] Part of the motivation was administrative simplification. Claimants no longer have to apply to multiple programs, each with different rules and deadlines, and pretty much the only information that they need is their income, working hours, and number of children. The creation of the ICC also allowed the government to eliminate contradictory policies and focus its resources on the working poor, especially working poor families. Finally and perhaps most interesting, the ICC reflects an effort by the Labour government to build an electoral constituency that will support aid to low-income families. Given the structure of the British economy, the government believes that Britain cannot afford a Swedish-style, generous, universal welfare state. The problem is that if benefits are paid only to the poor, the programs will lack political support. Labour's gambit, which it labels "progressive universalism,"[63] is that by giving small amounts of aid to everyone, it can gain political support for an ICC that concentrates the lion's share of resources on poor families. The ICC provides roughly £16 per week ($24) to all families (universal child benefit) and £26 per week ($39) to 90 percent of families (child benefit + family element of child tax credit), so even the affluent receive something. Low-income families receive considerably more, however. The 50 percent of families at the bottom of the income scale get an additional £29 per week ($45) (per child element of child tax credit) for a total of £55 per week ($83). These families are also eligible for income support and working tax credits worth as much as £90 per week ($135). Taken together, the combination of a higher minimum wage and tax credits raised the minimum weekly income guarantee for a family with one child and one full-time worker by almost one-third in four years, from £182 in 1999 ($273) to £241 in 2003 ($362).[64]

The British case shows the possibilities for a more supportive, thick approach to labor market activation within a liberal welfare world and political economy. Like the U.S. welfare reform, Britain's New Deals have tightened the surveillance and pressure on those outside the labor force to take a job. Britain has also emulated the U.S. practice of extending tax credits to make work pay and relieve family poverty. But Britain has gone further in supporting working families, in part because the goal is to reduce child poverty, not just the welfare rolls. Tax cuts have been targeted at the lowest income brackets, rather than the highest; leaving welfare does not mean leaving health insurance as well; and the government has boosted spending on training and especially child care. More generally, whereas PRWORA aimed to cut spending by $54 billion, British authorities have made no secret of the fact that the costs of activation may exceed those of passive income support. As a result, the well-being of welfare leavers is less dependent on the vicissitudes of the economy in Britain and is more protected by public policy.

Activation has by no means been confined to countries in the liberal welfare world. Just about every government in Europe, from Sweden to Denmark to Germany, has tightened job search requirements in an effort to move unemployed youths, single mothers, the long-term unemployed, and other groups into the labor market. Once again, though, activation need not be synonymous with the thin, neoliberal approach. Recent reforms in Sweden exemplify the progressive, new social liberal alternative.

The Swedish approach has revolved around three sets of policies. The first is the commitment to traditional "active labor market policy," as pioneered by Sweden in the 1950s: heavy investments in job training, job matching, and geographical relocation for displaced workers.[65] This approach was bolstered during the 1990s by the Adult Education Initiative (described above), which allowed the unemployed to pursue higher education full time while still receiving their unemployment benefits. The university population doubled in the 1990s,[66] and many young Swedes were able to reenter the labor market with a stronger knowledge and skill base.

The second strand of Swedish activation was a reform of the unemployment insurance system in 1999.[67] The reform established a so-called "activity guarantee." This initiative corresponded more closely to the thin neoliberal approach, tightening supervision and increasing the demands on claimants. Even so, the activity guarantee was not entirely coercive. The reform simultaneously increased unemployment benefits by up to 30 percent and was supported by the LO trade union.

The "activity guarantee" was designed to remedy the problem of the quaintly named "benefits carousel." Formally, unemployment benefits in Sweden expire after two years. In practice, however, whenever benefits were about to end, recipients would be placed in a training program. They would remain in the program for six months, thereby requalifying for another two years of unemployment benefits. Thanks to this "carousel," there was no effective time limit on the receipt of unemployment benefits.

Another problem with the benefits carousel was that the unemployed received the attention of public authorities only at the end of their two-year benefit period. The rest of the time, they were left to their own devices. This benign neglect by public authorities created opportunities for fraudulent unemployment claims. It also left many unemployed workers isolated, discouraged, and depressed.

The activity guarantee broke with the logic of the benefits carousel and lax public supervision. After 100 days of unemployment, claimants are no longer allowed to remain at home. They must be "active" for eight hours per day, with "activity" defined as a job, a training program, a public internship, or some other kind of structured routine outside the home. The activity guarantee has helped some unemployed people by providing contact with caseworkers and placement opportunities. It has also made it more difficult to cheat the system. Claimants can no longer receive unemployment benefits while holding a job under the table, because they must account for their actions eight hours per day. Not coincidentally, recent Swedish statistics reveal a sharp drop-off in the unemployment rolls at the 100-day mark.

The third dimension of the Swedish activation strategy has centered on carrots, instead of sticks. The goal has been to reduce the financial penalties on employment—to lessen the "poverty trap," as it is commonly called. The thin neoliberal strategy for "making work pay" is to slash unemployment benefits (the principle of "less eligibility"), while perhaps tendering some kind of tax credit to low-income earners. As we have seen, Sweden increased unemployment benefits, rather than cutting them. Consequently, in order to make work pay, Swedish authorities needed to also boost the financial payoff from holding a job.

One way of making work pay, in line with standard neoliberal prescriptions, has been to reduce taxes on labor income. A 7 percent employee payroll tax, which had been imposed as part of the austerity measures of the 1990s, was phased out over a four-year period, from 1999 to 2003.[68] Although few would argue with the need to cut taxes in Sweden, the most heavily taxed country in the world, the Social Democrats' strategy was not without critics. During the 1990s, the government had raised the top personal income tax rate to 55 percent, but promised to reduce it below 50 percent once the economy improved. Given this pledge and given that mobile investors tend to be very sensitive to personal income tax rates, one might have expected the Social Democrats to reduce the top rate once the Swedish budget returned to surplus in 1998. Instead, the government announced that the 55 percent bracket would be retained permanently and concentrated its tax-cutting efforts on employee payrolls. This approach put money in the pockets of Social Democratic constituents, while also increasing the payoff for moving from welfare to work.

Swedish authorities have done more than cut taxes. They have also lowered "taper rates," that is, the rate at which transfer payments are withdrawn when a claimant earns money from work. Swedish policy has always been based on the assumption that the best way to combat poverty is to allow people to combine government transfer payments with earnings from work. This orientation is especially important for single mothers, who often can work only part time because of their child-rearing responsibilities. Poverty rates among single-parent households have been kept at very low levels by allowing lone parents to combine earnings from a (typically part-time) job with social benefits.[69]

The third way in which Swedish authorities have increased the returns to employment has been by phasing out means-tested benefits. Swedish Social Democrats despise means-tested programs, not only because they see such programs as stigmatizing, but also because the means test functions as an additional income tax, one that is concentrated on the poor. Typically, as a person moves from welfare to work, means-tested benefits are reduced, sometimes drastically. Most Swedish social programs are, therefore, organized on a universal basis. In contrast to the United States, the unemployed in Sweden do not have to worry that they will lose health care or child-care benefits should they take a job, because these benefits are available to all citizens at little or no cost. Nonetheless, means-tested programs have always existed around the edges of the Swedish welfare state, and they were expanded in the 1990s, as fiscal austerity made it more difficult to provide universal benefits at an adequate level. With the return to more flush fiscal times in the past few years, the Social Democrats have made it a priority to curtail means testing.

In 2002, a sliding scale for child-care fees was replaced by the "maximum fee," which limits the maximum parental contribution to about $150 per month, cutting costs for the average family by 40 to 50 percent.[70] Children of the unemployed also became eligible for public child care, so that their parents would be able to search for work. The Social Democrats attempted to reform another means-tested program, the housing allowance. Arguing that housing costs are primarily a problem for households with one income, they proposed to turn the means-tested housing allowance into a nonmeans-tested benefit for single mothers. Even in "woman-friendly" Sweden, however, this proposal proved politically unfeasible. As a fallback, the Social Democrats have frozen the housing allowance, allowing it to wither on the vine, while channeling the savings into a universal child allowance that is not means tested. The result, again, is to phase out means testing.

The thick, Swedish approach to activation has activated public authorities as well as the nonemployed. Under the activity guarantee, the nonemployed are held accountable for their actions during the workday. But the government is also held accountable. The unemployment benefits of people who genuinely cannot find jobs have been increased by up to 30 percent. Swedish public authorities have also forged expensive new instruments, such as the Adult Education Initiative, to boost the human capital and employment prospects of job seekers. Most important, the Social Democrats have retooled public policies across a range of areas to improve the financial returns from employment: lowering taxes on labor; allowing people to combine substantial earnings from work with social transfers; providing high-quality, universal services virtually free of charge; and phasing out means-tested programs. In short, the thick, Swedish policy has been geared not only to move people from welfare to work, but also to improve their welfare in the process.

CONCLUSION

This chapter has shown that there are real differences among strategies for activating labor markets—whether closing off early retirement, promoting atypical (part-time or temporary) employment, or inducing the unemployed and nonemployed to take a paid job. The impact of activation on society and on the activated individual varies tremendously, depending on whether the activation strategy is thick or thin. The thick activation strategy deployed in Sweden, Holland, and to a lesser degree Britain moves beyond the thin, neoliberal agenda of coercion, "less eligibility," and scaled-back state protections. It regulates as well as deregulates labor markets; it promotes good jobs as well as more jobs; it increases the income and opportunity of the activated as well as their obligations; and it forces state authorities to rethink and expand their interventions across a range of policy areas, including areas outside formal labor market policy (taxation, social services, and means-tested benefits, to name just a few).

Thick, new social liberal activation is a very different set of policies, with very different economic and social consequences, as compared to thin, neoliberal activation. For this reason, labor market activation should not be seen as inherently opposed to progressive principles and the needs of the disadvantaged. Stated in more general terms, there are varieties of economic liberalization. Neoliberalism is a subset of liberalism, not a synonym, and *how* a country liberalizes is as important as *whether* it liberalizes.

The bitter lesson of the French unemployment insurance reform is that if progressives are disinclined to reform in line with their principles and constituent interests, other actors with different principles and interests stand ready to act in their place. The Dutch, Swedish, British, and other European cases tell a more hopeful tale, demonstrating that there is room for progressive priorities within an activating or liberalizing agenda. Given this opportunity and given the stakes of liberalizing reform, it would be a shame for progressive politicians and thinkers to abdicate the terrain.

NOTES

1. Geoffrey Garrett, *Partisan Politics in the Global Economy* (New York: Cambridge University Press, 1998).

2. Carles Boix, *Political Parties, Growth, and Equality: Conservative and Social Democratic Economic Strategies in the World Economy* (Cambridge: Cambridge University Press, 2001).

3. Peter Hall and David Soskice, eds., *Varieties of Capitalism: The Institutional Foundations of Comparative Advantage* (New York: Oxford University Press, 2001).

4. Throughout this essay, it should be clear that I am using the word "liberalism" in the European sense—a belief in limited government, maximum individual liberty, and free markets—as opposed to the contemporary U.S. usage, conveying faith in government activism and social programs. I mean the liberalism of John Locke, Adam Smith, or *The Economist* magazine, not of Lyndon Johnson and Edward Kennedy. The closest American approximation of the concept would probably be "libertarianism."

5. Desmond King, *In the Name of Liberalism: Illiberal Social Policy in the United States and Britain* (Oxford: Oxford University Press, 1999).

6. For a discussion, see Bruno Palier, "Defrosting the French Welfare State," *West European Politics* 23, no. 2 (2000):113–36.

7. Joel Handler, "Social Citizenship and Workfare in the U.S. and Western Europe: From Status to Contract," *Journal of European Social Policy* 13, 3 (2003); King, *In the Name of Liberalism: Illiberal Social Policy in the United States and Britain.*

8. Christopher Green-Pedersen, *The Politics of Justification: Party Competition and Welfare-State Retrenchment in Denmark and The Netherlands* (Amsterdam: Amsterdam University Press, 2002); Paul Pierson, "Coping with Permanent Austerity: Welfare State Restructuring in Affluent Democracies," in *The New Politics of the Welfare State*, Paul Pierson, ed. (New York: Oxford University Press, 2001), 410–56.

9. OECD, *Netherlands, 1997–1998* (Paris: OECD, 1998); Jelle Visser and Anton Hemerijck, *"A Dutch Miracle": Job Growth, Welfare Reform, and Corporatism in The Netherlands* (Amsterdam: Amsterdam University Press, 1997).

10. Sven Steinmo, *Taxation and Democracy: Swedish, British, and American Approaches to Financing the Modern State* (New Haven, CT: Yale University Press, 1993).

11. Swedish Government, *Action Plan for Employment* (2002).

12. Visser and Hemerijck, *"A Dutch Miracle."*

13. Green-Pedersen, *The Politics of Justification: Party Competition and Welfare-State Retrenchment in Denmark and The Netherlands.*

14. Bernhard Ebbinghaus, "Any Way Out of 'Exit from Work'? Reversing the Entrenched Pathways of Early Retirement," in *From Vulnerability to Competitiveness: Welfare and Work in the Open Economy*, Fritz Scharpf and Vivien Schmidt, eds. (Oxford: Oxford University Press, 2000), 511–53; Gøsta Esping-Andersen, "Welfare States without Work: The Impasse of Labour Shedding and Familialism in Continental European Social Policy," in *Welfare States in Transition: National Adaptations in a Global Economy*, Gøsta Esping-Andersen, ed. (Thousand Oaks, CA: Sage, 1996), 66–87; Martin Kohli et al., eds., *Time to Retire: Comparative Studies on Early Exit from the Labor Force* (New York: Cambridge University Press, 1991).

15. Ebbinghaus, "Any Way Out of 'Exit from Work'? Reversing the Entrenched Pathways of Early Retirement"; Eskil Wadensjö, "Sweden: Partial Exit," in *Time for Retirement: Comparative Studies of Early Exit from the Labor Force*, Martin Kohli, et al., ed. (New York: Cambridge University Press, 1991), 284–323; Eskil Wadensjö, "Sweden: Revisions of the Public Pension Programmes," *Industry and Trade* (1999):101–15.

16. Visser and Hemerijck, *'A Dutch Miracle': Job Growth, Welfare Reform, and Corporatism in The Netherlands.*

17. Fritz Scharpf and Vivien Schmidt, eds., *Welfare and Work in the Open Economy: From Vulnerability to Competitiveness*, vol. 1 (Oxford: Oxford University Press, 2000).

18. Esping-Andersen, "Welfare States without Work: The Impasse of Labour Shedding and Familialism in Continental European Social Policy."

19. Karen Anderson, *The Welfare State in the Global Economy: The Politics of Social Insurance Retrenchment in Sweden, 1990–1998* (Ph.D. diss., University of Washington, 1998).

20. Although conducted for other reasons, Sweden's shift from a defined-benefit to a defined-contribution pension system in the late 1990s also reduced incentives for early retirement. Under the old pension regime, a worker acquired full pension rates after thirty years of contributions, and the pension was calculated on the basis of the fifteen best years of earnings. Consequently, most workers in their fifties were no longer accruing pension credits. Under the new pension regime, by contrast, employees receive one kronor of pension credit for every kronor of contributions, hence prolonging one's career translates into a bigger pension.

21. Sven Hort, "Sweden—Still a Civilized Version of Workfare?," in *Activating the Unemployed: A Comparative Appraisal of Work-Oriented Policies*, Neil Gilbert and Rebecca Van Voorhis, eds. (New Brunswick, NJ: Transaction, 2001), 243–66; OECD, *Sweden, 2000–2001* (Paris: OECD, 2001).

22. Anders Björklund, "Denmark and Sweden—Going Different Ways," in *Why Deregulate Labor Markets?*, Gøsta Esping-Andersen and Marino Regini, eds. (Oxford: Oxford University Press, 2000), 148–80.

23. Office of the Prime Minister, *A Programme for Halving Open Unemployment by 2000* (Stockholm, 1996).

24. Ibid.

25. Bo Rothstein, *Just Institutions Matter: The Moral and Political logic of the Universal Welfare State* (Cambridge: Cambridge University Press, 1998).

26. Joakim (Chair) Palme, *Summary: Interim Balance Sheet for Welfare in the 1990s* (Report to the Minister for Health and Social Affairs, Government of Sweden, 2000).

27. Swedish Government, *Action Plan for Employment* (2001).

28. OECD, *Sweden, 2000–2001*, 96.

29. Olivier Blanchard, "Hysteresis and the European Unemployment Problem," in *NBER Macroeconomics Annual* (Cambridge, MA: MIT Press, 1986), 15–78; Assar Lindbeck and Denis Snower, *The Insider-Outsider Theory of Unemployment* (Cambridge, MA: MIT Press, 1988).

30. Palme, *Summary: Interim Balance Sheet for Welfare in the 1990s*.

31. Ibid.

32. Without denying that men are sometimes the primary caregivers, for purposes of linguistic simplicity, I am equating caregivers/part-time workers with women and breadwinners/full-time workers with men.

33. Milton Friedman, *Free to Choose: A Personal Statement* (San Diego: Harcourt Brace Jovanovich, 1990), chapter 8; Lindbeck and Snower, *The Insider-Outsider Theory of Unemployment*; OECD, *The OECD Jobs Study: Facts, Analysis, Strategies* (Paris: OECD, 1994).

34. Lindbeck and Snower, *The Insider-Outsider Theory of Unemployment*; Mancur Olson, *The Rise and Decline of Nations* (New Haven, CT: Yale University Press, 1982).

35. Jonah Levy, "Vice into Virtue? Progressive Politics and Welfare Reform in Continental Europe," *Politics & Society* 27, no. 2 (1999):239–73; OECD, *Netherlands, 1997–1998*; Visser and Hemerijck, *'A Dutch Miracle': Job Growth, Welfare Reform, and Corporatism in The Netherlands*.

36. Perhaps for this reason, Dutch women voice considerable satisfaction with part-time work. According to a recent survey, only 7 percent of part-time female employees wish to work full time; conversely, 35 percent of those working full time would like to work part time; OECD, *Netherlands, 1997–1998*. In other words, if the Dutch labor market perfectly mirrored the expressed preferences of the female population, the result would be *more* women working part time, not fewer. This satisfaction with part-time work may be a product of false gender consciousness among Dutch women or the absence of quality child-care facilities that would make full-time work more attractive. Still, one cannot ignore the fact part-time employment is unusually attractive in The Netherlands, owing to the alignment of (hourly) wages and benefits on the rates paid to full-time workers. Indeed, part-time employment is not just attractive to women. One-sixth of all Dutch men work part time, the highest figure in the OECD by far and more than double the OECD average.

37. This strategy is generally described as "welfare to work" in the United States and "labor market activation" in Europe. The two notions are not strictly synonymous. Welfare to work in the United States has centered on single mothers, whereas European labor market activation has usually started with unemployed youths, before being extended to older unemployed workers, single mothers, and the disabled. In this section, for purposes of syntactic variation, I use the phrases "welfare to work" and "labor market activation" interchangeably to designate strategies designed to move claimants from passive programs, such as unemployment, disability, or support for single mothers, to paid employment.

38. Handler, "Social Citizenship and Workfare in the U.S. and Western Europe: From Status to Contract," 229–43; King, *In the Name of Liberalism: Illiberal Social Policy in the United States and Britain*.

39. Roger Cloward and Frances Fox Piven, *Regulating the Poor: The Functions of Public Welfare* (New York: Vintage Books, 1971).

40. Visser and Hemerijck, *'A Dutch Miracle': Job Growth, Welfare Reform, and Corporatism in The Netherlands*.

41. Ann Shola Orloff, "Ending the Entitlements of Poor Single Mothers: Changing Social Policies, Women's Employment, and Caregiving," in *Women and Welfare: Theory and Practice in the United States and Europe*, Nancy Hirschmann and Ulrike Liebert, eds. (New Brunswick, NJ: Rutgers University Press, 2001).

42. David Ellwood, *Poor Support: Poverty in the American Family* (New York: Basic Books, 1988); Margaret Weir, ed., *The Social Divide: Political Parties and the Future of Active Government* (Washington, DC: Brookings, 1998).

43. Walter Korpi and Joakim Palme, *New Politics and Class Politics in Welfare State Regress: A Comparative Analysis of Retrenchment in 18 Countries, 1975–1995* (paper presented at the annual meeting of the American Political Science Association, San Francisco, CA, August 30–September 3, 2001); Paul Pierson, *Dismantling the Welfare State? Reagan, Thatcher, and the Politics of Retrenchment* (New York: Cambridge University Press, 1994).

44. R. Kent Weaver, "Ending Welfare As We Know It," in *The Social Divide: Political Parties and the Future of Active Government*, Margaret Weir, ed. (Washington, DC: Brookings, 1998), 361–416; R. Kent Weaver, *Ending Welfare As We Know It* (Washington, DC: Brookings, 2000); Weir, ed., *The Social Divide: Political Parties and the Future of Active Government*. The Bush administration's reauthorization proposal for TANF in 2002 also reflects a thin, neoliberal approach. Margy Waller, *TANF Reauthorization 2003: Lessons from Block Grants* (presentation in New York City, June 13, 2003); Margy Waller, *Welfare Reform: Building on Success* (testimony to Senate Committee on Finance, March 12, 2003). The

administration sought to increase work requirements from thirty hours per week to forty hours per week, despite the post–September 11 recession and growing unemployment. Moreover, many training and education activities would no longer count toward the work requirement. According to the Congressional Budget Office (CBO), to meet the new work requirements, states would have to spend an additional $8 billion to $11 billion over five years, principally on child-care and public works programs. Yet, the Bush administration proposed no increase in funding.

45. Weaver, "Ending Welfare As We Know It."

46. Thomas Gais and R. Kent Weaver, "State Policy Choices under Welfare Reform," in *Welfare Reform and Beyond: The Future of the Safety Net*, Isabel Sawhill et al., eds. (Washington, DC: Brookings, 2002), 39.

47. Isabel Sawhill et al., eds., *Welfare Reform and Beyond: The Future of the Safety Net* (Washington, DC: Brookings, 2002); Alan Weil and Kenneth Finegold, eds., *Welfare Reform: The Next Act* (Washington, DC: Urban Institute Press, 2002).

48. Sawhill et al., eds., *Welfare Reform and Beyond: The Future of the Safety Net*.

49. Waller, *TANF Reauthorization 2003: Lessons from Block Grants*; Waller, *Welfare Reform: Building on Success*.

50. R. Kent Weaver, "The Structure of the TANF Block Grant," in *Welfare Reform and Beyond: The Future of the Safety Net*, 98.

51. Jørgen Goul Andersen and Per Jensen, eds., *Changing Labour Markets, Welfare Policies, and Citizenship* (London: Policy Press, 2002); Neil Gilbert and Rebecca Van Voorhis, eds., *Activating the Unemployed: A Comparative Appraisal of Work-Oriented Policies*, International Social Security Series, vol. 3 (New Brunswick, NJ: Transaction, 2001); Ivar Lødemel and Heather Trickey, eds., *'An Offer You Can't Refuse': Workfare in International Perspective* (London: Policy Press, 2000).

52. Jacob Torfing, "Workfare with Welfare: Recent Reforms of the Danish Welfare State," *Journal of European Social Policy* 9, no. 1 (1999):5–28.

53. British Government, *National Action Plan for Employment* (2002); Ken Judge, in *Activating the Unemployed: A Comparative Appraisal of Work-Oriented Policies*, Neil Gilbert and Rebecca Van Voorhis, eds. (New Brunswick, NJ: Transaction, 2001), 1–28; Lødemel and Trickey, eds., *'An Offer You Can't Refuse': Workfare in International Perspective*.

54. Torfing, "Workfare with Welfare: Recent Reforms of the Danish Welfare State."

55. British Government, *National Action Plan for Employment*.

56. Robert Chote, Carl Emmerson, and Helen Simpson, *The IFS Green Budget* (Institute of Fiscal Studies Commentary 92, January 2003).

57. Mike Brewer and Paul Gregg, *Eradicating Child Poverty in Britain: Welfare Reform and Children since 1997* (Institute of Fiscal Studies Paper, May 3, 2001).

58. British Government, 2003 budget.

59. Isabel Sawhill and Ron Haskins, "Welfare Reform and the Work Support System," in *Welfare Reform and Beyond: The Future of the Safety Net*.

60. British Treasury, *Budget 2003 Press Notices* (April 9, 2003).

61. David Piachaud and Holly Sutherland, *Changing Poverty Post-1997* (Centre for Analysis of Social Exclusion (CASE) Paper No. 63, London School of Economics, November 2002).

62. British Treasury, *The Child and Working Tax Credits* (2002); Chote, Emmerson, and Simpson, *The IFS Green Budget*.

63. British Treasury, *The Child and Working Tax Credits*; Edward Miliband, *Presentation to the Institute for Fiscal Studies* (1999).

64. British Government, *2003 Budget* (2003), 90.

65. Hort, "Sweden—Still a Civilized Version of Workfare?"

66. Björklund, "Denmark and Sweden—Going Different Ways."

67. OECD, *Sweden, 2000–2001*; Swedish Government, *Action Plan for Employment*.

68. Swedish Government, *Action Plan for Employment*.

69. Siv Gustafsson, "Single Mothers in Sweden: Why Is Poverty Less Severe?," in *Poverty, Inequality, and the Future of Social Policy*, Katherine McFate, Roger Lawson, and William Julius Wilson, eds. (New York: Russell Sage Foundation, 1995), 291–325.

70. OECD, *Sweden, 2000–2001*; Swedish Government, *Action Plan for Employment*.

IMMIGRATION REFORM IN COMPARATIVE PERSPECTIVES

Sunshine and Shadow Politics in the United States and Europe

VIRGINIE GUIRAUDON

INTRODUCTION

THE IMMIGRATION ISSUE HAS RISEN ON THE POLITICAL AGENDA ON BOTH SIDES OF THE Atlantic in the last decade, which also witnessed a flurry of legislative changes and new operational initiatives backed by budget increases. Starting with the 1994 successful campaign for the Save Our State Initiative (proposition 187) in California and culminating in the 1996 presidential campaign where the immigration issue loomed large in the election, U.S. developments seemed comparable to those of its counterparts in Europe, where populist politics have also weighed on immigration policy debates. The September 11 attacks on New York and Washington heralded a security-oriented overhaul of immigration controls in the United States and brought U.S. policies closer to those of the emerging European Union (EU) immigration regime while transatlantic cooperation in this area gained new momentum.

Analytically, we can distinguish *immigration* policy that regulates entry and exit flows from *immigrant* policy that concerns foreigners' rights once they have arrived, including access to citizenship, antidiscrimination laws, and policies that seek to "integrate" populations of migrant origin. This chapter focuses on immigration policy, yet it includes reforms—popular in the 1990s—that consist of rolling back the rights and social benefits enjoyed by foreigners to explicitly deter migration.

Immigration policy falls into two broad categories: policies either seek to "solicit" or to "stem" international migration.[1] In the case of stemming, immigration policy becomes "control" policy. In Europe, the 1973 oil crisis marked the end of the recruitment of guest worker and postcolonial migrants, although migrants' families and asylum seekers were still allowed to enter.[2] The focus was on "control," and soliciting was confined to seasonal workers and some highly skilled workers. Since the resumption of wanted settler immigration in the United States in the mid-1960s, the imperative of soliciting has prevailed over that of stemming. Yet, in the 1990s, it coexists with efforts at controlling illegal migration,[3] and bills to reduce legal migration were only narrowly defeated in Congress. In any case, the 1990s mark the end of a period of "benign neglect" toward the issue of illegal immigration.[4]

The key question is why immigration policy is consistently more expansive than electoral politics and surveys would predict. In this respect, immigration policymaking resembles the situation highlighted in other chapters in this volume: it is largely about avoiding blame for unpopular policies (in this case, expansive immigration policies).[5] Yet, politicians will not be equally able to make it hard for voters to trace the responsibility of reforms by seeking a consensus or by lowering their visibility.

The comparative query that this chapter addresses is why the United States has continued to solicit important levels of migrants (although the 1990s was also marked by beefed-up border controls and harsher measures against illegal aliens and asylum seekers), whereas, in Europe, the migrants who are allowed to stay are unsolicited humanitarian categories (migrants' families, asylum seekers, and refugees).

The chapter compares major reforms adopted during the 1990s in the United States with those in France and Germany. The goal is to identify the key determinants of reforms in the United States and see whether their presence or absence in the European cases can help us account for policy outcomes, corresponding to the same underlying logic of policy reform.

A simple framework of analysis to map out the determinants of immigration reform in advanced industrial liberal democracies is to consider the triangular tensions between law, politics, and economics. Democratically elected governments have an electoral incentive to appease public anxieties over immigration. The temptation to scapegoat migrants is greater during periods of socially costly industrial restructuring or in the face of rising unemployment. One such period started in Europe in the late 1970s and in the United States in the first part of the 1990s. At the same time, governments also have to cater to business interests. This includes the tourism industry and more traditional sectors such as textile, agriculture, and related industries—for example, the meatpacking business—that rely on cheap foreign, mostly unskilled labor. It also concerns the new demands for importing highly skilled workers such as computer programmers in the new information technology industries. In addition, governments in a "globalizing" world engage in free-trade policies that contradict calls for closing the borders and necessarily have implications for the movement of people.

Liberal democracies are equally marked by a tension between popular sovereignty and liberal norms that restrict the discretion of majoritarian governments. Since the 1970s, constitutional guarantees and activist high courts on both sides of the Atlantic significantly circumscribed both the authority and the capacity of states to prevent family reunion or to dispose of migrants at will. The response to the migration control dilemma can be assumed to vary cross-nationally, depending on the relative weight of legal, political, and economic factors that the institutional and ideational makeup of receiving states.

Reforms that protect foreigners' rights of entry and stay or increase immigration levels generally result from "shadow politics." In brief, they are enacted without much salience in public opinion, media interest, or public debate. Conversely, reforms that restrict immigration levels and foreigners' rights belong to the realm of "sunshine politics." In the first section, I further specify the hypotheses that derive from this view of policymaking and present the comparative framework. I then turn to policy developments in the United States and contrast them with the situation in Europe.

Courts, a particular type of restricted venue of debate, have served as a last resort to protect foreigners' rights and circumscribe the actions of migration control agencies. Most of the policy innovations in Europe and the United States regarding migration-control instruments has been aimed at circumventing the judiciary. This is the case of "remote-control" policies that seek to prevent undesirable aliens from reaching the territory of the state where they could access legal help and the asylum process. They include increased cooperation with third countries, visa requirements, and carriers' sanctions. The United States has served as a model for European states in this respect. This contrasts with the policy tools imported to the United States from continental Europe on internal controls that include employers' sanctions and identity papers. They are examined in the last section of this chapter as part of a wider reflection on shifts in the locus of policymaking away from the central state, *upward* to the supranational level and *downward* to regional and local authorities, and shifts in the implementation of control policy *outward* to private actors.

COMPARATIVE FRAMEWORK AND HYPOTHESES

Some may consider that including the U.S. and European cases in the same research design on immigration policy amounts to comparing apples and oranges. The United States is a settler nation, a land of immigrants, whereas the German mantra has been until 2000 that it "was not an immigration country." The Dutch called postwar migrants "guest workers." Even in France, which first welcomed a migration of settlement in the nineteenth century to remedy an early demographic deficit and slow down the transition from country to city, immigration is not part of national self-understanding. Although these historical differences resulting in dissimilar conceptions of nationhood cannot be denied, empirically, it does not result in striking differences in the percentages of new arrivals or foreign-born inhabitants in the population (see table 4.1).[6] Attitudinal surveys also show that U.S. citizens are not significantly and systematically more in favor of migration

Table 4.1. Immigration and Asylum Data in Selected OECD States

Country	Foreign/Foreign-Born Population	Immigrant Inflow	Total Population	Annual Immigrant Inflow per 1000 Inhabitants	Annual Average Asylum Applications per 1000 Inhabitants (1992–2001)	Ranking of Annual Average out of 30 Industrialized Nations
United States	9.8% foreign-born	660,500	288,511,264	2.29	0.45	17
Germany	8.9% foreigners	605,500	82,499,000	7.34	1.94	5
France	7.6% foreign-born, 5.6% foreigners	138,100	59,191,000	2.33	0.48	14
The Netherlands	9.6% foreign-born, 4.2% foreigners	81,700	16,171,520	5.05	2.27	3
Canada	17.4% foreign-born	174,100	31,100,000	5.60	0.94	12
Australia	21.1% foreign-born	77,300	19,000,000	4.07	0.47	15
Switzerland	19% foreigners	74,900	7,400,000	10.12	3.30	1

Date of reference: 1998. Sources: OECD, Trends in International Migration: Continuous Reporting System on Migration (Paris: OECD, 2001); census (various countries), UNHCR and UN population division.

than their European counterparts. A majority of persons surveyed in U.S. polls think that immigration levels are too high, just as Eurobarometer respondents in our European cases do.[7]

These figures show that, although outcomes in the United States and Europe are only partially convergent, there are the same general pressures in the countries compared. Therefore, differences and similarities do not originate in a difference in the structure of the "problem" to be addressed. Of course, one could surmise that perhaps there is a greater need for foreign labor in the United States, explaining the demands of employers. The jury is still out among economists.[8] The need for skilled labor in certain sectors is felt everywhere.[9] Given the importance of the service sector in Europe, the need for unskilled labor is as great as in the United States, compared to the industrial sector where one finds few low-skilled jobs in Germany, given the production system. The importation of labor does not seem to correspond to a particular job-training system. Otherwise, France should recruit the same types and levels of foreign labor as the United States.[10]

The empirical reality that need to be accounted for is twofold. In Europe and in the United States, calls for closure have been numerous. Notwithstanding, policy outcomes reflect a significant degree of openness, with the United States continuing to recruit high numbers of workers. My ambition is to solve the enigma by finding out the key suspects. The goal is therefore to focus in a parsimonious fashion on the distinctive features of the U.S. case and, then, through paired comparisons with the European ones, see which factors are remarkably absent in Europe. Conversely, when two countries have the same prominent institutional feature (e.g., the United States and Germany are both federal states), I examine whether the same dynamics are at work.

The visibility of policy change was first theorized in E. E. Schattschneider's seminal work, *The Semi-Sovereign People*.[11] He argued that the scope of a policy debate was an important determinant of its outcome and that political "conflicts are frequently won or lost by the success that the participants have in getting the audience involved in the fight or in excluding it as the case may be." Roger Cobb and Charles Elder have described this process as the mobilization of larger and larger constituencies, aimed at destroying policy monopolies by engaging attention publics, then the informed public, and finally the general public.[12]

My first hypothesis is that reforms that favor immigration and foreigners' rights are not highly salient in public opinion and the media, and they occur when there is no open debate in the electoral arena. In the latter, important participants hold systematic negative biases against foreigners (public opinion and the media) and antiforeigner parties or politicians such as Patrick Buchanan (who did well in the 1992 and 1996 primaries on an antiforeigner stance) can voice their opinions in ways that they cannot in a debate restricted to administrative circles or congressional committees. Conversely, migrant associations and their allies have secured access to institutional actors that gives them a weight that they do not have in the electoral sphere. For all these reasons, large-scale debates on foreigners' rights are not likely to tip in their favor.[13]

Yet, not all policy debates are salient, and "the mass public represents but one of the many potential venues for a policy debate."[14] Scholars who have stressed "autonomous state contributions to policy-making even in constitutional polities nominally directed by legislatures and political parties" and analyzed the insulation of policymaking from external actors in society.[15] Be they technocratic, bureaucratic, or judicial, debates with less public exposure involve different participants and institutional settings with different modus operandi. My second hypothesis purports that one of the venues that is biased toward protecting aliens' rights in a measurable and systematic way is the judicial sphere (high courts). This positive bias of courts toward foreigners' rights derives from the distinct mode of functioning and reasoning. A crucial element if courts want to establish their legitimacy is consistency. In other words, if they treat different groups or constituencies differently, they will not be credible as neutral arbiters. Martin Shapiro has argued that the "triadic model of justice" implies that judges must act neutrally to ensure their legitimacy.[16] All the decisions on aliens are presented in the courts as a balancing of state interests and individual freedoms based on the notion of proportionality. This mode of reasoning specific to the legal world contrasts with the power relations that migrants face in the electoral sphere.

TRANSATLANTIC DIVERGENCE: ENDURING "CLIENT POLITICS" OF THE UNITED STATES VS. "POPULIST POLITICS" IN EUROPE?

In the United States, the Immigration Act of 1990 had increased the limits on legal immigration, and the 1986 Immigration Reform and Control Act (IRCA) that sought to fight illegal migration through employer sanctions and border reinforcement had clearly lacked teeth. The beginning of the decade suggested that the "client politics" linking organized interest and public officials that had characterized immigration policymaking would endure.[17] By 1994, with California voters passing proposition 187 to deny benefits to illegal aliens and political entrepreneurs in other states such as Texas campaigning on an anti-immigration ticket in the midterm election that saw the Republicans win control of both houses of Congress, a restrictionist agenda had never seemed more popular and feasible. Several reforms passed in 1996, including the Illegal Immigration Reform and Immigrant Responsibility Act (IIRIRA) (illegal immigration reform), the Personal Responsibility and Work Reconciliation Act (PRWORA) (welfare reform), and the antiterrorism act, contained provisions that boosted the fight against illegal migrants and asylum seekers but also denied benefits to legal migrants. Since then, the nativist upsurge has in part receded, and legislation has suffered rollbacks or died in the courts.

A starting point is Gary Freeman's "Towards a Theory of Migration Politics."[18] Seeking to explain the puzzle of how expansive immigration policies could arise in spite of anti-immigration public sentiment, Freeman adapted the political economy framework of James Q. Wilson and the public policy typology of Theodore Lowi to offer this explanation. Based on the role of costs and benefits (interests and incentives), Wilson's framework shows that the intensity of political conflict over a particular policy depends on distribution of the benefits and costs of that policy in society.[19] When benefits are concentrated and costs are diffuse, a low-conflict mode of politics called "client politics" is the result: the organized beneficiaries of concentrated benefits prevail over the unorganized bearers of diffused costs.

Freeman argues that this situation applies to immigration policy in the United States and other settler nations. Although public opinion in these nations has at times been strongly anti-immigration, the flow of immigration has continued relatively unabated. This is because

> [t]he combination of concentrated distributive policies and client politics should produce low levels of conflict, since the majority of citizens and groups is inattentive. The 'clients' develop highly institutionalized and regular relationships with the agencies and decision-makers responsible for policy.[20]

Freeman adds Lowi's distributive, redistributive, and regulatory typology[21] because

> Policies have substantive content, but this content is experienced differently by various groups and over time. Defining the terms of debate is critical. Adversaries in a particular policy arena may seek to shape public discussion in such a way as to turn a distributive policy, for example, into one that is understood to entail redistribution, thus mobilizing new constituencies or demobilizing others.[22]

While acknowledging the possibility of populist upsurges ("entrepreneurial politics"), Freeman views them as either transitional or affecting policy only partially. Client politics are deemed more significant than party politics. The United States has known both expansionary/inclusive and restrictive/exclusive moments in its history.[23] Yet what is striking in Dan Tichenor's view is that the recent restrictionist upsurge of the 1990s has been short-lived and its gains relatively modest.[24] He thus concurs with Freeman and explains it by two dynamics, "one rooted in immigrant enfranchisement and competitive democratic elections, the other in the insulation of elite decision makers from mass publics."[25] Catering to enfranchised migrants and interest groups, therefore, is a powerful characteristic of U.S. immigration politics—for Christian Joppke, its distinguishing feature in comparative perspective.[26] It accounts for the disjuncture between the more lukewarm or hostile attitudes of public opinion and policy outcomes that opinion studies have highlighted.[27]

THE DYNAMICS OF POLITICIZATION

Jeannette Money in *Fences and Neighbors: The Political Geography of Migration* makes a convincing case for taking electoral dynamics into account to show how the political right sought to win votes in constituencies of the left with a high proportion of immigrants.[28] Because of the local concentration of immigrants, costs are indeed (geographically) concentrated rather than diffuse as in Freeman's model. Thus, if immigrant localities are crucial for electoral majorities, restriction is likely.[29]

Money's point on the geographical distribution of migrants and the electoral weight of these localities is well taken in the U.S. case, where most migrants settle in six states. In the first part of the 1990s, immigration became a central issue in high-immigration states (California and Texas). When Republican Governor Pete Wilson promoted proposition 187, which barred illegal aliens from schools and public services, as the central motif of his reelection bid and presidential aspirations, California had become the first destination state for migrants: 35 percent of the 7.4 million new legal immigrants between 1980 and 1990 settled in California.[30] The success of proposition 187 in 1994, including among Latinos and Asians, has been attributed to the economic recession with a spectacular drop in foreign (Japanese) investment and high unemployment (almost 10 percent in 1993), 250,000 defense sector workers having been made redundant after the end of the cold war. This situation made it more convincing to argue that immigration was a case of "concentrated costs" for the resident California population. The impact of proposition 187 on agenda setting at the national level cannot be underestimated: it received extensive media coverage and was emulated by Republicans in other states. When the new Republican-dominated Congress convened in 1995, the redistributive take on the "costs" of illegal immigration gained support among Republicans.[31] Lamar Smith, a Texas Republican restrictionist, became chairman of the House immigration subcommittee.

The California story is a case of "sunshine politics" and, as expected, it was restrictive of aliens' rights. Both policy venues and policy frames are important to understand its success. The rules of the game mattered to the extent that direct democracy is an important tool in the United States in the hands of political entrepreneurs to shed light on policy issues, whereas only Switzerland in Europe also has extended use of referenda and popular initiatives. Second, the federal/state cost imbalance is a significant source of politicization. As in Germany, there is a tension between the (federal) state that decides on entry and stay and the (decentralized) welfare state that ensures that migrants are included in society and get housing, education, jobs, etc.[32] In the U.S. case, this is not compensated by migrants' taxes and social security payments that end up in federal coffers. In California, 60 percent of migrants' contributions goes to the federal government and 3 percent to the counties.[33]

In Germany, in the early 1990s, as the number of refugees, asylum seekers, and ethnic Germans arriving skyrocketed, states that received the bulk of the newcomers also complained. The solution adopted was "burden sharing" among the Länder. This coupled with internal migration within Germany to more prosperous industrial centers meant that soon northern states far from the border sided with southern ones to denounce "costs" and called for a stricter asylum policy, which was adopted in 1993. A more somber part of the story is that asylum seekers were dispatched all over the German territory, including in problem-ridden rural towns in the former East Germany. For example, in August 1992, in Rostock, with the complacency of the police and the sympathy of the population, skinheads engaged in arson attacks against asylum seekers and migrant workers. The lesson that the national government drew from the Rostock riots, which drew considerable public attention, was to call for a revision of the constitutional article on asylum.[34]

FROM POLITICIZATION TO REFORM

In the United States in 1994, when the Republicans won control of the House, many first-term Republicans from Texas and California with strong ideological sentiment were motivated to take strong steps to reduce legal migration, deny benefits to aliens that they saw as exploiting state budgets, and step up the fight against illegal migration. Yet, there were strong divisions among House Republicans. Over in the Senate, Lamar Smith's counterpart was more moderate: Alan Simpson (R-WY) was skeptical about the benefits of migration and wished to overhaul the whole system but had declared earlier that he refused to withdraw benefits from legal aliens. In the Senate, there were strong immigration defenders from both parties (Edward Kennedy and Orrin Hatch in particular). There were thus differences between the two chambers: this allowed the Clinton White House to play one against another and provided multiple access points to lobby groups. After a year of feverish activity, in March 1996, the House agreed to split the bill into two parts, adopting measures against illegal migration but not amending the legal program (the Senate Judiciary Committee followed suit a few days later by sending two bills to the floor). This critical decision was a response to an impressive coalition against changes in the legal program: the usual suspects (employers, ethnic groups, churches, immigrant rights groups, and immigration lawyers) allied with a coalition of high-tech businesses and, briefly, the Christian Coalition and profamily groups who had access to Republican lawmakers.[35] High-tech businesses wanted to recruit highly skilled workers, and Christian groups were worried about proposals to cut down on family migration, both issues linked to the legal immigration program.

By splitting the bill into two, House Republicans acknowledged that they would not go against these groups and thus renounced reducing legal immigration. Yet, they split the coalition when distinguishing between legal and illegal migration. IIRIRA revamped the enforcement process, made asylum claims more difficult, limited the rights of illegal aliens to reenter legally, required the Immigration and Naturalization Service (INS) to exclude aliens without judicial review, and barred the agency from granting removable aliens from suspending expulsion for humanitarian purposes. It was a radical reform adopted quickly without much debate. The immigration lawyers and rights groups that denounced the measures were quite alone now that the rest of the coalition had obtained what they wanted. IIRIRA even toughened the provisions of the Anti-Terrorism and Effective Death

Penalty Act adopted a few months before in the wake of the Oklahoma bombings, which created secret deportation tribunals for suspected terrorists.[36] The new law already linked to terrorism issues has been called "harsh and unjust" by moderate immigration legal scholars such as Peter Schuck.[37] In fact, federal courts stepped in to declare parts of IIRIRA unconstitutional and prevented the retroactive application of the antiterrorism law.[38]

This 1995–96 story of congressional politics shows that, even with both houses under Republican control, riding on a populist wave, compromise and tit-for-tat strategies prevailed. The next electoral episode bears another lesson. After the success of Buchanan in some primaries, Republican nominee Bob Dole raised the immigration issue to win the crucial state of California, the state where the debate had started, portraying illegal aliens as welfare abusers. Bob Dole lost and polls showed that 71 percent of Latino voters in California and nationwide had supported Clinton. A page was turned and the lesson learned—Texas Governor George W. Bush, who had always appealed to the Latino vote, pursued this strategy in the next election. In the meantime, a number of programs expanded the number of legal immigrants: the number of H-1B visas for nonimmigrant skilled workers was raised every year by law, illegal migrants were regularized, and persons with a Temporary Protection Status were given permanent asylum status. As to the benefits taken away from legal migrants, most states stepped in to compensate for the lost income. Courts rescinded a number of the 1996 legal provisions. This was done outside public purview. It was back to shadow "politics as usual" in the immigration field, except for a strong commitment to border control.

THE EUROPEAN CASES

In Europe, when immigration is exploited by political entrepreneurs such as populists and leaders of the extreme right, their agenda is taken up by mainstream parties. The clearest examples stem from countries where political responsibility can easily be traced. In the United Kingdom, the prime minister, supported by a disciplined single-party majority, cannot diffuse blame to others. The United Kingdom was the first European country in the 1960s to enact laws that restricted immigration to nip in the bud the British National Front and populists such as Enoch Powell.

In France, party competition between left and right was exacerbated in the 1980s and 1990s by the rise of the National Front. Immigration was featured in each electoral campaign, and each change of government resulted in the passing of a law reforming immigration reform (1981, 1986, 1989, 1993, 1997, 2003). Whereas in the United States the possibility that naturalized immigrants may vote tames the discourse of both Republicans and Democrats, in France, immigrants and their descendants have not been wooed. Instead, both parties of the left and right seek to recapture voters lost to the National Front of Le Pen since 1984. Among the voters of the extreme right, young men either working in the industrial sector or who are unemployed are overrepresented. These socioeconomic categories used to support parties of the left. Ethnocentrism cuts across partisan cleavages in such a way that the fear of immigrants can be found among voters of all parties.[39] The weight of populist forces on partisan politics is not compensated, as in the case of the United States, by the influence of interest groups such as migrant associations, legal since 1981, and business lobbies on the legislative process. The persistence of high unemployment has not led French business to demand more expansive legal immigration.

Given that the political support coalitions for an expansive immigration policy were absent in the French case, there was no means of compensating for the politicians' fear of being blamed for "lax" entry policies. Instead, foreigners' rights have been protected through the intervention of high courts: the Council of State, the highest administrative court, and the Constitutional Council. This dates back to 1977–78 when 37 decrees, circulars, and memos regarding foreigners were issued to reverse migration flows by all means including forced returns and nonrenewal of residence permits. This set the stage for the entrance of the Council of State into the immigration debate. In 1978, the Council of State struck down many dispositions contained in circulars and other regulatory texts. Most strikingly, on December 8, 1978, the council voided the decree of November 10, 1978, on family reunification. In 1993, the Constitutional Council decided to annul eight of the dispositions of a restrictive law on the entry and stay of aliens known as the *lois Pasqua*. On this occasion, it confirmed the Council of State's stance on family reunion, elevating it to a constitutionally guaranteed right. The pattern according to which aliens' rights were restricted to be reasserted later hinges on the role that the judicial sphere has played after governments sought to establish strict migration controls. In the end, contested rights in the electoral sphere were guaranteed in judicial venues.

In Germany, just as in France, ethnocentric voters are present in all parties. Polls have repeatedly shown that SPD (*Sozialdemokratische Partei Deutschlands* [social democrat—party of the left]) voters are almost as likely as CDU (*Christlich-Demokratische Union* [Christian democrat—party of the right]) voters to believe that there are too many foreigners in Germany. Although the German extreme right is not as electorally successful as in France, it weighs heavily on local and regional elections and has influenced national party platforms.[40] Between 1965 and 1990, there was no major legislative reform on immigration in Germany, although labor recruitment had been stopped in 1973. The SPD had shied away from reform while the CDU-led coalition that came in power in 1983 after waging a xenophobic campaign was internally divided as the liberal party (the FDP [*Freie Demokratische Partei*]) fought against the most restrictive legislative proposals.[41]

Throughout that period, legal immigration continued, thanks to the rulings of the German Federal Constitutional Court and the administrative courts based on the fact that, as stated in Article 20 of the Basic Law, the interest of the state had to be balanced against the constitutional interests of the foreign worker. The landmark decision of the Federal Constitutional Court came on September 26, 1978, in a case involving a construction worker from India who had been denied a renewal of residence permit in 1973 by the local alien police while he had lived and worked lawfully in Germany since 1961.[42] The Federal Constitutional Court stated that prior routine renewals of a foreigner's work permit had created a constitutionally protected "reliance interest" in continued residence. This could not be overridden by the official thesis that "Germany was not an immigration country." The reversal in migration policy after 1973 did not justify the expulsion of foreign workers given that the government had induced their de facto settlement. Furthermore, other courts affirmed that residence and permit renewal guarantees had to be granted to foreigners based on their right to freely develop their personality as it is stated in Article 2 of the German Constitution and thus must be given the opportunity to plan their future.

In decisions regarding deportation, the Federal Constitutional Court also took into consideration the family situation of the alien and, in particular, in a 1979 case involving a married Turk convicted of selling hashish. Article 6 of the Basic Law provides for explicit protection of marriage and protection of the family (sections 1 and 2), which are defined as "natural rights." The court upheld that this constitutional guarantee applied to all marriages, whether between aliens or between an alien and a citizen. Judges asserted that the German government's violation of the right to a family life could not be justified as part of a general crime deterrence policy. The court ruled in 1987 on three cases in which non–European Community aliens appealed state implementation of 1981 federal recommendations regarding the granting of residence permits for foreign spouses of second-generation resident aliens.[43] Two states (Bavaria and Baden-Württemberg) set a three-year waiting period for family reunion. The court found it excessive.[44]

In 1990, the CDU–FDP coalition passed a law that took into account the jurisprudence of German high courts on foreigners' rights, securing the residence status of foreign legal residents, enhancing the rights of family members, and easing naturalization criteria. It did so under particular circumstances that allowed "shadow politics" to dominate. In 1990, unification dominated people's attention and the foreigners' bill went unnoticed. This exceptional event overshadowed other issues in a way that explains why the 1990 law seems to have received little attention. Based on the Politbarometer surveys, Manfred Küchler discusses the salience of the foreigners' issue as follows:

> By early 1989, the issue topped the political agenda, but quickly faded as the unification issue gained in salience. . . . One may speculate that the issues of unification and "foreigners" are two manifestations of the same underlying concern for West Germans, who feel they must closely guard their affluence.[45]

The exceptional circumstances of the 1990 reform are the exception that confirm the rule. In 1993, a constitutional reform of Article 16 restricting Germany's unique subjective right to asylum was adopted one year before the 1994 general election. The reform required the approval of the SPD *Bundestagsfraktion* [parliamentary group]. Under pressure from CDU politicians who spread the motto "every other asylum seeker is an SPD asylum seeker," SPD party leaders realized that they had to swim with the tide or risk losing the election. Because 50,000 SPD members had sent back their party cards over the issue, the SPD had its own way of measuring the electoral risks if it refused to reform asylum law.

Since 1998, an SPD–Green coalition has been in power, and a reform of the immigration law has been on the table. For the first time, business interests were voicing their concerns that they needed to recruit foreign workers, leading the government to create a "green card scheme" to hire 20,000 workers for the information technology industry, mainly Indian computer programmers. The situation could be likened to the U.S. situation to the extent that business interests were influencing parliamentary politics. Another feature of the German political system that resembles the U.S. case is that it allows for blame sharing and the diffusion of responsibility among government coalition partners but also among the two houses of parliament (the *Bundestag* and *Bundesrat*). This supposes that a cross-party compromise be found because the opposition had the majority in the upper house. Consensus building takes a long time, and the Schroeder government did not want to risk running into the next electoral campaign with this issue unresolved. In the end, the coalition government resorted to a voting procedure in the *Bundesrat* that was struck down as unconstitutional by the constitutional court. The possibility of "shadow politics" provided by the rules of decisionmaking is undermined in the German case by the fact that brokering a compromise can be so slow that the "sunshine politics" that characterize electoral campaigns every four years eventually wins out.

In sum, the European cases reveal the specificity of the U.S. case, the combination of congressional lobbying politics and coalition building between business and migrant interests that have also persuaded politicians of their electoral clout. Therefore, in Europe, immigration laws that willingly augment the legal admission of foreigners have not been politically palatable. Still, populist politics have not resulted in the expulsion of unwanted migrants. Instead, mainly through the intervention of high courts, the rights of foreigners have been guaranteed in such a way as to allow humanitarian immigration of family members and refugees.

TRANSATLANTIC POLICY TRANSFERS: EXTERNALIZING AND DELEGATING CONTROL

I have depicted the immigration dilemma as a triangular relationship between populist politics, liberal legal norms, and a global economy. In this section, I examine common responses to escape this conundrum by border control advocates, responses that involve the delegation of authorities away from the border and outside the state. This is the occasion to analyze cases in which one side of the Atlantic emulated the other. The different fate of similar policy instruments should help us reflect on crossnational differences.

SHIFTING POLICY OUTWARD

In all the cases above, immigration policy seeks to resolve conflicting goals (open trade, tourism, recruitment of highly skilled workers, seasonal labor recruitment, *and* restricted family and asylum migration), and contradictory pressures (electoral populism *and* business lobbying). Policy instruments often address only part of the pressures that governments are under. Such is the case of highly visible border management.[46] This strategy restores the appearance of control yet cannot be reconciled with the opposite objective of facilitating the movement of welcome people and goods. "Remote control" is a strategy that aims at preventing unwanted migrants from accessing the system of legal protection and the asylum process, thereby avoiding the domestic and international legal norms that stand in the way of restricting migration flows. This strategy, which operates *before* aspiring migrants and potential refugees reach the border, also allows for less control at the point of entry itself, thus facilitating the movement of inhabitants of the first world, tourists and business people. It has taken various forms: visa regimes, carrier sanctions, as well as cooperation with transit and sending countries, with the goal of erecting "buffer zones" around postindustrial liberal democracies.

The idea of selecting migrants before they reached one's territory is an old U.S. idea: the 1902 Passenger Act forced steamship companies to retransport at their own cost inadmissible passengers, and the 1924 Immigration Act charged American consuls abroad with managing quotas and delivering visas. In the Ellis Island era, steamship companies took measures to ensure that would-be emigrants would pass muster when arriving at U.S. ports, thus acting as "sheriff's deputies."[47] U.S. laws on fining carriers that bring in "any alien who does not have a valid passport or an unexpired visa" (section 273, Immigration and Nationality Act) have been reactualized. The 1990 Immigration Act increased the amount of the fine per passenger from $1,000 to $3,000. After using the stick, Congress came out with a carrot in 1994 with the Immigration and Nationality Technical Corrections Act, which mitigated fines for airlines that showed "good performance"—a reward for efficacy in screening passengers.

European countries have imitated the older U.S. legislation. The first government to act was the United Kingdom, the country most likely to look for models across the Atlantic, which passed a law in 1987. Germany, France, and Benelux signed the Schengen Implementation Agreement in 1990. Article 26 called for the adoption of laws on carriers' sanctions. All European countries adopted legislation in this area in the 1990s, and EU candidate countries had to comply with that Schengen *acquis*. In 2000, with Schengen incorporated into the EU framework, the French submitted a directive proposal to reinforce and harmonize sanctions against carriers, which was adopted as Directive 2001/51 in May 2001.[48] Carrier sanctions have been adopted to comply with Schengen norms even in countries where migrants come mostly through nonconventional means of transport (such as Spain or Italy) or where there is no international airport to speak of (such as Luxembourg). This shows the limit of policy transfers.

This involvement of private companies as "immigration officers" complements that of public officials working in consulates abroad who deliver visas. The visa system developed a long time ago in the United States is quite sophisticated. In the 1980s, Europe reintroduced visa requirements. In the 1990s, visas became a generalized and elaborated instrument to screen the "huddled masses" in sending countries. Already inscribed as one of the main goals of the 1990 Schengen agreement, it is now within the competence of the European Community. In fact, contrary to other areas of the common migration and asylum policy where unanimity votes are required and member states can initiate legislation, common visa rules are adopted by the Council of Ministers with a qualified majority on a proposal of the European Commission after consultation of the European Parliament. The Council Regulation 539/2001 of March 15, 2001, lists the third countries whose nationals must be in possession of visas when crossing the external borders of the European Union.[49] The Common Consular Instructions, which were incorporated into the European Community framework and published in 2000, call for close consular cooperation in establishing more informal lists of bona fide applicants and "migration risks," a synonym for poor persons.[50] Consular personnel are instructed to be "particularly vigilant when dealing with [. . .] unemployed persons and those with irregular income" (Common Consular Instructions, section V). The applicant and his host in the EU country have to provide many supporting documents on his income and "social and professional status." In addition, Schengen countries have devised a common computerized data bank (Schengen Information System), with over two million entries of "inadmissible foreigners" whose visa requests were denied.

Finally, another means to prevent unwanted migrants from reaching Europe or the United States has consisted of enlisting third countries. In the United States, the idea that migration control requires cooperation with sending countries gained prominence after a number of migration "crises" with sea-bordering countries when the federal government realized that its policy of interdiction at sea was ineffective and politically costly and turned to diplomatic and military solutions with the source countries, including an agreement with Cuba and a 1994 military intervention in Haiti to change the regime and stem emigration to U.S. coasts.[51] Cooperation with land neighbor Mexico stepped up as the migration issue gained salience in the 1990s, and it became linked to the North American Free Trade Agreement (NAFTA) debate. Indeed, although the U.S.–Mexico Binational Commission set up in 1981 included working groups such as the Border Relations Action Group, the frequency of meetings stepped up after 1994 with the Working Group on Migration and Consular Affairs, which serves as a forum of cabinet-level officials to resolve border problems of mutual interest. There are now joint U.S.-Mexican border patrol task forces. With the 1997 launch of border control Operation Gatekeeper III in October 1997, U.S. and Mexican officials formed a multiagency group.

The U.S.–Mexico relationship is not one of equal partners and resembles greatly that of EU countries with accession states in East and Central Europe. Soon after the fall of the Berlin wall, at the behest of Germany a myriad of bilateral re-admission agreements were signed with Eastern Europe. With the treaty of Amsterdam, the imposition of EU standards goes well beyond that because candidate countries must comply with the totality of the Schengen *acquis* and harmonize their policy with that of EU states. Ten percent of the aid money given to states acceding to the European Union (€130.7 million in 2000) goes to Justice and Home Affairs issues, half of which concern border issues, especially east of Poland.[52] EU member states, which themselves have already supranationalized their immigration policies, are now delegating the bulk of frontier control enforcement to the East.

The trend has also been to use multilateral negotiations between the European Union and other regional entities to diffuse instruments such as readmission agreements. For instance, Interior and Justice ministers insisted that the Cotonou agreement of 2000, between the European Union and 71 African, Caribbean, and Pacific countries, include a standard clause whereby countries commit themselves to taking back their nationals deported from an EU member state. At the Seville EU summit, the Spanish proposed that countries that did not readmit their nationals would face financial sanctions such as cuts in aid. The summit conclusions mention the possibility of retaliatory measures against noncooperating countries, using trade as a bargaining chip with developing-world countries.

The enlisting of third actors in external controls has been mirrored by a redeployment of state prerogatives and the incorporation of new policy implementers in "internal controls." Like artificial tentacles added on to the central body of the state, mayors, employers, and local services are all urged to reach deep into societies to uncover undocumented foreigners.

An interesting case study regards that of employer sanctions whereby employers face penalties if they hire undocumented workers—an old policy instrument in Europe that the United States tried to set up in the 1990s. France is the first country to have instituted penalties against employers that did not declare workers, back in 1926. In 1975, the Netherlands and Germany and, in 1976, France again adopted legislation that prohibited the employment of illegal aliens.[53]

In the United States, at the behest of Texas growers, the 1952 Immigration and Nationality Act (INA) stipulated that employing illegals did not constitute the criminal act of harboring (the so-called Texas proviso). In 1986, the Immigration Reform and Control Act first made the knowing hire of unauthorized workers a federal labor law violation. This was the stick that accompanied the carrot of amnesty (three million illegal aliens were legalized). Hispanic interest groups argued that they were the main target of the reform, which they equated with ethnic discrimination. They successfully mobilized to be joined by "strange bedfellows": employers and antistatist civil rights groups that called the checking of work documents totalitarian and likened it to the star Jews had to wear during the Nazi era.[54] In the end, the 1986 scheme was innocuous for employers. First, employers needed to check only one of twenty-nine acceptable documents to verify the identity of the employee and file an I-9 form to be considered not to have made a knowing hire of an undocumented alien. Moreover, asking for a specific identification could constitute a discriminatory practice.

In the mid-1990s, the Commission for Immigration Reform deemed a nationwide employment verification system the crux of the fight against illegal migration. Yet, during the 1996 reform process, a Kennedy amendment delayed the scheme for eight years and called instead for voluntary pilot programs. Meanwhile, an amendment by Utah Republican Senator Orrin Hatch eliminated the increase in fines against employers. In Christian Joppke's terms, the 1996 scheme resembled a "Swiss cheese, with big holes eaten into it by America's clients of immigration policy."[55]

When studying the "institutional transplant" of employers' sanctions from Europe to the United States, it is clear that it is largely cosmetic. The tradition of internal controls remains a "continental" phenomenon in Europe, as the U.K. government is still divided over imposing the kind of identification cards necessary for its functioning. The same can be said of the United States, where lobbies opposed to these measures can point to a tradition of opposition to state meddling in business affairs. From a principal-agent perspective, monitoring compliance is much easier and less costly in the case of carrier sanctions than that of employers' sanctions. The personnel resources required to check the status of workers in the thousands of businesses likely to hire illegal aliens are colossal. The risk of being caught during one of the spectacular INS raids of Operation SouthPAW (Protect American Workers) or Operation Restore is too small to deter employers that calculate the payoff of hiring a cheap, docile labor force. In Europe, fines and jail terms are much more severe for employers,[56] yet there is a stronger incentive to avoid paying employer payroll contributions that are much lower in the United States. The U.S. case also shows that, once again, although the adoption of employers' sanctions illustrated a political incentive to fight illegal migration, the details of the law and its implementation are testimony to the enduring strength of "client politics." The promigration lobby lost a battle but not the war. The United States adopted employer sanctions only in the 1980s and the system of employer identification verification is only partly in place because of the lack of a national identification card. By 2003, 900 city police forces and many businesses were accepting the so-called "matricula card" issued by Mexican consulates, showing the lax implementation of identification verification policies.[57]

SHIFTING POLICY DOWNWARD

Migration control policy reforms have also tended to give local or regional governments certain prerogatives.[58] This is flagrant in unitary states such as France and the Netherlands. In federal states, the relationship between state and federal governments had been more clearly laid out prior to that period, yet both in Germany and in the United States, the states that receive the largest share of migration have expressed disgruntlement with existing institutional and financial arrangements and called for stricter rules.[59]

To understand why in the 1990s subnational leaders called for restrictive migration policies and devolution in this policy area: the concentration of migrants in certain areas leads to an uneven distribution of the costs involved in the reception of foreigners. In the United States, this tension can be illustrated by the case of asylum seekers. States were responsible for the reception of asylum seekers, who were always more numerous than planned, while there were no extra funds to match. The federal–local imbalance arises as the higher levels of government deflect costs to the next lower level until "local governments have nowhere else to run, they end up paying most of the costs of immigration."[60]

Not all states asked to partake in the fight against illegal migration. In contrast with California, in East Coast states such as New York and New Jersey, for instance, the myth of the nation of immigrants symbolized by the Statue of Liberty lives on: elected officials have been more willing to listen to those who predicted crime and health problems if undocumented aliens were afraid of the police or public hospitals. In Germany, border states have built their identity more strongly on their differentiation from outsiders and, to this day, there is systematic anti-immigrant ideological bias in the leadership of these receiving regions (in Baden-Württemberg and Bavaria).

In the United States, federalism has tended to take the form of federal agents applying federal laws and state agents, state laws. In the area of migration, states until the mid- to late nineteenth century still carried a number of prerogatives including the rights granted to aliens.[61] During most of the twentieth century, Supreme Court decisions have emphasized the exclusive federal prerogatives in the area of immigration regulation through the "plenary power" doctrine. Seeing calls in the 1980s and 1990s emanating from governors in Texas and California for a state role in immigration policy is therefore a return to the past. As legal scholar Peter Schuck has argued, it is ultimately up to Congress to authorize states to play a role in immigration policy as they did in 1996 with respect to the welfare benefits of legal aliens.[62] One concrete example of devolution can be found in the 1996 federal immigration law. The IIRRA permits the INS to deputize and train local police officers to enforce immigration laws. So far, small borderland towns in states such as Arizona have asked the U.S. Attorney General to grant local police and sheriff's deputies the right to work as border patrol agents.[63] Police chiefs in larger cities such as Salt Lake City have also expressed interest.

In centralized states, electoral politics has driven calls for devolution as that issue has been seen as lucrative by local political entrepreneurs. In France, politicians often hold at least two elected positions such as member of parliament (MP) and mayor or president of the regional council. In 1996, a group of right-wing MPs endorsed a report on illegal migration proposals that gave mayors a greater role in migration control. Many were local elected officials who had built their political careers on the issue. The immigration law of December 30, 1993, that included measures against "marriages of convenience" gave mayors the right to call on the *Procureur de la République* to suspend or annul a wedding involving a foreigner. That same year, a housing certificate that had to be obtained and approved by the mayor became necessary to request a short-term visa.

Migration control now involves a number of public and private actors, at the local, national, and transnational level. It thus resembles the kind of multilevel governance system that describes other policy fields discussed in this volume. This development should not be overlooked: controlling who enters, stays, and leaves one's territory has long been emblematic of national sovereignty and considered a founding prerogative of the modern nation-state. State "monopoly over the legitimate means of movement" characterized the last century. The role of local and private actors was a limited one and, at the behest of states and national control agencies such as the U.S. Immigration and Naturalization Agency, expanded and developed their bureaucratic autonomy.[64]

Still, for several reasons, it would be misleading to consider migration control policy as a new illustration of "new public management." First, the cooptation of noncentral state actors *complements* rather than *replaces* the prerogatives of traditional national agencies. Their budget and personnel increased throughout the 1990s, especially in the United States[65] and, in the wake of the end of the cold war, public civil servants that feared to outlive their utility (intelligence, army . . .) quickly invested that policy domain.[66] On both sides of the Atlantic, there are more rather than less bureaucratic resources dedicated to migration control than before 1989. Second, the delegation of control functions to the private sector shifts liability to third actors but does not imply that "principals" relinquish operations to these "agents."[67] This is particularly clear in the case of private actors. The latter are enlisted through legislation mostly based on sanctions. To comply, airline personnel are trained by public security agencies and hire former civil servants with a police, intelligence, or army background to head the security departments of major airline and railway companies.[68] On the ground, at airports considered as "hot spots" for migration risks, European countries have sent "liaison officers."[69] Although there is liability and blame shifting at work here, the goal is to reinforce state capacity.

SHIFTING POLICY UPWARD: THE CASE OF THE EUROPEAN UNION

Since the coming into force of the Treaty of Amsterdam in 1999, the immigration and asylum policies of thirteen EU states are due to be progressively harmonized within the community framework, incorporating the relevant Schengen *acquis*. At the 1999 Tampere EU summit, chiefs of state stated that the elaboration of a common European policy "in the distinct, yet closely related, fields of asylum and migration" was the European Union's next major project after the single market and the Euro.[70]

Migration control policies that sought to stem or even revert migration flows after the first oil crisis were curtailed by judicial constraints and ran counter to the goals of social bureaucracies. Civil servants in the ministries of interior and justice responded in the mid-1980s by seeking to elaborate control policy in trans-governmental settings that excluded their national bureaucratic adversaries and made judicial oversight of decisions difficult (supranational clubs such as Trevi attended by civil servants and police officials). The secretive negotiations excluded other ministries in a way that changed the balance from a national setting and gave the Interior ministries more degrees of freedom. The cooperation forums include experts, international organizations, non-EU governments, and even subnational governments such as German *Länder* and excludes a number of actors with better access in a horizontal national policy process. The process was difficult to oversee and national parliaments were presented with agreements such as the 1990 Schengen agreement a couple of weeks before a vote of ratification that did not permit any amendments. Multitiered governance in the European Union has not empowered national promigrant coalitions that must now muster the know-how involved in transnational activism.

The form of EU cooperation still privileges intergovernmental bargains over supranational institutional actors although EU institutions have been progressively incorporated in the process. In 1992, the Treaty on European Union created the third pillar on justice and home affairs with one full working group dedicated to asylum, visa, and migration, yet the framework required unanimous decisions by the council and remained outside the community legal order. After the treaty of Amsterdam, the form of international cooperation remains largely intergovernmental because unanimity is required and EU institutions have a limited role (coinitiative for the commission, consultation role for the European Parliament). This makes sense because the main advantage of transgovernmentalism is to avoid "veto points"[71] and increase the leeway of law and order agencies. The content of the emerging European regime is restrictive, emphasizing concerns about asylum fraud and migrant smuggling rather than the importance of achieving internal free movement. Interior and justice officials were the first to define the meaning of a common "immigration policy" and continue to dominate, thereby emphasizing security concerns.

These officials have sought to avoid the judge's eye, as can be seen by the limited role given to the European Court of Justice (ECJ) in this policy area. The ECJ did not have a role to play in the Maastricht "third pillar" framework. In the post-Amsterdam era, the application of preliminary rulings in areas covered by Title IV on migration and asylum is restricted. The ECJ cannot rule on national measures adopted in relation to border crossing in order to maintain law and order and safeguard internal security. Moreover, the decisions taken in international settings have also diminished the role of national courts. I have mentioned visas and carrier sanctions. Regarding asylum seekers, accelerated procedures were adopted in 1993 in France, Germany, and The Netherlands on the basis of European decisions on "manifestly unfounded claims" and "safe third countries" so that asylum seekers will not have access to asylum-granting agencies and appeals courts.

The end of the cold war rather served as a cognitive frame justifying trans-governmental cooperation in the 1990s as security agencies invoked "new" trans-national threats that included in their view immigration, which they linked to criminal activities. The single-market project of the European Union was also used as a justification for cooperation on border controls, migration, and asylum even though EU member states that supported and participate in single-market policies (the United Kingdom, Ireland, and Denmark) have opted out of Amsterdam's Title IV on the harmonization of migration and asylum regulations and only selectively opt in. The constitution of the immigration policy domain thus depended on the windows of opportunity constituted by the emergence of new frames and contextual changes. Today's winners may yet face challenges at the next constitutional moment. Notwithstanding, they have accumulated legitimacy capital, and the policy domain has been institutionalized in a way that cannot be easily undone.

After September 11, a security frame with restrictive policy outcomes still prevails. For politicians, calling for a common EU immigration policy is a convenient way of shifting responsibility for an issue that the success of populist parties has turned into a hot potato. Yet, harmonization is slow, and EU measures have resulted in an increase in illegal immigration. In the end, this strategy may be as dangerous as activating xenophobia at the national level. Populist parties, which are generally both anti-immigrant and anti–European Union, will be further strengthened by the promises of European leaders that they do not fulfill. If the European Union as a new policy venue has benefited law-and-order bureaucrats, it is less clear that the corresponding "blame-avoidance" strategy of political leaders will be fruitful.

CONCLUSION

In the 1990s, U.S. legislative changes did not question the continued high levels of legal immigration, and many proposals and amendments targeted at illegal migrants failed. Still, the 1996 reforms have given new financial and regulatory means to control borders and denied legal migrants certain benefits. For U.S. scholars, the last decade resembles a half-empty, half-full glass: more border controls but more legal migration. There is also the feeling that a more restrictive agenda failed to materialize in Congress. In Europe, policy reform privileged migration "stemming" over "soliciting," and restrictive control policies were supra-nationalized. Yet, rights-based politics helped by activist high courts allowed humanitarian migration to continue, and legal migrants saw their rights confirmed rather than rolled back.

During the intense congressional debates of the mid-1990s, ethnic and business lobbies mobilized in the United States. They convinced enough politicians that reducing migration would be politically costly by invoking the importance of the "ethnic" (Latino) vote in close elections and their reliance on business support as campaign financers. In Europe, migrant-origin voters are not wooed as they are in the United States; instead, parties seek to contain the anti-immigrant populist vote. Nor do we find business groups actively lobbying for foreign labor in any manner equivalent to that in the United States. Migrant associations, to the extent that they mobilize, are not focusing on demanding more entries. This striking difference between the two continents warrants further enquiry. Yet, it means that in Europe, the promigrant field has been mostly occupied by human rights groups including churches and leftist parties and movements engaging in the defense of rights rather than in the increase of economic migration. The only actors that have adopted a proimmigrant stance on both sides of the Atlantic are trade unions.[72] Moreover, on both sides of the Atlantic, courts have also been active guarantors of migrant rights since the late 1970s, which has lead to the same avoidance strategies by migration-control bureaucrats in the form of "remote control" policies.

Clearly, some ideational differences are stable: as the case of employer sanctions shows, state intervention in the economy and in identification cards is much less acceptable in the United States than in Europe (high unemployment levels make the question of foreign labor recruitment taboo), whereas, even in "populist" Europe, taking away social benefits from *legal* foreigners seems anathema. Nevertheless, in the United States, the splitting of the immigration bill into two in 1996 ushered in a new era, where border-control policy is discussed separately from legal immigration, depriving promigrant groups of their business allies to water down measures against undocumented aliens or refugees.

Moreover, the reframing of the issue in the United States seems "European" as security concerns gain new ground. In this respect, the effects of September 11 on migration-control policy should not be overlooked. This "focus event" had an effect on the INS bureaucracy that can be compared to the explosion of *Challenger* for NASA. More important, it has ushered in an era in which migration is linked to internal and external security issues just as has been the case in Europe for almost two decades now.

The minutes of the EU–U.S. meeting on immigration issues that took place right after September 11 state,

> The U.S. delegation indicated that since the events of 11 September 2001, the whole system of visas, border controls, management of legal migration, etc. had come under close scrutiny and there was a consensus in the U.S. on the need for an effective system across the board, not targeted specifically at terrorism, but taking the events of 11 September as the trigger for developing a new approach.[73]

EU institutions have been extremely cooperative with the United States in the area of justice and home affairs. To comply with demands, the EU Commission has violated the EU data protection law by asking European airline companies to provide U.S. authorities with 39 information fields from their passenger information data records. Moreover, since the Patriot Act came into force, the EU Commission has issued proposals for a new EU passport with heightened security features so that EU citizens can avoid having to apply for a $100 visa when traveling to the United States.[74]

NOTES

1. Virginie Guiraudon and Christian Joppke, "Introduction" in *Controlling a New Migration World*, ed. Virginie Guiraudon and Christian Joppke (London: Routledge, 2001), 2.

2. EC citizens have the right to move to another member state and therefore a special legal regime applies to them.

3. The INS estimates that there are about six million illegal aliens living in the United States, a number that increases by more than 200,000 per year. California is home to 40 percent of the undocumented population. The INS estimates that 40 percent of illegal residents entered the United States legally but overstayed their visas.

4. Philip Martin, "The United States: Benign Neglect towards Immigration" in *Controlling Immigration*, ed. Wayne Cornelius, Philip Martin, and James Hollifield (Stanford: Stanford University Press, 1994), 83–100.

5. See chapters 4 and 8. See also R. Kent Weaver, "The Politics of Blame Avoidance," *The Journal of Public Policy* 6, no. 4 (1986):371–98; and Paul Pierson, *Dismantling the Welfare State: Reagan, Thatcher, and the Politics of Retrenchment* (New York: Cambridge University Press, 1994).

6. About a million and a half legal migrants arrive in the European Union each year (374 million inhabitants), proportionally almost twice as much as in the United States with its 288 million inhabitants. With its 650,000 annual legal newcomers, the United States receives the same number of new migrants as 82-million strong Germany. In its 2000 *World Migration Report*, the International Organization for Migration (IOM) estimates the upper limit of unauthorized migrants in Europe at three million in 1998, as compared to less than two million in 1991. Depending on the calculation methods used, illegal migrants are thought to represent between 10 percent and 15 percent of migrants already present and between 20 percent and 30 percent of inflow. In the countries studied here, they constitute about a half percent of the total population.

7. For U.S. data, see Rita Simon and Susan Alexander, *The Ambivalent Welcome: Print Media, Public Opinion and Immigration* (Westport, CT: Praeger, 1993). For EU data, see Eurobarometer, *Public Opinion in the European Community: Racism and Xenophobia* (Brussels: Commission of the European Communities, 1989, 1994, 1997). For comparative assessments, see Rita Simon and James P. Lynch, "A Comparative Assessment of Public Opinion toward Immigrants and Immigration Policies," *International Migration Review* 33, no. 2 (1999):455–67; and Joel Fetzer, *Public Attitudes toward Immigration in the United States, France, and Germany* (Cambridge: Cambridge University Press, 2000).

8. George J. Borjas, *Heaven's Door: Immigration Policy and the American Economy* (Princeton : Princeton University Press, 1999); H. Brücker, Gil Epstein, B. McCormick, G. Saint-Paul, A. Venturini, and K. Zimmermann, "Managing Migration in the European Welfare State," part 1, in *Immigration Policy and the Welfare System*, ed. T. Boeri (Oxford: Oxford University Press for Fondazione Rodolfo de Benedetti, 2002), 3–151.

9. OECD Working Group on Employment, *Foreign Labor: Perspectives and Issues in OECD Member States* (Paris: OECD, 2001).

10. See Pepper Culpepper, *Creating Cooperation: How States Develop Human Capital in Europe* (Ithaca, NY: Cornell University Press, 2003). The United States is not saving on education by "brain draining" given the number of foreign students in U.S. universities.

11. E. E. Schattschneider, *The Semi-sovereign People: A Realist's View of Democracy in America* (New York: Holt, Rhinehart and Winston, 1960).

12. Roger Cobb and Charles Elder, *Participation in American Politics: The Dynamics of Agenda-Building* (Baltimore: John Hopkins University Press, 1983), 105–29.

13. See Virginie Guiraudon, *Policy Change behind Gilded Doors: Explaining the Evolution of Aliens' Rights in Contemporary Western Europe* (PhD diss., Harvard University, 1997).

14. Frank Baumgartner and Bryan Jones, *Agendas and Instability in American Politics* (Chicago: Chicago University Press, 1993), 36.

15. Theda Skocpol, "Bringing the State Back in: Strategies of Analysis in Current Research," in *Bringing the State Back In*, ed. Peter Evans (New York: Cambridge University Press, 1985); Hugh Heclo, *Modern Social Politics in Britain and Sweden* (New Haven, CT: Yale University Press, 1974).

16. Martin Shapiro, *Courts: A Comparative and Political Analysis* (Chicago: University of Chicago Press, 1981).

17. Gary Freeman, "Client Politics or Populism? The Politics of Immigration Reform in the United States" in *Controlling a New Migration World*, ed. Virginie Guiraudon and Christian Joppke (London: Routledge, 2001), 65–95.

18. Gary Freeman, "Towards a Theory of Migration Politics" (paper presented at the International Conference for Europeanists, Chicago, March 14–17, 2002).

19. James Wilson, ed., *The Politics of Regulation* (New York: Basic Books, 1980).

20. Freeman, "Towards a Theory of Migration Politics," 5.

21. Theodore Lowi, "American Business, Public Policy, Case Studies and Political Theory," in *World Politics* 16: (1964):677–93.

22. Freeman, "Towards a Theory of Migration Politics," 4.

23. Aristide Zolberg, "From Invitation to Interdiction: U.S. Foreign Policy and Immigration since 1945" in *Threatened Peoples, Threatened Borders: World Migration and U.S. Policy*, ed. Michael Teitelbaum and Myron Weiner (New York: W. W. Norton, 1995), 117–59; Dan Tichenor, *Dividing Lines: The Politics of Immigration Control in America* (Princeton, NJ: Princeton University Press, 2002).

24. Dan Tichenor, "Voters, Clients, and the Policy Process: Two Faces of Expansive Immigration Politics in America." Paper presented at the conference "Magnet Societies: Immigration in Postwar Germany and the United States," Evangelische Akademie Loccum, Hannover, Germany, June 14–18, 2000.

25. Tichenor, "Voters, Clients, and the Policy Process: Two Faces of Expansive Immigration Politics in America," 3.

26. Christian Joppke, *Immigration and the Nation-State: The United States, Germany, and Great Britain* (Oxford: Oxford University Press, 1999).

27. Simon and Alexander, *The Ambivalent Welcome: Print Media, Public Opinion and Immigration;* and Fetzer, *Public Attitudes toward Immigration in the United States, France, and Germany.*

28. Jeannette Money, *Fences and Neighbors: The Political Geography of Immigration Control* (Ithaca, NY: Cornell University Press, 1999).

29. Anthony M. Messina, *Race and Party Competition in Britain* (Oxford: Clarendon Press, 1989).

30. Richard Walker, "California's Collision of Race and Class," *Representations* 55 (1996):167.

31. James Gimpel's account of the congressional politics of immigration finds that, since the late 1970s, immigration has become increasingly a partisan issue precisely because of the redistributive costs of some of the programs developed then (e.g., the program for refugee assistance) that Republicans denounced. See James Gimpel, "From Consensus to Controversy: The Congressional Politics of US Immigration Policy" (paper presented at the Murphy Institute conference on the political economy of migration, Tulane University, New Orleans, March 23–24, 2000).

32. Michael Bommes, "Migration, Nationalstaat und Wohlfahrtsstaat: Kommunale Probleme in föderalen Systemen," in *Migration Ethnizität Konflikt*, ed. Klaus Bade (Osnabrück: Institut für Migrationsforschung und Interkulturelle Studien, 1996).

33. Joppke, *Immigration and the Nation-State*, 80.

34. Dietrich Thränhardt, "The Political Uses of Xenophobia in England, France and Germany," in *Immigration into Western Societies*, ed. Donald Puchala and Emek Uçarer (London: Pinter, 1997).

35. James G. Gimpel and James R. Edwards, Jr., *The Congressional Politics of Immigration Reform* (Boston: Allyn & Bacon, 1998).

36. The bombers turned out to be U.S. citizens.

37. Peter Schuck, *Citizens, Strangers and In-Betweens: Essays on Immigration and Citizenship* (Boulder: Westview Press, 1998), 144.

38. Federal judges also blocked the implementation of the measures of proposition 187, except regarding criminal penalties for the use of fraudulent documents. Freeman, "Client Politics or Populism? The Politics of Immigration Reform in the United States."

39. Nonna Mayer, "Ethnocentrisme, racisme et intolérance," in *L'électeur français en questions*, CEVIPOF (Paris: Presses de la FNSP, 1991).

40. Michael Minkenberg, "Context and Consequence: The Impact of the New Radical Right on the Political Process in France and Germany," *German Politics and Society* 16, no. 3 (1998).

41. Thränhardt, "The Political Uses of Xenophobia in England, France and Germany."

42. *Entscheidungen des Bundesverfassungsgerichts* 1978, 168–85. See also decision of January 7, 1979, in *Entscheidungen des Bundesverfassungsgerichts* 1979, 166, 175.

43. Decision of May 12, 1987 in *Entscheidungen des Bundesverfassungsgerichts* 76, 1.

44. Gerald Neuman, "Immigration and Judicial Review in the Federal Republic of Germany," *New York University Journal of International Law and Politics* 23 (1990).

45. Manfred Küchler, "Framing Unification: Issue Salience and Mass Sentiment, 1989–1991," in *The New Germany Votes*, ed. Russell Dalton (Providence, RI: Berg, 1993), 47.

46. Peter Andreas, *Border Games: Policing the U.S.–Mexico Divide* (Ithaca, NY: Cornell University Press, 2000).

47. Aristide Zolberg, "The Great Wall against China: Responses to the First Immigration Crisis, 1885–1925," in *Migration, Migration History, History: Old Paradigms and New Perspectives*, ed. Jan and Leo Lucassen (New York: Peter Lang, 1997); John Torpey, *The Invention of the Passport* (Cambridge: Cambridge University Press, 2000).

48. *Official Journal of the European Communities*, L187 (July 10, 2001), 45–6.

49. *Official Journal of the European Communities*, L81 (January 23, 2001).

50. *Official Journal of the European Communities*, L239 (September 2000).

51. Christopher Mitchell, "The Political Costs of State Power: U.S. Border Control in South Florida," in *The Wall around the West: State Borders and Immigration Controls in North America and Europe*, ed. Peter Andreas and Tim Snyder (Lanham, MD: Rowman and Littlefield, 2000), 81–97.

52. House of Lords Select Committee on European Union, *Seventeenth Report on Enlargement and EU External Frontier Controls* (London: House of Lords, October 24, 2000), part 3, 4.

53. Mark Miller, *Employer Sanctions in France: From the Campaign against Illegal Alien Unemployment to the Campaign against Illegal Work* (Washington, DC: U.S. Commission on Immigration Reform, 1995).

54. Christian Joppke, "Why Liberal States Accept Unwanted Immigration," *World Politics* 50, no. 2 (1998):274.

55. Joppke, "Why Liberal States Accept Unwanted Immigration," 280.

56. Penal sanctions do vary across Europe, from a six-month jail term in The Netherlands to a five-year term in Germany, although administrative fines are comparable.

57. Rachel L. Swarns, "Old ID Card Gives New Status to Mexicans in U.S.," *New York Times*, August 25, 2003.

58. Local authorities have also been contracted out to detain illegal migrants. In the United States, nine national centers out of thirteen holding illegal aliens or asylum seekers in 1996 were run by local and state actors with the support of government funds, and the INS rents thousands of beds in local jails. Virginie Guiraudon and Gallya Lahav, "A Reappraisal of the State Sovereignty Debate: The Case of Migration Control," *Comparative Political Studies* 33, no. 2 (2000):163–95.

59. In Germany, states implement federal laws such as the federal aliens law. In their role as arbiters between state and federal government, courts have given states some leeway in the interpretation of federal mandates and ruled that the fact that states applied federal guidelines differently did not constitute a violation of equality before the law or federalism. See Gerald Neuman, "Immigration and Judicial Review in the Federal Republic of Germany," *New York University Journal of International Law and Politics* 23, no. 1 (1990):59.

60. Thomas Espenshade and Eric Rothman, "Fiscal Impacts of Immigration to the United States," *Population Index* 58, no. 3 (1992):410.

61. This stemmed from the fact that states with slave populations wanted control over their population and some of these state rights were taken away from them by courts after the Civil War. See Gerald Neuman, *The Effects of Immigration on Nationality Law*, European Forum seminar series (Florence: EUI, 1998).

62. Schuck, *Citizens, Strangers and In-Betweens: Essays on Immigration and Citizenship*.

63. Vincent J. Schodolski, "Ranchers Round Up Immigrants: What Border Patrol Doesn't Do, Locals Do," *Chicago Tribune*, May 12, 1999.

64. See Kitty Calavita, *Inside the State: The Bracero Program, Immigration and the INS* (New York: Routledge, 1992); John Torpey, "Coming and Going: On the State Monopolization of the 'Legitimate Means of Movement,'" *Sociological Theory* 16, no. 3 (1998):239–59.

65. The INS budget grew from $1.1 billion in 1990 to $2.6 billion in 1995.

66. Didier Bigo, "Migration and Security" in *Controlling a New Migration World*, ed. Virginie Guiraudon and Christian Joppke (London: Routledge, 2001).

67. Agency theory is directed at the relationship, in which one party (the principal) delegates work to another (the agent), who performs that work. It comes from the work of Oliver Williamson on transaction costs and has been influential in law and politics. See Oliver E. Williamson, "Transaction Cost Economics and Organization Theory," *Industrial and Corporate Change* 2 (1993):107–56.

68. To illustrate this point, the Air France security head is an Interior Ministry official from the border control agency (*Police de l'air et des frontières*), his KLM counterpart was a police chief in Amsterdam in the counterterrorism unit that has been trained by the FBI, and the German security agencies at airports recruit among the German border police (*Bundesgrendschütz*). Eurotunnel, the company that manages the tunnel crossing between France and the U.K., hired a retired British army general in 2001 to prevent foreigners from trying to reach Great Britain.

69. *Official Journal of the European Communities*, L239 (September 22, 2000).

70. See Virginie Guiraudon, "European Integration and Migration Policy: Vertical Policy-making as Venue Shopping," *Journal of Common Market Studies* 38, no. 2 (2000): 249–69.

71. Ellen Immergut, *Health Politics: Interests and Institutions in Western Europe* (New York: Cambridge University Press, 1992).

72. Leah Haus, *Unions, Immigration and Internationalization: New Challenges and Changing Coalitions in the U.S. and France* (New York: Palgrave, 2002).

73. Council of the European Union, "Outcome of Proceedings of the Strategic Committee on Immigration, Frontiers and Asylum Meeting with the United States dated 26 October 2001," doc. 13803/01 ASIM 21 USA 24 Brussels (November 12, 2001).

74. Sharon Spiteri, "Commission Pressed over Airline Data Exchange," *EU Observer*, October 9, 2003.

THE EUROPEAN UNION AND THE DIFFUSION
OF DISABILITY RIGHTS

THOMAS F. BURKE

THE UNITED STATES IS RIGHTLY KNOWN AS THE NATION IN WHICH, AS ALEXIS DE
Tocqueville put it nearly 170 years ago, "there is hardly a political question in the
United States that does not sooner or later turn into a judicial one."[1] The United
States has a comparatively large number of *litigious policies*, laws that promote the
use of litigation in resolving disputes and implementing public policy.[2] American
public policy uses litigious policies to address social problems that in other nations are handled solely by bureaucratic regulation and welfare programs. Thus
litigation is an often-overlooked stratagem of governance in the United States,
comparable to the tax credit and "private social benefit" schemes about which Jacob Hacker and Christopher Howard have written.[3] As they suggest, arguments
about the weakness of the American state often miss techniques by which U.S.
public policy steers the actions of nonstate actors. Litigious policies steer by creating incentives for private actors to implement and enforce laws, an approach that
is attractive to American politicians because it serves as an alternative to an expanded welfare-regulatory state.

It should be no surprise, then, that the United States is the birthplace of a litigious approach to the problem of disability. Beginning in the 1960s and 1970s,
the disability rights movement aimed to recast disability as a civil rights issue:
people with disabilities, the movement argued, suffered more from social discrimination than from their impairments. Like African Americans, they were burdened
by social attitudes and structural barriers that excluded them from the mainstream
of social life. Further, as with African Americans, the solution to the problems of
people with disabilities lay in litigation: they must be given the ability to sue for
discrimination. Thus in the United States a series of disability rights laws have
provided the right to sue: Section 5 of the 1974 Rehabilitation Act, the 1975 Education for All Handicapped Children Act, and, most prominent of all, the 1990
Americans with Disabilities Act (ADA). Disability rights litigation in the United

States has become commonplace, and some plaintiffs—Casey Martin, the professional golfer with a mobility disability, for example—have even become minor media celebrities.

Thus far the story of disability politics fits neatly with the familiar pattern Tocqueville and so many commentators after him have noted, as the United States has embraced a court-oriented approach to basic problems in social policy. But the past few years have seen a new development that, at least in disability policy, may undermine the portrait of American legal exceptionalism: the diffusion of antidiscrimination rights proposals and policies across the globe. Disability organizations, academic lawyers, and activists have used international conferences, publications, and the Internet to spread the key concepts of the disability rights movement. International organizations, most prominently the United Nations, have embraced the new emphasis on inclusion and participation in disability policy pioneered by the United States and have promulgated a series of resolutions and proclamations on disability rights. But many nations have gone beyond "soft" laws to enact enforceable antidiscrimination provisions. In Europe, the crowning example is the European Union's 2000 Equal Treatment in Employment and Occupation Directive. This law was nicknamed the "Horizontal Directive" because it requires all EU nations to adopt antidiscrimination laws across several grounds— not just disability, but also age, religion, and sexual orientation. The Horizontal Directive gives aggrieved individuals the right to bring a complaint against a party that discriminates.[4]

Like many chapters in this book, then, this one features a public policy idea— "disability rights"—that has swept across the Atlantic to fuel political discourse in both Europe and North America. Yet, as the other chapters in this book suggest, common terms of debate do not necessarily lead to convergent outcomes. Like "administrative reform" or "pension privatization," the concepts of disability rights translate differently depending on the structures of national institutions and political alignments. It seems unlikely, for example, that the Horizontal Directive, standing by itself, will lead Europe to American-style disability rights litigation. That is because most European nations thus far lack the legal machinery required to vigorously implement litigious policies. Contingency fees, large verdicts, a corps of aggressive plaintiff lawyers—the taken-for-granted requisites of litigious policy in the United States—are in short supply in Europe. Until they appear, disability rights implementation seems poised to take a different direction, indeed several different directions, among European nations. Yet, the adoption of the Horizontal Directive, and the growing embrace of antidiscrimination laws in Europe, create at least the possibility of a turn to litigation in European social policy.

Scholars in recent years have speculated about the extent to which the American emphasis on litigation could spread to Europe, creating a convergence in public policy style. They have suggested some likely "carriers." Some observers, for example, point to international commercial law, which has brought American and European lawyers into closer contact. Perhaps, it is theorized, American lawyers could infect their European colleagues with a more aggressive, enterprising approach to the practice of law, leading to novel, more complex, and more sweeping forms of litigation.[5] In a globalizing, competitive economy, this more aggressive legal style may prove advantageous, so that trade liberalization and the attendant neoliberal policy style might lead to expanded litigation.[6] Other researchers, detecting the "judicialization of politics" in Europe, focus on the proliferation of higher-law constitutionalism and the building of national constitutional courts.[7] Still others look to declining trust in the executive and legislative institutions, the gradual drift from a corporatist to a pluralist mode of interest representation, or the growth of legal capacity within interest groups.[8]

The mechanism I focus on in this chapter is the European Union (EU). The establishment of the European Union creates in Europe some of the very same structures that in the United States promote court-oriented public policy, in particular a division of authority analogous to federalism. Federalism creates an incentive for policymakers at the national level to create rights that can be enforced against states and localities. Similarly, within the European Union, politicians at the center can claim credit for delivering benefits to constituencies while passing the burdens on to national-level governments.[9] By creating rights, in this case a right against discrimination on the basis of disability, politicians and bureaucrats in the European Union can satisfy constituencies, extend their role in disability policy, and build the legitimacy of their institution at minimal cost to themselves. These incentives would seem to operate in spheres far beyond disability and thus raise the specter of litigious policymaking across policy realms in Europe.[10] Indeed, the case of disability may be just one small part of a broad rise of "adversarial legalism" that some observers have detected in Europe, both within statutory and EU constitutional law. At the very least, the case of disability suggests that the many national-level institutional and cultural barriers to litigious policies in Europe will be matched against the interest of some EU actors in creating new rights mandates.

REFRAMING DISABILITY POLICY

"Disability" is a huge problem for any polity. Depending on how one defines disability—and there are seemingly as many definitions as there are disabilities—as many as one in five Americans count as disabled.[11] In Europe, one recent report produced a report finding that 13 percent of people within the EU nations were disabled.[12] Whatever the estimate, disability is a huge social problem. People with disabilities can be considered the largest and poorest "minority" in the United States and, along with the elderly, the biggest consumer of state services. Monroe Berkowitz, in an analysis of the 1995 federal budget, estimated that nearly $184 billion dollars are spent on people with disabilities, roughly half on health care and a little less than half on income maintenance.[13] In Europe, as pressure on the welfare state has grown, the expanding cost of disability pensions has been an increasing concern. The most notorious example is The Netherlands, where by the early 1990s more than one of every seven people of working age was collecting disability benefits, and nearly 5 percent of gross national product was consumed by disability income transfer programs.[14]

Traditional policy responses to disability are all based on the notion that disabled people are helpless victims who need aid, either from the state, the family, or helping institutions. The three main tracks of disability policy in the twentieth century were compensation, institutionalization, and rehabilitation. Each of these tracks shares the core premise that disabled people are defective; the response is either compensation for lost wages, segregation from the normal, or rehabilitation to fix the problem. The disability rights movement has attempted to reframe disability as a matter of discrimination. The key premise of the movement is that people with disabilities are disabled more by attitudinal and physical barriers than by their impairments. Failing to accommodate people with disabilities is not merely bad manners or uncharitable policy, but a violation of the norm of equal treatment. The solution is to create a right against discrimination and allow disabled people to sue for violations of their rights. The easiest way to sum up all this is to think of disability as a problem society creates rather than a problem individuals have—a so-called "relational" view of inequality.[15]

In the United States, this movement is sometimes summarized as "from needs to rights" or "from charity to rights."[16] In Europe, where there is a much stronger tradition of social rights—rights to welfare payments, technical aids and treatment—it really is a matter of "rights to rights." The differences between the two sets of rights, social and civil, are substantial, however. Social rights are more general norms of state behavior that are not individually enforceable. Civil rights claims are individual demands that can be brought to a court or agency for enforcement and can involve claims against nonstate actors. Moreover, many of the theorists of the civil rights movement argue that the welfarist approach is part of the problem; people with disabilities need to be treated as capable of work. If the civil rights model becomes dominant, all the traditional components of disability policy will have to be rethought and reorganized. Thus, although the reframing of disability is, even in the United States, still in its infancy, it has the potential to transform every aspect of disability policy.

DISABILITY RIGHTS IN THE UNITED STATES

How did American disability activists, not a particularly strong constituency, enact into law a major social reform? The story of the American disability rights movement has now been well chronicled by both academics and journalists.[17] Disability historians have located various struggles against forms of disability discrimination throughout the twentieth century—for example, campaigns by the blind to allow guide dogs on public transportation, or protests over inadequate job opportunities for people with disabilities in New Deal work programs.[18] A leader of the blind community, law professor Jacobus ten Broek, conceptualized disability in part as a problem of legal rights and discrimination back in the

1960s.[19] But most would concede that the disability rights movement became coherent only after the passage of the 1973 Rehabilitation Act. Stuck into this omnibus law, the main vehicle for federal funding of rehabilitation programs, was
Section 504, a single sentence that passed by unnoticed by nearly everyone:

> no otherwise qualified individual in the United States . . . shall, solely by
> reason of his handicap, be excluded from participation in, be denied the
> benefits of, or be subjected to discrimination under any program or ac-
> tivity receiving Federal assistance.

The initiative for Section 504 came from liberals in Congress and their staffs.[20]
They first considered amending the Civil Rights Act of 1964 to bar discrimination
on the basis of disability but reconsidered, either because they feared the consequences of opening up the act for amendment or because they recognized that
disability was distinctive enough to merit separate treatment. In the hands of the
civil rights division of the Department of Health, Education and Welfare, charged
with writing the regulations based on Section 504, and the federal courts, called
on to interpret it, this obscure sentence became a full-fledged antidiscrimination
law. The Ford and Carter administrations held up implementation of Section 504
regulations, but the Carter administration relented after a celebrated moment in
the history of the disability rights movement: a cross-disability sit-in at a San Francisco federal building.

In the wake of Section 504, a disability rights movement, complete with academic theorists and a public law organization (the Disability Rights Education and
Defense Fund) styled after the National Association for the Advancement of
Colored People (NAACP) grew up. The premises of the disability rights model
were enunciated and began to be diffused, first in the disability community and
among civil rights advocates, then in the wider policy and academic circles. Section 504 covered only federal agencies and those receiving federal funds. In the af-
termath of Section 504, a number of state laws creating a general right against
discrimination were enacted, but for disability activists these laws were piecemeal,
often weakly enforced, and thus unsatisfactory.

Moreover, implementation of Section 504 was considered weak, and there
was a backlash against it in the early Reagan administration. In the midst of this,
disability activists hit on a marvelous strategy for advancing their rights message.
They found that they could pitch the disability rights model to Reaganites as a
kind of welfare reform: disability welfare programs, they told Reagan administration officials, reduce disabled people to dependency. By empowering disabled
people and releasing them from the chains of government handouts, disability
rights laws would launch disabled people "toward independence."[21]

That became the basis of a strong alliance between disability activists and
Reagan and Bush administration officials. A Reagan administration commission
drafted the first (more radical) version of the ADA, and George H. W. Bush endorsed it during his 1988 presidential campaign. Bush's endorsement foreclosed
debate over the basic premises of the ADA; after the ADA was introduced into

Congress, business interests picked away at the edges of the bill but never contested the rights frame, and the law was enacted with bipartisan support in 1990.

The disability rights movement lacked fearsome political resources, but its leaders wisely mustered their few advantages. Disability activists had a handy template for both the problem and the solution to disability. They drew on the experiences and imagery associated with the civil rights movement and analogized the problems of disabled people to those of African Americans, in the process gaining the support of the civil rights lobby. The activists were able to sustain this recasting of disability in large part because of the unity of the disability lobby. Despite the extraordinary diversity of the community of people with disabilities, disability groups held together largely on the need for a rights law. But most of all, disability activists benefited from the political virtues of their proposal. The civil rights remedy they suggested had the great advantage of costing the federal government relatively little; by extending rights, politicians transferred most of the costs of the rights laws to state and local governments and the private sector. Indeed, disability activists were able to convince conservatives in the Reagan and Bush administrations that the ADA would *save* the federal government in the long run because it would help move disabled people off welfare to work. As a result, the ADA, a major social reform, was adopted relatively quickly and by large majorities in both houses of Congress.[22]

Implementation has proven another matter. ADA enforcement has deeply disappointed disability activists, as federal courts have interpreted the law narrowly and, in so doing, created a series of barriers for plaintiffs. Moreover, the law has not led to the wholesale transformation of traditional disability policy as its most vigorous advocates had hoped. Supplemental Security Income (SSI) and Social Security Disability Income (SSDI), the two main disability welfare programs, have ballooned in the years following the ADA's enactment, and employment among people with disabilities has continued to fall.[23] Yet in the rest of the world the ADA is considered a groundbreaking law. This is no accident, as American activists have consciously attempted to export the disability rights model, using international organizations, conferences, and field visits to convey the rights message.

DIFFUSION TO EUROPE

The effort to export the disability rights message was successful in generating international attention. European disability activists made pilgrimages to the main centers of disability activism in the United States, particularly Berkeley, California, to learn the precepts of the "disability rights model." The arguments and techniques of American disability activists were spread through academic writings and international disability conferences. Lobbied by disability nongovernmental organizations (NGOs), international organizations—most prominently the United Nations—created proclamations and resolutions endorsing the civil rights approach, such as the 1993 "Standard Rules on the Equalization of Opportunities for Persons with Disabilities."

Yet by 2000, within Europe only Britain, Ireland, and Sweden had civil disability rights laws. Some other nations had largely symbolic constitutional or criminal provisions protecting against discrimination, but American-style antidiscrimination laws, where they had been proposed, had been stalled. The slow progress of European disability activists at the national level is unsurprising. They started in an even weaker position than their counterparts in the United State. In Europe, there is no strong civil rights tradition, and in many nations, no civil rights template at all. Thus, unlike their American colleagues, European disability rights activists had a much tougher time explaining their argument to policymakers. They faced the daunting prospect of building antidiscrimination laws and institutions from the ground up, rather than simply building on established practices. (Sweden and Britain, two of the three nations that adopted rights laws, had already built antidiscrimination enforcement agencies covering gender and race.) Moreover, in contrast with the relatively unified American disability rights movement, in most European nations there are strong, state-supported disability organizations that are ambivalent about, if not hostile to, the civil rights approach. Disability rights activists were sometimes insurgents within their own disability community.[24] For some European disability policy leaders, the whole idea of a judicially based, rights-oriented approach to disability was considered a noxious foreign import.

And yet as national-level rights campaigns were being thwarted, a small network of academics and activists, probably no more than a few dozen, proved far more successful at the EU level. Their campaign began in the early 1990s. Within the European Union, British disability activists were the first to raise nondiscrimination issues, according to European Commission staff. The British campaign for a disability rights law had begun in the 1980s, and the British activists, like their American counterparts, had an evangelical zeal to expand the scope of antidiscrimination policy. Their pleas for action, however, were met by a powerful argument: the treaties that establish the European Union simply did not grant it power in this realm. In Eurospeak, disability rights laws were beyond the European Union's "competence." Indeed, under the traditional view, disability was a matter of "social policy"—welfare, rehabilitation, and education—a realm in which the European Union was supposed to play only a minor role. The place of the European Union in social policy was a matter of great disagreement and some fluidity, but deliberations surrounding the Maastricht Treaty had emphasized "subsidiarity," leaving less room for EU social policy initiatives.[25]

Nevertheless, nondiscrimination advocates found a way to move forward. As part of a broader policy initiative on social exclusion and joblessness in Europe, the European Union had created a series of "action programs" that funded conferences and information sharing on disability-related issues. The early action programs were criticized for wasting money on ill-considered projects and for failing to involve people with disabilities. This was addressed in "Helios II," a package of grants for research and cross-national consultation on the problems of unemployment among people with disabilities. It was Helios II money that created the European Disability Forum (EDF), an association of member-state disability groups dedicated to the civil rights model.[26] The formation of the EDF was a key move. It became a central resource for European disability rights activists, tying them together in a network and providing a clearinghouse for idea-sharing and advocacy. EDF lobbied both the European Commission and Parliament, producing reports and research designed to promote the disability rights message and arguing that a Europe-wide solution to disability discrimination was appropriate.[27] The first sign of success was a 1993 green paper on European social policy that argued that segregation of people with disabilities, "even with adequate income maintenance and special provision, is contrary to human dignity."[28] This was followed by the Commission's 1994 white paper, the first EU publication to mention discrimination in connection with disability. The white paper also specifically mentions "the positive experience of the European Disability Forum" in building accessibility for people with disabilities.[29] Thus with the arrival of EDF at the EU, disability began to be seen as a matter fit for nondiscrimination policies, a mechanism that the European Union had before considered only in the context of race and gender.

With growing support from within the European Commission, disability rights advocates lobbied to expand EU competence to cover antidiscrimination measures during the 1997 revisions to the EU treaty in Amsterdam. Groups representing racial and ethnic minorities, gays and lesbians, and religious minorities also lobbied for nondiscrimination powers. Although there was discussion about creating a treaty-based, quasiconstitutional right against discrimination, treaty negotiations stopped well short of this. The Amsterdam Treaty did, however, produce Article 13, which specifically granted the European Union competence to take action on discrimination across a range of grounds, including disability.

Armed with the Amsterdam Treaty, disability rights advocates worked within the European Commission to draft a "directive"—a rule requiring nations to make rules. In late 1999, two directives were proposed by the European Commission.[30] The first, covering racial and ethnic discrimination, was broad in scope, governing goods and services, employment, and education. The second, the Horizontal Directive, covered more grounds (religion, sexual orientation, age, and disability) but governed only employment and professional education. The campaign for an EU antidiscrimination measure gained ground during the controversy over the appointment of Jorge Haider to a position in the Austrian cabinet. Haider was a populist right-wing Austrian parliamentarian whose party was widely seen as racist. The Haider appointment served to highlight the new politics of race in Europe, and EU officials resolved to make a strong antiracist statement. The race directive was enacted in June 2000, just seven months after it was introduced.[31] To a large extent, proponents of nondiscrimination policies on other grounds (religion, sexual orientation, age, and disability) simply followed in the wake of the strong push for antiracist action, and the Horizontal Directive was enacted four months later, in October 2000.[32]

The Horizontal Directive gave member nations until 2003 to create enforcement systems, but they can get a waiver for age and disability until 2006. The Directive does not specify what procedural form enforcement should take. It could

be administrative or judicial, or some combination of both. The directive also does
not require that compensation be paid to victims, but it does provide substantive
standards. It specifies that penalties for discriminatory conduct must be "effective,
proportionate and dissuasive."[33] Moreover, the disability antidiscrimination policy must include some requirement for "reasonable accommodation" of people
with disabilities, as in the ADA, and it must forbid "indirect" as well as direct
discrimination—provisions that, though seemingly neutral, disproportionately
burden people with disabilities. The directive is just one way in which nondiscrimination ideas have influenced EU policy and, some observers think, is not
necessarily the most consequential in the short run. That is because it is a "framework" directive, which merely instructs member states that they must take "effective" action against discrimination and specifies some standards. The directive
does not create a right against discrimination at the EU level, and it is not clear
what the remedy will be if the actions taken by member states are deemed "ineffective." But the directive is part of a series of actions at the EU level that is changing the terms in which disability policy is debated within Europe.

Already the move to a rights model of disability has spurred the adoption of
further laws, some with greater immediate impact than the Horizontal Directive.
For example, a new transportation directive requires that member states make
their buses accessible to wheelchairs.[34] Disability activists now know that if they
are blocked within their home nations, they can lobby the European Union instead, hoping to get a rule that they can then enforce at the national level—the
so-called "boomerang" maneuver that Margaret Keck and Kathryn Sikkink have
identified in their study of transnational advocacy.[35] Finally, through the creation
of the European Disability Forum, the European Union has brought together disability activists from around Europe who can help mobilize EU directives and
standards within their home countries. EDF officials have drafted a second, more
far-reaching disability directive that would, like the ADA, go beyond employment
to cover the accessibility of transport and public facilities, a key concern of the disability rights movement—and a potentially much more expensive matter for national governments.[36]

THE EUROPEAN UNION AS RIGHTS MANUFACTURER

The progress that disability rights activists have made in the European Union
can be traced to several factors. First, disability advocates to a large extent rode in
the slipstream of growing concern about racism and discrimination on the basis of
ethnicity. Once this concern generated the energy necessary to enact an antidiscrimination directive for race, the sponsors of the Horizontal Directive, including disability activists, found their path already paved for them.

Second, there simply was no strong opposition to the reframing of disability as
a civil rights issue. The main employer organizations never mounted a campaign
against the Equal Treatment Directive, and most member nations that might have

had their doubts chose not to push the issue in a visible way. The lack of *visible* opposition to disability rights proposals is a pattern one sees in all the polities in which such proposals have reached the legislative agenda. Once an issue is conceived as a matter of rights, it is not easy for politicians or even interest groups to oppose them. This may be doubly true when politicians are attempting to "deny rights" to people with disabilities, a particularly difficult enterprise. There are scattered criticisms of the turn to nondiscrimination rights in disability policy, but no one has yet mounted a coherent campaign against it. This is a striking illustration of the fact that new policy ideas, even when advanced by weak political forces, can gain ground when there is no politically effective argument against them.

Perhaps most important for the success of disability advocates, however, was a congruence between their agenda and that of EU officials. The transformation of disability into a matter of civil rights coincided with the institutional interests of the European Union in at least two respects.[37] First, the protection of rights has become a legitimating project for the European Union. With criticism of the European Union's corruption, bureaucracy, and lack of accountability continuing, many have argued that the European Union needs to go beyond its founding mission of lowering barriers to economic exchange in Europe to reshape its image. One new mission is the protection of rights. There is much talk within the European Union of building a "European citizenship" and much discussion about what that would involve. As T. H. Marshall famously observed, citizenship and rights are intimately related, and some have argued that the creation of EU-protected rights could become part of the foundation of a new European identity.[38] A European Commission committee report in 1996 concluded that "[i]nclusion of civic and social rights in the Treaties would help to nurture [European] citizenship and prevent Europe from being perceived as a bureaucracy assembled by technocratic elites far removed from daily concerns."[39] In 2000, the European Union adopted a nonbinding Charter of Fundamental Rights;[40] some version of this bill of rights may one day be part of a grand constitutional reform that is being proposed for the union. Below the grand level of the charter, meanwhile, smaller rights are regularly being manufactured at the European Union. Although, for example, the U.S. Congress recently decided not to enact an "airline passengers bill of rights," the European Union now has such a law, and its provisions are prominently displayed at all European airports. The airline law may be mere symbolism, but it is symbolism that builds the image of the European Union as a rights protector. Similarly, and more substantively, with the passage of the two discrimination directives, the European Union has put itself at the forefront of civil rights protection in Europe—and for gays and lesbians, religious minorities, people with disabilities, and the other groups protected, the European Union suddenly looks like much more than a trade liberalizer.

EU officials have a more specific interest in disability rights. The embrace of disability rights has greatly enlarged the EU role in disability policy. As long as disability was defined in traditional ways, there was little role for EU involvement in member state policies. The European Union does not have competence to intervene in social security matters, or education, or caregiving, or even most aspects of labor policy. Until the 1997 Amsterdam Treaty, the European Commission's Social Affairs Directorate, the unit responsible for disability, could only sponsor research or initiate information sharing among member states. By embracing the rights model, the directorate suddenly had a new mission, one entirely compatible with founding EU principles. If the problem of disability resulted from social exclusion and discrimination, then it was a matter of market barriers, and the European Union has lots of experience in knocking down such barriers. Disability has become one of a number of policy areas in which the Social Affairs Directorate has justified a stronger role for itself by focusing on exclusion.[41] As Employment and Social Affairs Commissioner Anna Diamantopoulou has argued, because "social exclusion imposes costs which an inclusive society can avoid," social policy has become economic policy.[42] This redefinition of disability as an issue of economic competitiveness has a venerable tradition at the European Union: it parallels the primary rationale for EU-level action on gender equality that began in the 1970s. A series of court rulings and directives on gender equality were justified as market integration measures. In the absence of EU-level action, it was argued that nations that continued to discriminate against women might gain a competitive advantage over their more egalitarian neighbors.[43] As with gender, in disability EU action on discrimination has been justified as compatible with the European Union's founding goal of market liberalization.

Armed with the rights model, EU officials can now attack problems such as inaccessible transport systems and public facilities, and discrimination in the marketplace. If disability is a matter of rights and discrimination, then the European Union, and in particular the European Commission, has a central role to play in European disability policy.[44] The development of the Horizontal Directive, and the disability rights agenda at the European Union, nicely fits Mark Kleinman's description of the way the Commission has expanded its powers in social policy:

> The Commission has shown itself to be an "adept strategist", a "purposeful opportunist". . . . It utilizes the skills and advantages of a bureaucracy, promoting marginal, incremental change. Day by day, through drafting regulations, Eurocrats construct a public policy formulation for further envisaged integration. Hence, non-binding "soft" law creates preconditions for further action. The Commission's research funding role is crucial in expanding the agenda. Having commissioned relevant research, it is able to act at politically opportune moments.[45]

COMPARISONS/CONCLUSIONS

Scholars have identified federalism as a significant cause of litigious policymaking within the United States. Federalism means that in at least some policy realms the center cannot directly command subnational units. In the United States, for example, policing and schooling are primarily local matters, and the attorney general and secretary of education are relatively powerless to command local police and school districts. There are only two techniques national officials can use to steer localities in these realms: bribery, through the provision of federal aid, and regulation, through the creation of rights. The attraction of the second strategy is clear. By creating rights, politicians at the center do good things for constituencies at little cost to themselves. For activists, meanwhile, the rights strategy allows them to simultaneously make progress across many subnational units—the alternative, of reforming each local unit one by one, is a Herculean task. Thus, the rights strategy in the ADA attracted both disability activists and conservatives in the Bush and Reagan administrations.

The development of the European Union as a social policymaking institution makes it analogous in some respects to the national government in the United States, and thus creates the same incentives for activists and policymakers. The European Union has limited budgetary resources and cannot possibly make a significant impact on a huge policy realm such as disability by spending money. Its main power is to regulate.[46] By embracing disability rights, European Commission staff and European Parliament politicians have vastly expanded their power over the disability field, at little cost. They do not even have to worry much about enforcing the regulations they enact, because those tasks are delegated to national governments—and to private litigants. EU officials get all the credit and little of the blame if the implementation process proves controversial. For disability rights activists, meanwhile, the European Union represents a new political opportunity structure that has led to a new form of organization, the transnational European Disability Forum.[47] The forum has created new capacities and resources for disability activists in Europe, facilitating information sharing among national-level disability groups, the development of new policy proposals, and coordination of political efforts. Taken together, the relationship of the forum, disability-sympathetic parliamentarians, and EC staff is beginning to resemble the "public interest triangle" that scholars observed in the 1960s and 1970s in the United States. Each side of the triangle supports the expansion of disability rights and reinforces the efforts of the others.

Further, the case of disability shows that smart, creative activists are reframing social issues as matters of rights while the opposition is more or less dormant—a pattern observed in the United States during the "rights revolution."[48] Indeed, R. Dan Kelemen detects the beginnings of an "EU rights revolution" in Europe, of which disability is just one small component.[49] The most celebrated area of expanding litigation is EU constitutional law, and the development of EU constitutional law offers intriguing parallels to the story told in this chapter. The European Union became "constitutionalized" by rulings at the European Court of Justice (ECJ) that gave private parties the right in some cases to enforce the treaty agreements that form the basis of the European Union. This supplemented the main mechanism for keeping member nations in line with their treaty obligations, the European Commission's infringement process. Because the European Commission cannot handle all the infringement complaints that come before it, it has encouraged private parties to bring such complaints to court and more generally has conducted a campaign to advise citizens, firms, and public interest groups of the opportunity to vindicate European rights in court.[50] Here we see the common element with the disability case: a lack of capacity at the EU level is addressed by giving private parties the right to bring claims against nations. Just as in the United States, the creation of rights to litigate is a way by which a weak center can nonetheless steer the periphery. Multiply this mechanism across realms such as the environment, securities regulation, and civil rights, and it does not seem far-fetched to forecast that courts and law will play a growing role in European social policy.[51]

Yet, there is good reason to be skeptical that American-style adversarial legalism will cross the Atlantic, because European legal systems offer an array of barriers to potential plaintiffs—and alternatives to litigation. Implementation of the Horizontal Directive, for example, will be mediated by national-level legal institutions and practices that discourage litigation. Those institutions and practices vary across Europe, so that implementation, rather than converging on the American model, will likely diverge. Some nations, such as Britain and The Netherlands, have preexisting administrative institutions designed to handle discrimination complaints and will adapt these institutions to meet the requirements of the Horizontal Directive. Others will start from scratch and build a combination of administrative and litigation mechanisms. The case of Sweden, the first continental European nation to adopt a disability rights law that allows individuals to sue, is instructive. Although individual Swedes have the right to bring lawsuits, implementation of the discrimination law is mainly through trade unions and through a specialized government mediator, the disability ombudsman. Sweden, like most European nations, has a "loser pays" rule so that unsuccessful plaintiffs incur not only their own legal fees but also those of defendants. Loser-pays systems can under some circumstances *encourage* litigation, because they allow plaintiffs with small but worthy claims to proceed, knowing that they will win lawyers' fees in addition to a court judgment. But a loser-pays system can also discourage risk-averse plaintiffs, particularly if there is no exception built in for plaintiffs who have few resources to pay a defendant's fees in the event of a loss. Moreover, Swedish law provides comparatively small winnings for a successful plaintiff. Swedish discrimination law has no provision for punitive damages, and "pain and suffering" awards are, by American standards, tiny. There is no provision for an injunction ordering an employer to hire (or rehire) a successful plaintiff and only limited ability to claim lost wages. Because the disability ombudsman and the trade unions have greater capacity than individuals, they can, despite these obstacles, more credibly threaten to sue, but even they are likely to resort to litigation in only a tiny percentage of cases.

Sweden's use of the ombudsman is distinctive, but its plaintiff-unfriendly legal institutions are typical of Europe. Just the lack of a contingency fee—where plaintiff lawyers agree to be paid through a percentage of the winning verdict—represents a major barrier to American-style rights litigation.[52] Could policymakers in the European Union, frustrated with the barriers faced by plaintiffs in discrimination cases, intervene to alter national legal practices toward the more litigious American policy style? In several prominent cases in the late 1980s and early 1990s, the ECJ appeared to do just that. For example, in *Marshall II*, a British cap on awards in sex discrimination cases was struck down because, the ECJ concluded, it made EU antidiscrimination laws ineffective.[53] In *Francovich,* the ECJ held Italy responsible for failing to properly transpose a directive and granted damages to a plaintiff damaged by this failure.[54] For a time it appeared that the requirement of an "effective" remedy could become a lever for harmonization of national legal systems. But in subsequent cases, the ECJ appears to have backed off, and the resulting case law on remedies and procedure is complex, even contradictory.[55] Thus, according to Lisa Conant, "national courts have tremendous discretion over remedies and individuals face unpredictable procedural requirements" in vindicating EU-based rights, and attempts by the European Commission to harmonize rules for remedies and state liability have been turned back by the member nations.[56] Although EU institutions have pushed European legal systems in a slightly more litigious direction, it would take a rather large shove to make disability rights enforcement a court-centered enterprise in Europe. Indeed, disability may be one of the realms in which convergence toward American adversarial legalism is *least* likely, because the legal institutions required to advance it seem most fundamental and resistant to change. Convergence toward the American experience would require the European Union to mandate vastly expanded remedies, abolition of restrictions on contingency fees, and modification of the loser-pays rule. Kelemen sees several developments that could facilitate litigation, including liberalized rules of standing, changes in the organization of law firms, and expansions in government-supplied legal aid.[57] These developments may encourage some disability organizations to bring cases (and employers and managers to defend such lawsuits vigorously), but they are not likely to make nondiscrimination litigation attractive to private parties.

That, however, is not the end of the story. The embrace of nondiscrimination law in Europe can have substantial effects even in the absence of a "litigation explosion." The consequences depend on whether the nondiscrimination ideal, now enshrined in a modest law, will be extended further to reshape other aspects of disability policy. The Horizontal Directive was, even for the national governments, a relatively easy step, because it involved no great governmental costs and no disruption of existing programs. Disability advocates are now pressing for a nondiscrimination law covering programs and services, a policy that might involve huge expenses and much greater social change, especially in transportation. Beyond this, there is the question of whether the nondiscrimination ideal will penetrate European labor and welfare policy. As many observers have noted, there is a tension between the civil rights approach to disability and the traditional social welfare disability policies of Europe.[58] Polities often live with such tensions, and there is no reason to believe that there will be a grand collision between the rights and social welfare models. But there may be smaller crashes. For example, the sheltered-workshops and wage-subsidy programs that help raise the level of employment among people with disabilities in many European nations do not grant participants standard labor law protections and thus may run afoul of antidiscrimination laws. It is quite conceivable that a judge at the national level, or even at the European Court of Justice, might one day rule them illegal. Even in the absence of widespread American-style discrimination litigation, then, a few key cases might challenge the basic premises of the social welfare approach to disability. At that point there would be no question of the power of the nondiscrimination ideal in European disability policy.

NOTES

1. Alexis de Tocqueville, *Democracy in America*, trans. George Lawrence, ed. J. P. Mayer (New York: Harper and Rowe), 167.

2. Thomas F. Burke, *Lawyers, Lawsuits and Legal Rights: The Battle over Litigation in American Society* (Berkeley: University of California Press, 2002); Robert A Kagan, *Adversarial Legalism: The American Way of Law* (Cambridge, MA: Harvard University Press, 2001); and Robert A. Kagan and Lee Axelrad, *Regulatory Encounters: Multinational Corporations and American Adversarial Legalism* (Berkeley: University of California Press, 2000).

3. Jacob S. Hacker, *The Divided Welfare State: The Battle over Public and Private Social Benefits in the United States* (New York: Cambridge University Press, 2002); Christopher Howard, *The Hidden Welfare State: Tax Expenditures and Social Policy in the United States* (Princeton, N.J.: Princeton University Press, 1997).

4. European Commission, *Council Directive 2000/78/EC of 27 November 2000 Establishing a General Framework for Equal Treatment in Employment and Occupation*, [2000] O.J. L. 303/16.

5. Bryan Garth and Yves Dezelay, "Merchants of Law as Moral Entrepreneurs: Constructing International Justice from the Competition for Transnational Business Disputes," *Law and Society Review* 29 (1995):27–64.

6. Robert A. Kagan, "Should Europe Worry about Adversarial Legalism?" *Oxford Journal of Legal Studies* 17 (1997):1.

7. Alex Stone Sweet, *Governing with Judges: Constitutional Politics in Europe* (New York: Oxford University Press, 2000).

8. C. Neil Tate and Torban Vallinder, eds., *The Global Expansion of Judicial Power* (New York: New York University Press, 1995); Charles R. Epp, *The Rights Revolution: Lawyers, Activists, and Supreme Courts in Comparative Perspective* (Chicago: University of Chicago, 1998).

9. Kagan, Adversarial Legalism; Burke, Lawyers, Lawsuits and Legal Rights, 15.

10. R. Dan Kelemen's chapter on environmental policymaking in this book raises this specter in another context.

11. Using questions from federal surveys—the Survey on Income and Program Participation, the Current Population Survey, and the National Health Interview Survey—one can estimate the percentage of people with disabilities widely, from a low of 8.2 per-

cent to a high of 21.5 percent. Richard V. Burkhauser, Andrew J. Houtenville, and David C. Wittenberg, "A User Guide to Current Statistics on the Employment of People with Disabilities," paper presented to the Conference on the Persistence of Low Employment Rates of People with Disabilities—Cause and Policy Implications, October 18–19, 2001, Washington, D.C., table 1A. The preamble of the ADA, enacted in 1990, claims there are 43 million people with disabilities (*U.S. Code*, vol. 42, sec. 12101(a)1). On the complexity of operationalizing "disability," see Glenn T. Fujiura and Violet Rutkowski-Kmitta, "Counting Disability" in *Handbook of Disability Studies*, ed. Gary Albrecht et al. (Thousand Oaks, CA: Sage Publications, 2001), 69–96.

12. European Disability Forum, *Disability and Social Exclusion in the European Union: Time for Change, Tools for Change* (2002). A recent OECD report estimates that 14 percent of working-age people in OECD nations are disabled. OECD, *Transforming Disability into Ability: Policies to Promote Work and Income Security for Disabled People* (2003), chart 3.1, 24.

13. Cited in Richard Scotch and Sharon N. Barnartt, *Disability Protests: Contentious Politics, 1970–1999* (Washington, DC: Gallaudet University Press, 2002), 275.

14. Leo J. M. Aarts, Richard V. Burkhauser, and Philip R. de Jong, "Introduction and Overview" in *Curing the Dutch Disease*, ed. Leo J. M. Aarts (Brookfield, VT: Avebury, 1996), table 1.1, 5; table 1.2, 7. On policy responses to the "Dutch Disease," see Wim Van Oorschot and Kees Boos, "The Battle against Numbers: Disability Policies in The Netherlands" in *Disability Policies in European Countries*, ed. Wim van Oorschot and Bjorn Hvinden (The Hague, Netherlands: Kluwer, 2001), 53–71.

15. Martha Minow, *Making All the Difference: Inclusion, Exclusion, and American Law* (Ithaca: Cornell University Press, 1990).

16. A variant is the title of Richard Scotch's book on Section 504, *From Good Will to Civil Rights* (Philadelphia: Temple University Press, 1984).

17. Scotch and Barnartt, *Disability Protests: Contentious Politics, 1970–1999*; Thomas F. Burke, "On the Rights Track: The Americans with Disabilities Act," in *Comparative Disadvantages? American Social Regulation and the Global Economy*, ed. Pietro Nivola (Washington, DC: The Brookings Institution, 1997); Doris James Fleischer and Frieda Zames, *The Disability Rights Movement: From Charity to Confrontation* (Philadelphia: Temple University Press, 2001); Robert A. Katzmann, *Institutional Disability: The Saga of Transportation Policy for the Disabled* (Washington, DC: Brookings Institution Press, 1986); Ruth O'Brien, *Crippled Justice: The History of Modern Disability Policy in the Workplace* (Chicago: University of Chicago Press, 2001); Joseph P. Shapiro, *No Pity: People with Disabilities Forging a New Civil Rights Movement* (New York: Times Books, 1993).

18. Paul K. Langmore and David Golberger, "The League of the Physically Handicapped and the Great Depression: A Case Study in the New Disability History," *Journal of American History* 87 (2000):888–922.

19. Jacobus ten Broek, "The Right To Live in the World: The Disabled and the Law of Torts," *California Law Review* 54 (1966):846.

20. Katzmann, *Institutional Disability*, 46–47; Scotch, *From Goodwill*, 41–43.

21. National Council on the Handicapped, *Toward Independence* (1988).

22. Burke, "On the Rights Track."

23. Richard V. Burkhauser, Marcy C. Daly, and Andrew J. Houtenville, "How Working Age People with Disabilities Fared over the 1990s Business Cycle," paper presented at the National Association on Social Insurance Conference on Ensuring Health and Income Security for an Aging Workforce, January 26–27, 2000, Washington, D.C.

24. Douwe Van Houten and Conny Bellemakers, "Equal Citizenship for All: Disability Policies in The Netherlands: Empowerment of Marginals" (unpublished manuscript, 2002).

25. Mark Kleinman, *A European Welfare State? European Union Social Policy in Context* (New York: Palgrave, 2002), 90. Writing in 1995, Paul Pierson and Stephan Liebfried argued, "The institutional, political, cultural and technical barriers to extending EU social policy are high." Nonetheless, Pierson and Liebfried foresaw several mechanisms that would lead to the continued expansion of EU social policymaking. Paul Pierson and Stephan Liebfried, "The Making of Social Policy," in *European Social Policy: Between Fragmentation and Integration* (Washington, DC: Brookings Institution Press, 1995), 11. Some of the mechanisms Pierson and Liebfried describe, in particular the role of EU organizations in advocating social policy expansion and the activity of nonstate European-level actors, are important in my account of disability politics. But the key mechanism in my narrative is the *redefinition* of disability policy as a matter of either trade liberalization or fundamental human rights.

26. Lisa Waddington, "The European Community's Response to Disability," in *Disability, Diversability and Legal Change*, ed. Melinda Jones and Lee Anne Basser Marks (London: Kluwer, 1999), 139–52; Gerard Quinn, "The Human Rights of People with Disabilities under EU Law," in *The EU and Human Rights*, ed. Philip Alston (London: Oxford University Press, 2000), 303–10.

27. For example, disability advocates established a "European Day of Disabled Persons" and used the organizing committee to publish a report focusing on discrimination against people with disabilities and the lack of a European remedy (European Day of Disabled Persons 1995, *Invisible Citizens: Disabled Persons' Status in the European Treaties*, December 7, 1995; European Day of Disabled Persons 1996, *Towards the Equalisation of Opportunities for Disabled People: Into the Mainstream?* 1996.

28. European Commission, *Green Paper: European Social Policy—Options for the Union*, COM(93)551 final.

29. European Commission, *White Paper: European Social Policy: A Way Forward for the Union*, COM(94)333 final.

30. *Proposal for a Council Directive Establishing a General Framework for Equal Treatment in Employment and Occupation*, COM(99)565 final.

31. Mark Bell, *Anti-Discrimination Law and the European Union* (New York: Oxford University Press, 2002), 74.

32. Bell, *Anti-Discrimination Law and the European Union*, 113.

33. *Council Directive 2000/78/EC of 27 November 2000*, Article 17.

34. *Council Directive 2001/85/EC of 20 November 2001*.

35. Margaret E. Keck and Kathryn Sikkink, *Activists beyond Borders: Advocacy Networks in International Politics* (Ithaca, NY: Cornell University Press, 1998).

36. *The EDF Proposal for a Disability-Specific Directive*. www.edf-feph.org/en/policy /nondisc/nondflpol.htm.

37. Deborah Mabbett and Helen Bolderson, "A Significant Step Forward? EU Social Policy and the Development of a Rights-Based Strategy for Disabled People" (unpublished manuscript, 2002).

38. T. H. Marshall, *Citizenship and Social Class* (Cambridge: Cambridge University Press, 1950); Philippe C. Schmitter, "The Scope of Citizenship in a Democratized European Union," in *European Citizenship: Between National Legacies and Postnational Projects*, ed. Klaus Eder and Bernhard Giesen (New York: Oxford, 2001), 86–121.

39. *For a Europe of Civic and Social Rights*, report by Comité des Sages, cited in Catherine Bernard, "Article 13: Through the Looking Glass of Union Citizenship," in *Legal Issues of the Amsterdam Treaty*, ed. David O'Keeffe and Patrick Twomey (Portland, OR: Hart Publishing, 1999), 376.

40. *Charter of Fundamental Rights*, www.europarl.eu.int/charter/defaultflen.htm.

41. Bryan Wendon, "The Commission as Image-Venue Entrepreneur in EU Social Policy," *Journal of European Public Policy* 5 (June 1998):339–53.

42. Anna Diamantopolou, European Commissioner for Employment and Social Affairs, "New Social Trends in Europe," speech to the Foreign Correspondent's Club of Japan, Tokyo, Japan, March 7, 2000.

43. Mark Bell describes the premises of the "market integration model" of EU anti-discrimination rights in his book, *Anti-Discrimination Law and the European Union*, 7–12.

44. Interview with European Commission staff.

45. Kleinman, *A European Welfare State?* 121.

46. Laura Cram, "Calling the Tune without Paying the Piper? Social Policy Regulations: The Role of the Commission in European Community Social Policy," *Policy and Politics* 21 (1993):135–46.

47. On the role of political opportunity structures in social movement theory, see Sidney Tarrow, "States and Opportunities: The Political Structuring of Social Movements," in *Comparative Perspectives on Social Movements: Political Opportunities, Mobilizing Structures, and Cultural Framings*, ed. Doug McAdam, John D. McCarthy, and Mayer N. Zald (Cambridge: Cambridge University Press, 1996).

48. See generally Marc K. Landy and Martin A. Levin, eds., *The New Politics of Public Policy* (Baltimore: Johns Hopkins University Press, 1995).

49. R. Daniel Kelemen, "The EU Rights Revolution: Adversarial Legalism and European Integration," in *The State of the European Union: Law, Politics, and Society*, ed. Tanja A. Borzel and Rachel A. Cichowski (New York: Oxford University Press, 2003), 221–34.

50. Tanja A. Borzel, "Guarding the Treaty: The Compliance Strategies of the European Commission," in *The State of the European Union: Law, Politics, and Society*, ed. Tanja A. Borzel and Rachel A. Cichowski (New York: Oxford University Press, 2003), 205; Lisa Conant, *Justice Contained: Law and Politics in the European Union* (Ithaca, NY: Cornell University Press, 2002), 78.

51. Kelemen suggests another way in which the structure of the EU encourages the use of courts: the multiple-veto structure of EU institutions both makes it hard to revise policies once enacted into law and gives bureaucrats considerable discretion. This in turn encourages legislators to draft detailed laws and use courts to try to enforce them. Kelemen, "The EU Rights Revolution," 223. Robert A. Kagan and I have proposed similar accounts to explain the use of litigation in American public policy; see Burke, *Lawyers, Lawsuits and Legal Rights*, and Kagan, *Adversarial Legalism: The American Way of Law.*

52. David S. Clark reports that although the contingency fee is "making inroads," it is still banned in most civil law countries. Clark, "Comparing the Work and Organization of Lawyers Worldwide: The Persistence of Legal Traditions," in *Lawyers' Practice and Ideals: A Comparative View*, ed. John J. Barcelo and Roger C. Cramton (The Hague, Netherlands: Kluwer, 1999), 143–44.

53. Case C271/91 *Marshall v. Southampton & South West Area Health Authority* [1993] ECR 1-4367.

54. Cases C-6 and 9/90 *Francovich and Bonifaci v. Italy* [1991] ECR 1-5357.

55. Takis Tridimas, "Enforcing Community Rights in National Courts: Some Recent Developments," in *The Future of Remedies in Europe*, Claire Kirkpatrick, ed. (Portland, OR: Hart Publishing, 2000), 35–50.

56. Lisa Conant, *Justice Contained*, 61.

57. Keleman, "The EU Rights Revolution," 225–29.

58. See, for example, Lisa Waddington and Matthew Diller, "Tensions and Coherence in Disability Policy: The Uneasy Relationship between Social Welfare and Civil Rights Models of Disability in American, European and International Employment Law," in *Disability Rights Law and Policy: International and National Perspectives* (New York: Transaction, 2002), 241–308.

THE HARE AND THE TORTOISE REVISITED

The New Politics of Risk Regulation in Europe and the United States

DAVID VOGEL

INTRODUCTION

IN THIS CHAPTER, I DESCRIBE AND EXPLAIN AN IMPORTANT SHIFT IN THE PATTERN OF consumer and environmental protection policies in Europe and the United States. From the 1960s through the early 1990s, American regulatory standards tended to be more comprehensive, risk averse, and innovative than in either individual European countries or in the European Union (EU). However, since the mid-1990s, the reverse has often been the case: during the last fifteen years, a number of significant regulatory standards promulgated by the European Union have been more comprehensive, risk averse, and innovative than those adopted by the United States.

To borrow Lennart Lundqvist's formulation, which he used to contrast American and Swedish air pollution control standards during the 1970s, since around 1990 the American "hare" has been moving forward at a tortoise pace, while the pace of the European "tortoise" more closely resembles that of a hare.[1] To employ a different metaphor, in a number of significant respects European and American regulatory politics have traded places. Previously, regulatory issues were more politically salient and civic interests more influential in the United States than in most individual European countries or the European Union. More recently, the reverse has been true. Consequently, over the last ten to fifteen years, the locus of policy innovation with respect to many areas of consumer and environmental regulation has passed from the United States to Europe.

In an essay published in 1990 titled "American Exceptionalism and the Political Economy of Risk," Jasanoff writes that while "the U.S. process for making risk decisions impressed all observers as costly, confrontational . . . and unusually open to participation," in Europe, "policy decisions about risk, remained, as before, the preserve of experienced bureaucrats and their established advisory networks."[2] Her generalization about European and American policy styles and the policy consequences that flow from them are echoed in virtually every comparative regulatory study published during the 1970s and 1980s.[3] This generalization must now be reexamined. The "American approach" to health, safety, and environmental regulation is no longer as distinctive as it appeared to scholars during the 1970s and 1980s.[4]

Yet the result has not been increased policy convergence, because recent European regulatory politics and policies resemble those of the United States of the 1970s and 1980s, not the 1990s. Since the early 1990s, consumer and environmental problems in the United States have lost much of their sense of urgency, and regulatory issues have become less politically salient. As a result, political pressures for additional regulation have declined. Yet, at the same time, there is little support for rolling back previously enacted standards. The result has been political stalemate: after more than two decades of relatively steady expansion, American consumer and environmental regulation has changed only marginally since the early 1990s.

But while the regulatory policy window has narrowed in the United States, it has opened wider in Europe. Thus, notwithstanding the powerful pressures of economic globalization, many important European and American risk management policies in the areas of consumer and environment protection remain divergent.

This chapter focuses primarily on changes in regulatory policies and politics in Europe. It argues that these changes are caused by three interrelated factors: a series of regulatory failures that have created a substantial gap between public expectations and policy effectiveness, the increased political influence of proregulation interest groups and political parties within several member states and the European Union, and the growing regulatory competence of the European Union. The latter's institutional structure and political environment have facilitated the development of an expanded European "regulatory state" in a number of ways. In particular, its decision-making structure has both magnified the political influence of the "greener" member states and provided representatives of civic interests with multiple points of access to the policy process, in part by increasing the policy role of the European Parliament. Politically, the European Union's commitment to the maintenance of a single market has provided policymakers with an important incentive to support relatively stringent standards in order to maintain public support for European integration—a policy commitment that has been reinforced by each successive constitutional treaty.

This chapter begins by exploring the emergence and significance of the precautionary principle within Europe. It then describes some of the specific ways in which the relative stringency and scope of European and American regulatory standards have shifted since around 1990. The final sections of the chapter explain why regulatory politics and policies have changed in both Europe and the United States—although in opposite directions.

THE PRECAUTIONARY PRINCIPLE AND REGULATORY REFORM

The increased legal and political influence of the precautionary principle represents an important dimension of the new European approach to health, safety, and environmental standards. This principle legitimates regulation when

> potentially dangerous effects deriving from a phenomenon, product or process have been identified, and . . . scientific evaluation does not allow the risk to be determined with sufficient certainty [because] of the insufficiency of the data or their inconclusive or imprecise nature.[5]

Originally developed in Germany during the 1970s and 1980s, it was incorporated in the 1993 Treaty of the European Union and, since 1994, it has been referenced in more than thirty reports and resolutions of the European Parliament.

Although the precautionary principle cannot be divorced from science, because "a scientific view of the risk is an essential component of the evaluation of risk that the principle anticipates," its growing popularity in Europe reflects the perception that scientific knowledge is an inadequate guide to regulatory policy.[6] It requires the extension of scientific knowledge while simultaneously acknowledging "the possible intrinsic limitations of scientific knowledge in providing the appropriate information in good time."[7] In effect, it reduces the scientific threshold for regulatory policymaking. By mandating or precluding regulatory action, in advance of scientifically confirmed cause–effect relationships, the principle "curtails the ability of politicians to invoke scientific uncertainty as a justification for avoiding or delaying the imposition of more stringent protection measures."[8]

Although its legal significance at both the EU and national level remains unclear, the practical effect of the precautionary principle has frequently been to permit, or even mandate, the adoption of more risk-averse policies. It explicitly acknowledges the inherently political nature of regulatory decision making by enabling policymakers to take into account a wide variety of nonscientific factors, including public opinion and social values. As Jordan and O'Riordan observe,

> The stringency with which the precautionary principle is applied depends upon and is also a useful barometer of deeper social and economic changes. Precautionary measures, for example, are most likely to be applied when public opinion is instinctively or knowledgeably risk-averse.[9]

The frequency with which the precautionary principle has been evoked in Europe among both activists and policymakers also has an ideological dimension. It reflects not only a decline in the role of science as a guide to policymaking, but also a decrease in public confidence in the benefits of technological innovation. Frequently underlying its invocation is the assumption that modern technology poses dangers of which we are unaware and that to avoid future harm we need to introduce new technologies more cautiously. As Corrine Lepage, the former French environment minister, writes in her coauthored book on the precautionary principle, "The precautionary principle precisely responds to the need for prudence when faced with the consequences of technological progress, whose repercussions are exponential and unknown."[10] For many environmentalists, this is precisely one of its most important attractions.

Yet, somewhat paradoxically, European regulatory administration is also becoming more scientifically rigorous. At both the national and the EU levels, there is increased recognition of the need to strengthen the capacity of government agencies to conduct risk assessments and to improve the quality of scientific information available to decision makers. An important factor underlying this development is an increase in judicial review of regulatory decisions at both the European and international levels.[11] Just as American regulatory agencies conducted risk assessments in order to be able to defend their decisions in federal court from challenges by both public interest groups and industry, so Europe's national authorities and the European Union are undertaking similar steps in order to defend their decisions before the European Court of Justice (ECJ) and World Trade Organization (WTO) dispute panels.

European regulatory institutions have also changed. In particular, to improve the quality of regulatory decision making, risk assessment is increasingly being separated from risk management. The former is the advice and information scientists provide to policymakers; the latter is what policymakers decide. This separation has been institutionalized at the EU level by the establishment of regulatory agencies such as the new food safety agency, which will perform risk assessments, with policy decisions made by the commission. Similar models have been adopted for food safety agencies in France and Britain. This separation has a number of purposes. Most obviously, it is designed to prevent "regulatory capture" by making regulatory policymaking more transparent: when risk assessments are made public, the public can determine the extent to which political officials are accepting or ignoring the relevant scientific advice. Second, it enables policymakers to take into account considerations beyond science in making regulatory decisions, such as public attitudes. Third, it protects the integrity of the risk assessors because their only role is to provide scientific information to policymakers. But perhaps most important, it makes policymakers more politically accountable for regulatory policymaking: if irreversible harm results from their decision or nondecision, it is now clearer whom to blame.

THE HISTORICAL CONTEXT

From the 1960s through the early 1990s, consumer and environmental protection standards were typically more stringent in America than in Europe. According to a comprehensive comparative study of chemical regulation published in 1985, more often than not, the United States was the first country to take significant restrictive action on suspected or confirmed human carcinogens.[12] For example, the U.S. Environmental Protection Agency (EPA) found the pesticides aldrin and deildrin to be carcinogenic, although on the basis of the same studies

British authorities concluded that they did not present a risk of cancer.[13] The United States subsequently banned most uses of these pesticides, whereas Britain imposed no restrictions. Red Dye No. 2 was banned in the United States, whereas its use was only restricted in Europe.[14] In 1971, the EPA banned DDT, whereas its use was only restricted in Britain, Germany, and France; nearly a decade elapsed before it was banned by the European Union.

Furthermore, many American chemical regulations were also more stringent and comprehensive. The 1958 Delaney clause to the Food, Drug and Cosmetic Act, which banned the use of any food additive if tests revealed that it caused cancer in either laboratory animals or humans on the grounds that such chemicals could cause irreversible harm, had no counterpart in any European country. The 1976 American Toxic Substances Control Act (TSCA) established regulations for both new and existing chemicals, whereas the European Union's 1979 Sixth Amendment only established regulatory procedures for approving new chemicals. (French, British, and German national law did contain provisions for reviewing existing chemicals, but only in exceptional circumstances.) A similar pattern held with respect to pesticide approval and renewals; American statutes enacted in 1972 and 1978 required more comprehensive reviews of existing pesticides than did either EU regulations or those of any member state.[15]

In the critical area of automotive emission standards, the American standards enacted in 1970 and 1977 were consistently stricter than the five increasingly stringent standards enacted by the European Union between 1970 and 1985.[16] For example, while the United States enacted legislation requiring all new cars to be equipped with catalytic converters and thus use only unleaded gasoline in 1970, the European Union did not adopt a similar requirement until 1989. During the 1980s, Sweden, Denmark, and Germany, three of Europe's most consistent environmental innovators, phased in standards comparable to those of the United States.[17]

During the mid-1970s, the issue of ozone layer depletion emerged as a major political issue in the United States. Although there was considerable unscientific certainty about both the causes and magnitude of this environmental problem, the 1977 Clean Air Act Amendments authorized restrictions on chlorofluorocarbons (CFCs) on the grounds that a "reasonable expectation" of harm was sufficient to generate regulatory action.[18] However, even before this law was passed, the EPA, acting under authority of TSCA, moved to prohibit the use of CFCs as aerosol propellants in nonessential applications. This decision affected nearly three billion dollars' worth of household products. Within three years, nearly the entire U.S. aerosol market had switched to non-CFC technologies. By contrast, in Europe, the issue of ozone depletion was less politically salient and the political influence of chemical producers much greater. The European Union initially refused to act, but in 1980, in response to American pressures, it agreed to a 30 percent decrease from 1976 levels by 1981—a reduction characterized by one European scholar as "a minimum solution."[19] Subsequently, the Montreal Protocol phased out the use of ozone-depleting chemicals on both sides of the Atlantic.

In the area of consumer protection, the United States established more stringent standards for the approval of prescription drugs than did any European country. After the scandal surrounding the near approval of thalidomide by the Food
and Drug Administration (FDA), in 1962 Congress enacted the Kefauver amendments to the Food, Drug and Cosmetic Act. This legislation significantly increased
both the time and expense for securing approval for new prescription drugs in the
United States. The result was a substantial cross-Atlantic "drug lag," with new
drugs typically approved years earlier in Germany and Great Britain than in the
United States.[20] According to a U.S. Government Accounting Office study that
tracked the introduction of fourteen significant new drugs, thirteen were available
in Europe years before they were approved for use in the United States.

In sum, "studies of public health, safety and environmental regulation published in the 1980s revealed striking differences between American and European
practices for managing technological risks." Moreover, "these studies showed that
U.S. regulators were quicker to respond to new risks, more aggressive in pursuing
old ones."[21] But since the early 1990s, in a wide range of policy areas, it is now European regulators who have become "quicker to respond to new risks, more aggressive in pursuing old ones."

THE NEW EUROPEAN RISK REGIME

One important area in which EU policies have become more stringent than in
the United States is food safety. Europe and the United States have historically had
different food cultures, with many European consumers and some governments
more willing to accept the risks of traditional foods such as raw milk cheeses and
cured meats than the United States, whereas Americans have been more open to
new food technologies.[22] However, differences between European and American
food safety regulations have since become more pronounced. A 1985 Council of
Ministers directive banned the use of all growth hormones for cattle. The directive's approval followed a vigorous public campaign led by the Bureau of European Consumer Unions, a coalition of national consumer unions. Although the
European Union's own scientific advisory bodies subsequently concluded that the
five disputed hormones did not pose a threat to human health, and the European
producers of the hormones vigorously opposed the ban, in the end public pressures proved decisive. As Franz Andreissen, the EC's farm commissioner, put it,
"Scientific advice is important, but it is not decisive. In public opinion, this is a
very delicate issue that has to be dealt with in political terms."[23] By contrast, in the
United States, the safety of the five growth hormones never entered the political
agenda.

A related area in which the European Union and the United States adopted divergent policies involved BST, a hormone designed to boost milk production. The
European Union imposed a moratorium on its use in 1989, which was made permanent in 1999. According to an EU official, the Commission feared a "consumer

backlash. . .it's not easy to explain to consumers that everything is all right when you are injecting drugs into cows."[24] By contrast, notwithstanding a determined effort by consumer groups, and some small milk producers, BST was approved for use in the United States in 1993.[25] Similarly, in 1989, the European Union banned the use of most antibiotics in animal feed and in 2001 announced plans to ban all use of antibiotics as growth-promoters by 2006. No comparable restrictions have to date been imposed in the United States. American regulations governing food irradiation have also been more permissive than those adopted by the European Union in 1997. Although the European Union banned the use of mammal-based proteins (farines) for all animals in 2000, the United States continues to permit their use in feed for farm animals other than cattle.[26]

The European Union has adopted a much more extensive array of animal protection measures than the United States, including, for example, banning the use of leg-hold traps for capturing wild animals in 1991. In contrast, the United States adopted only a partial ban following pressures from the European Union in 1997.[27] In 1999, the European Union issued strict standards for the size of cages for battery hens and for the treatment of animals in transit. Such rules remain nonexistent in the United States.

The regulation of genetically modified (GM) foods and seeds in Europe and America provides a striking illustration of the pattern of recent European and American approaches to consumer and environmental regulation.[28] The United States initially chose to regulate both GM foods and seeds under existing laws, whereas EU legislation established a distinctive and complex set of new regulatory requirements that apply only to this new agricultural technology. However, when EU standards for the commercial authorization of agricultural biotechnology were first issued in 1990, they did not differ substantially from those of the United States. But after opposition to GM seeds and foods surfaced in Europe in the mid-1990s, European regulatory policies became increasingly restrictive. To date, whereas the European Union has issued eighteen licenses for biotechnology products, including for nine GM crops,[29] the U.S. Department of Agriculture has approved fifty[30] and the EPA has approved eight.[31] Nearly three-quarters of the world's GM crop acreage is in the United States; hardly any is in Europe. The European Union and a number of member states have enacted strict labeling requirements for GM products, but the United States requires only that such products be labeled if they differ from their non-GM counterparts. As of December 2003, the European Union had not approved any new seed strains for more than five years, and the marketing of new food products under the Novel Foods Regulation (1997) was effectively halted. Foods grown from GM seeds are seldom found in European stores, largely because of EU labeling requirements, but their use is pervasive in the United States, where there are, in effect, no labeling requirements.

Recent cases of more stringent or innovative European consumer and environmental regulations are not confined to food safety or agriculture. Although public or quasipublic ecolabeling schemes spread from Germany and Sweden to much of Europe during the second half of the 1980s and were adopted by the European

Union in 1992, they continue to play little role in the United States.[32] In 1994, both inspired and pressured by policies previously adopted by Germany and Denmark, the European Union established ambitious recycling targets for glass, paper, plastics, and aluminium.[33] In the United States, there are no federal regulations governing packaging wastes, and recycling requirements remain governed by local laws, which are typically less stringent and comprehensive than the 1994 EU directive.

In 2000, the European Union approved an automobile recycling directive, which, in addition to providing for the collection of vehicles at the end of their useful life, requires car makers to recycle or reuse 80 percent of car weight by 2006 and 85 percent by 2015. It also bans the use of heavy metals such as lead, mercury, and cadmium as of 2003.[34] A 2003 EU directive made manufacturers responsible for the "life cycle" of all electronic products. This directive mandates collection standards for ten categories of products including all household appliances and telecommunications equipment. A related directive phases out and ultimately prohibits the use of heavy metals such as lead, mercury, and cadmium in electronic products and batteries in order to promote recycling and reduce the toxicity of solid wastes and thus protect landfills. Neither regulation is on the national political agenda in the United States, and there have been only limited policy initiatives at the state level. The 1990 U.S. Clean Air Act Amendments did continue the pattern of more stringent American automotive emission standards, although in the case of heavy-duty vehicles, EU standards adopted in 1998 are more stringent than those of the United States.[35]

The European Union has also replaced the leadership role of the United States in addressing global environmental problems. Through the 1980s, most major international environmental agreements—most notably the London Convention on Dumping at Sea (1972), the Conventional on International Trade in Endangered Fauna and Flora (1973), and the Montreal Protocol (1987), which phased out the use of CFCs to protect the ozone layer—were both initiated and strongly supported by the United States and subsequently ratified by either individual European countries or the European Union. "Since the early 1990s, however, effective U.S. international environmental policy leadership has lapsed."[36] By contrast, by 1994 the Basel Convention on Hazardous Wastes (1989) had been ratified by every EU member state but has yet to be ratified by the United States. Both the Convention on Biological Diversity (1992) and the Biosafety Protocol (2000) were signed by the European Union, but not by the United States.

The European Union, as well as each of the member states, has ratified the Kyoto Protocol (2002–03) an international treaty to reduce emissions of greenhouse gases, and a number of European nations have established policies to reduce carbon emissions. The United States refused to ratify the 1997 Kyoto Protocol, was not a party to the 2001 Bonn agreement, and has no federal controls on carbon emissions. Nor are any likely in the foreseeable future.

The change in the relationship between European and American consumer and environmental standards can also be seen in the pattern of trade disputes between the European Union and the United States.[37] Earlier transatlantic trade disputes typically involved complaints by the European Union or its member states about the American use of regulatory standards as nontariff barriers. Thus, complaints were filed about American automotive fuel economy standards (adopted in 1975), Superfund taxes (adopted in 1986), and a ban on tuna imports to protect dolphins (adopted in 1990). But for complaints based on policies of more recent origin, it is the United States that has typically challenged European regulations as nontariff barriers. With the exception of the 1985 beef hormone ban, the European policies about which the United States has complained have been enacted since 1990. These include the EU's leg-trap ban (1991), ecolabeling standards (1992), and, most important, restrictions on the sale and labeling of foods grown from GM seeds (1990, 1997 through present).

Table 6.1 provides a schematic overview of changes in the relative stringency of European and American consumer and environmental regulations.

In some cases, American standards have remained more stringent, whereas in other cases European and American standards have both become more stringent. But compared to the 1970s and 1980s, since around 1990 European standards are more likely to be relatively more stringent than their American counterparts.

Table 6.1. Relative Stringency of European and American Regulations

	1970s–1990		1990s–2002	
	EU	*U.S.*	*EU*	*U.S.*
Agriculture				
1. Beef hormones	x[a]			
2. Milk hormones	x	x	x	
3. Antibiotics in animal feed			x	
4. Genetically modified agriculture			x	
5. Battery hen cages			x	
6. Leg-hold traps			x	
Industry				
7. Automobile emissions		x		x
8. Chemicals		x		x
9. Packaging recycling			x	
10. Automobile recycling			x	
11. Electronics recycling			x	
12. Ozone protection		x	x	x
13. Curb on greenhouse gases			x	
14. Ecolabeling			x	
15. Ban on heavy metals in electronics and cars			x	

[a]Denotes a relatively stringent standard.

EXPLAINING THE NEW EUROPEAN REGULATORY REGIME

What accounts for these changes in European regulatory policies and institutions? Explaining a complex set of developments over a period of nearly two decades presents a difficult analytical challenge. However, three interrelated factors appear to have contributed to these policy shifts. They are a series of regulatory failures and crises, the broadening of political support for more risk-averse regulatory policies within Europe, and the growth of the regulatory competence of the European Union.

THE REGULATORY FAILURE CYCLE

A key factor contributing to the increased stringency of health, safety, and environmental regulation in Europe has been a series of regulatory failures and crises that placed new regulatory issues on the political agenda and pressured policymakers to adopt more risk-averse or precautionary policies. The effect of each crisis has been cumulative, making public opinion progressively more risk averse, more skeptical of scientific expertise, and more mistrustful of existing regulatory institutions. Each crisis has also spilled over into unrelated policy areas.

The year 1986 witnessed both the nuclear accident at Chernobyl and the Sandoz chemical fire on the Rhine, both of which had significant transborder health and environmental consequences. The *Washington Post* observed in December 1988: "Dead seals in the North Sea, a chemical fire on the Loire, killer algae off the coast of Sweden, contaminated drinking water in Cornwall. A drumbeat of emergencies has intensified the environmental debate this year in Europe, where public concern about pollution has never been higher."[38] According to Elizabeth Bomberg,

> These disasters made an impact. In 1992, the protection of the environment and the fight against pollution had become an "immediate and urgent problem" in the view of 85% of EU citizens. . . . Eurobarometer surveys in 1989 and the early 1990s registered up to 91% of EU citizens expressing support for a common European policy for protecting the environment. . . . Questions on the environment evoked stronger and more positive support for unified EU action than did questions concerning any other area of policy.[39]

During the latter half of the 1990s, Europeans experienced a second wave of crises, this time involving food safety. The most important of these was mad cow disease.[40] When BSE (bovine spongiform encephalopathy) was first detected in cattle in the U.K. in 1982, the European Commission accepted assurances from the British Ministry of Agriculture that it posed no danger to humans. Subsequently, Britain was forced to notify other EU member states of a potential food safety problem, especially after scientific studies showed the disease was transmittable to mice. Following a massive outbreak of BSE in 1989–1990, the European Community banned human consumption of meat from the affected cattle. Although concern among the British public over the health effects of eating meat of BSE-diagnosed cattle continued to grow throughout the 1990s, the British government denied the legitimacy of the public's concerns. Its position was accepted by the European Commission, which placed only limited restrictions on the sale of British beef.

The crisis over BSE broke in 1996 in the United Kingdom, when the British government announced that ten cases of Creutzfeld-Jakob disease had been diagnosed in humans and that these cases were likely related to exposure to cattle with BSE. The commission responded by issuing a global ban on the export of British beef and requiring widespread slaughter of cattle in Britain and, to a lesser extent, in other member states. Although both the commission and its scientific advisory body subsequently certified British beef as safe for human consumption, the European Union's belated recognition of its potential health hazards severely undermined public trust in EU food safety regulations and the scientific expertise on which they were based. It also led to the deaths of approximately 100 people, primarily in the United Kingdom.

As one British scholar put it, "the BSE scandal represents the biggest failure in UK public policy since the 1956 Suez Crisis."[41] It also emerged on the heels of a long line of food scares in the United Kingdom, including an outbreak of E. coli in Scotland, salmonella in eggs, and listeria. In 1999, a major public health scare emerged over dioxin contamination of food products produced in Belgium, leading to both the fall of the Belgian government and the removal of all Belgian food products from stores throughout Europe, as well as a crisis involving the safety of Coca Cola, although the latter turned out to have no scientific basis.[42] A senior European official noted in 2000,

> the past years have seen a big dip in consumer confidence in the safety of the food supply and, as a consequence, in Member State authorities tasked with the job of overseeing the food industry. There seems to be an endless supply of [food scares].[43]

The regulatory failure associated with mad cow disease had important political consequences. It dramatically exposed the gap between the single market— which exposes all European consumers to goods produced anywhere within the European Union—and the inability of European institutions to ensure the safety of the products sold within that market. At the EU level, it led to the decision in December 2000 to create a European food safety agency. It also called into question the functioning of the "comitology" system, the European Union's term for the structure of advisory bodies that it relies on for expert advice, because the European Commission had relied on the advice of the Scientific Veterinary Committee, which was chaired by a British scientist and primarily reflected the thinking of the British Ministry of Agriculture, Fisheries and Food—advice that subsequently proved flawed.[44] Many of the changes in European regulatory administration reflect the effort to establish institutional arrangements that will reduce the future likelihood of regulatory capture, as does the European Union's official endorsement of the precautionary principle.

There have also been regulatory failures in Europe in other policy areas. During the early 1990s, the French government was severely criticized for responding too slowly to the public health and workplace dangers associated with the use of asbestos.[45] In spite of overwhelming evidence that asbestos constituted a serious health hazard, killing approximately 2,000 people a year, according to a French government study, its manufacture, importation, and sale were not severely restricted until 1996, nearly two decades after the United States began to take regulatory action and after it had been banned in seven other European countries. Another, far more consequential scandal was the apparent failure of French governmental officials and doctors to protect hemophiliacs from blood contaminated with the human immunodeficiency virus (HIV).[46] This issue, which became highly visible during the early 1990s, led to the resignation and criminal indictment of three senior government officials, including the prime minister. Three senior medical officials were convicted of criminal negligence and fraud and were sentenced to prison. Officials were accused of failing to adequately screen blood donors, delaying the approval of an American technology to test blood in order to benefit a French institute, and knowingly allowing contaminated blood to be given to patients. The deaths of more than 300 hemophiliacs were linked to these decisions. Although hemophiliacs were given contaminated blood in several countries, the rate of HIV inflection was significantly higher in France. As in the case of its regulation of asbestos, the French government's regulatory failure was widely attributed to its placing domestic economic interests over public health.

"Le sang contaminé" (the contaminated blood) scandal in France, like mad cow disease in the United Kingdom, had significant domestic repercussions. It shocked French public opinion, calling into question the public's historic high regard for the competence of the public sector in a highly paternalistic state. It also continues to haunt French politicians, making them highly risk averse, particularly with respect to potential threats to public health. Significantly, ministers have accepted nearly every recommendation of L'Agence Française de Securité Sanitaire des Aliments (AFSSA), France's recently established food safety agency, which has statutory responsibility for reviewing all government food safety policies—lest they be accused of (again) endangering public health and possibly face legal penalties. The French decision to maintain its ban on imports of British beef, made in defiance of the European Union and against the advice of the Ministry of Agriculture, was taken in response to the recommendations of the AFSSA. (This decision has since been rescinded.) The haste with which the French government responded to an increase in the number of BSE cases among French cattle in November 2000 by banning the feeding of farines to all animals—without even waiting for a scientific assessment by AFSSA—reflects the continuing impact of the contaminated blood scandal on French health and safety policies, as in part do French policies toward genetically modified organisms (GMOs).[47]

Regulatory failures or crises are not by themselves politically determinative. After all, Europe had experienced regulatory failures prior to the mid-1980s. But the policy impact of the regulatory failures and crises during the second half of the 1980s and the 1990s has been broader and deeper. Their cumulative impact has been to increase the public's sense of vulnerability to and anxiety about the risks associated with modern technology and this in turn has affected the political context of regulatory policymaking, making public officials more precautionary or risk averse. As the *Washington Post* observed in the spring of 2001:

> wealthy, well-educated Europe is regularly swept by frightening reports of new dangers said to be inherent in contemporary life. . . . Americans have health concerns, too, but not on this scale. The year is two months old and already in 2001 public opinion and public officials have been rattled by alarms over risks—proven and not—from genetically modified corn, hormone fed beef and pork, "mad-cow" disease, a widely used measles vaccine, narrow airline seats said to cause blood clots and cellular phones said to cause brain damage.[48]

A SHIFTING POLITICAL LANDSCAPE

A second, related explanation for the change in European regulatory policies and institutions has to do with political developments within individual European countries. During much of the 1980s, support for strict environmental, health, and safety regulations in Europe was geographically polarized. Typically, Germany, The Netherlands, and Denmark favored stricter and more risk-averse regulations, whereas Britain, France, and Italy opposed them.[49] Much of EU environmental policymaking thus represented a struggle between the European Union's three "green" member states, where constituencies representing civic interests enjoyed considerable public support and influence, and Britain, France, and Italy, where they did not. Germany, The Netherlands, and Denmark continue to play a role as environmental "pioneers" within the European Union, joined in 1995 by Sweden, Austria, and Finland.

In part as a result of a series of regulatory failures, strong public interest and support for stricter health and environmental standards have spread south and west within Europe. This change in public and political preferences has been particularly significant in Britain and France, which are no longer regulatory "laggards" within Europe. "Britain has clearly emerged from the more minimalist and hostile stance of the early 1980s to emerge as a medium-positioned state in the league of environmental leaders and laggards."[50] And French public opinion and public policy have been among the most hostile in Europe to GMOs.[51]

In 1999, the Green Party was represented in four European governments: Germany, where it has historically been strong, and France, Italy, and Belgium, where it previously was not. All told, the party had nearly 150 members in eleven of the

European Union's fifteen national legislatures.[52] Although the party is no longer a member of the governing coalition in either Italy or France, national policymakers in both countries have continued to support and adopt a range of relatively risk-averse regulations. In sum, although substantial national differences in regulatory priorities persist within the European Union, political support for more stringent protective regulations has become more widespread in Europe. When viewed in a broader historical perspective, the increasing importance of regulatory politics within much of Europe reflects a decline in the importance of class-based politics, which suggests that European politics are becoming increasing postindustrial.

THE EUROPEAN UNION: STRUCTURAL DEVELOPMENTS

In addition to a series of regulatory failures and related broadening and deepening of political support for more stringent regulatory polices within Europe, the emergence of the European Union as a more important source of regulatory policymaking has also affected the stringency and scope of European regulatory policies. Institutional changes in European regulatory governance are both a cause and effect of changes in European regulatory policies. Significantly, the changes in European regulatory policies and politics described in this chapter began around the time of the enactment of the Single Europe Act (SEA) in 1987. This amendment to the Treaty of Rome enabled directives to be enacted by a system of qualified majority voting instead of unanimity. This significantly increased the European Union's ability to harmonize regulations. The European Union has played a critical role in changing the dynamics of European regulatory policies: each subsequent revision of the Treaty of Rome has accorded civic interests greater weight in the policy process. Combined with growing public support for risk-averse policies, these institutional changes have increased the influence of civic interests within the governance of the European Union.

The SEA gave environmental policy a treaty basis for the first time, specifying that preventive action should be taken whenever possible and requiring that harmonized standards take as a base "a high level of protection." The Treaty on the European Union (1993) made precaution a guiding principle of EU environmental policy:

> Community policy shall aim at a high level of protection taking into account the diversity of situations in the various regions of the Community. It shall be based on the precautionary principle and on the principles that preventive action should be taken.[53]

The Treaty of Amsterdam (1997) called on the council and the parliament to achieve high levels of health, safety, environmental, and consumer protection in promulgating single-market legislation, and Article 153 explicitly defined consumer policy and health protection as "rights." It also extended the precautionary principle to consumer protection.

As Majone has noted, the European Union is primarily a regulatory state: issuing rules is its most important vehicle for shaping public policy in Europe.[54] Notwithstanding frequent criticisms of the European Union's "democratic deficit," its institutions have played an important role in strengthening the representation of civic or diffused interests, although, in general, consumer and environmental pressure groups have more limited influence on the commission than do representatives of business. There are, however, some notable exceptions.[55] The European Consumers Union led a successful campaign calling for the EU beef hormone ban, while Greenpeace effectively worked with Green parties and other interest groups to mobilize public and political opposition against the approval of GMOs in Europe. In addition, the "European Court of Justice has often played a crucial role in promoting civic interests" and has been repeatedly willing "to be influenced by consumer and civic concerns in reaching its judgments."[56]

EU treaties have also steadily expanded the role of the European Parliament, a body in which consumer and environmental interests have been relatively influential, in shaping European legislation.[57] The SEA granted parliament legislative power under "cooperation" procedures, and these were expanded by the Maastricht Treaty, which established "co-decision" procedures, thus giving the parliament and the Council of Ministers coresponsibility for writing legislation. The parliament's purview over environmental legislation was expanded by the Amsterdam Treaty. "Despite the limitations of co-decision, its use as the legislative procedure for environmental measures considerably strengthens the Parliament's role in the adoption of new environmental legislation."[58] The Green Party has been an important political presence in the European Parliament since 1989, when it captured thirty-seven seats; following the June 1999 election, it had thirty-seven members. The Parliament has often been an effective source of pressure on the council for the adoption of more stringent regulations.

The European Union's decision-making structure has also magnified the influence of the "greener" member states. As Heritier argues, an important key to understanding the dynamics of EU policymaking lies in the logic of diversity, "which initiates a spontaneous acceleration of policymaking by regulatory competition and mutual learning."[59] Formally, EU policy is highly centralized: directives are approved in Brussels and the member states are obligated to transpose them into national law and then enforce them. But in fact EU policymaking is highly fragmented. If supporters of more stringent regulatory standards can persuade decision makers in one or more member states that their ideas have merit, "these policymakers will carry this point of view into the EU process."[60] Accordingly, "the significant participation of the member states means that the various ideas that circulate at the national level may in turn diffuse into the EU level."[61] This is also the case when member states unilaterally enact more stringent regulatory standards—a dynamic that has often contributed to a "trend toward higher and tougher standards by Brussels."[62]

The European Union's quasifederal structure, along with the fragmentation of authority among the commission, the council, the European Parliament, and the

ECJ, has provided representatives of civic interests with multiple points of access. An entrepreneurial coalition favoring more stringent regulatory standards

> needs ready access to only one part of the EU system (as long as that structural position provides a visible and vocal platform for the coalition's cause). Because EU institutions encompass such a wide array of interests, finding one sympathetic access point is relatively easy.[63]

Obviously, a fragmented political system also provides opponents of policy change with multiple veto points. The European Union's constitutional structure does not automatically privilege civic interests any more than does the fragmented American system. But, as the American experience of the 1970s illustrates, the multiple points of access offered by a fragmented political system, when combined with a highly mobilized public, can lead to a significant strengthening and broadening of regulatory standards.

Finally, the strengthening of regulatory standards at the European level has also been affected by the dynamics of the single market. An important consequence of the single market has been to make European consumers increasingly dependent on, and thus vulnerable to, the regulatory policies of all fifteen member states as well as Brussels. This has increased political pressures on the European Union to promulgate stricter Europe-wide rules because regulatory failure in any member state endangers the single market as a whole. For Europeans, Brussels represents an important response to policy failures at the national level. In addition, protecting the health and safety of Europeans as well as the European environment has become critical to the European Union's legitimacy and its claim to represent the broader interests and concerns of Europeans. As Breyer and Heyvaert suggest,

> [Regulatory] Centralization may be the expression of a growing feeling of unity among the citizens of Europe, of a growing desire to protect the common European heritage across national boundaries, and of a rising expectation among Europeans that, when they move from one country to another, they will benefit from the same high level of health and environmental protection.[64]

Moreover, the European business community has a strong stake in harmonized standards in order to capture the efficiencies of the single market. Accordingly, there is often a convergence of interest between representatives of civic interests and business at the European level; the latter may not want more stringent European standards, but they typically prefer a harmonized standard to fifteen different ones.

THE EUROPEAN PRESENT AND THE AMERICAN PAST

There are a number of similarities between regulatory policies and politics in Europe and those in the United States during the 1970s and 1980s. During those decades, an influential segment of American elite and public opinion became more risk averse, often focusing on the dangers of new technologies rather than their potential benefits. One British journalist wrote in 1971:

> We saw the Americans thrashing around from one pollution scare to the next, and we were mildly amused. One moment it was cyclamates, mercury the next, then ozone, lead, cadmium—over there they seemed set on working their way in a random manner through the whole periodic table.[65]

A British social scientist observed in 1979, "Americans seem to have taken an excessively strict interpretation of risk, reducing 'reasonable risk' practically to 'zero risk.'"[66] Douglas and Wildavsky wrote in *Risk and Culture*, published in 1982:

> Try to read a newspaper or news magazine . . .; on any day some alarm bells will be ringing. What are Americans afraid of? Nothing much, really except the food they eat, the water they drink, the air they breathe. . . . In the amazingly short space of fifteen to twenty years, confidence about the physical world has turned into doubt. Once the source of safety, science and technology has become the source of risk.[67]

The argument in the United States against public funding of a supersonic passenger airplane is similar to that made by many Europeans against granting regulatory approval for GM agricultural products nearly a quarter-century later: in both cases, a significant segment of the public saw no benefits associated with the proposed new technology, only increased environmental and health risks. The political salience of ozone depletion in the United States during the 1970s parallels the high level of European concern over global climate change during the 1990s. The political setbacks experienced by the American chemical and automotive industries during the 1970s and 1980s are similar to those experienced by agricultural biotechnology firms in Europe since the late 1990s.

The United States, like Europe, also experienced a series of widely publicized regulatory failures, or credible reports of regulatory failures, whose cumulative effect was to increase public support for more effective and stringent regulation. The thalidomide scandal (1962), Rachael Carson's *Silent Spring* (1962), Ralph Nader's *Unsafe at Any Speed* (1965), Love Canal (1977), and Three Mile Island (1979) were the American counterparts to Europe's Chernobyl, the contamination of the Rhine, mad cow disease, dioxin in the food supply, and contaminated blood. The significant membership expansion and increased political influence of public interest lobbies in the United States during the 1970s and 1980s parallel the increased influence of representatives of civic interests, including Green parties, in Europe beginning in the 1980s and accelerating during the 1990s. And the centralization of regulatory policymaking in Brussels parallels the federalization of regulatory policymaking in the United States. On both sides of the Atlantic, institutional changes also made regulatory policymaking more fragmented, which in turn strengthened the influence of proregulation constituencies and reduced the ability of business to dictate regulatory outcomes.[68] Significantly, the fragmented constitutional structure of the European Union, with its quasiseparation of powers and quasifederal division of regulatory responsibilities, more closely resembles the United States than it does any member state.

WHAT HAPPENED IN AMERICA?

This raises a critical question: what happened to American regulatory politics and policies after 1990? After all, EU regulations could have become more stringent and comprehensive while the United States also continued to enact relatively stringent and comprehensive regulations, thus producing policy convergence. Or each could have adopted more stringent and innovative policies in different areas, with the result that on balance, the consumer and environmental standards adopted since around 1990 would have been no more or less stringent or innovative on either side of the Atlantic. But neither scenario has occurred. Why?

Before addressing this question, it is important to note that few of the relatively stringent and comprehensive statutes enacted in the United States through 1990 have been repealed. Indeed, some highly risk-averse regulations continue to be issued pursuant to these laws, including, for example, the 1997 ambient air standards for ozone and particulates promulgated by the Clinton administration and the arsenic in drinking water standards (reluctantly) adopted by the Bush administration. (The latter is similar to the standard earlier adopted by the European Union.) What *has* changed is the rate at which significant new regulatory laws have been approved. The last major legislative expansion of environmental regulation in the United States was the Clean Air Act Amendments of 1990; not since the emergence of the modern consumer and environmental movement in the 1960s has Congress gone so long without enacting a significant new regulatory statute.[69]

It is thus primarily with respect to consumer and environmental issues that have emerged since around 1990 that America has become a regulatory laggard. Here the contrast with the European Union is particularly striking. It is not that federal standards for eco-labeling, packaging wastes, automobile and electronic recycling, the use of heavy metals in autos and electronic equipment, and carbon emissions are less stringent than those of the European Union; in each of these critical policy areas *American federal regulation is nonexistent*. And in the case of GMOs, European standards are notably more stringent than in the United States. Why then did the American hare start moving like a tortoise after around 1990?

The American structure of regulatory policymaking has not changed. The legal and administrative reforms that opened up the American regulatory process during the 1970s—namely, enhanced congressional oversight, increased opportunities for nonbusiness interests to participate in administrative rule making, and more extensive judicial review, including the granting of standing to representatives of civic interests—remain in place. Rather, the slowdown in the rate of new regulatory policy initiatives in the United States since the early 1990s has to do with politics.

One critical difference between Europe and the United States is the relative absence of politically salient regulatory failures in the latter. (The last such regulatory failure in the United States was the 1989 *Exxon Valdez* oil spill, which affected only a narrow range of policies.) There have been periodic consumer safety and environmental crises since then, but, unlike in Europe, their policy impact has been limited. In sharp contrast to the 1970s and 1980s, when high levels of public anxiety frequently impacted public policy—recall, for example, the critical role Love Canal played in prompting congressional passage of the Superfund or the successful media campaign of the Natural Resources Defense Council to ban Alar—more recent allegations of harm have had much less political resonance.[70] A notable example is genetically modified foods and crops. Notwithstanding periodic intense media coverage of their possible threat to public health or the environment, policymakers have imposed few additional restrictions, and public concern has been episodic rather than sustained.[71] In short, compared to the 1970s and 1980s, the number of crisis-induced policy windows in the United States has declined.

American attitudes toward risk and regulation appear to have changed. In contrast to the 1970 and 1980s, during the 1990s Americans were more likely to view technological innovation as a source of progress and wealth creation rather than increased risk. They also became more skeptical of claims by activists that particular business activities threatened their welfare. Public opinion polls also reveal an increase in public satisfaction with the accomplishments of the nation's environmental policies, even though these policies have changed relatively little. For example, between 1993 and 1999, the portion of Americans who "say they are generally satisfied with the state of environmental protection in the U.S." increased from less than half to two-thirds.[72] Likewise, the percentage of Americans who worried "a great deal" about air pollution declined from 64 percent in 1989 to 42 percent in 1997.[73] Equally important, Americans became now more trusting of government regulation than Europeans. Thus, whereas 90 percent of Americans believe the U.S. Department of Agriculture's statements on biotechnology, only 12 percent of Europeans trust their national regulators.[74] Finally, according to one polling firm, America's faith in major corporations rose in the 1980s and 1990s, helping to "produce a politics that has been reluctant to impose new regulatory burdens on business that might diminish corporate profits."[75]

These changes in public attitudes have changed the incentives of politicians. Democratic politicians, who have traditionally been the strongest supporters of more stringent regulations, have perceived fewer political advantages in advocating the expansion or strengthening of regulatory controls. Significantly, the 103rd

Congress (1993–1995), with a Democratic majority and a Democratic president, produced, according to one analyst, "the worst environmental record in 25 years."[76] Throughout the eight years of his presidency, Bill Clinton invested relatively little political capital in expanding the scope of regulation; he gave fewer speeches on the environment than any president since John Kennedy, saving his most important environmental policy initiative—a significant expansion of western lands on which development was restricted—to the closing weeks of his presidency.[77] Although Clinton announced his strong support of the Kyoto Protocol, he never submitted it to Congress. Nor did he seek to mobilize public support for legislation to reduce greenhouse gases. For his part, Vice President Albert Gore, not withstanding his reputation as a strong support of environmentalism, failed to focus on environmental issues either while in office or during his 2000 presidential campaign. Not surprisingly, the Clinton–Gore administration's environmental record disappointed the American environmental community.[78]

Although the initial expansion of environmental regulation during the late 1960s and early 1970s reflected a bipartisan consensus, differences in the environmental policies of the Republican and Democratic parties subsequently increased, with congressional Republicans more opposed to environmental policy initiatives than Democratic legislators.[79] Nonetheless, because public support for environmental regulation remained strong, Ronald Reagan paid a political price for his initial efforts to weaken environmental enforcement and spent much of the remainder of his presidency trying to overcome his anti-Green reputation by not opposing Democratic regulatory initiatives. Significantly, in 1988, Republican presidential candidate George H. W. Bush ran on a campaign promising to be a "Republican president in the Teddy Roosevelt tradition, a conservationist. An environmentalist," in order to distinguish his record from Reagan's.[80] And he delivered on this promise by securing congressional passage of the Clean Air Act Amendments of 1990, breaking a thirteen-year deadlock over this critical dimension of environmental regulation.

Five years later, during the mid-1990s, the newly elected Republican majority in Congress made a determined and largely unsuccessful effort to weaken the nation's environmental laws. This effort was strongly and effectively challenged by the environmental community, and the party paid an electoral price in the 1996 congressional elections.[81] But in marked contrast to the late 1980s, the Republican Party did not seek to become "greener" by supporting additional environmental regulation; rather, it moved closer to the center by abandoning its efforts at regulatory "reform."

These examples suggest that the preferences of the median voter changed during the 1990s. In contrast to the 1970s and 1980s, when median voters often supported regulatory expansion, more recently they support the regulatory status quo. They still consider themselves strong environmentalists, but the political salience of environmental policy has diminished. While they continue to oppose the weakening of regulation, since the early 1990s they have also become less persuaded of the need for strengthening or expanding it, hence the political deadlock that has characterized American regulatory policy since the early 1990s.[82]

CONCLUSION

The policy preferences of Europeans and Americans have diverged. Whereas the number and significance of politically unacceptable risks have increased in Europe, they have stabilized or decreased in the United States. As a result of a crisis facing European regulatory institutions, regulatory officials and politicians increased opportunities for public participation and became more responsive to public pressures and perceptions, hence the adoption of the precautionary principle and the increasing willingness to enact relatively risk-averse regulations. By contrast, the intensity of public concern about the inadequacies of existing regulatory laws and institutions has diminished in the United States. This in turn has made regulatory decision making more technocratic, less responsive to short-term public pressures and anxieties, and frequently less risk averse. To use Ulrich Beck's influential formulation, whereas Europe has become more of a "risk society"—one in which citizens perceive themselves to be faced with an endless series of unintended risks generated by advances in technology—America has become less of one.[83] Wildavsky and Douglas's previously quoted depiction of America in the early 1980s now more accurately describes Europe than the United States.

We are now in a better position to generalize about the dynamics of regulatory policymaking on both sides of the Atlantic. Consumer and environmental regulations are likely to become more innovative, comprehensive, and risk averse as a response to widespread public perceptions of regulatory failures. Such a cycle of regulatory failures have a spill-over effect: they both make public opinion more sensitive to the risks associated with new technologies and undermine public confidence in existing regulatory institutions. Each new demonstrated failure makes allegations of future harms more credible. They also increase the demands for political access of constituencies who favor more stringent regulatory policies and often increase their influence at the expense of business. Institutional changes in the policy process both are caused by and contribute to shifts in regulatory policy.

The American experience suggests that this policy dynamic can persist for an extended period of time. It persisted for more than two decades in the United States, and the momentum for increased regulatory stringency in Europe has now lasted nearly fifteen years. However, it does not last indefinitely. As new procedures for making regulatory policies are established and appear to be functioning reasonably effectively, the political salience of consumer and environmental regulation declines and public pressures for more stringent standards diminish. At the same time, the influence of industry on regulatory policymaking again increases as policymakers become more sensitive to the costs of relatively stringent standards.

As long as the institutional changes that made policymaking more open and publicly accessible remain in place, the result is not so much a rolling back of existing consumer or environmental regulations, but rather policy gridlock. This took place in the United States after 1990 and will at some point occur in Europe as well. Even hares cannot keep running forever.

NOTES

Portions of this chapter first appeared as "The Hare and the Tortoise Revisited: The New Politics of Consumer and Environmental Regulation in Europe," in *British Journal of Political Science* 33 (2003):557–80; reprinted by permission of Cambridge University Press ©2003.

1. Lennart Lundqvist, *The Hare and the Tortoise: Clean Air Policies in the United States and Sweden* (Ann Arbor: University of Michigan Press, 1980).

2. Shelia Jasanoff, "US Exceptionalism and the Political Acknowledgement of Risk," in *Risk*, ed. E. J. Berger (Ann Arbor: University of Michigan Press, 1993), 63, 66.

3. See for example, Ronald Brickman, Shelia Jasanoff, and Thomas Ilgen, *Controlling Chemicals*, (Ithaca, NY: Cornell University Press, 1985); Lundqvist, *The Hare and the Tortoise*, and David Vogel, *National Styles of Regulation* (Ithaca, NY: Cornell University Press, 1986); Joseph Badaracco, Jr., *Loading the Dice: A Five Country Study of Vinyl Chloride Regulation* (Boston: Harvard Business School Press, 1885); Steven Kelman, *Regulating America, Regulating Sweden* (Cambridge, MA: MIT Press, 1981); and Graham Wilson, *The Politics of Safety and Health: Occupational Safety and Health in the United States and Britain* (Oxford: Clarendon Press, 1985).

4. Breyer and Heyvaert make a similar point in a more recent comparison of American and European institutions for managing risk. Stephen Breyer and Veerle Heyvaert, "Institutions for Managing Risk," in *Environmental Law, the Economy and Sustainable Development*, Richard Revesz, Philippe Sands, and Richard Stewart, eds. (Cambridge: Cambridge University Press, 2000), 283–352.

5. Communication from the commission on the precautionary principle, February 2, 2000, 15.

6. James Cameron, "The Precautionary Principle," in *Trade, Environment and the Millenium*, ed. Gary Sampson and W. Bradnee Chambers (New York: United Nations University Press, 1999), 244.

7. Oliver Godard, "Social Decision-Making under Conditions of Scientific Controversy, Expertise and the Precautionary Principle," in *Integrating Scientific Expertise into Regulatory Decision-Making: National Traditions and European Innovations*, ed. Christain Joerges, Karl-Heinz Ladeur, and Ellen Vos (Baden-Baden: Nomos Verlagsgesellschaft, 1997), 65.

8. Andrew Jordan and Timothy O'Riordan, "The Precautionary Principle in UK Environmental Law and Policy," in *UK Environmental Policy in the 1990s*, ed. Tim Gray (London: Macmillian Press, 1995), 71.

9. Ibid., 61.

10. Corinne Lepage and Francois Guery, *La Politique de Precaution* (Paris: Presses Universitaires de France, 2001), 144 (translation by author). For a collection of essays generally sympathetic to this position, primarily by Americans, see *Protecting Public Health and*

the Environment: Implementing the Precautionary Principle, ed. Carolyn Raffensperger and Joel Tickner (Washington, DC: Island Press, 1999). For a wide-ranging critique of the precautionary principle as both law and philosophy, see *Rethinking Risk and the Precautionary Principle*, ed. Julian Morris (Oxford: Butterworth, 2000).

11. Joanne Scott and Ellen Vos, "The Juridification of Uncertainty," in *Good Governance in Europe's Integrated Market*, ed. Christian Joerges and Renaud Dehousse (Oxford: Oxford University Press, 2002), 253–88.

12. Brickman, Jasanoff, and Ilgren, *Controlling Chemicals*, 48.

13. Ibid.

14. Ibid., 47.

15. Ibid., 37.

16. Henning Arp, "Technical Regulation and Politics: The Interplay between Economic Interests and Environmental Policy Goals in EC Car Legislation," in *European Integration and Environmental Policy*, ed. J. D. Leifferink, P. D. Lowe, and A. P. J. Mol (London: Belhaven Press, 1993), 15–174; David Vogel, *Trading Up: Consumer and Environmental Regulation in a Global Economy* (Cambridge, MA: Harvard University Press, 1995), 63–77.

17. Lundqvist, *The Hare and the Tortoise*, 170–71; Arp, "Technical Regulation," 155.

18. Richard Elliot Benedict, *Ozone Diplomacy* (Cambridge, MA: Harvard University Press, 1991, 1998), 25.

19. Ibid., 25.

20. The data in this paragraph are summarized in David Vogel, "When Consumers Oppose Consumer Protection," *Journal of Public Policy* 10, no. 4 (October–December 1990):458.

21. Jasanoff, "American Exceptionalism and the Political Acknowledgement of Risk," 63.

22. See Marsha Echols, "Food Safety Regulation in the European Union and the United States," *Columbia Journal of European Law* 4 (1998):525–43.

23. Quoted in Vogel, *Trading Up*, 158.

24. Quoted in ibid., 172.

25. Ronald Libby, *Eco-Wars: Political Campaigns and Social Movements* (New York: Columbia University Press, 1998), 27–52.

26. Steve Stecklow, "Despite Assurances, U.S. Could be at Risk For Mad-Cow Disease," *Wall Street Journal*, November 18, 2001.

27. David Vogel, *Barriers or Benefits? Regulation in Transatlantic Trade* (Washington, DC: Brookings Institution Press, 1997), 44–46.

28. For a more extensive discussion of the differences between European and American regulations of GMOs, see Thomas Bernauer and Erika Meins, "Scientific Revolution Meets Policy and the Market: Explaining Cross-National Differences in Agricultural Biotechnology Regulation," Adelaide University, Centre for International Economic Studies (unpublished paper, November 2001); Mark Pollack and Gregory Shaffer, "The Challenge of Food Safety in Transatlantic Relations," in *Transatlantic Governance in the Global Economy*, ed. Mark Pollack and Gregory Shaffer (Oxford: Rowman & Littlefield, 2001), 162–70; and David Vogel, "Ships Passing in the Night: GMOS and the Politics of Risk Regulation in Europe and the United States" (INSEAD: Centre for the Management of Environmental Resources Working Paper, 2002).

29. CNN Headline News, June 24, 1999, and "Genetically Modified Food: Food for Thought," *The Economist*, June 19, 1999.

30. Marian Burros, "U.S. Plans Long-Term Studies on Safety of Genetically Altered Foods," *New York Times*, July 14, 1999.

31. Nikki Tait, "EPA Sued over Genetic Crop Approval," *Financial Times*, February 19, 1999.

32. See David Vogel, *Barriers or Benefits*, 46–52.

33. Markus Haverland, *National Autonomy, European Integration and the Politics of Packaging Waste* (Amsterdam: Thela, 1999).

34. Michael Mann, "Brussels Acts over Missed Scrap Car Deadlines," *Financial Times*, July 30, 2002.

35. European Conference of Ministers of Transport, *Vehicle Emission Reductions* (Paris: European Conference of Ministers of Transport, 2001), 22–31.

36. Robert Paarlberg, "Lapsed Leadership: U.S. International Environmental Leadership Since Rio," in *The Global Environment*, ed. Norman Vig and Regina Axelrod (Washington, DC: Congressional Quarterly Press, 1999), 236.

37. For a detailed discussion of each of these trade disputes, see David Vogel, *Barriers or Benefits*.

38. Robin Herman, "An Ecological Epiphany," *Washington Post National Weekly Edition* (December 5–11, 1988).

39. Elizabeth Bomberg, *Green Parties and Politics in the European Union* (London: Routledge, 1998), 13.

40. There is an extensive literature on this subject. See, for example, Scott Ratzan, ed., *The Mad Cow Crisis: Health and the Public Good* (New York: New York University Press, 1998).

41. Erik Millstone, "Comment and Analysis," *Financial Times*, October 6, 2000.

42. The links are observed by journalists with titles such as "Mad Coke Disease," John Lanchester, *New York Times Magazine* (July 4, 1999):7–8.

43. "Back to the Future," *Consumer Voice*, special ed. (2000).

44. See Graham Chambers, "The BSE Crisis and the European Parliament," in *EU Committees: Social Regulation, Law and Politics*, ed. Christian Joerges and Ellen Vos (Oxford: Hart Publishing, 1999), 95–108.

45. For an extended discussion of this issue, see *Les Sombres Precurseurs (The Dark Forerunners)*, Francis Chateauraynaud and T. Didier (Paris: Editions de L'École des Hautes Études en Sciences Sociales, 1999), ch. 3–7.

46. The extensive literature on this issue includes Michel Setbon, *Pouvoirs contra Sida* (Paris: Éditions du Seuil, 1993); Blandine Kriegel, *Le sang, la justice, la politique* (Paris: Plon, 1999) ; and Olivier Beaud, *Le sang contaminé* (Paris: Behemoth, 1999). It should be noted that many scholars believe the scandal has been overblown and the prosecution of government officials for it was both ethically and legally problematic. But this point of view has not affected public perceptions.

47. For a discussion of the origins of French policies toward GMOs, see David Vogel and Olivier Cadot, "France, the United States and the Biotechnology Debate," Brookings Institution *Foreign Policy Studies* (January 2001).

48. T. R. Reid, "Be Careful What You Eat, Where you Sit and. . ." *Washington Post National Weekly Edition* (May 12–18, 2001).

49. See Mikael Andersen and Duncan Liefferink, eds., *European Environmental Policy* (Manchester, UK: Manchester University Press, 1997).

50. B. Flynn, "EU Environmental Policy at a Crossroads? Reconsidering Some Paradoxes in the Evolution of Policy Content," *European Journal of Public Policy* 5 (1998):696.

51. See, for example, Pierre-Benoit Joly and Claire Marris, "Les Americans ont-ils accepté les OGM? Analyse compare de la construction des OGM comme problème public en France et aux États-Unis" (unpublished paper, 2001).

52. John McCormick, *Environmental Policy in the European Union* (New York: Palgave, 2001), 61.

53. Jordan and O'Riordan, "The Precautionary Principle," 68–69.

54. Giandomenico Majone, *Regulating Europe* (London: Routedge, 1996).

55. Wyn Grant, Duncan Matthews, and Peter Newell, "Business and Environmental Interests," *The Effectiveness of European Union Environmental Policy* (London: Macmillan, 2000).

56. Alasdair Young and Helen Wallace, *Regulatory Politics in the Enlarging European Union* (Manchester, UK: Manchester University Press, 2000), 19.

57. See Elizabeth Bomberg, *Green Parties and Politics in the European Union* (London: Routledge, 1998).

58. Wyn Grant, Duncan Matthews, and Peter Newell, *The Effectiveness of European Union Environmental Policy* (London: Macmillan, 2000), 35.

59. Andrienne Heritier, *Policy-Making and Diversity in Europe* (Cambridge: Cambridge University Press, 1999), 2.

60. Anthony Zito, *Creating Environmental Policy in the European Union* (London: Macmillan, 2000), 23.

61. Ibid.

62. Young and Wallace, *Regulatory Politics in the Enlarging European Union*, 9.

63. Zito, *Creating Environmental Policy in the European Union*, 192.

64. Breyer and Heyvaert, "Institutions for Managing Risk," 327.

65. Stanley Johnson, *The Politics of the Environment: The British Experience* (London: Tom Stacey, 1971), 170–71.

66. Quoted in Vogel, *National Styles*, 182.

67. Mary Douglas and Aaron Wildavsky, *Risk and Culture* (Berkeley: University of California Press, 1982), 10.

68. The changes in the United States are explored in detail in Vogel, *Fluctuating Fortunes* (New York: Basic Books, 1989), ch. 5.

69. Michael Kraft, "Environmental Policy in Congress: From Consensus to Gridlock," in *Environmental Policy*, ed. Norman Vig and Michael Kraft (Washington, DC: Congressional Quarterly Press, 2002), 127–50.

70. Aaron Wildavsky, *But Is It True?* (Cambridge, MA: Harvard University Press, 1995).

71. Kathleen Hart, *Eating in the Dark* (New York: Pantheon Books, 2002).

72. Lydia Saad, "1999 Earth Day Poll: Environmental Concern Wanes," *The Gallup Poll Monthly* (April 1999):38.

73. Glen Sussman, Byron Daynes, and Jonathan West, *American Politics and the Environment* (New York: Longman, 2002), 63.

74. Juan Enriquez and Ray Goldberg, "Transforming Life, Transforming Business: The Life Science Revolution," *Harvard Business Review* (March–April 2000):103.

75. David Callahan, "Private Sector, Public Doubts," *New York Times*, January 15, 2000.

76. Jessica Matthews, "Earth First at the Polls," *Christian Science Monitor*, November 11, 1996.

77. Sussman, Daynes, and West, *American Politics*, 164.

78. Jedediah Purday, "Planet Bush, Planet Gore," *American Prospect*, November 20, 2000.

79. Charles Shipan and William Lowry, "Environmental Policy and Party Divergence in Congress," *Political Research Quarterly* (June 2001):245–63.

80. Sussman, Daynes and West, *American Politics*, 171.

81. Matthews, "Earth First at the Polls."

82. Richard Morin, "A Lighter Shade of Green," *Washington Post National Weekly Edition* (June 5–11, 1995):36–37.

83. Ulrich Beck, *World Risk Society* (Cambridge: Polity Press, 1999).

THE POLITICS OF ENVIRONMENTAL POLICY IN THE UNITED STATES AND THE EUROPEAN UNION

Coercive Federalism?

R. DANIEL KELEMEN

INTRODUCTION

DURING THE 1990S, MUCH OF THE DEBATE OVER ENVIRONMENTAL POLICY IN BOTH THE United States and the European Union (EU) focused on two common sets of questions. The first set of questions concerned the allocation of regulatory authority. Policymakers in the United States and the European Union debated how state (member state) and federal (supranational) levels of government should divide regulatory authority. The second set of questions concerned what regulatory instruments (i.e., command and control, economic, or voluntary instruments) should be used in pursuit of environmental policy objectives. In other words, policymakers in the United States and European Union debated (1) *Who should regulate?* and (2) *How should they regulate?* The rhetoric invoked by policymakers engaged in these debates often emphasized that efficiency considerations should determine the answer to these questions. Scholars have largely followed policymakers, in that much of the academic literature on environmental federalism and regulatory instruments focuses on identifying the most efficient forms of regulation. However, in practice, decisions over the allocation of regulatory competences and the selection of policy instruments often had little to do with efficiency and, instead, much to do with politics.

This chapter analyzes the politics behind these policy choices. On the question of who should regulate, I show that the European Union and United States moved in opposite directions during the 1990s. Formerly weak EU regulators substantially increased their control over member state regulation, while powerful federal regulators in the United States devolved considerable power to the states. These opposing trends are leading to a convergence in the way the United States and European Union allocate regulatory authority between levels of government. I argue that this convergence can be attributed largely to similarities in the federal institutional structure of the two political systems. In the context of the federal structures common to both systems, the desire of both levels of government to claim credit for addressing environmental concerns while shifting blame for costs of policies to one another leads to the emergence of shared division of competences whereby the federal level plays an active role in policymaking and state-level governments conduct most implementation and enforcement.

On questions of how regulation should be conducted, the United States and European Union have converged to some degree as well. The United States, which has long been distinguished by its reliance on detailed command-and-control regulations and its rigid, adversarial approach to implementation, has introduced a number of "second generation" market- and information-based policy instruments and has promoted more flexible approaches to regulation. In the European Union, too, command-and-control regulation has been supplemented by a range of new policy instruments such as environmental taxes, ecolabeling, and environmental management and audit schemes. Many policymakers have also placed great emphasis on the use of environmental agreements in the European Union. The range of policy instruments used in both the U.S. and EU environmental policy has certainly increased over the past decade. Nevertheless, it is clear that command-and-control regulation backed by an adversarial, litigious approach to policy enforcement continues to dominate U.S. policy style and that this approach has become far more prevalent in the European Union as well. Again, I argue that the prevalence of this policy style in both cases stems from similarities in their basic institutional structures. In both polities, the fragmentation of political power encourages the drafting of detailed, inflexible regulations and an emphasis on judicialized enforcement. In this institutional context, efforts to promote flexible, voluntary approaches to regulation are likely to meet with only limited success.

WHO REGULATES? ENVIRONMENTAL FEDERALISM IN THE UNITED STATES AND EUROPEAN UNION

During the 1990s, control over environmental policy in the United States and the European Union moved in opposite directions. In the European Union, the "federal" (supranational) level of government steadily expanded its role in environmental policy throughout the 1990s. A number of major EU environmental directives and regulations were adopted, and, perhaps most important, the European Union asserted a powerful role in enforcing EU environmental law against intransigent member states. Despite a great deal of rhetoric concerning the principle of "subsidiarity," the European Union clearly moved toward greater centralization in the 1990s. In the United States, by contrast, control over environmental policy shifted toward state governments. Although there was no major rollback of existing federal legislation, a series of developments decreased the federal role in monitoring and enforcement and increased the flexibility that state governments enjoyed in implementing federal law. Although the European Union and the United States were moving in opposite directions during the 1990s, they were heading toward a similar destination. With the expansion of the European Union's authority and the loosening of federal controls in the United States, the manner in which regulatory authority is divided between state and federal regulators in the two polities is coming to look more and more alike.

By the start of the 1990s, the European Union's role in environmental policymaking was well established. The European Union's environmental competence had expanded over the course of two decades as a result, primarily, of pressure from Green member states and from EU institutions. Member states that adopted high environmental standards beginning in the late 1960s feared that their standards might put them at a competitive disadvantage vis-à-vis laxer member states, or that the European Court of Justice (ECJ) might strike down their standards as illegal nontariff barriers to trade. These Green states pushed for the adoption of stringent standards on a communitywide basis. The European Commission and the European Parliament, eager to expand EU competences and to claim credit for addressing an issue of great concern to citizens across Europe, consistently worked to expand the scope of EU environmental policy. The ECJ, too, supported the commission's expansive agenda. Together these actors built up a body of community environmental law that encompassed most of the major areas of contemporary environmental policy, including regulation of air and water pollution, toxic chemicals, nature conservation, and waste disposal.[1]

In the late 1980s, with its environmental policymaking competence well established, the commission began intensifying its monitoring and enforcement activities.[2] Most significantly, the commission dramatically increased its use of the infringement procedure, whereby it could bring member states before the ECJ for noncompliance with EU law. With the commission taking an increasingly stringent, adversarial stance, it became clear to member states that the European Union's environmental directives and regulations could not be treated merely as nonbinding, or loosely binding, frameworks.

Reacting to this growing EU power, in 1992 the United Kingdom seized on the principle of subsidiarity, which had been given such a prominent place in the Maastricht Treaty, and led an effort to roll back EU environmental laws. The subsidiarity principle established a federalism balancing test, requiring that the community could take action "only if and in so far as the objectives of the proposed action cannot be sufficiently achieved by the Member States and can therefore, by reason of the scale or effects of the proposed action, be better achieved by the Community."[3] The United Kingdom argued that many EU environmental measures did not satisfy this test. Initially, pressure from the United Kingdom led the commission to withdraw some pending proposals.[4] However, ultimately the United Kingdom found insufficient support among other member states, and its effort to roll back community environmental regulation, or even more modestly to stem its growth, proved a failure. No established areas of community competence have been turned back to the member states. Neither of the subsequent treaty revisions, at Amsterdam and Nice, witnessed major efforts to roll back existing environmental policy. Rather, the Amsterdam Treaty (Article 175 (ex Article 130s)) extended the use of the codecision procedure in environmental policymaking. To date, the principle of subsidiarity has not provided the bulwark against the expansion of community competence that some had hoped for.[5]

Quite to the contrary, during the 1990s, the European Union has taken a number of ambitious legislative initiatives and has continued to strengthen its monitoring and enforcement activities. The European Union has amended and expanded existing regulations in areas such as air and water pollution and has adopted new legislation in areas such as recycling of packaging waste and recycling of automobiles. In 1990, the community established a European Environment Agency (EEA) to coordinate information gathering on the state of the environment across the community.[6] Although the EEA plays no direct role in enforcement, it has significantly improved the European Union's ability to monitor member state progress on environmental protection. The commission has continued to strengthen its enforcement regime. Most recently, it has invoked a provision of the Maastricht Treaty (Art. 228 (ex 171)) that empowered it to request that the ECJ impose penalty payments on member states that fail to comply with ECJ rulings. Although this procedure applies to all areas of community law, the commission has used it most vigorously in environmental policy. In 1997, the commission brought its five first such cases to the ECJ, all of them involving member state violations of EU environmental policy. Subsequently, the commission has initiated dozens more of these cases, and the threat of financial penalties has pressured member states to come into compliance rapidly in most cases.[7] One case, involving Greece's ongoing violations of EU waste-management directives on the island of Crete, reached the final stage of the penalty procedure. On July 4, 2000, the ECJ imposed the European Union's first-ever penalty payments on a member state for failure to implement community law, ordering Greece to pay 20,000 euros per day until it came into compliance. By February 2001, when the commission finally found Greece to be in compliance, Greece had accrued a penalty of 4.8 million euros, which it paid to the Commission.[8]

In the United States, pressure for devolution increased in the early 1990s as state governments lashed back against the burdens of federal environmental mandates. Although President Ronald Reagan had come to office promising a deregulation and devolution in the area of environmental protection, Democrats in Congress were able to block most of his agenda.[9] In fact, the number of federal mandates calling for state implementation enacted in the 1980s exceeded that in any previous decade.[10] One area where Reagan did succeed was in cutting federal funding to states for implementation of federal environmental programs.[11] This transformed programs that had originally been accompanied by substantial federal funding into unfunded (or at least severely underfunded) mandates. To fulfill their mandates, state governments were pressured to increase funding and staffing of state environmental protection departments substantially during the 1980s and early 1990s. By the early 1990s, states collectively provided twice as much funding for environmental programs as the federal government, had nearly four times the staff of the Environmental Protection Agency (EPA), and conducted the overwhelming majority of environmental inspections.[12]

As the federal government increasingly shifted the costs of its regulatory programs to states, states lashed back. State and local officials mounted a nationwide campaign culminating in an October 1993 "National Unfunded Mandates Day" to protest the burdens placed on them by federal mandates, particularly in the area of environmental regulation.[13] The Clinton administration responded by issuing an executive order (E.O. 13083) restraining administrative mandates and by making programs that promised states more flexibility in implementation a central element of its plan to "reinvent" environmental regulation. The most prominent EPA initiative targeted at the states was the National Environmental Performance Partnership System (NEPPS). Under this 1995 program, states may sign agreements with their EPA regional office in which the state promises to collect data on specific environmental indicators, to provide regular self-assessment reports, and to engage in monitoring activities, and in exchange, the EPA office promises to afford the state more flexibility in implementing and enforcing policy, particularly if the state shows improvements on the agreed environmental indicators. This system also extends to federal grants, and as part of an agreement, the federal government may offer Performance Partnership Grants (PPGs) that permit states greater flexibility in allocating federal funds among environmental programs.

Republicans in the 104th Congress responded to state concerns about unfunded mandates as well. Along with its general calls for deregulation, House Speaker Newt Gingrich's *Contract with America* placed great emphasis on devolution. In 1995, Congress enacted the Unfunded Mandate Reform Act (UMRA),[14] which promised to restrict the adoption of unfunded mandates. Most recently, the Bush administration has moved to grant states greater control over environmental policy. Bush's EPA chief, former New Jersey governor Christine Todd Whitman, has promised to grant states increased flexibility in meeting federal mandates.[15] The Whitman EPA has proposed delegating to states the power to designate "impaired water bodies" under the Clean Water Act and granting them considerable discretion as to how to achieve the "highest attainable" uses of them.[16]

Together, all of these federal initiatives have certainly served to increase flexibility for state governments in implementing federal statutes. However, we should be careful not to exaggerate the degree of devolution that has occurred. Unfunded mandates remain the primary form for federal policymaking. Moreover, citizen suit provisions of existing statutes continue to allow private parties to sue states for noncompliance with federal mandates. For instance, just as federal officials were working to increase flexibility for states, environmental groups initiated a wave of lawsuits seeking to force states to enforce long-ignored provisions of the Clean Water Act concerning overall water quality in watersheds.[17] Without a major revision of existing environmental statutes that would increase flexibility for states and limit third-party suits, more far-reaching devolution is unlikely. Given the difficulty of assembling the legislative coalition necessary to enact such far-reaching reforms in the Unites States' fragmented institutional structure, such change is unlikely.

Today, the United States and European Union find themselves in roughly similar positions concerning the allocation of regulatory authority. Certainly, the U.S. federal environmental bureaucracy dwarfs the European Union's, and U.S. federal agencies carry out some implementation and enforcement activities that their EU counterparts do not. For instance, the EPA directly implements some programs, such as Superfund, and has the power to bring enforcement actions directly against polluters. In the United States, the federal government is empowered to preempt the state government role in implementing and enforcing federal statutes. However, the federal government practically never revokes state control, despite ample evidence that states routinely flout federal requirements.[18] The federal government strongly prefers to leave states in control, because doing so allows it to shift most implementation costs to the states.[19] The U.S. federal government lacks the staffing and resources necessary to implement its own policies, and both levels of government understand that the formal possibility of federal preemption will not be exercised. Thus, in both the United States and European Union, the federal (or supranational) level of government produces most major framework legislation, while state governments are responsible for the vast majority of implementation and enforcement. This allocation of regulatory authority is likely to prove a relatively stable equilibrium in both cases, because it provides both levels of government with opportunities to claim credit for addressing environmental concerns, while shifting blame for regulatory failures and for costs of regulation to one another.[20]

In both the United States and European Union, this allocation of authority has served to gradually force up the standards in laggard states (i.e., Greece, Portugal, and Spain in the European Union; Texas, Ohio, and Missouri in the United States) without forcing down the standards in Green states (i.e., Denmark, The Netherlands, and Germany in the European Union; California in the United States). In both polities, most federal standards have established floors rather than ceilings, allowing greener states to pursue stricter policies. Instances in which ceilings in federal legislation have forced green states to lower their standards, as was the case when the EU packaging-waste directive led Germany to reduce its recycling targets, are extremely rare. The fact that California has taken the lead in an otherwise anemic U.S. response to global warming is the latest reminder of the continuing power of green states to act as laboratories and agenda setters.[21] With green states as important backers of federal legislation, federal standards have tended to be set at high levels, creating upward pressure on laggard states. For countries of southern Europe, EU environmental policy has been a primary force behind advances in environmental protection, and the same is true today for the applicant countries of Eastern and Central Europe.

HOW DO THEY REGULATE?

On questions of regulatory style, as on questions of federalism, the United States and European Union seem to have moved in opposite directions in the 1990s. In the United States, federal policymakers have attempted to shift from a notoriously adversarial policy style toward one that emphasizes more cooperative and flexible policy instruments. Although EU policymakers have also extolled flexible, cooperative policy instruments and have introduced a handful of them at the EU level, in many respects the European Union seems to be moving in the opposite direction—pushing member states with traditionally cooperative styles to become more legalistic and adversarial.

Writing in the 1980s, Vogel and others noted that the U.S. approach to environmental regulation was more formal, litigious, costly, and slow than regulatory processes in various West European countries.[22] The American approach to environmental regulation had its roots in the landmark statutes of the 1970s that Congress had adopted in response to the rapid growth in public concern with environmental pollution. Statutes such as the Clean Air Act, the Clean Water Act, the Resource Conservation and Recovery Act (RCRA), and the Toxic Substances Control Act took an ambitious command-and-control approach, proscribing certain activities, establishing a variety of strict standards, requiring the use of particular technologies, and threatening polluters with penalties for noncompliance. The EPA was assigned the lead role in enforcing these statutes, and it worked to establish its credibility early on by taking an aggressive stance vis-à-vis polluters. Moreover, foreseeing that future administrations might backpedal on implementation and enforcement of environmental policy, environmental advocates in Congress attached citizen-suit provisions to a number of these statutes so that private parties could sue developers or polluters directly or sue the EPA to force it to fulfill its statutory mandate. The command-and-control nature of these statutes was intensified in the 1980s, as the Democratic Congress moved to force the intransigent Reagan administration to take action on the environment.[23] When crucial environmental statutes such as the RCRA, Superfund, and the Clean Air Act came up for reauthorization, Congress added more detailed, inflexible, justiciable provisions that would force the Reagan (and later the Bush) EPA to act.

By the end of the 1980s, however, the command-and-control approach to environmental regulation was coming under an increasingly widespread attack. A growing chorus of critics argued that command and control was economically inefficient, excessively rigid, slow, uncoordinated, and, ultimately, ineffective. Critics suggested that market-based mechanisms (such as emissions trading) and measures that provide greater flexibility for regulated entities to achieve pollution control targets in the most cost-effective manner possible would achieve superior results at lower costs. Initially, such critiques and reform proposals emanated from academia and industry circles, and they won the support of well-placed officials in the first Bush administration, including EPA chief William K. Reilly. The first major application of a market mechanism came with the 1990 Clean Air Act Amendments, which provided for the establishment of an emissions-trading scheme. The Bush EPA also began to promote cooperative relations with industry and voluntary pollution control through pilot schemes such as the "33/50 Program," which encouraged voluntary reductions in emissions of toxic chemicals, and the Green Lights program, which encouraged businesses to install energy-efficient lighting.[24]

Such reform efforts did not end with the return of Democrats to the White House. Quite to the contrary, the Clinton–Gore administration made the reform of environmental regulation central to their broader efforts to "reinvent" government by reducing red tape and improving the quality of regulation. The Clinton EPA, headed by Carol Browner, pushed ahead with a series of initiatives, sometimes labeled reinvention programs or second-generation policy instruments. The Clinton administration supported expanding the use of market mechanisms and labeling- and information-based approaches where applicable. The most significant program based on economic instruments is the emissions quota trading system for sulfur dioxide established by the 1990 Clean Air Act Amendments.[25] This program has proved successful. The EPA has instituted a similar trading scheme involving ozone-depleting substances, and a number of state governments are developing emissions-trading programs for issues such as volatile organic materials.[26] By contrast, the use of environmental taxes in the United States has not grown significantly. A limited number of variable user charges have been introduced by state governments, for instance in the area of waste disposal. However, proposals for more widespread introduction of environmental taxes have met with broad opposition, as the Clinton administration discovered with its failed 1993 effort to introduce a 1993 BTU ([British thermal unit] energy) tax as a measure to combat climate change. Federal agencies have introduced a few labeling schemes, such as the Energy Star program for labeling energy-efficient appliances. However, such programs remain limited in scope.

In addition to economic instruments and labeling programs, the Clinton EPA introduced a number of new programs designed to increase regulatory flexibility and cooperation between regulators, business, and other stakeholders. The most high profile of these programs was Project XL (eXcellence and Leadership), and others included Partners for the Environment, the Environmental Leadership Program, and the Common Sense Initiative. These initiatives share a number of key characteristics: first, all of them are voluntary, relying on industry to choose to participate. Second, they all promise regulated entities some form of greater flexibility in meeting environmental objectives, freeing them of normal regulatory requirements. Finally, they all promise not to allow for any diminution of environmental protection and to ensure some form of participation by nonindustry stakeholders such as community groups and environmental nongovernmental organizations (NGOs).

Although the Clinton administration called great attention to these programs,[27] they remained a decidedly marginal, experimental aspect of environmental regulation throughout the 1990s. The shortcomings of Project XL are typical of other reinvention initiatives and illustrate the difficulties of pursuing flexible regulation in the U.S. context. Launched in 1995, Project XL was designed as a pilot program to explore innovative approaches to achieving environmental protection. Under Project XL, businesses, local governments, representatives of industrial sectors, or federal agencies can propose a plan for delivering superior environmental results from those that would result from following existing federal regulations. If the EPA approves the project, it exempts the project's sponsor from existing regulations and allows them the flexibility to pursue the superior environmental performance they have promised.

Project XL has confronted a number of problems that highlight the impediments to applying its approach on a broader scale. First, Project XL has faced considerable criticism from environmental organizations that suspected it would provide a cover for regulatory laxity and "sweetheart" deals with industry and would not deliver the promised superior results.[28] The EPA sought to address such criticisms from the outset, requiring that Project XL proposals win the support of outside stakeholders such as environmental groups and community organizations. However, this commitment to stakeholder participation has led to considerable delays, with stakeholder negotiations involving hundreds of hours of meetings, and has sparked further controversy as some stakeholders maintain that they were marginalized during the negotiation process.

Second, Project XL has attracted only moderate interest from industry, and the number and quality of proposals submitted have been disappointing.[29] Although the promise of increased flexibility and exemption from command-and-control regulations provides a powerful incentive, the difficulties involved in winning stakeholder support for a project and the legal uncertainties surrounding XL have deterred many potential participants.[30] The primary legal uncertainty involves the potential for citizen suits against businesses participating in Project XL. Although government regulators can apply their discretion to pledge not to pursue enforcement litigation against Project XL participants for violations of existing regulations, they cannot prevent citizens' suits. In the absence of legislation exempting participants from citizen suits, the citizen-suit provisions of existing statutes continue to apply and participants risk being sued for violating existing law.[31]

In addition to such high-profile pilot programs, the Clinton administration extended a number of implementation practices that increased the flexibility of regulation. For instance, Regulatory Negotiation among stakeholders was used on a limited basis as an alternative to standard rule-making processes; Supplemental Environmental Project provisions included as part of settlements in enforcement actions allowed violators to undertake environmental projects as a substitute for some financial penalties; Prospective Purchaser Agreements allowed flexibility for Brownfield redevelopment under the Comprehensive Environmental Response, Compensation and Liability Act (CERCLA); and agreements on Habitat Conservation Plans have allowed developers some flexibility in complying with requirements of the Endangered Species Act.[32] Most of these initiatives lacked any legislative basis. Rather, these initiatives were undertaken as initiatives of the executive branch, leading to what Stewart calls a "dual-track" system of regulation with an official track involving the implementation of statutes and a separate, shadow track involving such flexible reform measures.[33]

The George W. Bush administration has intensified efforts to promote both emissions trading and cooperative approaches to regulation. Bush's "Clear Skies" initiative promises to extend emissions trading to a range of other pollutants.[34] On broader questions of regulatory style, Bush has taken a number of steps to bring to Washington the emphasis on flexibility and voluntary compliance that he was known for as governor of Texas.[35] Bush signaled this intention during his campaign and again early in his administration by nominating Christine Todd Whitman, who was well known for advocating a cooperative approach to regulation as governor of New Jersey, to head the EPA. During her confirmation hearing, Whitman called for a "new era of cooperation" among state and federal governments, businesses, and environmentalists.[36] The Bush administration has continued with the regulatory "reinvention" programs initiated by the Clinton administration. The Bush administration has also taken additional steps to increase flexibility that have proven more controversial. Moves to weaken "new source review" provisions of the Clean Air Act in order to give utilities more flexibility in modernizing aging, highly polluting power plants sparked an outcry from environmentalists and lawmakers in the northeastern states that lie downwind of most of the grandfathered plants.[37] These moves, coupled with broader efforts to downsize the EPA's enforcement staff, led to the highly publicized resignation of EPA's top enforcement official, who accused the administration of undermining the EPA's enforcement activities.[38] The environmental community continues to view the Bush administration's commitment to flexibility and cooperative approaches as a smokescreen for its deregulatory agenda.

While new regulatory instruments have proliferated, a major shift in American regulatory style in the area of environmental policy is unlikely. The underlying impediments to environmental agreements and other flexible forms of regulation are rooted in the structure of U.S. political institutions. Whether such measures are backed by sincere advocates of reform or by disguised backers of deregulation, they have difficulty taking hold in the institutional terrain of American government. First, given the separation of executive and legislative power in the United States, the legislature has incentives to minimize agency losses by limiting executive discretion. Given the independence of the judiciary in the fragmented American system, lawmakers have an incentive to empower private parties to use the courts to act as watchdogs of executive malfeasance. Indeed, these factors explain why detailed, action-forcing environmental statutes filled with citizen-suit provisions were enacted in the first place.[39]

Second, given the multiple veto players built into the U.S. Constitution, the federal executive is unable to promise chosen stakeholders the sort of privileged position that their counterparts in the most corporatist European countries would enjoy. Flexible approaches to regulation are built on a model of exchange whereby the government commits itself to allow regulated actors some measure of flexibility and forgo strict legislation in exchange for a commitment from the regulated actors to produce certain results. However, in the U.S. system, because firms and interest groups can pursue their interests in a variety of political and legal fora, the executive cannot make a credible commitment to restrain the exercise of public authority. For instance, if environmental NGOs distrust the executive, as is the case under the current administration, they will hardly be willing to support flexible, voluntary approaches to regulation. Instead, they are likely to turn to the courts and to invoke the action-forcing provisions of existing statutes to force the executive's hand.[40] In this context, the executive cannot make credible commitments to regulated industries.[41]

As in the United States, growing criticism of the inefficiency and ineffectiveness of command-and-control regulation in the European Union has led to calls for the introduction of "new" policy instruments, including pollution taxes and trading schemes, ecolabeling programs, and, above all, voluntary agreements.[42] Calls for the introduction of such instruments have stemmed primarily from industrial interests, with environmental groups remaining cautious or directly opposed to their use.[43] Some of these policy instruments, such as the European Union's ecolabeling program and the planned greenhouse gas emissions trading scheme,[44] do constitute innovations in the European context. However, the notion that flexible, negotiated agreements represent a departure from an entrenched command-and-control approach is ill founded. Recent calls for negotiating environmental agreements or covenants between government, industry, and other stakeholders look suspiciously like old wine in new bottles in the European context. As noted above, comparative studies of environmental regulation in the 1980s emphasized that European regulators took a much more flexible cooperative stance vis-à-vis regulated industries than their American counterparts.[45] More generally, the practice of negotiated rule making and delegation of self-regulatory powers to firms and sectoral organizations has a long tradition in the corporatist systems of western Europe.[46]

All of the rhetoric surrounding new, cooperative approaches to regulation notwithstanding, the most marked trend in the European Union is movement in precisely the opposite direction. In comparison to national-level policy styles that granted regulators wide administrative discretion in their dealings with regulated entities (for instance, in the United Kingdom) and discouraged recourse to litigation to settle disputes over regulation (for instance, in Germany), the European Union's approach to regulatory policy seems formal, inflexible, and adversarial. A number of "new" alternative policy instruments have spread throughout the European Union in recent years. However, this trend has been countered by a less-discussed but more-pronounced intensification of command-and-control regulation by the European Union.

The European Commission made calls for the use of "new policy instruments" central to its last two multiyear Environmental Action Programmes. The use of economic instruments such as ecotaxes and emissions trading has increased modestly across the community during the 1990s. A number of member states have adopted environmental taxes at the national level, including taxes on carbon dioxide emissions, other automobile emissions, waste disposal, and effluents.[47] Some member states are in the process of introducing more comprehensive "ecological tax reform" with the intention of shifting the tax burden away from labor and capital toward natural-resource consumption.[48] However, to date, environmental taxes have not emerged as major instruments of environmental policy on the national level.[49] Given the lack of EU competence on fiscal matters, the European Union has not played a significant role in this area, and a proposal for an EU-wide carbon tax scheme failed to win support.[50] The use of tradable permits has been much more limited in the European Union than in the United States. At the national level, the United Kingdom introduced a system for trading sulfur dioxide emissions, and, at the EU level, a proposal for introducing an emissions-trading system to reduce greenhouse gas emissions is currently moving through the legislative pipeline (under codecision).[51] A number of member states instituted ecolabeling programs at the national level since the late 1970s, such as Germany's Blue Angel and the White Swan used in Scandinavian countries. In 1992, the European Union introduced its own ecolabel, the EU flower, and the use of the EU ecolabel increased considerably in the late 1990s, extending to products such as washing machines, dishwashers, toilet paper, paper towels, lightbulbs, and bed linens.[52]

Environmental agreements, sometimes referred to as environmental covenants, voluntary agreements, or long-term agreements, have been concluded in a number of member states. The vast majority of environmental agreements were reached in The Netherlands, where they were a centerpiece of the National Environmental Policy Plan of 1989, and in Germany.[53] More generally, environmental agreements have found the most support in countries with cooperative, neo-corporatist policymaking traditions, and they have been pushed by representatives of industry and conservative parties.[54] They have been adopted in a variety of policy areas including energy efficiency, emissions, packaging waste, and organic food labeling. Unlike in the United States, where such agreements are typically concluded at the level of particular industrial sites, environmental agreements in Europe have tended to be concluded on a broader scale—for instance, at the level of industrial sectors. Generally, such agreements involve a bargain between regulators and regulated industry whereby the government promises to either exempt industry from existing regulations or to forestall the introduction of new command-and-control measures, and industry promises to use this increased flexibility to deliver superior environmental results. For instance, in a 1996 German agreement on greenhouse-gas emissions, representatives of industrial sectors made commitments to reduce emissions by 20 percent by 2005 in exchange for the government refraining from adopting pending regulations on waste heat and energy audits.[55] In The Netherlands, environmental covenants have generally taken the form of enforceable private law contracts signed by firms and the government; however, in most member states voluntary agreements lack any legal basis and essentially constitute "gentlemen's agreements." In the Flanders region of Belgium, early experiments with voluntary agreements yielded generally disappointing results and led to a shift to a more legalistic, contractual approach. However, as the agreements became legally binding, industry lost interest in participation.[56]

Environmental agreements could be applied in the EU framework in two ways: agreements at the member-state level might be used to implement EU law, or agreements might be concluded at the EU level. Although the European Commission advocates the use of voluntary agreements, the framework of EU policy-making and law actually discourages the use of such agreements at the national level. Where EU directives create rights for individuals, as is the case with many EU environmental directives, national implementing measures must guarantee legal certainty and effectiveness. The ECJ has maintained strict interpretation of this requirement. For instance, the ECJ forbade Germany's practice of implementing community air-quality directives with nonbinding administrative circulars, holding that member states must adopt measures "with unquestionable binding force, or with the specificity, precision and clarity required . . . to satisfy the requirement of legal certainty."[57] Clearly, voluntary agreements with industry would not meet this standard.[58]

In 1998, the commission concluded its first formal, voluntary environmental agreement at the EU level as part of its climate-change policy.[59] The European Automobile Manufacturers Association committed itself to cutting average carbon dioxide emissions from new cars sold in the European Union to 140 grams per kilometer by 2008, in exchange for which the commission committed to not proposing binding legislation on carbon dioxide emissions. This agreement evoked the wrath of the European Parliament, which saw the agreement as subverting the European Union's democratic processes. Given the commission's sensitivity to criticisms regarding issues of transparency and democratic accountability, it seems unlikely that the Commission will make such EU-level voluntary agreement a central policy tool in coming years.

As we have seen, the commission frequently declares its commitment to flexible, cooperative policy instruments and has issued a number of directives that aim to increase regulatory flexibility. However, most EU directives continue to include detailed substantive and procedural requirements and to fix rigid deadlines, and many create rights that individuals may later rely on in court. When existing EU environmental laws were amended during the 1990s, their inflexible, command-and-control approach was left in place,[60] and a similar approach was taken in most of the new environmental directives adopted in the 1990s.[61] As noted above, the European Commission consistently brings cases against member-state governments for infringements of EU environmental directives. Not only has the commission challenged member states on substantive violations, it has also forced them to adopt more inflexible, legally binding instruments to implement EU law. Recently, the commission has started to impose penalty payments on member states that fail to comply with ECJ judgments. Through such enforcement mechanisms, the European Union has forced significant shifts in the selection of policy instruments and policy styles in many member states.

In addition to enforcement actions brought by the commission, the European Union is creating both greater opportunities and greater incentives for private enforcement of environmental law. Many EU environmental directives create rights for individuals. These include substantive rights, such as rights to specified levels of environmental quality in water or air, and procedural rights, such as the right to be consulted in environmental impact assessments or the right of access to information on the environment.[62] When community directives have been transposed properly into national law, they are indistinguishable from purely national laws, and private parties can simply defend their rights under these laws before national courts as they would any other right. Even where national governments have failed to properly transpose EU directives, individuals can rely on the doctrines of direct effect and supremacy of community law to defend their rights under community law before national courts.[63] National courts may rule on these cases directly, or they may refer the cases to the ECJ via the preliminary ruling procedure (Art. 234 (ex Art. 177)). There are no comprehensive EU-wide statistics on environmental litigation rates across the member states; however, given the dominance of EU environmental law (relative to purely national environmental law) and given the abundance of justiciable rights in EU environmental law, EU environmental law has clearly increased opportunities for environmental litigation before national courts. As for references to the ECJ, as of 1999 only forty-six references for preliminary rulings in environmental cases had been sent to the ECJ.[64] Although the pace of referrals from national courts accelerated in the late 1990s and has started to play an important role in areas such as nature conservation policy,[65] overall the impact of the preliminary ruling procedure on EU environmental policy remains limited. One important reason for the infrequency of such cases is that many member state legal systems maintain restrictions on standing that prevent environmental NGOs from bringing suits before national courts.[66]

Recent commission initiatives and developments in European law promise to strengthen further the incentives and opportunities for private parties to initiate litigation. Since the mid-1990s, the commission and the European Parliament have pressured member states to harmonize their rules governing "access to justice" for private parties.[67] In 1998, EU member states and the European Union itself signed the United Nations Aarhus Convention, which includes a set of commitments concerning access to justice in environmental policymaking. The Commission and member state environmental inspectorates have interpreted the convention as demanding that environmental NGOs have at least some opportunity to challenge administrative decisions in the public interest.[68] The ECJ's case law concerning the principle of state liability has created the potential for environmental plaintiffs to sue member states for damages they suffer because of the nonimplementation of environmental law. In a series of rulings beginning with *Francovich*,[69] the ECJ has developed a doctrine of state liability that provides that under certain conditions member states can be held liable for damages suffered by individuals as a result of the member state's failure to implement Community law.

Although this principle has yet to be applied to environmental directives, considering the criteria for state liability, it seems likely that individual plaintiffs could successfully assert a basis for such damage claims. Moreover, the mere potential for such suits is likely to have an impact on states' implementation practices. Beyond these general principles of state liability, there has been an increase in the potential for environmental liability claims. At the national level, there has already been a marked trend to broaden the scope of environmental liability.[70] At the EU level, there is an ongoing discussion about adopting environmental liability rules on a community-wide basis.[71]

The European Union has developed an inflexible, adversarial, and judicialized approach to regulation for much the same reason as the United States. As in the United States, the institutional structure of the European Union is characterized by fragmentation of power at the center. Power is divided between two legislative bodies (the council and the parliament), an executive that also has the power to propose legislation (the commission) and a highly independent judiciary (the ECJ). The council's (and, increasingly, the Parliament's) distrust of the commission, its mutual distrust of the member state administrations, and the member states' distrust of each other all encourage the drafting of detailed directives and regulations that can later be enforced by the ECJ. For instance, the parliament's distrust of member state administrations helps explain its opposition to the use of voluntary environmental agreements as instruments of policy implementation and its demand for transparent, legally binding measures. The fragmentation of power in Brussels safeguards the ECJ against political attacks and emboldens it to play an active role in the regulatory process.

The United States and the European Union emerged from the 1990s with a wide variety of policy instruments in place. Although new voluntary agreements and other cooperative instruments have been introduced and have attracted attention in environmental policy debates, their impact remains marginal in the United States and in most of the European Union (with the exception of The Netherlands). Moreover, in the European Union, moves to adopt cooperative approaches to environmental policy have been overwhelmed by more powerful trends toward judicialization emanating from Brussels. This shift in policy style has occurred despite the existence of long traditions of cooperative approaches to regulation in many member states and despite the fact that many European policymakers have consciously sought to discourage an inflexible, adversarial, judicialized approach to policymaking. The fact that such a policy style has developed in the face of such powerful traditions and ideas suggests the power institutions in shaping policy styles.

Empirical studies on the effectiveness of various approaches to environmental policymaking are rare and do not yield a consistent set of findings. Certainly, some emissions trading schemes have already shown they can generate great cost savings.[72] There is little data on the effectiveness of the recent wave of voluntary environmental agreements.[73] In broader studies of the effectiveness of more neocorporatist, cooperative policy styles in the area of environmental policy,

Scruggs[74] and Crepaz[75] find statistical evidence that corporatist patterns of interest intermediation are conducive to pollution reduction, although case studies of particular policies have yielded contradictory findings.[76]

CONCLUSIONS

Comparing recent developments in environmental policy in the United States and European Union challenges our thinking about both polities. First, it suggests that the fact that EU member states retain near total control over implementation and enforcement need not be taken as a sign of the European Union's impotence. Even the powerful U.S. federal government lacks the administrative capacity to preempt state implementation and is quite eager to leave these competences overwhelmingly in state hands. The U.S. federal government has powers to enforce environmental law directly against polluters that the European Union lacks. However, the European Union is actually better positioned to bring legal action against its component states than is the U.S. federal government, given the constitutional limits on "commandeering" state governments in the United States. The comparison of environmental federalism trends in the United States and European Union cautions us not only against underestimating the power of Brussels, but also against overestimating the power of Washington.

As to the issue of policy style, the comparison again highlights the impact of institutional design. Powerful coalitions of industrial interests and academics backing the idea of "new policy instruments" including market-based instruments, information-based instruments, and voluntary agreements have been active in both the United States and the European Union. Their ideas have proven influential in both cases, leading to the introduction of some of these instruments. However, the fragmented constitutional structure common to both systems has limited the application of such instruments and encouraged the continuing dominance of an adversarial, legalistic approach to policy in the United States and the recent growth of such an approach in the European Union.

NOTES

1. R. Daniel Kelemen, *The Rules of Federalism: Institutions and Regulatory Politics in the EU and Beyond* (Cambridge, MA: Harvard University Press, 2004).

2. Fourth Environmental Action Programme [1987] OJ C328/1; Albert Weale, Geoffrey Pridham, Michelle Cini, Dimitrios Konstadakopulos, Martin Porter, and Brendan Flynn, *Environmental Governance in Europe: An Ever Closer Ecological Union?* (Oxford: Oxford University Press, 2000), 297.

3. Maastricht Treaty, Article 3b(2).

4. Jonathan Golub, "The Pivotal Role of British Sovereignty in EC Environmental Policy," EUI Working Paper, RSC No. 94/17 (Florence: European University Institute, 1994).

5. Ludwig Krämer, *E.C. Treaty and Environmental Law,* 2d ed. (London: Sweet and Maxwell, 1995), 60.

6. R. Daniel Kelemen, "The Politics of Eurocratic Structure and the New European Agencies," *West European Politics* 25, no. 4 (2002):93–118.

7. European Commission, *Second Annual Survey on the Implementation and Enforcement of Community Environmental Law: January 1998–December 1999.* Working document of the Commission Services, Directorate General XI, 2000.

8. "Legal Actions Announced over EU Waste Rules," *Ends Environment Daily* 1038 (July 30, 2001).

9. John Kincaid, "The New Coercive Federalism," in *The American Federal System: Federal Balance in Comparative Perspective*, ed. Franz Gress, Detlef Fetchner, and Matthias Hannes (Berlin: Peter Lang, 1994); Susan Rose-Ackerman, "Deregulation and Reregulation: Rhetoric and Reality," *Journal of Law and Politics* 6 (1990):287–309.

10. Timothy Conlan, James Riggle, and Donna Schwartz, "Deregulating Federalism? The Politics of Mandate Reform in the 104th Congress." *Publius* 25, no. 3 (1995):23–40.

11. Evan Ringquist, *Environmental Protection at the State Level: Politics and Progress in Controlling Pollution* (Armonk, NY: M. E. Sharpe, 1993), 62.

12. James Pfander, "Environmental Federalism in Europe and the United States: A Comparative Assessment of Regulation through the Agency of Member States," in *Environmental Policy with Political and Economic Integration: The European Union and the United States*, ed. John Braden, Henk Folmer, and Thomas Ulen (Cheltenham, UK: Edward Elgar, 1996), 88.

13. Conlan, Riggle, and Schwarz, "Deregulating Federalism?" 26.

14. 2 U.S.C. §1501 (1994).

15. Douglas Jehl, "Whitman Promises Latitude to States on Pollution Rules," *New York Times*, January 18, 2001.

16. Eric Pianin, "EPA Seeks Leeway in Rules about Dirty Water," *Washington Post*, August 8, 2002.

17. John Cushman, Jr., "Courts Expanding Effort To Battle Water Pollution," *New York Times*, March 1, 1998.

18. John Cushman, Jr., "EPA and States Found To Be Lax on Pollution Laws," *New York Times*, June 7, 1998.

19. Richard Stewart, "A New Generation of Environmental Regulation?" *Capital University Law Review* 29, no. 56 (2001):21–182; John Dwyer, "The Practice of Federalism under the Clean Air Act," *Maryland Law Review* 54 (1995):1199–1216. Susskind and Secunda report one such revocation involving the RCRA program in Connecticut; see Lawrence Susskind and Joshua Secunda, "The Risks and the Advantages of Agency Discretion: Evidence from EPA's Project XL," *UCLA Journal of Environmental Law and Policy* 17 (1998/1999):71.

20. Kelemen, "The Politics of Eurocratic Structure and the New European Agencies," ch. 1.

21. In July 2002, California adopted a law that will force carmakers to substantially reduce emissions of greenhouse gases such as carbon dioxide and methane by cars sold in the state after 2009. See Christopher Parkes, "California Leads Battle against Car Emissions," *Financial Times*, July 23, 2002; William Booth, "California Takes Lead on Auto Emissions," *Washington Post*, July 22, 2002.

22. David Vogel, *National Styles of Regulation: Environmental Policy in Great Britain and the United States* (Ithaca, NY: Cornell University Press, 1986); Joseph Badaracco,

Loading the Dice: A Five Country Study of Vinyl Chloride Regulation (Boston: Harvard Business School Press, 1985); Ronald Brickman, Sheila Jasanoff, and Thomas Ilgen, *Controlling Chemicals: The Politics of Regulation in Europe and the United States* (Ithaca, NY: Cornell University Press, 1985). For a review of such comparative studies, see Robert Kagan and Lee Axelrad, "Adversarial Legalism: An International Perspective," in *Comparative Disadvantages? Social Regulations in the Global Economy*, ed. Pietro Nivola (Washington, DC: Brookings Institution, 1997).

23. Stewart, "A New Generation of Environmental Regulation?" 24.

24. Susskind and Secunda, "The Risks and the Advantages of Agency Discretion," 82.

25. Stewart, "A New Generation of Environmental Regulation?" 103–10.

26. Ibid.

27. Lisa Lund, "Project XL: Good for the Environment, Good for Business, Good for Communities," *Environmental Law Reporter* 30 (2000):1040–41.

28. Rena Steinzor, "Reinventing Environmental Regulation: The Dangerous Journey from Command to Self-Control," *Harvard Environmental Law Review* 22 (1998): 125, 141.

29. Steinzor, "Reinventing Environmental Regulation," 188.

30. Stewart, "A New Generation of Environmental Regulation?" 78; Steinzor, "Reinventing Environmental Regulation," 131.

31. Stewart, "A New Generation of Environmental Regulation?" 68–71, 79.

32. Ibid., 68–94.

33. Ibid., 38.

34. Daniel Altman, "Just How Far Can Trading of Emissions Be Extended?" *New York Times*, May 31, 2002.

35. Cindy Skrzycki, "New Brand of Oversight: Bush's Regulatory Record in Texas Offers Clues to the Approach He'll Bring to Washington," *Washington Post*, January 21, 2001.

36. Jehl, "Whitman Promises Latitude to States on Pollution Rules."

37. Katharine Seelye, "White House Seeks a Change in Rules on Air Pollution," *New York Times*, June 14, 2002; Nancy Dunne, "Bush Plans To Relax Air Pollution Rules," *Financial Times*, June 14, 2002.

38. Katharine Seelye, "Top E.P.A. Official Quits, Criticizing Bush's Policies," *New York Times*, March 1, 2002; Faye Fiore, "Top EPA Enforcement Official Quits, Blasts Bush Policy," *Los Angeles Times*, March 1, 2002.

39. Terry Moe, "The Politics of Bureaucratic Structure," in *Can the Government Govern?* John Chubb and Paul Peterson, eds. (Washington, DC: Brookings Institution, 1989).

40. Douglas Jehl, "Fearing Bush Will Win, Groups Plan Pollution Suits," *New York Times*, December 7, 2000.

41. Magali Delmas and Ann Terlak, "The Institutional Context of Environmental Voluntary Agreements" (paper presented at Conference on Organizations, Policy and the Natural Environment, Kellogg School of Management, Northwestern University, April 28–30, 2000).

42. Jonathan Golub, "Introduction and Overview," in *New Instruments for Environmental Policy in the EU*, ed. Jonathan Golub (London: Routledge, 1998), 1–8; Arthur Mol, Volkmar Lauber, and Duncan Liefferink, eds., *The Voluntary Approach to Environmental Policy: Joint Environmental Policy-making in Europe* (Oxford: Oxford University Press, 2000);

Christoph Knill and Andrea Lenschow, eds., *Implementing EU Environmental Policy* (Manchester, UK: Manchester University Press, 2000).

43. Golub, "Introduction and Overview," 6; Duncan Liefferink, Mikael Skou Andersen, and Martin Enevoldsen, "Interpreting Joint Environmental Policy-making: Between Deregulation and Political Modernization," in *The Voluntary Approach to Environmental Policy*, ed. Mol, Lauber, and Liefferink, 13–14.

44. COM(2001)581, October 23, 2001.

45. See supra, note 22.

46. See, for instance, Wofgang Streeck and Philippe Schmitter, *Private Interest Government: Beyond Market and State* (London: Sage, 1985); Jeremy Richardson, ed., *Policy Styles in Western Europe* (London: George Allen & Unwin, 1982); Frans van Waarden, "Persistence of National Policy Styles: A Study of Their Institutional Foundations," in *Convergence or Diversity: Internationalization and Economic Policy Response*, ed. Brigitte Unger and Frans van Waarden (Aldershot, UK: Avebury, 1995).

47. See Organization for Economic Cooperation and Development (OECD), *Environmentally Related Taxes Database* (Paris: OECD, 2002), www.oecd.org; Kerstin Tews, Per-Olof Busch, and Helge Jörgens, "The Diffusion of New Environmental Policy Instruments," FFU-report 01-2002 (Berlin: Forschungsstelle für Umweltpolitik, Freie Universität Berlin, 2002), www.fu-berlin.de/ffu/.

48. Jos Delbeke and Hans Bergman, "Environmental Taxes and Charges in the EU," in *New Instruments for Environmental Policy in the EU*, ed. Golub.

49. Golub, *New Instruments for Environmental Policy in the EU*, 10; Delbeke and Bergman, "Environmental Taxes and Charges in the EU"; OECD, *Environmentally Related Taxes Database*.

50. Golub, *New Instruments for Environmental Policy in the EU*, 11.

51. COM(2001)581, Brussels, October 23, 2001.

52. Council Regulation No. 880/92, March 23, 1992; Eva Eiderström, "Ecolabels in EU Environmental Policy," in *New Instruments for Environmental Policy in the EU*, ed. Golub, 194–99; Tews, Busch, and Jörgens, "The Diffusion of New Environmental Policy Instruments."

53. Arthur Mol, Duncan Liefferink, and Volkmar Lauber, "Introduction," in *The Voluntary Approach to Environmental Policy*, ed. Mol, Lauber, and Liefferink; Peter Börkey and Francois Lévêque, *Voluntary Approaches for Environmental Protection in the European Union*, OECD, Working Party on Economic and Environmental Policy Integration, ENV/EPOC/GEEI(98)29/Final (Paris: OECD, December 10, 1998).

54. Volkmar Lauber, "The Political and Institutional Setting," in *The Voluntary Approach to Environmental Policy*, ed. Mol, Lauber and Liefferink.

55. David Grimeaud, "Are 'Voluntary Environmental Agreements' an Alternative or a Useful Complement to 'Classic' Policy Instruments in Europe and the USA?" in *Green Giants: Environmental Policy in the United States and the European Union*, ed. Norman Vig and Michael Faure (Cambridge, MA: MIT Press, 2004).

56. Kurt Deketelaere, "New Environmental Policy Instruments in Belgium," in *New Instruments for Environmental Policy in the EU*, ed. Golub, 111–22.

57. Ibid., 2602–03. The Court has made a number of similar rulings. C-131/88 *Commission v. Germany* [1991] ECR I-825; Case 58/89 *Commission v. Germany* [1991] ECR I-4893 concerning the surface waters directive; Case 59/89 *Commission v. Germany* [1991] ECR 2607.

58. European Commission, *Communication on Environmental Agreements*, COM (96) 561 final (1996); Jonathan Verschuuren, "EC Environmental Law and Self-Regulation in the Member States: In Search of a Legislative Framework," in *Yearbook of European Environmental Law*, ed. Han Somsen (Oxford: Oxford University Press, 2000), 112; Grimeaud, "Are 'Voluntary Environmental Agreements' an Alternative or a Useful Complement to 'Classic' Policy Instruments in Europe and the USA?"

59. 1999/125/EC, OJ L 40/49, February 13, 1999.

60. Andrew Jordan, Rüdiger Wurzel, and Anthony Zito, "European Governance and the Transfer of 'New' Environmental Policy Instruments in the European Union" (paper presented at the 2001 Biennial International conference of the European Community Studies Association, Madison, Wisconsin, May 29–June 2, 2001).

61. Berthold Rittberger and Jeremy Richardson, "(Mis-)Matching Declarations and Actions? Commission Proposals in Light of the Fifth Environmental Action Programme" (paper presented at the Seventh Biennial International Conference of the European Community Studies Association [ECSA], Madison, Wisconsin, May 31–June 2, 2001).

62. Dir. 85/337 [1985] OJ L 175/40.

63. For an overview of the development of the doctrines of supremacy and direct effect, see Joseph Weiler, "The Transformation of Europe," *Yale Law Journal* 100 (1991): 2403–83.

64. Han Somsen, "The Private Enforcement of Member State Compliance with EC Environmental Law: An Unfulfilled Promise?" in *Yearbook of European Environmental Law*, ed. Han Somsen.

65. Rachel Cichowski, "Litigation, Compliance and European Integration: The Preliminary Ruling Procedure and EU Nature Conservation Policy" (paper presented at the 2001 Annual Meeting of the European Community Studies Association, Madison, Wisconsin, May 31–June 2, 2001).

66. Somsen, *Yearbook of European Environmental Law*; IMPEL (European Union Network for the Implementation and Enforcement of Environmental Law), *Complaint Procedures and Access to Justice for Citizens and NGOs in the Field of Environment within the European Union*, 2000. http://europa.eu.int/comm/environment/impel/access_to_justice.htm.

67. European Commission, *Communication from the Commission: Implementing Community Environmental Law*, COM(96) 500 final (1996).

68. IMPEL, *Complaint Procedures and Access to Justice for Citizens and NGOs in the Field of Environment within the European Union*, 16, 160–63.

69. Joined cases C-6/90 and C-9/90, *Francovich and Others v. Italy* [1991] ECR I-5357; joined cases C-46/93 and C-48/93.

70. Gerrit Betlem and Michael Faure, "Environmental Toxic Torts in Europe," *Georgetown International Environmental Law Review* 10 (1998):855–90.

71. European Commission, *White Paper on Environmental Liability*, COM(2000)66 final (2000); Michael Mann, "Businesses May Be Liable for Environment Harm," *Financial Times*, November 25, 2001.

72. Altman, "Just How Far Can Trading of Emissions Be Extended?"

73. Börkey and Lévêque, *Voluntary Approaches for Environmental Protection in the European Union*, 21.

74. Lyle Scruggs, "Institutions and Environmental Performance in Seventeen Western Democracies," *British Journal of Political Science* 29, no. 1 (1999):1–31.

75. Markus Crepaz, "Explaining National Variations of Air Pollution Levels: Political Institutions and Their Impact on Environmental Policy-Making," *Environmental Politics* 4, no. 3 (1995):391–414.

76. See Vogel, *National Styles of Regulation*, and Robert Kagan and Lee Axelrad, eds., *Regulatory Encounters: Multinational Corporations and American Adversarial Legalism* (Berkeley: University of California Press, 2000), for studies that find cooperative approaches more effective, but see Liefferink, Andersen, and Enevoldsen, "Interpreting Joint Environmental Policy-making," 18–20, for a review of studies that find corporatism to be detrimental to environmental policy.

AUSTERITY POLITICS, THE NEW PUBLIC MANAGEMENT, AND ADMINISTRATIVE REFORM IN THE UNITED STATES, BRITAIN, AND FRANCE

ADAM D. SHEINGATE

INTRODUCTION

ACROSS THE INDUSTRIALIZED WORLD, POLITICAL LEADERS HAVE EMBARKED ON ADMINIS-
trative reform programs that promise to improve the efficiency, economy, accessibility, or quality of public services. Informed by the rhetoric of the "new public
management," these reform efforts emphasize increased management flexibility,
the use of performance and output measures, market mechanisms such as contracting out, the decentralization of government functions, and a "customer" orientation in the delivery of public services. The diffusion of new public management
rhetoric reflects, in part, the spread of private sector management ideas and insights from the new institutional economics into public administration. By bringing together elements of managerialism, public choice theory, and transaction cost
economics, the new public management provides, in the words of one observer, "a
dominant but loosely specified set of ideas . . . which can be applied to a very wide
range of contexts."[1]

But the attraction of these ideas also comes from their political usefulness. In
this chapter, I argue that administrative reform and the rhetoric of the new public
management are particularly well suited to the contemporary politics of public
policy in the United States and Europe. Specifically, I identify two related thrusts
to the politics of reform. On the one hand, administrative reform efforts consist of
visible, well-publicized initiatives closely identified with presidents and prime
ministers. Motivated by electoral considerations, such initiatives encompass a
variety of techniques and new technologies designed to address voter concerns
over the quality of public service delivery. At the same time, administrative reform
efforts have been part of less-visible, institutional struggles that alter the distribu-

tion of authority within government. Whereas public initiatives for reform often promise to decentralize policymaking or empower front-line managers of government programs, these institutional reforms often result in more centralized control over the political direction of public policy.

As I argue below, this seeming contradiction of administrative reform—decentralized management amid more centralized control—makes sense within the context of contemporary politics and public policy. As Paul Pierson has shown, policymakers are caught between the demographic and economic pressures on modern welfare states and the political resiliency of entrenched social programs—when an irresistible force meets an immovable object.[2] Specifically, programmatic policy retrenchment designed to ease fiscal pressures runs up against the politicians' incentive to avoid blame for unpopular measures.[3] Because of the status quo bias inherent in the politics of blame avoidance, welfare state retrenchment—cutting back on the scope of social provision—remains difficult even in the face of contrary economic and demographic trends.

As I explore in the cases of the United States, Britain, and France, financial constraints, increasing electoral volatility, and declining public trust in government are clearly reflected in the politics of administrative reform. Given the challenges and constraints of contemporary politics, politicians and policymakers seize on administrative reform both as an attractive political issue in an age when the range of alternatives is increasingly circumscribed, and as a device through which to pursue institutional changes that enhance the political direction of policy. Through reform, politicians in these countries hope to distance themselves from unpopular bureaucracies and public service shortcomings, while at the same time improve central coordination of policy so that elected leaders can secure policy accomplishments from an increasingly narrow range of credit-claiming opportunities.

Not surprisingly, the degree to which politicians can achieve this, as well as the precise mechanisms they employ, will depend on particular configurations of institutions, ideological traditions, and partisan politics. In sum, administrative reform in the United States, Britain, and France illustrates how similar political incentives and cross pressures are channeled through country-specific characteristics to produce distinct national outcomes. In this way, administrative reform sheds light on both the commonalities and differences in the politics of public policy in the United States and abroad.

VARIETIES OF ADMINISTRATIVE REFORM

To begin, it is helpful to specify what we mean by administrative reform. It is a mark of its political utility that the concept has come to include a wide variety of mechanisms, including reductions in the number of civil servants, changes in the structure and function of government agencies, and efforts to improve the quality of public services. In order to better organize the discussion, as well as provide a way to compare reform efforts across countries, I have grouped together the various mechanisms into three related activities. These three activities are overlapping, rather than exclusive, and are meant to suggest both the scope of reform and the different goals politicians hope to pursue through administrative reform programs.

First, some reforms are designed to *reduce the size and scope of government*. For example, governments have downsized the civil service in an effort to improve the economy and efficiency of the public sector or pursued savings through general cost-cutting measures such as office closures or streamlining procedures. Similarly, governments have used privatization to raise revenues through the sale of state-owned enterprises or reduce expenditures through the transfer of commercial activities to the private sector. In addition, governments have turned to contracts and competitive tendering in order to acquire or produce goods and services from the private sector previously provided by government itself.[4] What distinguishes these reforms are the ends; they are designed to shrink the state by cutting the number of employees, reducing expenditures, and transferring the production of goods and services to the private sector.

A second group of reforms attempt to *transform the structure of government*. For example, decentralization pushes responsibility for public functions downward toward subnational units of governments; deconcentration pushes responsibility toward lower administrative units within government.[5] Other reforms seek to transform the relationship between levels of bureaucracy—for example, by hiving off responsibility for policy implementation to newly created, semiautonomous agencies.[6] Often accompanying this "agencification" is the use of explicit contracts between parent ministries and agencies that stipulate precise functions as well as indicators for measuring performance. This "contractualization" replaces traditional hierarchical methods of bureaucratic accountability. In some cases, relations among governmental units are "marketized" in the sense that they must compete with one another in an internal market for the provision of public functions.[7] Finally, granting greater autonomy to agencies or bureaus often requires the loosening of rules and procedures, or internal deregulation, in areas such as personnel or budgeting. What unites each of these structural reforms is an attempt to alter the distribution of authority and responsibility within and between governmental units.

Third, reforms seek to *improve the performance of government*. Some reforms employ top-down mechanisms, such as the imposition of specific targets and the use of monitoring, regulatory bodies, and inspectorates to assess whether targets have been achieved. When combined with outcome- or performance-based budgeting, governments may attempt to link the budget process with the achievement of specific goals or targets.[8] Other reforms are more bottom-up in their orientation. For example, efforts to improve the responsiveness, accessibility, or transparency of public services can focus on those points of direct contact between government and citizens. In general, this "consumerization" of public service pro-

Table 8.1. Varieties of Administrative Reform

Reduce the size and scope of government

- Downsizing
- Privatization
- Contracting out
- Cost cutting

Transform the structure of government

- Decentralization/deconcentration
- Agencification
- Contractualization
- Marketizing
- Internal deregulation

Improve the performance of government

- Targets
- Monitoring
- Outcome/performance budgeting
- Access/transparency
- Customer orientation

---

vision identifies government performance with levels of "user" satisfaction. Similar measures might include the bundling of various functions into "one-stop shops" for government services, simplifying application procedures, or easing access to government information. Whether imposed from above through targets or encouraged from below through satisfaction levels, a common theme has been to develop specific outcome measures that can be used to assess government performance. Table 8.1 summarizes these three varieties of administrative reform.

As we will see, all three countries have experimented with reforms directed at the size, structure, or performance of government. Of course, some reforms pursue multiple objectives: granting an agency responsible for policy implementation greater autonomy (structure) may result in lower administrative costs (size) and enable bureaucrats to meet specific agency targets (performance). However, as I describe below, administrative reforms also fulfill explicitly political purposes. Promises to cut the number of bureaucrats or improve public sector performance can often provide a cheap political appeal designed to attract voters. At the same time, politicians might endorse structural change because it increases their capacity to direct policy from the center and extract whatever opportunities for credit claiming are available in an otherwise constrained policy environment. In this way, administrative reforms reflect the incentives and political cross pressures faced by politicians and policymakers.

AUSTERITY POLITICS AND THE NEW PUBLIC MANAGEMENT

Administrative reform has occurred against a backdrop of constraints characteristic of contemporary politics in advanced industrial countries. Demographic
pressures of an aging society, the financial commitments of mature pension and
health care policies, and the slowdown in growth associated with the transformation from manufacturing to service sector employment impose significant fiscal
burdens on mature welfare states. Deficit politics, or the fiscalization of public
policy, in turn severely limits the range of alternatives policymakers may reasonably consider, ruling out for example the creation of new programs—and the opportunities for credit claiming—that occurred during the heyday of welfare state
construction.[9] Instead, fiscal constraints impose difficult tradeoffs—for example,
between generous social policies and fiscal rectitude—that risk-averse politicians
are likely to avoid, especially given the blame generated when politicians directly
confront entrenched social programs.

Second, politicians face the rhetoric if not the reality of globalization, which
reinforces arguments in favor of fiscal austerity, low taxes, and liberal economic
policies in the pursuit of global or regional competitiveness. Like the demographic
pressures and policy commitments of mature welfare states, concerns over competitiveness constrain the range of plausible policy alternatives and sharpen the
tradeoffs politicians confront. Moreover, in the case of Britain and France, competition is on a European as well as global level and, at least for France, the fiscal requirements of monetary union add further austerity pressures.

In addition to the pressures of austerity, politicians in advanced industrial
countries must confront a transformed electoral landscape following the decline of
mass-based, patronage-driven parties anchored to class. One consequence of this
decline is greater electoral uncertainty: politicians can no longer rely on political
parties to mobilize voters with the same regularity as in the past, a fact that is com-
pounded by growing dissatisfaction among the electorate as evidenced by declining voting rates and rising support for extreme parties.[10] Austerity politics might
contribute to this trend in two ways: (1) fiscal constraints limit politicians' recourse
to the creation or expansion of programs that solidified voter attachments to parties, and (2) politicians' unwillingness or inability to address the difficult tradeoffs
associated with permanent austerity contributes to voter dissatisfaction.

THE POLITICS OF ADMINISTRATIVE REFORM

It is against this backdrop that politicians in the United States, France, and
Britain have turned to administrative reform programs. As I describe below, an
irony of administrative reform is the seeming contradiction between initiatives
that promise to devolve responsibility toward lower-level managers and release
the creative energies of bureaucrats from stifling rules and regulations on the one
hand, and the apparent centralization of policy authority through the introduc-

tion of various control mechanisms on the other. In fact, this contradiction makes sense in light of the cross pressures politicians face to claim credit and avoid blame. The constraints of contemporary public policy significantly limit opportunities to claim credit, and they have amplified pressures to avoid blame. Nevertheless, politicians still seek to do both, and the political appeal of administrative reform comes from its capacity to help political leaders negotiate the difficult terrain of austerity politics. Measures that appear to devolve responsibility can be an effective way for politicians to avoid blame for administrative failures or public dissatisfaction with bureaucracy. At the same time, the centralization of policy authority can facilitate the kind of steering necessary to ensure that whatever credit can be extracted from the system is claimed by those at the top. Indeed, the attraction of administrative reform and the rhetoric of the new public management lay precisely in its adaptability to these cross pressures of credit and blame.

It is these cross pressures, moreover, that distinguish contemporary administrative reforms from previous attempts to transform government. As a number of scholars point out, reform itself is hardly new; in the United States, for example, various initiatives date back to the struggles over civil service reform in the 1870s.[11] Paul Light has identified 141 federal management statutes signed into law from 1945 to 1995 that make up several "tides of reform" over the post–World War II period alone.[12] But beginning in the late 1970s, a notable change appears in the politics of administrative reform. In his study of presidential reorganization since 1905, Peri Arnold argues that, "beginning with Carter . . . administrative reorganization and reform have become expressions of populist concerns about government's size, cost, and performance."[13] This shift, moreover, coincides with the spread of enthusiasm for new public management ideas around the world noted by comparative scholars of public administration.[14] Thus, at a time when the fiscal constraints and political pitfalls of mature welfare states became increasingly apparent, presidents and prime ministers turned to administrative reform to position themselves apart from and, in some cases against, the very bureaucracy they ostensibly lead.

In the Unites States, Jimmy Carter is perhaps the first president to make administrative reform an electoral issue and in 1979 successfully pushed for congressional passage of the Civil Service Reform Act. Along with performance appraisals and merit-based pay, the act created a Senior Executive Service in the hope of providing a more responsive and efficient bureaucracy.[15] With Reagan's election in 1980, the White House initiated a number of visible attacks on the supposed fraud, waste, and inefficiency in the federal executive. These efforts included the President's Council on Integrity and Efficiency (1981) and his appointment of the Grace Commission in 1982, otherwise known as the President's Private Sector Survey on Cost Control.[16] Administrative reform was less prominent during the first Bush administration with the exception of the Council on Competitiveness (1989) and its efforts to streamline federal regulations. But with Clinton's election, administrative reform again became a prominent theme following inauguration of the National Performance Review (NPR) in 1993 (renamed the National Partnership for

Reinventing Government in 1998). Prompted in part by the Perot candidacy in 1992 and its appeal to voters dissatisfied with or disaffected by government, the Clinton–Gore embrace of "reinvention" included efforts to downsize the bureaucracy, reform the federal procurement process, and generally increase the customer orientation of public service delivery. The current Bush administration announced its management plan in September 2001, emphasizing greater private-sector competition for public service provision and better use of performance targets in budgeting decisions.[17] In short, presidents since Carter have used administrative reform as a political issue designed to attract votes.

Similarly in Britain, administrative reform has been a central component of consecutive governments, Conservative and Labour, since the late 1970s. Like Reagan, Thatcher portrayed the civil service as wasteful and inefficient, a move that shifted blame for poor government performance and high public-sector deficits onto self-serving bureaucrats. The 1982 Financial Management Initiative gave line managers within ministries greater control over resource allocation in exchange for more explicit budget and performance targets imposed from the center.[18] Subsequent reforms granted further responsibility for policy implementation to lower levels of the bureaucracy. The 1988 Next Steps Initiative created semiautonomous agencies responsible for the delivery of particular services and linked them to the central ministries through contracts that set overall policy goals. A similar strategy was employed in the National Health Service (NHS) reforms. Implemented in 1991, hospitals formerly under the immediate direction of NHS authorities became semiautonomous NHS trusts forced to compete in an internal market for patients and services.[19]

Another prominent theme in British reforms has been the customer focus in public service delivery. Governments throughout the 1980s and 1990s introduced new inspection services (e.g., Office for Standards in Education) and issued performance measures intended to track quality improvements in public service provision.[20] Similarly, the 1991 "Citizen's Charter" became a central focus of the Major government; it outlined a number of general principles for improving quality, with a particular emphasis on how users experienced various public services.[21] Public service renewal has perhaps reached its greatest prominence under the Blair Labour government. A 1999 White Paper titled "Modernizing Government" set forth a broad program for public services, emphasizing themes such as "making sure public service users, not providers, are the focus" and "delivering public services that are high quality and efficient."[22]

In France, administrative reform has taken place against the backdrop of decentralization. Beginning in the early 1980s, local and regional governments gained greater autonomy and responsibility over a host of policy areas.[23] In addition, a process of deconcentration gave local officers of central government, such as prefects, greater authority over policy decisions formerly decided in Paris. As political issues, decentralization and deconcentration promised to make administration less rigid and more easily adapted to the local concerns of citizens, a theme that dovetailed nicely with the administrative reform programs of the late 1980s and

1990s. In 1989, for example, Prime Minister Rocard announced a plan for administrative reform titled "Renewal of the Public Service." Rocard's program identified a number of reform goals, most prominently the delegation of authority for policy implementation to "responsibility centers" within ministries. In 1992, the Bérégovoy government issued its "Public Service Charter" establishing principles of transparency, simplicity, and accessibility in citizen's dealings with government.[24] And in 1995, Prime Minister Juppé issued a circular titled "Reform of the State and Public Services" that envisioned a more ambitious reorganization of state functions, whereby central government ministries would be responsible for resource allocation, policy formation, and evaluation, while local agencies would become responsible for actual service provision.[25] Although much of Juppé's plan foundered with the rest of his neoliberal reforms in 1995, administrative reform remained on the national agenda during the Jospin government (1997–2002). In 2000, parliament passed a law titled "Rights of Citizens in Relations with Government" that further codified issues of access and transparency in public administration.[26]

Alongside the more visible political initiatives that emphasize devolved responsibility and increased satisfaction with public services have been less-visible efforts to concentrate political control over policy at the center. For example, we have seen a general growth in the political staff of presidents and prime ministers in each country. In the United States, the Executive Office of the President employed more than 1,600 people in 2002, a number that has remained stable through the federal downsizing of the 1980s and 1990s. Of these, 397 work directly for the president in the White House Office, or West Wing.[27] Although expansion of the presidential bureaucracy is a well-documented institutional development in the United States, the rise in numbers of political advisers in Britain and France is perhaps more surprising given the traditions of a professional civil service in both countries. In Britain, for example, the number of advisers serving the prime minister has increased to the point that some critics of Tony Blair refer to the "presidentialization" of Number 10.[28] Although small when compared to the White House, the number of staff members working directly for the prime minister has increased from 71 in 1970 to 150 in 1999; of these, about 40 people work on policy and political matters.[29] French scholars of administration have also drawn attention to the politicization of policy advice, noting, for example, that the number of staff members who work in ministerial *cabinets*—the political advisers to each minister chosen personally from the senior civil service—increased since the inauguration of the Fifth Republic in 1959. Under the Jospin government, the number of such advisers averaged around 16 per minister, or 448 in all, twice the average during the 1970s. Meanwhile, the number of permanent staff attached to the prime minister's office increased by nearly 70 percent between 1980 and 2000.[30]

In addition to the growth in political staff has been the promotion of institutional mechanisms that further centralize control over policy. A number of these mechanisms have been either created or enhanced through administrative reforms often justified on the grounds of improved government performance or increased efficiency. In the United States, for example, the 1979 Civil Service Reform Act gave presidents "greater leverage to manipulate civil service personnel . . . [and] influence the staffing of departments critical to its policy objectives more effectively."[31] The Office of Management and Budget (OMB) has similarly become an instrument of political coordination of policy in the hands of some presidents. Through the Office of Internal Regulatory Affairs, OMB review of agency regulations enhanced presidential control over the bureaucracy, a tool used to great effect by the Reagan administration.[32] More recently, legislation passed in conjunction with the National Performance Review has strengthened OMB's oversight and coordination role. The Government Performance and Results Act (GPRA), passed in 1993, promised to "encourage greater efficiency, effectiveness, and accountability in federal spending by establishing a new framework for management and subsequently budgeting in federal agencies."[33] Specifically, GPRA requires agencies to set targets, design quantitative performance measures, and routinely report results to OMB. Along with an internal reorganization carried out in 1995, the GPRA can be used to link budgeting decisions with the presidential coordination of policy priorities.

Similarly in Britain, prime ministers have used administrative reform to strengthen policy coordination, especially through the Cabinet Office. For instance, prime ministers since Thatcher have served as the Minister of the Civil Service, a move accompanied by the disbanding of the Civil Service Department within the Treasury and the creation of a Management and Personnel Office within the Cabinet Office. In 1992, the Major government merged civil service functions with other Cabinet Office units responsible for administrative reforms such as Next Steps and the Citizen's Charter into a single Office of Public Service and Science.[34] Under New Labour, this trend has continued with the creation of new Cabinet Office units designed to ensure that the Blair government achieves its ambitious goals for public service provision. Under the most recent reorganization, the prime minister's "Reform and Delivery Team" now includes a strategy unit, a delivery unit, and the Prime Minister's Office of Public Services Reform.[35] Historically viewed as an "honest broker" between departments, the Cabinet Office is increasingly a tool for prime ministerial policy coordination: Cabinet Office staff increased by 56 percent between 1990 and 2001, a time of deep personnel cuts in the British Civil Service.[36] Meanwhile, the Treasury has developed a stronger policy coordination role. In 1998, Chancellor Gordon Brown introduced his first Comprehensive Spending Review, a three-year forecast of public sector expenditures including specific objectives for public service improvements. Finally, in an attempt to overcome departmentalism, the Blair government has promoted "joined up government," an effort to articulate policy goals that span ministries within the British executive.[37]

Under the French dual executive, constitutional authority over the bureaucracy rests somewhat ambiguously between the president and prime minister.[38] Consequently, administrative reforms can provide a way for prime ministers to assert themselves vis à vis parliament and the president. For example, Juppé's plans for state reform promised to reaffirm political control over a bureaucracy under the control of recalcitrant technocrats. To achieve his goals, Juppé created an independent Ministry for State Reform responsible for restructuring the bureaucracy apart from the Civil Service Ministry and secured several institutional innovations that lived on even after his plans for administrative reform stumbled.[39] The Interministerial Council for State Reform (CIRE), for example, is presided over by the prime minister and includes officials from the Ministry for Civil Service and State Reform, the budget office of the Finance Ministry, the Interior Ministry, and the Planning Commission. CIRE publishes studies and recommendations for administrative reform; a second interministerial body, also under the responsibility of the prime minister, oversees its implementation. More recently, the Jospin government required each ministry to submit a multiyear "modernization plan" (*programmes pluriannuels de modernization*) used in tracking performance and progress in the government's initiatives for public service reforms.[40]

To sum up, as politicians face the political, economic, and demographic constraints of mature welfare states, administrative reforms provide leaders with something they can actually *do*.[41] Politicians are attracted to reform for its political usefulness, because it provides them with a novel appeal to voters, one that cleverly taps into public dissatisfaction and skepticism toward government. Administrative reform reorients public debate away from the *content* of public policy, particularly the scope and generosity of social provision, toward the *process* of service delivery with its emphasis on quality, efficiency, and customer satisfaction. As Pollitt and Bouckaert describe it, administrative reform is "technical politics . . . streamlining, repackaging, marginally modifying or actually downsizing . . . existing programmes, rather than any heroic new efforts."[42]

These qualities run through the reform initiatives in United States, Britain, and France. Closely identified with presidents and prime ministers, administrative reform has been a highly visible, well-publicized attempt to address voter concerns over the quality of public service delivery. Although important differences exist, politicians across the political spectrum—Reagan and Clinton, Thatcher and Blair, Rocard and Juppé—have sought political advantage from administrative reform. In addition, administrative reform in all three countries drew on the rhetoric of the new public management, especially its emphasis on empowering managers, adopting output and performance measures, and orienting service provision toward the needs of the "user."[43] The National Performance Review in the United States, the Modernising Government White Paper in Britain, and the efforts at "reform" and "renewal" of the French public service all share, at least rhetorically, a belief in devolved responsibility and a focus on users in order to improve service delivery. More than simply reflecting faddish management ideas drawn from the private sector, however, these similarities illustrate the political appeal of administrative reform. A public embrace of administrative reform goals can be a useful device for avoiding the blame generated by unpopular bureaucracies.[44] At the same time, championing improvements in service delivery can be a cheap source of political credit among voters generally dissatisfied with the quality of public service provision.

Politicians are also drawn to administrative reform because it presents an opportunity to promote institutional devices that enhance central control over policy. In each country, the executive created or augmented administrative bodies with responsibility for policy coordination that report directly to the president or prime minister. All three countries have experimented with forcing ministries and departments to adopt performance agreements and modernization plans that, when tied to the budget process, can provide an additional tool for policy coordination. Students of administrative reform and the new public management rightly point out the apparent contradiction in granting line managers greater responsibility over implementation decisions at the same time that efforts are made to increase bureaucratic accountability to central authorities through performance measures or contractual relationships.[45] But this contradiction makes sense in the context of political cross pressures for blame avoidance and credit claiming. Administrative reforms at once distance political leaders from the blame-generating functions of government and provide ways to exploit the limited credit-claiming opportunities that arise within the complex and increasingly constrained policy environment of mature welfare states.

ADMINISTRATIVE REFORM IN COMPARATIVE PERSPECTIVE

Despite these similarities in the pressures and incentives driving reform, important differences remain in the experiences of the United States, Britain, and France. Returning to the three varieties of reform described above, we can identify a particular emphasis in the reform initiatives of each country. In the United States, reform efforts have focused primarily on reductions in the size and scope of government. In Britain, where the reform agenda has been the broadest, the most far-reaching changes transformed the structure of the British bureaucracy and significantly reduced its size. In France, administrative reforms have concentrated on public sector performance, along with the structural changes accompanying decentralization.

Table 8.2 summarizes these differences across countries. As indicated, the United States and Britain have been more active in efforts to reduce the size and scope of government than France. In the United States, for example, a summary report by the National Performance Review (renamed the National Partnership for Reinventing Government) issued in January 2001 listed "Ending the Era of Big Government" first among its "major accomplishments." Specifically, the report boasted a reduction of 426,000 in the size of the federal civilian workforce and savings of more than $136 billion through various cost-cutting measures such as the closure of field offices and the simplification of administrative procedures.[46] However, as Paul Light has shown, simple civil service head counts do not reveal the "true size of government" because they exclude a vast "shadow government" of individuals working for the government under contracts and grants. According to Light's estimates, the federal government employed over eight million people

Table 8.2. Comparison of Administrative Reforms in the United States, Britain, and France

A. Reduce the size and scope of government

	United States	Britain	France
Downsizing	X	X	
Privatization	X	X	X
Contracting out	X	X	
Retrenchment	X		

B. Transform the structure of government

	United States	Britain	France
Decen/Decon			X
Agencification		X	X
Contractualization		X	X
Marketizing		X	
Internal deregulation	X	X	

C. Improve the performance of government

	United States	Britain	France
Customer orientation	X	X	X
Targets	X	X	X
Budgeting		X	
Access/transparency			X

through contracts and grants in 1996, more than four times as many than the number of people employed through the civil service. Moreover, excluding Defense Department contracts and grants, the number of "shadow" employees increased by more than 16 percent between 1984 and 1996. In other words, at a time when the Clinton administration touted its personnel reductions, the federal government increased its reliance on contract workers in nondefense-related functions.[47] This trend will likely continue: the 1998 Federal Activities Inventory Reform Act (FAIR) strengthened rules that require federal agencies to seek commercial sources for products and services whenever possible. And in November 2002, the Bush administration announced that it would put up to 850,000 jobs—half of the civil service—up for competition with the private sector in coming years.[48]

British reforms have also reduced the size and scope of government. Between 1978 and 2001, total public sector employment declined by a third. This reduction has taken place through a combination of downsizing, privatization, and contracting out. Since 1979, privatization in sectors such as aerospace, telecommunications, gas, water, and rail transferred more than 1.6 million jobs to the private sector and accounts for nearly 70 percent of the decline in public sector employment over the period.[49] Contracting out—introduced through the program Competing for Quality in 1991 and further codified by the Deregulation and Contracting Out Act of 1994—also trimmed public sector employment, especially in the Ministry of Defense and in local government, the latter shedding 12 percent of its employees between 1979 and 2001 despite a 22 percent increase in the number of police. Finally, areas of the public sector less touched by privatization and contracting out have also declined; for example, employment in the core civil service decreased by 35 percent since 1979.[50]

Uniquely, public sector employment in France steadily increased over the last twenty years. Between 1980 and 1998, in fact, public sector employment in France increased by 19 percent.[51] We can place this growth in context by comparing it to public sector employment trends in the United States and Britain. Figure 8.1 traces civilian employment in central government ministries and federal government departments in the United States, Britain, and France between 1980 and 1998. As indicated, the number of employees per 1,000 individuals declined rather dramatically in Britain, from over 15 in 1980 to less than 10 in 1998.[52] In the United States, employment remained steady through the 1980s but declined during the 1990s, falling to just over 10 per 1000 individuals in 1998. In France, civilian employment in central government ministries remained steady, hovering around 30 per 1000 during the period.

A slightly different picture emerges if we consider employment at all levels of government or take into account the impact of federalism and the distribution of policy authority between central and local government.[53] In France, education is administered by the national government; teachers are employees of the Ministry of Education. If we exclude education from central government employment, as in figure 8.1, the size of the central French state appears less extraordinary, even if the trend remains the same. Figure 8.2 traces total public employment at all levels of government between 1980 and 1998. As indicated, the number of public employees per 1,000 in Britain declined rather dramatically beginning in the 1990s from 95 in 1980 to 77 in 1998. In France, public sector employment increased steadily during the period, growing from 74 in 1980 to 84 in 1998. Public sector employment in the United States increased in the late 1980s but remained steady through the 1990s at around 73 per 1,000 individuals. This suggests that the decline in federal employment in the United States was offset by the growth of state and local government. Put another way, administrative reforms that reduced the size and scope of the U.S. federal government pushed responsibilities downward to state and local government, and outward to contract and grant employees.

Turning to structural reforms, table 8.2 indicates that there has been greater emphasis on these kinds of reforms in Britain or France than in the United States.[54] Through the Next Steps program begun in 1988, for example, the major-

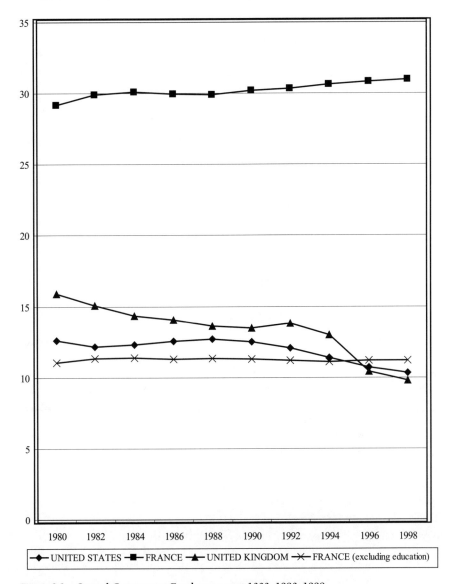

Figure 8.1. Central Government Employment per 1000, 1980–1998

Sources: Brenot Ouldali et al. (2000), *Séries longues*, 15, 27; Hardwidge (2002), "Jobs in the Public and Private Sectors," 43; OMB (2002), *Budget of the United States Government, Historical Tables*, 304; OECD, *National Accounts*.

ity of British government services are today provided by semiautonomous executive agencies linked to parent ministries through contracts that specify as precisely as possible agency responsibilities and measures for tracking performance. Between 1991 and 2001, permanent staff employed in Next Steps agencies increased from 37 percent to 76 percent of the civil service—this at a time when overall

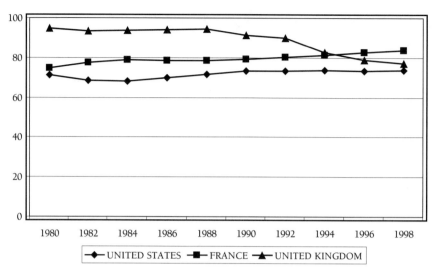

Figure 8.2. Total Public Employment per 1000, 1980–1998
Sources: See Figure 8.1.

employment in central government departments declined by 13 percent.[55] Next Steps transformed a bureaucracy long organized on traditional hierarchical lines into one based on contractual relationships between agencies responsible for implementation and the central ministries that set policy. In some cases, market-type mechanisms accompanied these structural changes. In health care, for example, reforms of the National Health Service begun in 1991 granted hospitals (providers) greater management independence from government health authorities (purchasers); by 1995, over 90 percent of the nearly 1.2 million people employed by the NHS worked for these semiautonomous hospital "trusts."[56] Alongside this "purchaser-provider split," the reforms of the early 1990s created an "internal market" in which NHS trusts competed with one another and with private hospitals for the care of patients as well as the provision of diagnostic and elective hospital procedures to large, office-based primary-care physician practices.[57]

Administrative reforms in France have also promoted the separation of policy formation from implementation, although the use of performance contracts has proceeded more slowly than in Britain. Each of the major reform initiatives—Rocard's program for "Renewal of the Public Service" in 1990, Juppé's plan for "Reform of the State" in 1995, and Jospin's "Program for Administrative Modernization" in 1998—called for greater use of contracts between ministries and the semiautonomous agencies (*établissements publics*) and local administrative units (*services déconcentrés*) responsible for service provision. A report by the body that oversees the implementation of administrative reforms (*Délégation Interministérielle à la Réforme de l'État*) noted that as of 2001 38 percent of the more than six hundred agencies under ministerial control had signed contracts. Progress was slower among local services, with only 19 percent forming contracts with parent ministries at the end of 2001.[58]

A more important transformation in the structure of French government has taken place through decentralization—the transfer of authority from central to subnational governments—and deconcentration—the devolution of authority to local officers of central government, such as departmental prefects. The 1992 Deconcentration Charter legally formalized the division between central administration and deconcentrated government services provided at the local and regional level. By 2000, governmental units responsible for deconcentrated services employed 98 percent of the French civil service working in ministries.[59] A government decree in 1997 gave departmental prefects greater authority over administrative decisions; by 1998, 73 percent of the nearly 4,000 administrative procedures on the books were decided at the local (departmental) level.[60] Meanwhile, as a result of the decentralization program begun in 1982, local governments now play a much greater role in decisions regarding public services (social policy, some aspects of education, and land-use planning), as do the elected members of the departmental and regional councils.[61]

Although reform programs in all three countries have pledged to improve the performance of government or better orient public services toward the needs of "users," subtle but important differences exist in the way government performance is understood and pursued in the United States, Britain, and France. For example, Britain has done the most in terms of government regulators responsible for the monitoring of public service delivery. According to Hood and his colleagues,[62] the number of staff employed by national regulatory bodies overseeing public sector bodies increased by 90 percent between 1976 and 1995—this at a time when overall public sector employment declined by a third.[63] British reforms have also gone further to link government performance with budgetary allocations. The 1998 Comprehensive Spending Reviews introduced the use of Public Service Agreements (PSAs), explicit performance targets for each department and agency that specify "departmental objectives and targets that have to be met, the stages by which they will be met, how departments intend to allocate resources to achieve these targets and the process that will monitor results."[64] Beginning with the 2000 Comprehensive Spending Review, departments and agencies are also required to submit Service Delivery Agreements that detail how the specific targets included in each PSA will be met. Although the U.S. government has made similar efforts to link performance and budgeting through the 1993 Government Performance and Results Act, forging such a link has been difficult. In 2002, the Bush administration introduced a Program Assessment Rating Tool to facilitate performance measurement, but this will cover only 20 percent of federal spending in fiscal year 2004.[65] Finally, in France, the introduction of multiyear modernization programs represents a similar attempt to employ explicit performance targets for government programs. And although most ministries have formulated performance goals, few have yet to develop any mechanism with which to measure whether goals are, in fact, met.[66]

Another difference is in how performance is itself understood. Reforms in the United States and Britain have tended to equate public sector performance with some notion of "customer" satisfaction, explicitly incorporating, for example, private sector standards to assess the quality of public services. In France, performance standards have emphasized the degree to which access is guaranteed across different communities, the simplification of administrative language, and the legal codification of citizens' rights in dealings with government agencies. In 1992, the Bérégovoy government issued a Public Service Charter, and in 1994 a joint declaration by central government and local authorities promised further improvements in public service delivery. One consistent theme, for example, has been the improvement of public service access to citizens in rural areas. Another is the improvement of Internet access to government and the simplification of administrative procedures. Finally, a new law promulgated in 2000 on the rights of citizens in their relations with government clarified a number of issues such as access to information and the timeliness of administrative procedures; the act also called for the creation of "one-stop shops" where several public services would be made available in one location.[67]

In sum, although reforms in the United States, Britain, and France have each addressed various issues related to the size, structure, and performance of government, distinct patterns are discernible in each country. In the United States, reforms reduced the size of the federal government—although, when we include numbers of contract workers and the size of state and local governments, it appears that administrative reforms mainly pushed responsibility downward and outward. In Britain, the size of the state also shrank, but even more dramatic has been the transformation in the structure of the British bureaucracy. Finally, in France, decentralization and deconcentration transformed the structure of government, but the emphasis on equality of access and citizens' rights in public service provision also distinguishes French reforms from the more consumerist orientation in the United States and Britain.

As I describe in the next section, a number of factors account for the specific characteristics of administrative reform in the United States, Britain, and France. These include ideas about the state and elite assumptions toward policy, institutions such as the organization of legislative and executive power and the distribution of authority between central and local government, and interests expressed through partisan competition and organized groups.

UNDERSTANDING THE NATIONAL CONTEXT OF REFORM

Differences in the reform experiences of the United States, Britain, and France reflect the ideological traditions, institutional structures, and partisan contexts in which administrative reform takes place. Although I consider each in turn, ideas, institutions, and interests come together to provide a national context for administrative reform. Specific outcomes—in terms of size, structure, or performance—depend on the kinds of rhetoric politicians may draw on in advancing reform programs, the formal powers and structural impediments institutions present, and the coalitions for and against administrative reform in each country.

To begin, there are distinct ideological traditions regarding the state and citizenship that impact the rhetoric politicians employ in promoting administrative reform. Given the tradition of antistatism in the United States, politicians can legitimately distance themselves from a supposedly wasteful, if not fraudulent, bureaucracy. A less hostile, but nevertheless skeptical view of the state is also found in Britain. In contrast, the view of the state as the embodiment of the public good in France may partly explain why we do not see reforms explicitly intended to reduce the size or scope of government and, instead, politicians are more likely to present themselves as champions of public service modernization than the outright critics of bureaucracy we find in the United States and Britain.[68] Similarly, differences between a liberal-individualist and republican-egalitarian conception of citizenship may help explain why we see a greater rhetorical emphasis on public service consumerism in the United States and Britain than in France, where the emphasis is on the equality of access to public services.[69]

Differences in ideological traditions are also reflected in the elite assumptions and academic ideas driving administrative reform. For example, elements drawn from the new institutional economics such as attention to transaction costs and principal–agent relations (with the underlying implication that one can counteract the venal tendencies of bureaucrats with properly structured incentives) have had a greater impact on reformers in the United States and Britain than in France. More than simply the relative sway of neoliberalism in each of the three countries, these ideational differences illustrate how widely held public beliefs (about the state or citizenship, for example) and elite assumptions about bureaucratic structure and incentives mutually reinforce one another in a way that magnifies the force of ideas in public policy.[70]

Second, divergence in the politics of administrative reform reflects the varying structure of political institutions: the organization of executive–legislative authority, the distribution of policy responsibility between state and local government, and the size and structure of national bureaucracies. In the United States, administrative reform proposals inevitably touch on the relationship between president and Congress. Many aspects of reform, for example, require congressional approval. Clinton proved generally successful in this area of legislative relations; during his eight years in office, Clinton signed more than ninety NPR-related bills.[71] But this simple success score belies the compromises necessary to navigate the legislative process and the exemptions and omissions that watered down reform goals. More substantively, presidential hopes that administrative reform will augment central political control over policy cannot escape the fact that both the president and Congress share authority over the bureaucracy. For example, the Clinton administration supported passage of the Government Performance and

Results Act in 1993 in part because requiring executive agencies to submit performance targets to OMB would enhance presidential control over the bureaucracy.
But soon after passage of GPRA, members of Congress quickly realized that these
same reporting requirements created a new mechanism for congressional oversight of executive departments.[72]

Moreover, federalism leaves the majority of public services well beyond the
reach of national administrative reform in the United States. Many issues related to
education, public service provision, or relations with public sector unions take
place mostly at the state and local level. Consequently, the national administrative
reform agenda in the United States has focused on personnel, procurement, and
the improvement of services in those agencies with the most direct relations to the
public such as the Internal Revenue Service and the Social Security Administration.

This contrasts quite clearly with the unitary British state, where the national
government has principal responsibility for health, education, transportation, and
police and fire. Coupled with the fusion of executive and legislative authority in a
Westminster system, the structure of center–local relations in Britain focuses accountability for public service performance on the national government. Consequently, the administrative reform agenda in Britain is much broader than in the
United States. Responsibility for train wrecks, medical horror stories, or police
misconduct ultimately fall on the central government and, in particular, the prime
minister. The flip side of this accountability, of course, is the relative absence of
veto points in the policy process that could present impediments to a government
dedicated to a reform program.

In France, administrative reforms often engage the ongoing political struggles
between prime ministers, presidents, and parliament engendered by the Fifth Republic Constitution. Efforts to assert prime ministerial authority within the constitutional system—essential if a prime minister is to secure parliamentary approval
of his or her agenda—often produces rivalries between presidents and prime ministers. Prime ministerial sponsorship of administrative reforms can be especially
problematic because questions of bureaucratic structure and control easily impinge on presidential prerogatives in matters of administration. For example,
Rocard's reform agenda ignited conflicts with President Mitterrand. When public
sector unions opposed elements of the Rocard plan, Mitterrand took sides with
the unions, going so far as to initiate salary negotiations without involvement by
his prime minister. And when Juppé began his efforts to secure political control
over the bureaucracy, he confronted ministers chosen by President Chirac on the
basis of rewarding supporters and distributing portfolios evenly among the two
principle right-wing parties.[73]

Put another way, institutional differences shape the opportunities for credit
and the likelihood of blame associated with administrative reform. The diffusion
of accountability in the U.S. system, and to a lesser degree in France, complicates
efforts by U.S. presidents or French prime ministers to claim credit for successful
reforms because other actors in these constitutional systems can legitimately claim

authority in administrative matters. Conversely, it is a widely recognized observation that the British system focuses accountability, and with it credit and blame, for reform successes and failures.[74]

But credit and blame are not simply a function of executive–legislative relations. Federalism permits U.S. presidents to enjoy asymmetric assignment of credit and blame in public sector reform. Consider the example of education reform. The attraction of education as a political issue for George W. Bush is in the fact that he can embrace performance measures and claim credit for addressing voter concerns over education even as local control shields him from blame for failing public schools. Such advantages are not available to Tony Blair, not because Britain has a parliamentary system, but because it is a unitary state.[75] Similarly, the ease with which U.S. presidents can distance themselves from an unpopular bureaucracy perhaps reflects the comparative paltriness of national administrative capacities until well into the twentieth century and the continued absence of a prestigious cadre of civil servants. In contrast, consider the French: one cannot easily shift blame onto an unpopular bureaucracy when one begins one's career in the senior civil service, as most politicians do in France.

Finally, the impact of ideological traditions and political structures—ideas and institutions—is mediated in important ways by partisan context. The politics of administrative reform looks different from the right or from the left; whether the same party controls national political institutions; and whether the size of the governing party's majority is large or marginal.[76]

For example, the political rhetoric surrounding administrative reform in the United States and Britain changed considerably with the election of a centrist Democrat and New Labour government, respectively. Whereas Republican and Conservative governments emphasized deregulation, privatization, and market mechanisms that would "shrink" the state, third-way governments emphasized themes of "reinvention" and "modernization."[77] Less hostile toward the public sector than their predecessors, third-way reforms advocated greater customer orientation, improved performance, and public–private partnerships in public service delivery. In fact, the reorientation of debate away from the content of social policy and toward the process of service delivery at the heart of administrative reform is particularly useful when governing from the center-left: it permits the simultaneous embrace of popular criticisms against bureaucracy without having to adopt a neoliberal position of privatization and deregulation that would alienate elements on the left such as public sector employees. Although less pronounced, a similar contrast can be made between the neoliberal reforms envisioned by Juppé and the more conciliatory tone struck by Jospin in matters of administrative reform.[78]

Second, the political dynamics surrounding administrative reform can change with partisan control of national political institutions. For example, as Kettl notes, the National Performance Review entered a distinct second phase with the election of a Republican Congress in 1994 and the return of divided government.[79] With the Republicans in control of the national political agenda, administrative reform became a way for the White House to find new relevance and defend presidential priorities in the face of congressional efforts at retrenchment and deregulation.

Finally, the size of the Labour Party's majority in Britain and the implosion of Conservative opposition inflamed whatever rivalry already existed between Tony Blair and his chancellor, Gordon Brown. Given the centrality of public service improvement at the heart of the current government's agenda, this rivalry inevitably touches on administrative reform. Recently, a rather open conflict emerged between Blair, Brown, and the Blairite Health Minister Alan Milburn over allowing high-performance hospitals to operate with little central oversight, including in matters of finance. Although the question of whether hospitals can borrow money without Treasury approval may be arcane, it points to larger debates over the appropriate public–private mix in a host of services such as health, housing, transportation, and education, on which Blair and Brown disagree.[80] The point is that the growing prominence of Treasury as a source of policy expertise beyond financial matters and as an instrument of central political coordination under New Labour interacts with a particular partisan context to produce institutional struggles and political rivalries over administrative reform.

Differences in ideas, institutions, and interests help explain the distinct characteristics of administrative reform in the United States, Britain, and France. In the United States, views about the state, the fragmentation of political authority, and the structure of political competition make reductions in the size of government relatively easy. Moreover, the relative weakness of public sector unions, especially at the federal level, where less than 20 percent of nonpostal employees are unionized, means there are few meaningful opponents to workforce reductions.[81] In addition, downsizing and contracting out present a number of advantages to a wide range of political actors. As Paul Light explains,

> Presidents have come to prefer the shadow government [contracting out] because it appears to strengthen their control over government against an increasingly reform minded Congress; Congress, because it provides an essential source of ongoing campaign support and incumbency advantage; Democrats because it provides a defense against their image as the party of big government; Republicans, because it strengthens their base of business support. . . . It is also the policy that caters to the public's core ambivalence about the size of government.[82]

At the same time, other types of reform confront various hurdles. Attempts to transform the structure of the bureaucracy—through greater use of semiautonomous agencies or performance contracts, for example—would conflict with established patterns of oversight and clientele relations between administrative agencies and congressional committees. A focus on government performance faces fewer obstacles but is limited in its impact by institutional fragmentation and the narrow scope of public services provided by the federal government.

In Britain, however, the structure of government institutions, especially the concentration of authority in the prime minister and the relative absence of veto points, makes it easier to transform the structure of government. As we have seen, progress of the Next Steps Initiative, begun in 1988, was impressive. This rather dramatic restructuring of the British civil service, the separation of service delivery from the central ministries where policy planning takes place, occurred with little opposition. As one senior civil servant interviewed in the mid-1990s reflected on the inauguration of Next Steps, "If the Prime Minister said she was going to do something it was going to be a brave minister who stood up to her. The reforms just went through."[83] This is commentary not only on Margaret Thatcher's political will but also on the institutional mechanisms at her disposal. These same institutional characteristics made possible reductions in the size of government, despite the fact that union membership density in the public sector is around 60 percent.[84]

However, the British case also illustrates the importance of partisan context. Because trade unions remain an important constituency of the Labour Party, the Blair government must take public sector union concerns over administrative reforms much more seriously than his Conservative predecessors. In particular, union opposition to the Private Finance Initiative, a program that contracts out building construction and other public services to private companies, has plagued the Blair government and contributed to the rift between the prime minister and his chancellor, Gordon Brown. This helps explains why the Labour government has put less emphasis on reductions in size and more on improvements in performance: over the last three years, in fact, public sector employment increased and the 2002 Comprehensive Spending Review promised an additional 61 billion pounds ($95 billion) in spending on education, health, transportation, and other public service priorities over the next three years.[85]

Finally, in France, with a positive view of state action that transcends right and left, the interpenetration of political and administrative elites, large levels of public sector employment, and a formidable public sector union movement (58 percent of central government employees), it is little surprise that reductions in the size of government have been virtually absent from the administrative reform agenda.[86] Even seemingly innocuous reforms can engender bitter political conflicts. For example, when the Jospin government announced plans to reform the Finance Ministry in 2000 by merging the separate bureaucracies responsible for tax assessments and tax collections into a single agency, opposition from public sector unions proved so great that Jospin shelved the reform plan and the finance minister handed in his resignation.[87] By contrast, promises to modernize or "renew" French administration confront far fewer obstacles and can in fact generate positive responses from politicians, bureaucrats, and voters. Consequently, the most substantive achievements of French administrative reform have been in the area of government performance. In contrast to the British and American cases, however, improving performance in the context of French reforms is principally about enhancing equity rather than efficiency in public service delivery. Thus, even the far-reaching changes in the structure of the French state wrought by decentralization can be understood as an attempt to bring administration closer to the user, where it can be adapted to the specific needs of a diverse population.

CONCLUSION

To sum up, the case of administrative reform reveals both commonalities and differences in U.S. and European public policy. On the one hand, we see distinct similarities in the pressures and political incentives for policymakers to address administrative reform issues. Fiscal austerity and public skepticism toward government make administrative reform well suited to the economic and political constraints of contemporary public policy. As a political issue, administrative reform helps politicians balance both the imperatives to avoid blame and claim credit; to distance oneself from an unpopular bureaucracy and fulfill voters' desires for better public service performance. At the same time, reform initiatives have produced institutional changes that enhance the capacity of central decision makers to direct policy and extract credit from a circumscribed policy environment.

On the other hand, comparative experiences with administrative reform highlight the differences that distinguish public policy in the United States, Britain, and France. In particular, the emphases placed on size, structure, and performance in each country reveal the impact of distinct ideological traditions, the structure of political institutions, and the patterns of partisan and interest group competition on administrative reform. In other words, common pressures and political incentives interact with different ideas, institutions, and interests to produce distinct policy outcomes. Because of the impact of these factors, it is easier to downsize government in the United States than address the administrative obstacles of a separated system; in Britain, it is easier to impose structural changes from above than improve public satisfaction with the state of health care, education, or transportation; and in France, it is easier to direct energies toward modernization and improving access and transparency than trim the size of an engorged public sector.

But herein lies another irony of administrative reform: if, for understandable reasons, politicians play to their strengths in choosing to emphasize certain aspects of reform over another, they do little to alleviate the source of public skepticism that generates pressures for administrative reform in the first place. In the United States, for example, the National Performance Review touted its success in ending the era of big government, especially the reduction in federal personnel. But the problem that spawned the first Gore report, "From Red Tape to Results," was the complexity and duplication of federal regulations. And by focusing on headcounts and budget amounts, administrative reform in the United States has done little to address the fact that this complexity and duplication is the product of separate branches sharing powers, especially struggles between the president and Congress for control of the bureaucracy and the administration of policy.[88] A focus on size completely neglects the problem of structure.

We find similar ironies in the cases of Britain and France. In Britain, administrative reforms have secured an impressive restructuring and downsizing of the British civil service, but public concerns persist, especially in health care. In fact, a paradox of administrative reform in Britain is the fact that performance measures and inspectorates designed to impose targets for improved service delivery may in fact increase public dissatisfaction. Publication of waiting lists for elective surgeries, the percentage of on-time trains, or the number of students attaining a certain score on exams may provide incentives for public sector employees, but they also quantify the misery some Britons experience in their daily life, adding to the skepticism that already exists toward segments of the public sector. Moreover, as the current Labour government has apparently learned, structural change alone will not improve services; it also requires government investment. Finally in France, reforms have brought administrative decisions closer to the individual and codified the rights of citizens in dealings with government. But in treating the symptoms of a large bureaucracy still predominantly under the control of a technocratic elite, these reforms have limited the possibility to renew public faith in a modernized French state.

Ultimately, the failure of administrative reform to address the core causes of public skepticism may not present a problem for politicians or policymakers. As critics of administrative reform caution, the creation of a consumerist, "user-friendly" government denotes a depoliticized conception of citizenship.[89] Where citizens are consumers, dissatisfaction with public policy is expressed through individual complaints to local service providers rather than national political leaders through the collective mobilization of party politics. And by replacing hierarchical relations with contractual ones in public bureaucracies, administrative reforms weaken the accountability that tied elected leaders to the outcomes and performance of state functions. Institutional innovations that centralize control over policy decisions serve a similar end. With the declining role of parties as mediating institutions between voters and politicians, contemporary political leaders have absorbed greater responsibility for the political direction of policy. But the absorption of political functions by presidents and prime ministers reinforces the consumerist conception of citizenship. Rather than express views through the collective organization of parties, citizens express their preferences as individual voters who choose among competing positions and issues crafted by political advisers.

It is too cynical to conclude that politicians pursue the political and institutional innovations of administrative reform purely to disempower voters. Nor is it accurate to simply dismiss the rhetoric of new public management as an administrative fad devoid of any real content. Some administrative reforms have increased efficiency, empowered managers, and improved public sector performance.[90] Rather, the key to understanding administrative reform is to appreciate the political motivations and constraints contemporary policymakers must face. Under conditions of continuing fiscal austerity where the opportunities for credit claiming are limited and the imperative to avoid blame is high, politicians will embrace "cheap" policy goals and attempt to enhance the political coordination of policy in the hopes of extracting whatever credit they can from an increasingly complex and constrained policy environment. Administrative reforms serve both goals nicely. By emphasizing process over content, shifting responsibility to lower levels of bureaucracy or government, and concentrating political control over policy at the center, politicians can claim credit for administrative reforms that simultaneously enhance the capacity for avoiding blame.

NOTES

1. Christopher Pollitt and Geert Bouckaert, *Public Management Reform: A Comparative Analysis* (Oxford: Oxford University Press, 2000), 943.

2. Paul Pierson, "Irresistible Forces, Immovable Objects: Post-Industrial Welfare States Confront Permanent Austerity," *Journal of European Public Policy* 5, no. 4 (1998): 539–60.

3. Here, Pierson builds on the work of R. Kent Weaver and his seminal 1986 article, "The Politics of Blame Avoidance," *Journal of Public Policy* 6, no. 4 (1986):371–98.

4. Although the boundary is far from clear, we might distinguish between the privatization of a purely commercial function, such as running a cafeteria in a federal office building, and the use of contract employment ranging from temporary support staff to the use of management consultants to perform specific, fixed-term quasigovernmental functions. See Paul C. Light, *The True Size of Government* (Washington, DC: Brookings Institution Press, 1999), 152.

5. In France, deconcentration specifically refers to the relocation of central government functions away from Paris and toward the *départements*, or regions.

6. OECD, *Distributed Public Governance: Agencies, Authorities, and Other Government Bodies* (Paris: OECD, 2002), 9.

7. Pollitt and Bouckaert, *Public Management Reform*, 176.

8. Vincent Wright, "Reshaping the State: The Implications for Public Administration," *West-European Politics* 17, no. 3 (1994):112.

9. Pierson, "Irresistable Forces."

10. Herbert Kitschelt, "Citizens, Politicians, and Party Cartellization: Political Representation and State Failure in Post-Industrial Democracies," *European Journal of Political Research* 37, no.2 (2000):149–79.

11. Stephen Skowronek, *Building a New American State: The Expansion of National Administrative Capacities, 1877–1920* (New York: Cambridge University Press, 1982).

12. Paul C. Light, *The Tides of Reform: Making Government Work, 1945–1995* (New Haven, CT: Yale University Press, 1997), 6. See also David Lowery, "The Presidency, the Bureaucracy, and Reinvention: A Gentle Plea for Chaos," *Presidential Studies Quarterly* 30, no. 1 (2000):79–108.

13. Peri E. Arnold, *Making the Managerial Presidency: Comprehensive Reorganization Planning, 1905–1996* (Lawrence: University Press of Kansas, 1998), 373.

14. Donald F. Kettl, "The Global Revolution in Public Management: Driving Themes, Missing Links," *Journal of Policy Analysis and Management* 16, no. 3 (1997):446–

62; Christopher Hood, "A Public Management for all Seasons?" *Public Administration* 69, no. 1 (1991):3–19; Donald J. Savoie, *Thatcher, Reagan, Mulroney: In Search of a New Bureaucracy* (Pittsburgh: University of Pittsburgh Press, 1994).

15. Joel D. Aberbach and Bert A. Rockman, *In the Web of Politics: Three Decades of the U.S. Federal Executive* (Washington, DC: Brookings Institution Press, 2000), 33.

16. Arnold, *Making the Managerial Presidency*, 375.

17. Ibid., 365; Donald F. Kettl, *The Global Public Management Revolution* (Washington, DC: Brookings Institution Press, 2000), 15–19. Office of Management and Budget, Executive Office of the President, *The President's Management Agenda, Fiscal Year 2002* (Washington, DC: Government Printing Office, 2001).

18. Savoie, *Thatcher, Reagan, Mulroney*, 121–23.

19. Pollitt and Bouckaert, *Public Management Reform*, 273.

20. Ibid.; Christopher Hood et al., "Regulation of Government: Has It Increased, Is It Increasing, Should It Be Diminished?" *Public Administration* 78, no. 2 (2000):283–304.

21. David Clark, "Citizens, Charters and Public Service Reform in France and Britain," *Government and Opposition* 35, no. 2 (spring 2000):152–69.

22. UK Cabinet Office, *Modernising Government* (London: HM Stationery Office, 1999).

23. Jonah Levy, *Tocqueville's Revenge: State, Society, and Economy in Contemporary France* (Cambridge, MA: Harvard University Press, 1999).

24. Alain Guyomarch, "'Public Service,' 'Public Management' and the 'Modernization' of French Public Administration," *Public Administration* 77, no. 1 (1999):171–93.

25. Philippe Bezes, "Defensive versus Offensive Approaches to Administrative Reform in France (1988–1997): The Leadership Dilemmas of French Prime Ministers," *Governance* 14, no. 1 (2001):99–132.

26. Lionel Jospin, "Declaration de Politique Generale" (speech before Parliament, June 19, 1997), www.archives.premierministre.gouv.fr/jospinflversion2/PM/D190697 .htm; Loi relative aux droits des citoyens dans leurs relations avec les administrations (Loi n° 2000-321), *Journal Officiel de la République Française* 88 (April 13, 2000):5646–54.

27. U.S. Office of Personnel Management, *Federal Civilian Workforce Statistics: Employment and Trends as of March 2002* (Washington, DC: Government Printing Office, 2002), 13.

28. For a critique of "President" Blair, see Jackie Ashley, "The Rise and Rise of President Blair," *New Statesman*, November 5, 2001.

29. Anthony Seldon and Dennis Kavanagh, *The Powers behind the Prime Minister: The Hidden Influence of Number Ten* (London: HarperCollins, 1999).

30. Jean-Patrice Lacam, *La France, une République de mandarins?* (Brussels: Éditions Complexe, 2000), 40; Annie Brenot Ouldali et al., *Séries longues sur l'emploi dans la fonction publique* (Paris: Direction générale de l'administration et de la fonction publique, 2000), 75; Délégation interministérielle à la réforme de l'Etat, *La Fonction publique et la réforme de l'État: Rapport annuel mars 2000–mars 2001* (Paris: La Documentation Française, 2001), 135.

31. Aberbach and Rockman, *In the Web of Politics*, 169.

32. Ibid., 35–36; Marissa Martino Golden, *What Motivates Bureaucrats? Politics and Administration during the Reagan Years* (New York: Columbia University Press, 2000), 7, 118–20.

33. Quoted in Aberbach and Rockman, *In the Web of Politics*, 150.

34. Pollitt and Bouckaert, *Public Management Reform*, 276.

35. Sir Andrew Turnbull, "Cabinet Office Reform and Delivery in the Civil Service" (paper delivered to the Civil Service Management Board June 24, 2002). www .cabinet-office.gov.uk/news/2002/020624flnewciv.asp.

36. UK Cabinet Office, *Civil Service Statistics 2001* (London: Office of National Statistics, 2002), 34; UK Cabinet Office, "Civil Service Staff in Post Summary Table 1 April 1990." www.civil-service.gov.uk/statistics/documents/pdf/apr90int.pdf.

37. On the Treasury, and centralization under Blair more generally, see Simon Lee and Richard Woodward, "Implementing the Third Way: The Delivery of Public Services under the Blair Government," *Public Money and Management* 22, no. 4 (2002):49–56.

38. Articles 20 and 21 give the prime minister leadership of the administration. However, presidents enjoy powers of appointment, a source of significant authority in administrative matters. See Bezes, "Defensive versus Offensive Approaches," 120–21.

39. Ibid., 113–14. Juppé reunited the Civil Service and State Reform ministries in his second government.

40. Ministère de la fonction public, "Le cadre de la réforme." www.fonction -publique.gouv.fr/reforme/structures/cadreflindex.htm.

41. Pollitt and Bouckaert, *Public Management Reform*, 6.

42. Ibid., 137.

43. Hood, "A Public Management for all Seasons?"

44. On the blame-avoiding functions of reform see Daniel Cohn, "Creating Crises and Avoiding Blame: The Politics of Public Service Reform and the New Public Management in Great Britain and the United States," *Administration and Society* 29, no. 5 (1997): 584–616.

45. See for example Aberbach and Rockman, *In the Web of Politics*; Kettl, *The Global Public Management Revolution*; and Pollitt and Bouckaert, *Public Management Reform*.

46. National Parternship for Reinventing Government, "History of the National Partnership for Reinventing Government: Accomplishments, 1993–2000." http://govinfo .library.unt.edu/npr/whoweare/appendixf.html.

47. Light, *The True Size of Government*, 198–99.

48. Ibid.,154; Richard W. Stevenson, "Government May Make Private Nearly Half of Its Civilian Jobs," *New York Times*, November 14, 2002.

49. Employment data expressed as full-time equivalents. Claire Hardwidge, "Jobs in the Public and Private Sectors," *Economic Trends* 583 (UK Office for National Statistics, June 2002), 43.

50. Organization for Economic Cooperation and Development, "Strategic Review and Reform—the UK Perspective" (paper prepared for symposium titled Government of the Future, Paris, September 14–15, 1999. www1.oecd.org/puma/strat/symposium/ UK.pdf, 3; Hardwidge, "Jobs in the Public and Private Sectors," 43.

51. Brenot Ouldali et al. (2000), *Séries longues*, 15.

52. Data for the UK include employees working for the National Health Service and, after 1990, employees for the NHS trusts.

53. Data for Britain and France exclude employees of government-owned firms.

54. Although reforms during the 1990s did streamline personnel procedures, simplify the procurement process, and provide greater management autonomy to the 350 "reinvention labs" created during the National Performance Review, the basic structure of the U.S. bureaucracy remained largely unchanged. For example, the 1995 Federal Reports Elimination and Sunset Act eliminated or modified more than two thousand reporting requirements, and in 1994 the Office of Personnel Management abolished its ten thousand–page

Federal Personnel Manual. See Frank J. Thompson and Norma M. Ricucci, "Reinventing Government," *Annual Review of Political Science* 1 (1998):251–52.

55. UK Cabinet Office, *Civil Service Statistics 2001* (London: HM Stationery Office, 2002), 4.

56. Hardwidge, "Jobs in the Public and Private Sectors," 43.

57. Susan Giaimo, "Who Pays for Health Care Reform?" in *The New Politics of the Welfare State*, ed. Paul Pierson (Oxford: Oxford University Press, 2001), 346.

58. Délégation Interministérielle à la réforme de l'Etat, *La contractualisation dans les administrations de l'État, Juin 2002.* www.fonction-publique.gouv.fr/communications /guides/BilanContractualisation.pdf, 120–21.

59. Délégation interministérielle à la réforme de l'Etat, *La Fonction publique et la réforme de l'Etat: Deuxième Partie—Bilan Social* (Paris: La Documentation Française, 2001), 136.

60. Commissariat à la réforme de l'État, *Rapport d'activité 1997* (Paris: La Documentation Française, 1998), 23.

61. Stephen Garrish, "Decentralization: The Reforms," in *An Introduction to French Administration*, ed. Institut International d'Administration Publique (Paris: La Documentation Française, 1996), 133–38.

62. Hood et al., "Regulation of Government."

63. Ibid., 96.

64. Gordon Brown, "Statement by the Chancellor of the Exchequer on the Comprehensive Spending Review, July 14, 1998." www.hm-treasury.gov.uk/Spending_Review /spend_csr98/spend_csr98_statement.cfm.

65. Executive Office of the President, Office of Management and Budget, "Memorandum for Heads of Executive Departments and Agencies, July 16, 2002—Program Performance Assessments for the FY 2004 Budget." www.whitehouse.gov/omb/budintegration /part_guidance_letter_agencies.doc.

66. Délégation interministérielle à la réforme de l'Etat, *Synthèse des bilans annuels des programmes pluriannuels de modernisation des ministères, 2001.* http://lesrapports .ladocumentationfrancaise.fr/BRP/024000052/0000.pdf, 15–17.

67. Organization for Economic Cooperation and Development, "Issues and Developments in Public Management: France—2000." www.oecd.org/dataoecd/28/43 /2344926.pdf, 16–19.

68. Pollitt and Bouckaert, *Public Management Reform*, 174–83.

69. Clark, "Citizens, Charters and Public Service Reform."

70. See John L. Campbell's discussion of ideas and public policy and, especially, the distinction he draws between ideas as "public sentiments" and ideas as "paradigms" in "Institutional Analysis and the Role of Ideas in Political Economy," *Theory and Society* 27, no. 3 (1998):377–409.

71. National Partnership for Reinventing Government, "History of the National Partnership." See also Christopher H. Foreman, Jr., "Reinventing Politics? The NPR Meets Congress," in *Inside the Reinvention Machine: Appraising Governmental Reform*, ed. Donald F. Kettl and John J. DiIulio, Jr. (Washington, DC: Brookings Institution Press, 1995), 164.

72. John Mercurio, "Nonprofit Group's Budget Workshop Hit by Staff," *Roll Call*, April 21, 1997; "Lack of Focus GOP in Learning-Curve Limbo," *Congressional Quarterly Weekly Report* (November 1, 1997):2649.

73. Bezes, "Defensive versus Offensive Approaches," 108–9.

74. Paul Pierson and R. Kent Weaver, "Imposing Losses in Pension Policy," in *Do Institutions Matter? Government Capabilities in the United States and Abroad*, ed. R. Kent Weaver and Bert A. Rockman (Washington, DC: Brookings Institution Press, 1993).

75. One must include policy legacies here as well. Although perhaps an obvious point, the scope of the administrative reform agenda in Britain is wider and the accountability for poorly performing public services more focused because of the legacy of the National Health Service, a fifty-five-year-old universal health system financed and managed by the central government. A slightly different legacy exists in transportation and the ghost of British Rail privatized by the Conservatives in the 1980s.

76. This finding is consistent with Weaver and Rockman's insights on the importance of partisan context, as well as a recent but growing literature on the impact of partisan factors on welfare state retrenchment (see, for example, Fiona Ross, "Beyond Left and Right: The New Partisan Politics of Welfare," *Governance* 13, no. 2 [2000]:155–83).

77. Pollitt and Bouckaert, *Public Management Reform*, 172*ff*.

78. Guyomarch, "'Public Service,'" 184.

79. Kettl, *The Global Public Management Revolution*, 17.

80. Will Hutton, "War Looms between Blair and Brown," *The Observer*, October 6, 2002.

81. Barry T. Hirsch and David A. Macpherson, "Union Membership and Coverage Database from the Current Population Survey: Note," *Industrial and Labor Relations Review* 56, no. 2 (2003):349–54. www.unionstats.com.

82. Light, *The True Size of Government*, 48.

83. Quoted in David Marsh et al., "Bureaucrats, Politicians, and Reform in Whitehall: Analysing the Bureau-Shaping Model," *British Journal of Political Science* 30, no. 3 (2000):470.

84. Abby Sneade, "Trade Union Membership 1999–2000," *Labour Market Trends*, no. 109 (UK Office for National Statistics, September 2001):433–44.

85. HM Treasury, *2002 Spending Review: New Public Spending Plans 2003–2006*. www.hm-treasury.gov.uk/media//F8FE5/SR2002%20leaflet.pdf.

86. Membership data calculated according to percent voting in elections to joint staff/management committees (*commissions administratives paritaires centrales*). Délégation interministérielle à la réforme de l'État, *Bilan Social*, 143, 259.

87. Robert Graham, "Unions Force Paris To Put Finance Plans on Hold," *Financial Times*, March 13, 2000.

88. Thompson and Riccucci, "Reinventing Government," 255.

89. Mathew A. Crenson and Benjamin Ginsberg, *Downsizing Citizens: How America Sidelined Its Citizens and Privatized Its Public* (Baltimore: Johns Hopkins University Press, 2002); James Carroll, "The Rhetoric of Reform and Political Reality in the National Performance Review," *Public Administration Review* 55, no. 3 (1995):302–12.

90. For a discussion of concrete, if only partial, accomplishments see James R. Thompson, "Reinvention as Reform: Assessing the National Performance Review," *Public Administration Review* 60, no. 6 (2000):508–21.

THE STATE OF THE CORPORATION

State Power, Politics, Policymaking, and Corporate Governance
in the United States, Germany, and France

JOHN W. CIOFFI

INTRODUCTION

DURING THE PAST TWENTY YEARS, CORPORATE GOVERNANCE HAS BECOME INCREASINGLY central to national economic policy agendas as governments initiated political–economic reforms and restructuring throughout the advanced industrial countries. The focus on corporate governance reform intensified during the 1990s as "shareholder capitalism" in the United States became more widely admired (and often feared and resented) for its apparent capacity to promote dynamic economic innovation and growth. As is painfully clear following the massive corporate financial scandals in the United States, the law and regulation of corporate governance constitute some of the core institutional structures of national political economies. Corporate governance affects the capacity of firms to adjust to changing economic conditions, influences the distribution of wealth and allocation of capital, and implicates the legitimacy of broader political–economic arrangements. The structure of corporate governance implicates the core interests of some of the most powerful interest groups in national politics: corporate managers, financial institutions, public shareholders, institutional investors, employees, and organized labor. Accordingly, the politics and policy of corporate governance provide a vantage point from which to view political and regulatory change more broadly. The importance of corporate governance is no less clear from the experience of European countries during the 1990s. Countries such as Germany and France have radically reformed their corporate governance systems to adopt more centralized and legalistic securities regulation and increase shareholder protections under company law, while trying to ameliorate the potentially disruptive and destabilizing effects of financially driven corporate restructuring.

Corporate governance regimes are the product of intense political and economic pressures ultimately embodied in legal relations, processes, and institutions. Increasing political competition over the "rules of the game" of governance indicates the centrality of law and regulation as political actors seek advantage through the modification of the legal rules defining the fundamental institutions of economic governance. The use of law and regulation to structure markets and firms (in other words, markets and hierarchies) is becoming an increasingly important, and perhaps dominant, mode of state intervention in the advanced industrial economies. Structuring economic institutions and relations through law has the potential to satisfy both political and economic demands on policymakers and managers, while avoiding more direct modes of intervention such as state ownership, bureaucratic control over finance and credit, and broad discretionary regulatory powers. This is the function of the governance structures and bargaining fora created by corporate governance law. The legal mechanisms of corporate governance do not *supplant* markets; they *restructure* markets and the organizational hierarchies of the firm to accomplish policy goals.[1]

This chapter examines the evolving dynamics and patterns of corporate governance policy in the United States, Germany, and France. Across these three major advanced industrial countries, policymakers have identified corporate governance reform as an increasingly important and salient area of public policy. Throughout the 1990s, policymakers have engaged in repeated efforts to reform their corporate governance regimes.

The chapter covers three broad areas. First, it briefly describes the basic frameworks of the American, German, and French postwar corporate governance regimes. Second, it summarizes the policy debates and reforms that have altered these national frameworks during the past twenty years, and particularly since the end of the 1980s. Third, the chapter presents a political analysis of these corporate governance reforms. This analysis explains why political elites identified corporate governance as requiring significant reform, the political forces that enabled and drove policy change, and the increasing centralization of public regulatory power and its expanding intervention into the workings of financial markets and firms.

NATIONAL INSTITUTIONAL STRUCTURES

The postwar political–economic organization of the United States, Germany, and France represents distinctive political–economic and associated corporate governance models. Thus, they form a comparative typology of corporate governance regimes associated with historically neoliberal, neocorporatist, and statist political economies, respectively.[2] In each case, characteristic institutional structures and relations are replicated at multiple levels of the state, market, and corporate firm. This multileveled ordering of juridical and economic structures and relationships within these national political–economic models is associated with established postwar models of corporate governance, discussed below and in table 9.1.

THE UNITED STATES

The United States possesses a highly fragmented state structure characterized by separation of powers, a bicameral federal legislature, federalist structures and traditions giving substantial policy authority to the states, and electoral and party systems that create little discipline and cohesion within parties and congressional delegations. The American regulatory structure reflects this political fragmentation. A multiplicity of competing (quasi-)independent federal regulatory agencies and levels of government carve up legislative and enforcement responsibilities for securities law, banking law, and corporate law. The American market structure recapitulates this fragmentation of power. Rules governing the ownership of corporate stock, the development of securities markets and investment funds alongside banks as financial intermediaries, and the absence of centralized or sectoral labor relations preclude the emergence and institutionalization of countervailing sources of power against that of senior management in firm governance. This absence of institutionalized representation of and negotiation among countervailing interest groups concentrates and centralizes power in the hands of the chief executive officer (CEO) and other senior managers. Market pressures are the primary check on managerial abuses, and this increases the incentive for policymakers to use market-reinforcing substantive legal rules to provide a functional framework for corporate governance.

The American political–economic structure favors arm's length, or transactional, economic relationships over longer-term relational ties, and a structurally similar pattern prevails with respect to state–corporate relations in the enforcement of corporate governance law. The tendency of law and regulation to preserve an expansive sphere of private organizational autonomy, while relying on highly developed and adversarially enforced frameworks of formal rights, constitutes a distinctive form of American legal liberalism.[3] What differentiates the American neoliberal conception of economic regulation from more statist or neocorporatist forms of political–economic ordering is that law generally has not *directly* modified and imposed mandatory, largely self-regulating *institutional structures* on the corporate firm. Instead, the relatively hands-off approach to corporate governance in American law allows greater latitude in the structuring of private institutions and affairs but uses more detailed, formal, prescriptive, legal rules to reduce and redress market failures. Regulators, prosecutors, and private litigants bringing disputes into courts are thus more important in American corporate governance than in Germany or France. In the absence of alternative institutional mechanisms to resolve governance conflicts, legal liberalism tends to emphasize and intensify the adjudicatory and prosecutorial modes of state intervention in the economy.

The United States created the world's first modern system of securities regulation. The Securities and Exchange Commission (SEC) provided a centralized federal securities regulator to protect investors from market manipulation and abuses through the drafting and enforcement of disclosure and transparency rules. As a result, the United States possessed unusually strong transparency, disclosure, and

Table 9.1. Postwar Corporate Governance Models in the United States, Germany, and France (ca. 1985)

Countries	Financial Market Regulation	Corporate/Company Law	Labor Law
United States (Neoliberal)	• Centralized national securities regulator. • Strong transparency and disclosure rules designed to correct market failures and protect minority shareholders. • Strong legal prohibitions on insider trading. • Fragmentation of equity ownership stakes and financial services (Glass-Steagall Act). • Pension and tax laws encouraged development of large equity-holding pension funds.	• Corporate law is permissive with few mandatory rules (enabling law approach grants wide latitude for contractual and charter-defined corporate governance structures and processes). • Pattern of state corporate law giving shareholders comparatively few rights to vote on important corporate decisions. • Strong elements of shareholder primacy enshrined in fiduciary duties enforceable by private rights of action, but diluted by "business judgment rule." • Vertically integrated firms rely on short-term contractual relations externally; law limits cross-shareholding, director interlocks, and business associations as sectoral coordinating bodies • Well-developed market for corporate control underpinned by fiduciary duty and disclosure rules.	• Strict separation of labor relations and firm management; labor law protects managerial prerogatives (sharp distinction between corporate and labor law). • No form of board or works council codetermination. • Fragmented labor organization with no sectoral or peak bargaining between employers and unions. • Weak protection for labor organizing.
Germany (Neocorporatist)	• Moderate to weak transparency and disclosure regulations • No federal securities regulator or regulation; reliance on state (*Land*) and self-regulation. • Regulation institutionalizes bargaining among insiders.	• Mandatory rules structure the corporation and governance processes. • Corporate interests legally superior to shareholder interests, corporation responsible for stakeholder employees, few effective privately enforceable legal protections for shareholders.	• Interpenetration of labor relations and firm management limits managerial autonomy and hierarchy (blurred boundaries between company and labor law). • Supervisory board and works councils codetermination gives

Table 9.1. *Continued*

Countries	Financial Market Regulation	Corporate/Company Law	Labor Law
	• "Universal banks" combine banking and securities business at core of financial system; substantial number of smaller peripheral local and regional financial institutions. • Public pensions predominate; private pensions insignificant and not encouraged by policy.	• Corporate networks underpinned by cross-shareholding, interlocking directorships, and strong employers and sectoral business associations. • Weak market for corporate control.	employees multiple institutional channels of representation. • Centralized labor organizations and employer associations; legal facilitation of sectoral-/industry-level bargaining. • Strong protection for labor organization and bargaining power (but not necessarily for strike activity).
France (Statist)	• Weak transparency and disclosure rules. • Administrative officials vested with extensive discretion over financial regulation (including discretionary allocation of capital). • Highly centralized and concentrated bank-dominated financial systems. • Public pensions predominate; private pensions insignificant and not encouraged by policy.	• More mandatory rules than neoliberal systems, but regulatory and interfirm relationships have most powerful impact on corporate governance. • Shareholder interests subordinate to "corporate interests" and state policies; few legal provisions for autonomous organization and representation of stakeholder interests or for effective protection of shareholders. • Hierarchical, vertically structured corporate networks linking large banks, core industrial firms, and suppliers. • Substantial state role in industrial and sectoral organization through administrative power and control over finance (no market for corporate control).	• De facto, if not de jure, separation of labor and strategic management of firm, and firm paternalism toward employees displaces employees' formal consultation and veto rights. • Fragmented organized labor limits coordination in bargaining; state-mandated labor and incomes policies more important than collective bargaining and partially implemented by more centralized employer associations. • Substantial legal employment rights combined with weak protection for autonomous labor organizing and bargaining.

insider-trading laws and regulatory rules designed to protect minority shareholders, facilitate market transactions, and buttress the perceived legitimacy of the country's securities markets.[4] The SEC also oversaw the stock exchanges, the Financial Accounting Standards Board (FASB), and thus the drafting of the exchanges' listing and disclosure rules and accounting principles that wield enormous influence over levels of financial disclosure and market behavior.

As argued by Mark Roe, statutory and regulatory restraints on the ownership of large equity stakes in corporations by financial institutions mandated the segmentation of financial services and *compelled* portfolio diversification that limited concentrated equity ownership as a means of checking the power of management.[5] As a result of this extensive financial market regulation to protect shareholders, the "external" capital markets in the United States are among the most developed and liquid in the world, with a high proportion of publicly traded firms and an extraordinary range of debt and equity financing options.[6] These innovations in financial instruments were driven by the very market segmentation imposed by the American regulatory regime; equity financing and financial innovation lagged where universal banks or the state dominated finance, as in Germany or France.[7] However, this legal framework encouraged institutional investors to respond to governance and management problems through exiting by selling their stakes rather than participating more actively through voice in firm governance.[8] The fragmentation of ownership thus created a mutually reinforcing relationship between the market-driven American financial system and a legalistic, transparency-based regulatory regime.

In contrast with the centralized structure of federal securities regulation, American company (or corporate) law has been the responsibility of the states. State company laws tend to take the form of broad enabling statutes that give corporate managers and directors wide discretion in how to structure the firm, its finances, and decision-making processes. State law typically gave shareholders comparatively few rights to vote on important corporate decisions, and managers also control the nomination of directors (their nominal superiors) and the proxy votes of shareholders so that they largely control the very institutions and processes designed to render them accountable to shareholders. This empowerment of managers and directors was partially counterbalanced by fiduciary duties that obligated them to run the corporation for the benefit of the shareholders alone, as opposed to any other corporate constituency, in a loyal and reasonably attentive and competent fashion.[9] These rights are enforceable by private lawsuits under a set of procedural rules, including derivative suits, class actions, and contingency fee retainers. However, fiduciary duties are substantially diluted by the "business judgment rule," which requires that decisions in the ordinary course of business are exempt from liability if made in good faith.[10] Accordingly, the legal liberalism characteristic of American law and institutions again favors adjudicatory forms of dispute resolution, even as practical constraints limit the utility of litigious mechanisms of resolving governance conflicts.

In light of the inexorable growth of the federal regulatory state, particularly in the twentieth century, the absence of a *federal* corporate law is an arresting feature of the American corporate governance regime. In this the United States is an exception and nearly unique among the advanced industrial countries. From the emergence of free incorporation in the early nineteenth century, the states have been responsible for the chartering and thus the regulation of the corporate firm. The emergence of truly national industrial corporations unleashed the political pressures for national regulation of business but did not reallocate authority over corporate law and chartering to the federal level. Ever since, periodic political debates have erupted over whether the legal authority for the creation and internal regulation of the corporation should be reallocated to the federal level. Serious consideration of federal corporate law legislation dates from the late nineteenth century but was defeated in every case by business and localized state interests.[11] Calls for a federal corporate law were renewed during the New Deal debates over the design and passage of the Securities Act of 1933 and the Securities and Exchange Act of 1934 as strengthened proregulation political and ideological forces that accompanied industrialization pressed for more fundamental and thoroughgoing corporate law reform.[12] However, even the passage of the federal securities laws and the creation of the SEC did not dislodge the preexisting federalist structure and the politics that lock it in place. Rather, the federal government entered those areas of law and policy that related to matters with the most direct impact on national capital markets and that the states had been unwilling or incapable of addressing through corporate law.[13]

The idea of a federal corporate law returned to the political stage repeatedly during the subsequent decades and was marked by intense conflict in each case. Proposals to enact a federal corporate law were mooted during the early 1940s and in the 1960s and 1970s in response to critiques of state law as representing a "race to the bottom" of regulatory laxity, and then during the ferocious legal and political battles set off by the takeover wave of the 1980s. These political struggles over the internal structure and governance of the corporation also extended to efforts to ensure greater uniformity in corporate law. The calls for a federal incorporation act in the 1940s were successfully resisted by business and state interest groups—but did ultimately result in the drafting of the American Bar Association's influential Model Business Corporation Act.[14] The American Law Institute's Principles of Corporate Governance project, in part undertaken to promote greater harmonization of state law in order to reduce pressure for federalization, triggered the most intense internal political conflict and business lobbying in the elite legal group's history.[15]

As a result of the repeated failures to enact a federal corporation law, federal securities regulation and state corporate law have remained in tension as they overlapped and blurred uneasily into one another with respect to subjects such as proxy solicitation and voting, tender offers, insider trading, and corporate accounting. However, despite the extraordinary economic and political importance of corporate law in industrial development and the constitution of corporate power, this odd and exceptional federalist legal structure persists. The internal affairs of the corporate firm are governed under the law of the state chartering the corporation, while its interactions with the securities markets (most importantly disclosure) are subject to federal regulation. Only with the political backlash against business and financial interests unleashed by the extraordinary stock market and corporate governance scandals of 2001–2002 and the subsequent passage of the Sarbanes–Oxley Act of 2002 did federal law finally penetrate the traditional sphere of state corporate law (discussed below).

For purposes of corporate governance, a striking characteristic of American labor law is its strict separation of labor relations and firm management. In the United States, labor law *protects managerial prerogatives* from encroachment by collective bargaining or union organization.[16] Matters such as investment, marketing and production strategy, design and production plans, and financial strategies are considered within the "core of entrepreneurial control" and not subject to collectively bargaining,[17] although these issues may have decisive importance for the future of the workforce. No legally mandated structures exist in American law at the state or federal levels to incorporate employees into firm decision making or provide for ongoing consultation processes, such as that provided by board representation or works council structures.[18] In this sense, the protection of managerial prerogatives by labor law parallels the empowerment of managers vis-à-vis shareholders by corporate law.

The prevalence of litigation in the American governance system (and its virtual absence in Germany) is thus a byproduct of distinctive political and legal regimes. From the comparative perspective, civil litigation (and its prevalence) in the United States appears as the legal mechanism most consistent with the structure of an advanced liberal political economy and not simply an arbitrary pathology that can be eradicated from it—although critics have fiercely attacked this view.[19] Structural mechanisms of regulation through institutionalized representational arrangements, as found in Germany, provide a functional equivalent of extensive legal regulation and blunt demand for legalistic enforcement mechanisms. Without recourse to such structural solutions, legal rules, procedures, and remedies fulfill regulatory functions in the United States. A paradox thus arises from the American solution: a system premised on maximizing the latitude of private power over capital and property has resulted in an extensive, expensive, and cumbersome regulatory regime largely administered by the courts and defined by complex rules, legalistic procedures, and adversarial relations.

GERMANY

The German corporate governance regime represents a stakeholder model of corporate governance that incorporates and protects the interests of nonshareholder constituencies, especially labor, within governance institutions.[20] Its long-established bank-centered financial system and pervasive corporate cross-shareholdings complemented the stakeholder model by encouraging the adoption of long-term adjustment and growth strategies by industrial enterprises. Germany is also often described as a highly legalistic country. However, German legalism more frequently *uses law to fashion representational structures and institu-*

tional frameworks that channel opposing interests into negotiation rather than formal enforcement processes.

The structure of the German state and political economy is more centralized than that of the United States and makes substantial use of centralized interest-group representation in the formulation of policy. The centralization of peak associations in neocorporatist bargaining compensates for the significant federalist reservation of authority to the *Länder* (state) governments and their representatives in the upper house of the Bundesrat. Historically, German corporate governance has been fashioned by balancing centralized regulation, neocorporatist economic governance, decentralized *Länder* regulation, and firm-level self-regulation.

The postwar legal framework of German corporate governance was the mirror image of the American. The American corporate governance regime was defined by centralized federal securities regulation and the dispersion of legal authority under state corporate laws that defined the internal structure and governance processes of the corporate firm. In contrast, a *uniform federal company law* and the *fragmentation of securities regulation* among the *Länder* and local self-regulating exchanges defined the legal framework of German corporate governance. Until the mid-1990s, German securities regulation remained undeveloped and rather feeble in its protection of shareholders. Transparency norms, disclosure regulations, and accounting rules remained weak and company finances opaque. In the absence of any provision for class actions, derivative suits, or contingency-fee retainers, the law provided few effective avenues for private litigation to enforce shareholder rights.

In contrast to the United States, Germany's federal company law relies heavily on mandatory rules that structure the corporation and its governance processes. In contrast to the single-tier American board of directors, the German corporation has a two-tier board structure. The highest authority in the German corporation is the supervisory board (*Aufsichtsrat*), the primary functions of which are the appointment and supervision of the managing board (*Vorstand*) of the corporation and the formulation and approval of corporate policy. German company law also gives the shareholders' meeting (Annual General Meeting, or AGM) the right to vote on and to receive relevant information regarding a broad range of issues, including mergers and acquisitions, capital increases, and major changes in business strategies. The law creates a private right of action to nullify any decision taken by the AGM where informational rights and procedures have been violated. Because these decisions usually concern the most important corporate strategic issues, managers are usually intensely concerned with settling suits quickly. Thus, German company law created a disclosure and transparency regime outside of securities regulation—although it functions only intermittently (i.e., when an AGM is held), rather than on a continuous basis as under securities law.

The most striking feature of German company law is employee representation through supervisory board codetermination.[21] Under the Codetermination Act of 1976, all stock corporations (*Aktiengesellschaft*, or AG) and close corporations (*Gesellschaft mit beschränkter Haftung*, or GmbH) employing over 2,000 employees must split their supervisory boards evenly between shareholder and employee representatives.[22] The chairman of the supervisory board is elected by the share-holders (and the banks that wield the voting rights of deposited shares) and wields a second tie-breaking vote.[23] Firms with 500 to 2,000 employees only need set aside one-third of the board seats for employee representatives.[24] Thus, the struc-ture of the board preserves shareholder (or managerial) dominance; employee representation serves only as an informational channel rather than an effective mechanism of control.[25]

A second, and more important, form of codetermination is created under Ger-man labor relations law. Works councils endow employees with substantial rights and power within the firm and workplace.[26] The works council wields influence by virtue of its power to demand compensation for economic injury suffered be-cause of a change in corporate policy and through its ability to use its informa-tional, consultation, and codetermination or codecision rights to substantially impede the implementation of managerial decisions.[27] German law mandates transparency in labor matters that the United States provides only to shareholders. The blending of company and labor-relations law under codetermination creates "microcorporatist"[28] structures that facilitate negotiation, compromise, coopera-tion, and consensus within firm governance.

German law provides shareholders few effective private rights of action to en-force these diffuse and undeveloped fiduciary duties. Private litigation is rare and ineffective as a mode of enforcing governance rights. Still, Germany has no deriva-tive suits, class, actions, or contingency-fee retainers that fuel corporate litigation in the United States. This is in part by policy design. German corporate gover-nance is constructed to facilitate cooperative relations and to avoid open conflict and to promote negotiation. Lawsuits to enforce rights to adequate disclosure to the AGM constitute the significant exception to this avoidance of litigation. Critics point out that this element of disclosure regulation through company law has pro-duced the same sorts of litigation abuses as American securities and company law: excess litigation rates, frivolous suits designed to extract quick settlements, and excess legalism and complexity in the heart of corporate operations.

This structuring of law and allocation of legal competencies between the fed-eral and state governments (along with the prevalence of self-regulation) formed the foundation for a bank-centered financial system, complemented by cross-shareholding networks, along with extensive sectoral organization of standards and labor relations, that defined a set of stable, interlocking ownership and gover-nance relationships. The major banks' central role in securities underwriting, bro-kerage, and trading gave them significant power over corporate affairs. In the absence of legislation separating commercial and investment banking, large Ger-man banks became "universal banks" that combined the banking and securities businesses at the core of the financial system. Consequently, large banks were si-multaneously important lenders to and major shareholders in publicly traded firms. Further, under German law, the banks' brokerage clients may deposit their shares and the banks may vote "deposited share voting rights" on authorization of the depositor–shareholder.[29] The combination of voting and financial power, along with long-term relational lender and shareholding relationships, contributed to a final source of bank influence: substantial representation on supervisory boards. Given the absence of strong shareholder protection and few incentives for major banks to cultivate equity financing, far fewer firms were publicly traded and many remained family owned.

FRANCE

Historically, France was the most highly centralized and statist of the political economies among the three country cases. Unlike the United States and Germany, the French state controlled a large number of the country's leading industrial and financial firms.[30] Not only was public ownership of enterprises common, but the state maintained control over the flow of credit to and from banks and thus over corporate finance.[31] The regulatory structure that administered these financial arrangements was correspondingly centralized and tended to serve the interests of state actors and the ends of state policy. Indeed, prior to the creation of the first securities markets regulator, the *Commission des Operations de Bourse* (COB) in 1967, securities regulation—a crucial foundation of market finance and component of corporate governance—was not even a recognized area of French law.[32] The state wielded de facto control over the governance of many major firms even where it did not exercise de jure ownership.

Prior to the late 1980s, France possessed weak and poorly enforced transparency and disclosure rules governing securities. Instead of a law- and regulation-based financial system that would allow and encourage the formation of market relationships among private economic actors, administrative officials exercised extensive discretionary control over financial regulation, finance, and credit. The postwar state organized a highly centralized and concentrated bank-dominated financial system, but, unlike Germany, used the banks as pliant instruments of state policy and power.

In 1967, France's first securities law created a national securities markets regulator, the COB, and provided a rudimentary framework for the disclosure of corporate financial information.[33] The law required companies to issue a prospectus (*note d'information*) subject to COB approval prior to an initial public offer or the listing of securities on an exchange.[34] The law also required the appointment of an official company auditor (the *commissaire aux comptes*) to assess and report on the corporation's financial results and internal controls.[35] Yet the overwhelmingly statist character of finance and corporate governance in practice limited the actual transparency of corporate accounts and the accountability of managers to shareholders and other stakeholders. Rather, firm finances remained opaque and its corporate management highly centralized and its discretionary power largely unchecked. French capitalism was known for its tightly knit political–bureaucratic–corporate elites that decided policy and corporate strategy behind closed doors.

This absence of transparency and regulatory enforcement, and thus accountability, was ripe for the corruption and financial market scandals that pervaded French politics and business.[36]

French public corporations are almost always legally organized as *societés anonymes* with a *unitary board* consisting of a board of directors (the *conseil d'administration*) chaired and dominated by the firm's CEO (the *President Directeur General*, or PDG).[37] Historically, this predominance of the unitary board structure brings the French corporate form closer to the American and British structure, rather than to the German dual-board structure. French company law imposes more mandatory rules on the country's firms than does American law, but they are not as stringent as under German law. Like German law, however, French company law subordinates shareholder interests to "corporate interests" and state policies. There are few legal provisions for fiduciary duties to effectively protect shareholders.[38] Boards protected the interests of controlling shareholders and were more attentive to the demands of state economic policy than the interests of minority shareholders. Further, the French company law framework, in combination with the securities law, did not, and was not designed to, produce an active market for corporate control. The substantial state role in industrial and sectoral organization along with the state's administrative control over finance left no room for autonomous sectoral and corporate reorganization through market mechanisms.

France has a history of ideologically driven labor militancy and uncooperative labor relations that has profoundly shaped the country's labor-relations system. In part, as in finance, the state stepped in to organized labor relations and wage bargaining through government-mediated national and sectoral collective agreements between fragmented unions representing a small percentage of the workforce and otherwise weak (although more centralized) employers' organizations. A history of chronic class conflict also has contributed to the de facto, if not de jure, exclusion of employees from firm governance. Instead, a tradition of firm paternalism toward employees took the places of employees' formal consultation and veto rights. Instead, substantial legal rights under national employment law (e.g., rights against arbitrary dismissal) combined with weak protection for autonomous labor organizing and bargaining to define labor relations in both more individualistic and more statist terms.

The highly centralized and concentrated market structure of the French corporate economy was dependent on state finance, cross-subsidies, or credit allocation (when not supplanted entirely by state ownership). Ownership structures were likewise centralized, either through state ownership or through the predominance of majority shareholders and family ownership of closely held firms.[39] In contrast with Germany, financial institutions historically have not played a prominent role in the control of corporate enterprise in France.[40] Markets remained truncated; market actors (e.g., firms, managers, banks, producer groups, unions) possessed little autonomy; and the highly centralized management structure of the firm matched the centralization of the state.[41] State administration of finance and widespread public ownership of enterprise supplanted market relations and constrained the development of markets independent of the state.[42] Shareholder rights, institutional investment, and strong codetermination laws would have limited managerial dominance but would have interfered with state control over the firm as an instrument of economic and industrial policy and so never developed under the *dirigiste* regime.

SUMMARY OF POLICY REFORMS

Across the three country cases, corporate governance reforms are strikingly similar in their focus on creating and/or strengthening the institutional and legal conditions for equity finance and investment.[43] Self-regulation and insider-dominated corporate governance have steadily given way to *increasingly legalistic regulation* in order to promote a more liberal market paradigm of corporate finance and governance.[44] Three common trends emerge from these developments. First, state actors have pushed forward the agenda of corporate governance reform through the growth and expansion of national-level legislation. Second, this expanded regulatory authority has been institutionalized through the creation or strengthening of increasingly centralized national securities regulators. Third, this legalism is embodied in the adoption of increasingly stringent substantive transparency and disclosure law and regulation to improve information flows to investors and financial markets. This trend represents the triumph of the American SEC model of securities regulation. Moreover, corporate governance reform has gone beyond securities and financial market regulation and extended more directly into reshaping the structure and internal operation of the corporation itself by strengthening the position of the board of directors vis-à-vis senior management. Legislative reforms in France during the 1980s, Germany during the 1990s, and the United States in 2002 extended beyond securities market regulation to company law itself. In each case, national governments have become more active in using law to restructure financial markets and the internal governance arrangements of the corporate firm. However, the structure of company law and the role of employees point to continued substantial divergence among the three countries and to the political and institutional differences that perpetuate them. These major legal changes in the American, German, and French corporate governance regimes are summarized in tables 9.2 through 9.5.

THE UNITED STATES

The contemporary corporate governance debate in the United States began two decades ago amid economic crisis and instability. The hostile takeover wave of the 1980s destabilized the American corporate governance regime and triggered a power struggle among managers, financial institutions, and shareholders

Table 9.2. Major Changes in Financial Market Law and Regulation (1985–2000)

United States	Germany	France
• 2002 Sarbanes-Oxley Act expands SEC authority over accounting rules and industry practices, creates Accounting Oversight Board, and requires certification of financial statements by CEOs and CFOs.	• 2001 legislation consolidates regulatory authority over all financial services (securities, banking, and insurance) within one agency (BAFin)	• French government reforms financial regulation to give up most discretionary power over allocation of finance.
• Institutional investors given more power and influence by 1992 reform of SEC proxy rules allowing greater cooperation in governance activism.	• Disclosure law passed in 1998 to increase transparency by allowing firms to issue financial statements using either IAS or US GAAP.	• EU increasingly restricts state's ability to finance and bail out firms. • 1988 and 1989 legal reforms expand COB power to oversee and enforce disclosure and reporting requirements.
• 1995 legislation granting institutional shareholders "lead shareholder" status in shareholder litigation.	• Securities Trading Law of 1995 requires disclosure of parties owning or controlling 5% of stock, but has significant loopholes.	• 1988 law establishes stock exchange authorities, the CMF and SBF, whose powers expand to include regulation of listing, brokerage, and tender offers.
• 1988 Treasury Department ruling requires ERISA pension funds to vote their shares as a fiduciary duty.	• KonTraG proxy voting rules more protective of shareholders, require internal bank procedures and offices to reduce conflicts of interest.	
• Federal Reserve and Treasury Department sanction erosion of Glass-Steagall separation of banking and securities business, ending in law's repeal.	• Frankfurt Stock Exchange increases stringency of internal disclosure and listing rules; its *Neue Markt* [New Market] for small-cap and high-tech securities issues requires use of IAS reporting standards.	

that has waxed, waned, and waxed again over the past two decades. The takeover wave of the 1980s transformed the relationship between corporate management and finance. Takeovers and the new power of investment banks encouraged the adoption of new financially driven management strategies and techniques of financial engineering that led to the practices and business culture of short-term strategic planning horizons, excessive leverage, a focus on immediate returns to

Table 9.3. Major Changes in Company Law (1985–2000)

United States	Germany	France
• Sarbanes–Oxley Act of 2002 extends federal law into internal corporate structure for first time; requires (1) auditors to report to board instead of management, (2) more independent board members, and (3) board must create and oversee firm's risk management policies. • 1999 NYSE and SEC rule amendments exempt most stock option plans from shareholder approval. • Antitakeover statutes in the late 1980s and early 1990s weaken shareholder rights and market for corporate control. • Takeover litigation during 1980s results in widespread judicial sanction of antitakeover defenses.	• 2001 Takeover Law permits stronger antitakeover defenses. • 2000 tax reform law designed to break up crossshareholdings. • 1998 KonTraG statute: (1) External auditors hired by and report to board instead of management (2) Limited voting of bank-controlled shares and proxies (3) Stronger fiduciary obligations of custodian bank in voting proxies (4) 1 share, 1 vote rule (5) Prohibition on voting cross-shareholding stakes in board elections (6) Stock repurchases allowed for first time • Courts infer existence of fiduciary duties to shareholders (1980s–1990s), but law remains undeveloped and conceptions of corporate interest distinct from shareholder interest persist.	• 1989 COB and exchange rules create bidding and disclosure procedures for tender offers. • Introduction of freeze-out and appraisal rules to protect minority shareholders. • Law requires shareholder vote on wide range of corporate decisions. • Proxy voting reform to facilitate shareholder voting and weaken management control over voting (too early to discern impact). • Private litigation enforcement mechanisms for shareholder rights considered but either rejected (e.g., class action) or not yet enacted. • Market for corporate control becomes very active (particularly in domestic market).

Notes: Provisions of French law have been allocated within the categories of company law and securities law according to their function. Securities law addresses the behavior of firms and individuals with respect to the securities markets and to the disclosure of information to regulators and the public. Company law provides for the institutional structure of the corporate firm and allocates rights and authority within it.

Table 9.4. Major Changes in Labor Relations and Labor Law (1985–2000)

United States	Germany	France
• No significant legislative changes. • Continued debate throughout 1990s over the legality of employee teams and "quality circles" under the NLRA § 8(a) prohibition on "company unions."	• 2002 law strengthens works council codetermination. • Court rulings strike down attempts to circumvent board codetermination. • Maintenance of board codetermination precludes proposed reduction of board size.	• No substantial legal change, despite continued employer criticism of job-protection legislation and litigation. • EU Works Council Directive introduces a weakened form of the institution to France (after 1982 Arroux laws introduce weak and ineffective works councils).

shareholders, successive booms in CEO empire building during the 1980s and 1990s, and—ultimately—manipulation of earnings and disclosures that would result in a corporate governance crisis following the collapse of the 1990s securities market bubble. Coming at approximately the nadir of American "deindustrialization," takeovers raised intense concerns over serious economic decline and social disruption caused by sudden and dramatic corporate restructuring, plant closings, and layoffs. The massive economic restructuring and redistribution of wealth driven by deindustrialization and the new variety of shareholder capitalism galvanized political opposition to the disruption and perceived injustice of takeovers. The suspicion of concentrated financial power, the crisis in the industrial economy during the 1980s, and the mobilization of politically powerful managers and local populist interest groups generated a potent policy backlash.[45]

During the 1980s and early 1990s, managers, corporate raiders, and shareholders fought fierce legal battles over the fiduciary obligations of managers and directors in resisting hostile tender offers and adopting antitakeover defenses. Courts significantly weakened fiduciary duties (most importantly in Delaware, the premier state of incorporation) by sanctioning the use of a proliferation of com-

Table 9.5. Degree of Change in Corporate Governance Law by Country and Category

Country	Financial Market Regulation	Corporate/Company Law	Labor Law
United States	High/Moderate	Moderate	Low
Germany	High /Moderate	Moderate	Low
France	High	High/Moderate	Low

plex and arcane takeover defenses. The political battles over takeover law further strengthened management and diluted fiduciary duties to shareholders, as many states (this time with the important exception of Delaware) adopted "corporate constituency statutes."[46] These statutes permitted directors responding to a hostile takeover attempt to consider and invoke the interests of other corporate stakeholders such as employees and local communities in opposition to those of shareholders. Yet, these laws granted no enforceable rights to these stakeholders.[47] Legal recognition of their interests served to strengthen the position of incumbent management, not their own.[48]

The backlash against takeovers set the stage for the ongoing policy debate over corporate governance. The result was an explosion of legal activity. Managers, unions, institutional investors, shareholder groups, financial institutions, and financiers sought to enshrine their policy preferences in the policy, statutory law, regulation, and legal doctrine. This politicization of the law and practice of American corporate governance during the 1980s marked the beginning of the contemporary international corporate governance movement. However, the battles over takeovers turned on the content and adequacy of company law and fiduciary duties, not federal securities law and regulation.

In reaction to the takeover wave of the 1980s, managers and directors began to award themselves lucrative "golden parachute" severance payments in de facto exchange for their prospective approval of a takeover. Further, following the prescriptions of economic theory, firms began to adopt stock options as a form of compensation to align the economic interests of mangers and directors with those of shareholders. Although this may be viewed as an efficient use of contracting to circumvent inefficient legal rules that entrench incumbent management, these payoffs also reveal the conflicts of interest inherent in takeover contexts and helped spark the dramatic rise in executive compensation that would play a prominent role in the scandals of the 1990s.

The politics of American corporate governance reform during the 1990s swerved between efforts to protect managerial interests and measures increasing shareholder protections. In 1995 and 1998, Congress enacted "tort reform" legislation designed to reduce the incidence of securities litigation. First, the Private Securities Litigation Reform Act of 1995 (PSLRA) raised the pleading requirements for securities fraud suits and largely abolished "aiding and abetting" liability under which law and accounting firms could be held liable for fraudulent statements and omissions by publicly traded companies. The PSLRA also authorized the appointment of a "lead plaintiff" in securities suits in hopes that the shareholder with the greatest alleged damages, almost always an institutional investor, could take charge of the litigation and thus press meritorious claims while quickly disposing of frivolous suits. The second law, the Securities Law Uniform Standards Act of 1998 (SLUSA), was even more sweeping. The SLUSA preempted state securities fraud laws that could have been used by plaintiffs' attorneys to circumvent the new, more demanding restrictions on federal securities suits. At a time when conservatives in Congress lauded federalism, Republicans pushed through a bill that dramatically increased centralized federal control over securities regulation. The laws were politically as much as economically motivated. They strengthened the position of managers, a predominantly Republican constituency, by weakening one of the most important mechanisms of transparency enforcement and managerial accountability, while attacking the financial base of a plaintiffs' bar that overwhelmingly supported Democrats.

However, throughout the 1990s, the SEC under Chairman Arthur Levitt initiated a series of reforms to improve managerial accountability and financial transparency. The first amended the SEC's proxy rules to eliminate the cumbersome requirement of filing a proxy statement whenever shareholders collectively owning more than 5 percent of a firm's stock communicated about governance issues.[49] The 1992 proxy reforms expressly recognized the growing political power of institutional investors and their expanding role in corporate governance. The SEC failed in its efforts to reform the regulation of accounting rules and the activities of accounting firms. In particular, the SEC sought to require the expensing of stock options and to address auditors' conflicts of interests when simultaneously acting as consultants. The accounting firms and "new economy" technology firms dependent on options enlisted allies in Congress to fight the regulatory proposals by bringing legislative pressure on the SEC until it was withdrawn.[50]

Finally, the SEC pushed through a regulatory change in direct tension with (and at least partially undid) the proxy reforms of 1992. Regulation Fair Disclosure (Regulation FD), adopted in August 2000, prohibited selective disclosure of material information by corporations in order to prevent favored analysts, financial institutions, and institutional investors from receiving information not released to the general public. While addressing the problem of informational asymmetries that disadvantage individual investors vis-à-vis large institutions, Regulation FD once again impeded the ability of institutional investors to pursue corporate governance activism by limiting their ability to communicate in private with managers about their concerns and demands.[51] By the end of 2000, it had become increasingly clear that transparency regulation and institutional activism, the two dominant paradigms of corporate governance regulation and reform, were operating at structural, legal, and political cross-purposes.

Only the post-1990s scandals of 2001–2002 would finally implicate the adequacy and legitimacy of the entire American corporate governance regime, including securities regulation, and inflame political support for more wide-ranging reform. With the enactment of the Sarbanes–Oxley Act in late 2002, following the Enron, WorldCom, Global Crossing, and other massive corporate scandals, the federal government instituted the most comprehensive corporate governance reform in the United States since the 1930s. Sarbanes–Oxley imposed a host of new regulatory requirements and measures on publicly traded corporations, corporate managers, accountants, and attorneys. Sarbanes–Oxley created an entirely new regulatory body appointed by and under the oversight of the SEC, the Public Company Accounting Oversight Board, to enforce a new set of regulations governing accounting standards and the activities of accounting firms in auditing and consulting. The law also required the SEC to draft new regulations requiring heightened disclosure of the financial condition of corporations that included off-balance sheet transactions, codes of ethics (and their waiver by the board), the reconciliation of "pro forma" financial results with generally accepted accounting standards, nonaudit services performed by the firm's auditor, and real-time disclosure of material financial information and developments.[52]

Under the act, federal law in the United States began *for the first time* to encompass the *internal* structure and affairs of the corporation—traditional subjects of state corporate law. Similar to German law (see below), Sarbanes–Oxley strengthens the auditing function of the board and its independence from management. Public firms are now required to appoint an auditing committee comprised *entirely* of independent directors, and the SEC is charged with writing and enforcing rules defining directorial independence.[53] To ensure the effectiveness of the committee, at least one member must be qualified as a financial expert under standards to be promulgated by the SEC, and the audit committee has direct responsibility appointing, compensating, and overseeing the outside auditors, resolving disputes between management and the auditors concerning financial reporting, and for approving all auditor services. Further, auditors must report directly to the audit committee, rather than management. This unprecedented—and underreported—centralization of corporate governance regulation represented a sharp break with traditions of American federalism, which suggests the extraordinary political potency of the financial and governance scandals of 2001–2002.

GERMANY

Germany has been widely regarded as lagging other advanced industrial countries such as France and the United Kingdom in reforming its financial market law. It delayed in enacting insider-trading laws as required by a European Union (EU) directive, preferring to maintain its voluntary Kodex rules that had been widely ignored and regarded as a failure. German accounting standards were known as lax and conducive to hiding cash and financial problems alike. Until the mid-1990s, there was no federal securities market regulator. Beginning in 1994, German policymakers transformed the country's securities and company law within a few years.[54]

The landmark securities legislation in Germany is the Second Financial Market Promotion Act of 1994.[55] The act transformed both the substantive law governing disclosure and securities transactions, and the institutionalization of securities regulation. It created a centralized federal securities regulator for the first time in German history.[56] The German Federal Securities Supervisory Office (*Bundesaufsichtsamt für den Wertpapierhandel*, or BAWe) replaced the decentralized system of state-level exchange regulators with a nationally centralized source of regulatory and enforcement power. The BAWe has not so much eroded the role of the *Länder* as it has created and/or enforced a comprehensive body of regulation for the first time in Germany. This has led to convergence on the SEC model of securities markets regulation in which a centralized regulator exercises jurisdiction over a fragmented federal political landscape and a consolidating national financial market structure.

The BAWe's history has been marked by two bursts of legislative expansion, followed by another massive consolidation of regulatory power. The first, from 1994 to 1995, created the agency and set out its primary functions and substantive enabling legislation. The second, from late 1997 to 1998, followed the BAWe's phase of initial organization and consolidation and markedly increased the agency's role in regulating and policing German securities markets by dramatically expanding the BAWe's jurisdiction and specific regulatory responsibilities.[57] The BAWe now oversees the filing of prospectuses, the disclosure and reporting of material information by public companies, insider trading, and the reporting of voting rights and ownership stakes. It also supervises financial services providers and the operation of the stock exchanges, and cooperates with other national securities regulators throughout the European Union and the rest of the world. In the short time of its existence, the BAWe regulators' authority and responsibilities have expanded to include a growing number of financial institutions and service providers, a widening array of substantive areas of regulation, and stronger enforcement powers.[58] Finally, in April 2002 the German parliament passed the Law on Integrated Financial Services Supervision[59] to consolidate and centralize all financial market and services regulation within one massive agency, the German Financial Supervisory Authority (*Bundesanstalt für Finanzdienstleistungsaufsicht*, or BAFin).[60] The BAFin combined the BAWe with the agencies responsible for banking supervision (*Bundesaufsichtsamt für das Kreditwesen*), insurance supervision (*Bundesaufsichtsamt für das Versicherungswesen*), and securities supervision under the BAWe into a single state regulator that supervises banks, financial services, and insurance institutions across the entire financial market.[61]

Following this massive overhaul of securities legislation in 1994, German policymakers enacted the Control and Transparency Act (*Gesetz zur Kontrolle und Transparenz im Unternehmensbereich*, or KonTraG) of 1998, the first substantial company law reform since 1965, in order to further modernize corporate finance and governance.[62] The KonTraG did not constitute a stunning break with the past, as did the Financial Promotion Laws, but it did advance and deepen the transformation of Germany's corporate governance regime and revealed the fundamental political shifts that underpinned the reform agenda. The law addressed the subjects of bank power, the role and power of the supervisory board, auditing, share voting rights, stock options, and litigation rules. At first glance, the KonTraG appears to attack the large universal banks. The law sought to trim the influence of Germany's powerful universal banks by forcing them to make a choice: if their holdings exceed 5 percent of a corporation's stock, they can vote their own equity stakes *or* vote the proxy votes of the shares deposited by their brokerage customers.[63] The KonTraG also requires that banks disclose all other board mandates held by their representatives and their ownership stakes in firms, inform their share depositors of alternative ways to exercise their votes, and strengthens their statutory fiduciary obligation to vote proxies in the best interests of the average share-holder.[64] These provisions sought to utilize and strengthen the German bank-based system of proxy voting, rather than undermine it, while creating opportunities for alternative mechanisms of proxy voting to emerge (such as shareholders' associations).

The KonTraG shifts information—and power—to the supervisory board by requiring that the external auditor be hired by, and report to, the supervisory board instead of the management board.[65] The annual audit must also now include an assessment of risk management and monitoring systems.[66] The law contains additional auditing reforms (of particular interest in the wake of the Enron scandal in the United States) to improve financial transparency by ensuring the independence and reliability of auditors.[67]

An equally important provision prohibited unequal voting rights among shares of common stock and therefore imposed a "one share, one vote" rule for the first time in Germany. The KonTraG also abolished voting caps that limited the maximum number of votes by one shareholder. The provision institutes shareholder democracy as a general principle of company law and weakens the control of insiders. In contrast to the general principle of one share–one vote, the KonTraG *prohibits the voting of cross-shareholding stakes above 25 percent in supervisory board elections.*[68] This provision was designed to prevent managers from wresting control from shareholders by engaging in reciprocal voting with the managers of other firms involved in cross-shareholding relationships. However, these new voting rights expose German firms to an unprecedented threat of hostile takeover by weakening their defensive ownership structures.

The KonTraG also incorporated Anglo-American concepts of shareholder value and financial practices by allowing stock repurchases and the use of stock options as executive compensation for the first time, although with stricter limitations on their terms and exercise to prevent excessive executive compensation and thus abuse. Finally, the law contained modest reforms of shareholder litigation rules. It lowered from 10 percent to 5 percent of shares or one million DM of nominal capital the minimum number of minority shareholders required to demand the filing of a claim against supervisory and management board members on behalf of the corporation for gross breaches of the fiduciary duty of loyalty.[69]

The modernization of securities markets and ownership structures that began with the KonTraG took an enormous leap forward when the Schröder government pushed through a major tax reform law (*Steuerreform*) in July 2000 that *abolished* capital gains taxes on the liquidation of cross-shareholdings. The government made a deliberate policy choice to undermine ownership structures that insulated German corporations from takeovers and other pressures to restructure and thereby invigorate German securities markets by increasing the proportion of shares actively traded on the market ("free float"). Despite the evidence that Germany's firms were increasingly vulnerable to takeover, German policymakers adopted a law designed to move corporate Germany from a network form of organization to a market form. In doing so, the tax reform of 2000 may be the most important corporate governance reform in German history.[70]

However, the takeover vulnerability created by the KonTraG and tax reform legislation triggered a backlash against the dramatic liberalization of German corporate governance. The first battle over neoliberalism in corporate governance was fought over the proposed EU Takeover Directive. Realizing that the EU directive would further increase takeover threats to German firms by foreign corporations protected by "golden shares" or protective ownership networks, German conservatives and left-wing Social Democrats alike mobilized to block the directive in the European Parliament. They succeeded in July 2001.

One week after the collapse of the EU Takeover Directive, the German Bundestag passed the Securities Acquisition and Takeover Act (the Takeover Act).[71] Opposition to takeovers across the political spectrum, from corporate managers backed by the Christlich-Demokratische Union (conservative party) to the leaders of organized labor supported by the left wing of the Sozialdemokratische Partei Deutschlands (social-democratic party), drove the government to accept expanded managerial powers to adopt takeover defenses. The domestic politics of takeover law ran parallel to the battle over the EU directive. Managers seeking defenses against raiders and unions demanding protection for jobs and codetermination politically overran the large banks and shareholders groups seeking to facilitate takeovers and consolidated the victory they had won in the European Parliament.[72] Managers won greater leeway to adopt takeover defenses, and labor secured greater procedural and informational rights.

The German cabinet approved the Securities Acquisition and Takeover Act on July 11, 2001, one week after the rejection of the EU Takeover Directive.[73] The Bundestag approved the legislation on November 15, 2001, and it came into effect on January 1, 2002. The Takeover Act covers public tender offers, takeover offers (offers to acquire 30 percent or more of a public firm's voting stock), and mandatory offers for remaining shares once the offeror's stake reaches the 30 percent control threshold. It imposes minimum bid requirements and a squeezeout rule that allows a majority owning 95 percent or more of a corporation to buy out the remaining minority shareholders.

The Takeover Act contains a general "duty of neutrality" that prohibits the management board from taking any action that would prevent the success of the hostile bid.[74] However, the statute also *expanded* the latitude of management to deploy defensive tactics against a hostile takeover.[75] The supervisory board now has potentially vast discretion to defend against takeover, similar to the reallocation of legal authority to the boards of American corporations during the 1980s. Yet, the act does not explicitly authorize a German equivalent of the poison-pill defense common in American practice, and the legal status of such mechanisms remains subject to some doubt.[76]

The Takeover Act also extended the BAWe's regulatory authority to corporate takeovers.[77] The Takeover Act does not disturb the core of the stakeholder corporate governance scheme. Codetermination and fiduciary obligations remain undisturbed. The law's drafters relied instead on bidding procedures and disclosure requirements to facilitate and ensure the fairness of takeovers. The details of take-over bids must be fully disclosed in a filing with the BAWe (similar to an SEC fil-ing in the United States) and through publication, along with any plans the acquirer has for the firm following a change of control.[78] The target's management must respond with a public report assessing the adequacy of the offer and the bid-der's business strategy. In addition, the bid must remain open between four and ten weeks, with an additional two-week "sweep-up" period for dilatory share-holders to tender their shares. Far from recognizing shareholder primacy, the Takeover Act obliges both the offeror and the target's management to disclose in-formation to either the works council or directly to the employees concerning the terms of the offer and its implications for the firm and employees and their collec-tive representation.[79] Thus, the act makes use of and may reinforce the institu-tions of works council codetermination even as it expanded the supervisory board's power.

Finally, to signal the preservation of Germany's stakeholder form of corporate governance, the foregoing reforms were accompanied in 2001 by a modest strengthening of works council codetermination legislation. Although the legisla-tion does not effect substantial change in the form or power of the works council, it does marginally expand its competence and makes it somewhat easier for em-ployees to form one. The Social Democratic government passed this legislation as a form of repayment to the unions and left-wing Social Democrats who had sup-ported or acquiesced in the far more important and influential securities, com-pany, tax, and takeover law reforms in recent years. On the symbolic level, if not in any significant practical sense, the works council reform illustrates the contin-ued significance of labor relations issues in the country's corporate governance regime.

FRANCE

The upheaval and epochal reform of corporate governance in France cannot be understood apart from the privatization of state-owned enterprises during the 1980s and 1990s. The elimination of capital controls that ushered in the opening and internationalization of financial markets eroded the capacity of the state to control the allocation of finance as a mechanism of industrial policy. The French state steadily lost its ability to utilize the ministry of finance to control access to capital to implement the highly interventionist industrial policies of the past. More precisely, even could it have done so, the French government did not have a sufficient reason to pursue policies that would restore its control over financial flows. The political costs of choosing economic winners and losers began to rise throughout the 1970s and 1980s. The "national champions" created with these fi-nancial policy mechanisms proved increasingly uncompetitive in European and world markets.[80] Consequently, the state ceased its allocation and rationing of credit as a component of a comprehensive industrial policy in the mid-1980s as state actors sought to escape the increasing burden of the declining firms' financial demands.

This need to separate firm and government finances led to two waves of privatizations and drove corporate governance reform in France.[81] Two waves of privatization swept the French economy, the first in 1986–1987 under Minister of Finance Eduoard Balladur and the second in 1993 under Balladur as prime minister.[82] On returning to power in 1988, the Socialists did not seek to renationalize privatized enterprises. In fact, government holdings continued to decline through the sales of minority equity stakes in state-owned companies. And despite campaigning on a platform pledging to halt the sale of state holdings, the Jospin government briefly *accelerated* the privatization program after it took power in 1997, and the privatization continues at present.[83] The privatizations of 1986–1987 were largely a product of ideological politics in which the new conservative government sought to reverse the 1982–1983 nationalization program of Mitterrand's Socialists. In doing so, the conservatives privatized the state's better-performing companies.[84] By the 1990s, ownership of the remaining, more poorly performing state-owned companies and financial demands by large French corporations overburdened the French state,[85] while the liberalization and integration of financial markets eroded the state control over finance that had underpinned the postwar French corporate economy. At the same time, successive corporate and political scandals undermined the legitimacy of established links between firms and the state financial bureaucracy. State actors were no longer responsible for "picking winners" or constructing and promoting "national champions," but were instead faced with increasing demands for financial support from market losers that appeared less and less capable of competing in a more open and competitive international economy.[86] Privatization (sometimes under cover of EU obligations), financial system modernization, and corporate governance reform served the purpose of extracting the state from responsibilities for corporate and economic outcomes that taxed its capacities and resources while producing diminishing political and economic returns.[87]

Market developments drove financial liberalization even further. The state attempted to restructure the French corporate economy into protective cross-shareholding networks by strategic placement of equity with banks and other firms during the privatization of state-owned firms. Known as les *noyaux durs* (the hard core), these cross-shareholding networks linked large banks, core industrial firms, and suppliers in an attempt to replicate the self-protective and stable ownership structures of German industry. In France, however, the network of cross-shareholding broke down during the mid to late 1990s as firms and financial institutions, under increasing pressure for greater financial liquidity—and not locked into their cross-shareholdings by capital gains taxes like their German counterparts—sold off these holdings. The result has been the emergence of a more active equity market with higher levels of "free float" (the percentage of shares actively traded and not locked into immobile holdings) and greater market liquidity.[88] This new market structure was reinforced by legal and regulatory reforms that transformed the institutional and juridical terrain of French corporate governance.

Led by state policymakers, a general consensus had emerged by the late 1980s across interest group and ideological lines that the development of capital markets in place of statist financial control was essential. This agreement on the general policy agenda ameliorated conflicts that might have been expected between economic actors with experience and expertise in market finance and those who remained reliant on the state.[89] As a direct consequence of privatization through public share offerings, state actors had to confront the need for reform of the financial system and corporate governance in order to ensure that French firms could find financing and function once state finance and planning were withdrawn. More-stringent securities regulation and shareholder-protective company law would promote greater investor trust and assuage the doubts of a public unused to equity investment and foreign investors suspicious of underdeveloped, insider-dominated French markets. Thus, corporate governance reform followed from a state policy of disengaging from direct control over economic affairs.

French corporate governance reforms began in the area of securities markets regulation. As a prelude, in 1984 the government substantially amended the law governing independent auditors, the *commissaire aux comptes*, to expand their oversight and reporting functions and to ensure their independence from management.[90] In 1987 brokers were allowed to trade in securities on their own account to increase the liquidity of French markets.[91] However, the critical juncture that placed France on the path to appropriating the American model of securities markets regulation came with the enactment of the Law on Security and Disclosure in the Financial Markets of 1988 and the Security and Disclosure Law of 1989.[92] The reforms formed an extended part of the epochal turn away from orthodox socialist and Keynesian policies that began in the mid-1980s and immediately followed two highly publicized, and highly politicized, financial market scandals.[93] These reforms targeted not only private abuses of the markets, but also the corruption and manipulation that emanated from the state's control over finance and the privatization process.

The 1988 reforms substantially expanded the enforcement power of the COB and imposed stricter disclosure, market manipulation, and insider-trading rules. The law also established two largely self-regulatory bodies, the *Conseil des Bourses de Valeurs* and the *Société des Bourses Françaises*, to oversee the stock exchanges in matters such as broker regulation, listing procedures, and tender offers.[94] The Security and Disclosure Law empowered the COB to impose steep fines and to search any private or public premises, question suspects, and impound any documents relating to an investigation (with the approval of the *Tribunal de Grande Instance* and the assistance of a judicial police officer).[95] The COB may also seek an order from the *Tribunal* to seize property, freeze assets, place funds in escrow, issue injunctions, and temporarily suspend persons from their professions.[96] Finally, the Security and Disclosure Law authorizes the COB to cooperate with and conduct investigations at the request of foreign securities regulators.[97] Following this extraordinary strengthening of regulatory authority, the COB's enforcement power exceeded that of the SEC in many respects.

As in securities regulation, French company law has changed with surprising swiftness and magnitude. Company law reforms have appropriated Anglo-American company law structures to a surprising degree, given the *dirigiste* tradition in French economic policy and governance. In October 2000, a bill was submitted to the senate to provide a new option in the unitary board by permitting the board of directors to decide whether to separate the two roles of president of the board of directors and the PDG. The law also requires the annual general meeting of shareholders to approve company accounts. Most surprisingly of all, these changes in law and state policy have triggered a dynamic market for corporate control, including tender offers and hostile takeover battles reminiscent of those in the United States.[98] The French government transformed the political economy by privatizing large numbers of public firms. However, it also deliberately structured the ownership stakes and governance relationships among these privatized firms to reorganize entire sectors of the French economy and to protect firms from takeover.[99] This strategy proved ineffective as firms found themselves dependent on capital markets for finance at the same time their share prices began collapsing and sought to raise cash by selling off stock holdings. This led to an unraveling of the state's meticulously crafted cross-shareholdings, the growing presence of foreign shareholders in French firms, and a wave of consolidating takeovers that is continuing. This takeover wave dramatically increased the practical importance of corporate governance in France.

The most far-reaching reforms of internal governance structures and processes in France have not been the subject of legislation or regulation, but have been the province of "codes of best practice" drafted by a private commission. The Viénot Report of 1995 was the product of a commission established by France's two main employer bodies (the *Conseil National du Patronat Français* and the *Association Française des Enterprises Privées*) and named for its chair, Société Générale chairman Marc Viénot. The report set forth a *voluntary* code of best practices, without formal legal force or regulatory enforcement. The Viénot Code recommended, *inter alia*, that

- boards should actively participate in strategically important corporate decisions;
- the board should have at least two independent directors;
- cross-shareholding should be eliminated;
- companies should not have interlocking directorates, and reciprocal directors should not serve on audit or compensation committees;
- firms should disclose annually their decision-making processes and the number of audit, compensation, and nomination committee meetings;
- the board should have audit, compensation, and nomination committees, composed of at least three members and at least one independent director;
- executive and employee representatives should not sit on the audit or compensation committees;

- at least one independent director and the board chairman should sit on the nomination committee; and
- directors should own a "significant" number of company shares.

In July 1996, a government commission chaired by Senator Philippe Marini issued a parliamentary report proposing sweeping reforms in French corporate law.[100] Just one year after the Viénot Report rejected formal changes to French company law, the Marini Report proposed significant legal reforms in corporate governance—including a number of the Viénot recommendations. The Marini Report expressly advocated the embrace of Anglo-American corporate governance practices and norms in French finance and law in order to remain competitive in an increasingly international financial system.[101] In keeping with this Anglo-American approach, the report pressed for company law reforms that avoided rigid mandatory rules and instead *enabled* firms to strengthen their boards and adopt more efficient corporate governance structures. Significantly, the Marini agenda largely stalled in parliament.

Parliament did enact a law requiring pension funds to vote their shares to ensure some level of institutional activism.[102] This law emulated a 1988 American Department of Labor ruling requiring pension funds under the department's jurisdiction to vote their proxies. However, on the basis of the American experience, the formal requirement of voting by itself does not ensure shareholder activism, or even attentiveness. The effects of the French law are especially unlikely to alter governance practice, given that government policy has not yet resolved the intense conflicts over pension reform, and private funds remain undeveloped.

Finally, although most French industry has been privatized, the state has not completely relinquished its grip on industry and the economy. Foreign institutional investors hold 35 percent to 40 percent of the French equity market, but the French government retains extensive powers to control transactions and can intervene selectively in merger and acquisition activity. The state holds a number of "golden shares" with disproportionate voting (or veto) power that give it control rights over some privatized companies. In addition, the Ministry of Finance can block the acquisition of more than 20 percent of a French firm by a non-EU party. Hence, the state combined liberalizing and interventionist policies in overseeing sectoral consolidation to ensure that French industry remains largely in the hands of French managers.[103]

However, the French state has adopted a *deliberate policy* of allowing market forces to drive consolidation and adjustment if managers cannot come to voluntary agreements. The BNP-Paribas merger that transformed the French financial sector also signaled the French government's policy choice to allow market forces, and in particular a new market for corporate control, to reshape French finance.[104] The emergence of hostile takeovers, restructuring and consolidation, and increased management turnover reflects the profound shift in government policy and the growing power and influence of the COB and the Banque de France in favoring the interests of shareholders over *dirigiste* traditionalists in the *Trésor*

Public (within the Ministry of Finance) and the interests of incumbent managers.[105] The business and political culture of insulated, self-protective elite networks that defined the postwar political economy is eroding rapidly in the absence of the institutional arrangements that perpetuated it.[106]

THE NEW POLITICS OF REFORM: NEW POLICIES OUT OF OLD INSTITUTIONS
PRESSURES FOR REFORM

Beginning in the mid-1970s, policymakers in all the advanced industrial countries faced a set of common destabilizing pressures that undermined established institutional arrangements and approaches to economic policy. Keynesian policies sparked domestic "stagflation" in an increasingly open and competitive international market environment. The American managerial capitalism that had dominated the industrialized world during the postwar era could not match the performance of Asian and German competitors by the mid-1970s. French industrial policies had created national champions but could not maintain their competitiveness in world markets. Germany's neocorporatist supply-side policies fared better for a time, but by the late 1980s (and especially after the reunification of East and West Germany) could no longer effectively sustain a high-growth, high-wage, and high-employment economy. The internationalization of financial markets further eroded established monetary and fiscal policies and sparked fiercer competition within the financial sector that spurred the pursuit of higher returns to capital. With the decline of state industrial policy and macroeconomic management, financial services became an increasingly important private industry at the same time that it lost its effectiveness as a tool of policy. Finally, recurrent financial scandals in each country were instrumental in mobilizing support for corporate governance reform by prompting popular backlash against corrupt insider-dominated dealings of corporate and financial hierarchies. However, corporate finance scandals could not have mobilized successful far-reaching reform efforts without the preconditions of broader political and economic problems that altered the balance of political power in favor of policy change.[107]

Under these economic pressures, policymakers came to recognize the need for more rapid firm-level adjustment in pursuing markets, restructuring, and improving financial flexibility and performance. Corporate governance reform, embracing the relationship between industry and finance but not reliant on state expenditures or monetary policy, responded to these common pressures by facilitating economic restructuring, financial market efficiency, and higher returns to capital while avoiding direct political conflict over potentially explosive issues such as labor relations and social welfare policy.

Notwithstanding their importance, these common pressures do not explain the specifics of corporate governance reform in particular countries. They do not explain the timing, the politics, or the substantive content of the reforms that ultimately were adopted. Aside from the important common pressures for reform acting on policymakers and the effects of European integration, policymakers in the United States, Germany, and France also faced nationally distinctive pressures and constraints that both induced and shaped their governance reforms. These nationally distinctive pressures for reform have far more explanatory power in a comparative analysis of policy change and structural reform.

POLITICS OF REFORM: MOTIVATIONS, INTERESTS, AND MODELS

The above discussion of corporate governance reforms, even in so stylized a form, helps to explain why corporate governance has become an area of increased policy activity across different countries with divergent political–economic structures. Policymakers in the United States, Germany, and France used corporate governance reform as a means to address both common and nationally distinctive economic and policy problems.

In France, state policymakers undertook corporate governance reform as a logical consequence and institutional necessity following the privatization of state-owned enterprises and the state's withdrawal from economic planning and the allocation of finance. In the absence of statist financial control, France was left without an available institutional foundation, such as that long established in Germany, on which to build reformed financial and corporate governance frameworks. Market institutions in post-*dirigiste* France had to be constructed nearly from scratch. Further, given the failure of the government to fashion and maintain German-style national networks of corporate ownership, the liberal market model possessed the advantages of conforming to the emerging international financial marketplace while being technically and administratively simpler to accomplish through policy mechanisms.

France is distinctive among the three cases considered here in that it is the only country in which fiscal constraints played a significant role in the origins and evolution of financial market and corporate governance policies. These budgetary constraints interacted with growing problems of economic competitiveness. The expense and opportunity costs of state-allocated finance became prohibitively burdensome on the treasury and economy as French firms failed to compete successfully internationally. Under these conditions, privatization and the reform of financial markets and corporate governance solved two pressing policy problems—a budget constrained by a post-Keynesian macroeconomic policy and poorly performing firms in need of greater market discipline to improve their competitiveness.

France's highly statist political–economic structure, however, enabled state policymakers to accomplish comprehensive and far-reaching reforms very quickly once an elite consensus had been reached.[108] No powerful constituency such as commercial or investment banks, institutional investors, or shareholders' associations developed in the statist environment of *dirigiste* France, and so none could significantly contribute to or detract from this policy agenda. This points to a final distinctive characteristic of French corporate governance reform. Just as the economy was exceptionally state-led during the heyday of government planning and credit allocation, the state led the process of reform with remarkably little accommodation of conflicting interest groups.

In Germany, financial-system reform began later but evolved into a comprehensive and fundamental transformation of the corporate governance system. The sustained surge of legislation extending and buttressing the powers and jurisdiction of the BAWe and leading to the consolidation of all financial market regulators within the BAFin indicates the existence of a stable and effective political coalition favoring financial and regulatory modernization dating back to the Kohl era. State actors responded initially to EU pressures for regulatory harmonization,[109] but then came to appreciate the reform of capital markets and securities law as necessary to improve macroeconomic performance. The European Union's powerful influence on policy was most apparent in the centralization of securities law and regulation at the federal level.[110] During the same period, excessive domestic competition, traditional lending, and increasing competition from British and American investment banks in higher value-added financial services triggered a shift in the policy preferences of large German banks. By the early 1990s, the large German universal banks began to look to the modernization of the financial system, the expansion of their securities markets and investment banking capacities, and greater integration with international markets as ways of reversing their declining profit margins. This shift altered the political terrain of policymaking as a powerful and well-organized set of economic actors and their political allies no longer saw themselves as the underwriters of the "German model" and sought to pursue policies of securities market and corporate governance reform. They gave their support to regulatory reforms that would channel domestic savings into the equities markets and foster demand for more investment banking services by firms.

By the late 1990s, the Social Democrats on the center-left used company law and corporate governance reform to claim the policy agenda of economic modernization as their own and adopted the cause of corporate governance reform as a way of advancing a general economic competitiveness policy. German Social Democrats and administrative policymakers mobilized the popular resentment of recurrent corporate financial scandals to address the systemic inefficiencies and risk aversion of the country's financial system, sluggish corporate restructuring, and a perceived slippage in technological innovation and prowess.[111] The politics of corporate governance reform in Germany thus rested on two major supports: politicians and policymakers who saw reform as necessary to preserve and improve the economic performance of the national economy in an increasingly competitive international environment, and major financial institutions that came to see their traditional business models as an economic trap and sought policies of structural reform as their exit into more lucrative international markets.

The European Union's single market directives aimed at unifying the capital and financial services markets may have contributed to the inception of this modernization program, but it became a central component of domestic policy. The steady opening of financial markets also reinforced domestic political pressures for legal restructuring as Frankfurt sought to remain competitive in attracting international capital (and retaining German investment capital) and German business and shareholder interests sought financial market changes that would benefit their constituents. However, where domestic policy preferences of labor and managers conflicted with those of the European Commission and major financial institutions, as in the area of corporate takeovers, national politics trumped commitments to the European Union and limited the scope and extent of corporate governance reform.

The United States in some ways presents the most puzzling case. The country that developed modern securities regulation and had the most elaborately developed corporate governance regime in the world lagged behind other advanced industrial countries in pursuing reforms of its own, and, when it did so, it appears that these reforms were less systematic and are more contested by interest groups and political factions within various levels of government. The structure of political institutions and interest groups in the United States imposed significantly different pressures for regulatory reform than those in Germany and France. The long and extensive development of securities markets, mass shareholding, and investment funds in the United States meant that financial interests (i.e., large, sophisticated financial institutions and institutional shareholders) were far more powerful, but also divided on the question of corporate governance reform.

Governance reform remained largely off the political agenda throughout the 1990s because of opposition of powerful managerial and financial services interests, the largely neoliberal and antiregulatory ideology of institutional investors and corporate governance advocates, and the fragmented character of the American government, which impedes substantial and comprehensive policy reform. Ultimately, deliberative policy debates did not drive American corporate governance reform. When massive market and regulatory failures and the most serious wave of corporate finance scandals since the Great Depression threatened the integrity and legitimacy of American political–economic arrangements, political paralysis yielded to public outrage and interest-group pressures for reform.

During the 1990s, the vicissitudes of financial market and corporate governance policy could be attributed to hubris. Political elites in the United States came to see the American regime as the polestar defining the "best practice" and best policy in corporate governance—and elites in France and Germany to some extent appeared to agree. By the time the securities market bubble burst in 2000 and the corporate finance scandals became public in 2001, this complacency could no longer be justified. Yet, the political struggle over Sarbanes–Oxley reforms suggests that the policy dynamic in the United States was the product of a more fragmented political structure and divisive interest-group politics. Unlike the German and French corporate governance reforms, the Sarbanes–Oxley reforms reflected no overarching coherent policy agenda. Rather, the law was the product of a political struggle in which Democrats sought to use financial scandals against the Republicans in the White House and Congress, and Republicans sought to dilute the legislation in accord with their deregulatory agenda and loyalty to their corporate supporters. Interest-group politics were even more fractious—both within and among groups. Corporate managers resisted the imposition of new legal rules that directly threatened their autonomy and material interests, but many wanted to remove the taint of scandal. Financial institutions such as investment banks were dependent on public faith in the integrity of the securities markets but were also privileged insiders that benefited from the status quo and stood to lose from reform. Institutional investors were long committed to an essentially voluntaristic form of corporate governance activism, but the majority of them espoused a neoliberal policy stance that was skeptical of, and often hostile to, increased securities and corporate governance regulation. Accounting firms, having perhaps the most to answer for and the most to lose in the new regulatory climate, fought back even at the risk of further alienating public opinion. Under such fractious political circumstances, state actors dominated the policy debate.

This political impasse over corporate governance reform has not been resolved yet. The continuing struggle over accounting regulation and the Public Company Accounting Oversight Board has already resulted in the resignation of SEC Chairman Harvey Pitt, the first chairman of the Accounting Oversight Board, and former FBI and CIA Director William Webster and threatens to inflict long-term damage to the prestige, legitimacy, and perceived competence of the SEC. Internationally, the American corporate governance model appears less appealing, less efficient, and more tarnished than at any time in decades. Domestically, resentment of Sarbanes–Oxley regulation and post-bubble government investigations is sparking a backlash led by corporate managers and financial services firms. In place of a resolute federal response, state regulators, led by New York State Attorney General Eliot Spitzer, have begun to fill the vacuum left by an ineffective and politically hobbled SEC. As the center has failed to hold at the federal level, the United States now appears to be partially *reversing* the centralization of corporate governance policymaking and regulatory enforcement that has been the dominant cross-national institutional and policy trend.[112]

CONCLUSION

None of these corporate governance systems have been left intact by reform efforts of the past decade. Their development displays features of convergence on a more centralized and legalistic form of corporate governance regulation and on the American transparency and disclosure model of securities market regulation, but each retains substantially distinctive regulatory and corporate structures. Nor can the changes be described solely in terms of reinforcing comparative economic advantages or reflecting the simple sum of economic interests. Politics and state actors intervened decisively in the reform of the corporation and its governance.

Politicians responded to a variety of policy imperatives and interest-group pressures but in confronting a context of interests and interest-group alignments in flux displayed substantial autonomy in policymaking. This observation points to a key distinction between the American case and the cases of Germany and France. The United States has not embarked on a course of fundamental policy reform in the area of corporate governance and financial market regulation. Fractious interest-group politics and fragmented state institutions limited the capacity of policymakers to formulate and pursue reform. Legislators and regulators have acted to satisfy popular outrage and address some of the most egregious financial abuses of the 1990s, but they have been tightly constrained by politically potent corporate managers and financial services firms and by sharp ideological and political divisions among political actors.

In contrast, Germany and France embarked on more fundamental reforms and institution-building efforts that broke more decisively with the past and are premised on a more fundamental realignment of policy preferences by powerful political–economic actors. The destabilization of established interests and political alliances, the greater centralization of policymaking institutions, and the pressures of EU integration gave German and French policymakers a freer hand in fashioning policy and could do so in a more comprehensive—and arguably coherent—fashion than their counterparts in the United States.

NOTES

This chapter is a distillation of some of the ideas and arguments developed at greater length in John W. Cioffi, "Public Law and Private Power: The Comparative Political Economy of Corporate Governance in the United States and Germany," PhD diss., University of California, Berkeley, 2002. See also John W. Cioffi, "Restructuring 'Germany, Inc.': The Corporate Governance Debate and the Politics of Company Law Reform," *Law & Policy* (December 2002), and "Governing Globalization? The State, Law, and Structural Change in Corporate Governance," *Journal of Law and Society*, 27, no. 4 (December 2000):572–600.

1. *Cf.* Klaus Hopt and Gunter Teubner, eds., *Corporate Governance and Directors' Liabilities: Legal, Economic, and Sociological Analyses on Corporate Social Responsibility* (Berlin and New York: Walter de Gruyter, 1985).

2. For a classic expression of this typology of political economic types, see John Zysman, *Governments, Markets, and Growth* (Ithaca, NY: Cornell University Press, 1983). An updated analysis of national corporate governance regimes from this typological perspective is presented in John W. Cioffi, "Governing Globalization? The State, Law, and Structural Change in Corporate Governance," *Journal of Law and Society*, 27, no. 4 (December 2000):572–600; and John W. Cioffi and Stephen S. Cohen, "The Advantages of Forwardness: The Interdependence of the State, Law, and Corporate Governance in an Age of Globalization," in *Corporate Governance and Globalization*, ed. Stephen S. Cohen and Gavin Boyd (Cheltenham, UK, and Northhampton, MA: Edward Elgar, 2000).

3. Robert Kagan calls this regulatory model "adversarial legalism." The emphasis on private autonomy here favors emphasis on the term liberalism. Robert A. Kagan,

Adversarial Legalism: The American Way of Law (Cambridge, MA, and London: Harvard University Press, 2001).

4. See, e.g., *Dirks v. Securities and Exchange Commission*, 463 S.Ct. 3255 (1983) (federal securities regulation covers insider trading). Under the SEC's rules, disclosure became a continuous process encompassing quarterly, annual, and proxy disclosure statements that kept shareholders abreast of important corporate developments. Together, these requirements compel the disclosure of all material information to the public via a complex system of public filings administered by the SEC. See *TSC Industries v. Northway Inc.*, 426 U.S. 438, 449 (1976) (defining materiality as whether a reasonably prudent investor would regard the information as important in making a particular investment decision).

5. The Glass–Steagall Act severed investment banking from commercial banking and traditional lending; the Investment Company Act of 1940 and the Employee Retirement Income Security Act of 1974 placed limits on the size of the stakes that investment firms and funds could hold as a percentage of their own capital and of outstanding corporate equity. Under these market conditions, shareholders cannot solve the collective action problem of coordinating and defraying the costs of monitoring efforts. See generally Mark J. Roe, "Codetermination and German Securities Markets," in *Comparative Corporate Governance: The State of the Art and Current Research*, ed. Klaus J. Hopt, Hideki Kanda, Mark J. Roe, Eddy Wymeersch, and Stefan Prigge (New York and Oxford: Oxford University Press, 1998); Mark J. Roe, *Strong Managers, Weak Owners: The Political Roots of American Corporate Finance* (Princeton, NJ: Princeton University Press, 1994); Mark J. Roe, "Some Differences in Corporate Structure in Germany, Japan, and the United States," *Yale Law Journal* 102 (1993b):1927; Mark J. Roe, "A Political Theory of American Corporate Finance," *Columbia Law Review* 91 (1991):10.

6. John C. Coffee, Jr., "Liquidity versus Control: The Institutional Investor as Corporate Monitor," *Columbia Law Review* 91 (1991):1277, 1286–87.

7. See Stephen K. Vogel, *Freer Markets, More Rules: Regulatory Reform in Advanced Industrial Countries* (Ithaca, NY: Cornell University Press, 1996), 31, 250.

8. See, e.g., Roe 1991; Coffee 1991. For the classic analysis of the use of exit and voice in governance relationships, see Albert O. Hirschman, *Exit, Voice, and Loyalty: Responses to Decline in Firms, Organizations, and States* (Cambridge, MA: Harvard University Press, 1981).

9. Fiduciary duties in American corporate law form a massive and complex subject far beyond the scope of this chapter. For leading treatises on the subject in all its myriad permutations and complications, see Dennis J. Block, Nancey E. Barton, and Stephen A. Radin, *The Business Judgment Rule: The Fiduciary Duties of Corporate Directors* (Englewood Cliffs, NJ: 1994); William E. Knepper and Dan A. Bailey, *Liability of Corporate Officers and Directors*, 7th ed. (Newark, NJ: Lexis Nexis, 2002). For an incisive, brief analytical overview and provocative theory of fiduciary duty law, see William T. Allen, "The Corporate Director's Fiduciary Duty of Care and the Business Judgment Rule," in *Comparative Corporate Governance,* ed. Hopt, Kanda, Roe, Wymeersch, and Prigge. These duties may also bind, under certain circumstances, majority shareholders in order to protect the minority. See, e.g., *Pepper v. Litton*, 308 U.S. 295, 306 (1939); *Kahn v. Lynch Comm. Sys. Inc.*, 638 A.2d 1110, 1113–14 (Del. 1994) (majority shareholders, in addition to corporate officers and directors, held to fiduciary standards).

10. The rule underscores the ultimate ineffectiveness of fiduciary duties as a mechanism of governance. The liabilities at issue in corporate fiduciary are potentially so enormous that rational individuals would refuse to act as directors if not granted a very broad safe har-

bor from personal liability and insurers would refuse to write "directors' and officers'" insurance policies at acceptable rates.

11. During the Progressive Era, the federal government repeatedly considered the passage of a federal incorporation act during the (first) Roosevelt, Taft, and Wilson administrations. The constitutionality of legislation that would intrude into such a well-established sphere of state authority as corporation law also was subject to substantial doubt given the conservative federalism jurisprudence of the *Lochner* Era Supreme Court.

12. See Louis Loss, *Securities Regulation,* vol. 1, 2d ed. (Boston: Little, Brown and Co., 1961), 109 (noting that the legislative history of the Securities and Exchange Act of 1934 contains recommendations favoring a federal incorporation act).

13. See Loss 1961; *cf.* Edward Ross Aranow and Herbert A. Einhorn, "Proxy Regulation: Suggested Improvements," *George Washington Law Review,* 28 (1959):306 (state inaction on proxy vote regulation induced Congress to address these issues under the Securities and Exchange Act of 1934).

14. See Robert B. Thompson, "Challenges to Corporate Governance: Preemption and Federalism in Corporate Governance: Protecting Shareholder Rights to Vote, Sell, and Sue," *Law & Contemporary Problems,* 62 (summer 1999):215, note 50 (citing American Bar Association, Committee on Corporation Law, Section on Corporation, Banking, and Mercantile Law, Preliminary Draft of a Federal Corporation Act [August 1943]). However, the Model Act fails to eliminate the fragmentation, the interstate competition for charters, or interest group politics that favor state-based managers to which corporate law federalism gives rise. It is thus not the equivalent of a federal corporation law.

15. For accounts of the lobbying and conflicts triggered by the ALI Corporate Governance Project, see Roswell B. Perkins, "Foreword," in American Law Institute, *Principles of Corporate Governance* (Philadelphia: American Law Institute, 1994); Richard B. Smith, "An Underview of the Principles of Corporate Governance," *Business Lawyer* 48 (August 1993):1297–311; Rita Henley Jensen, "Navigating Turbulent Waters at ALI: The American Law Institute Brings Its Corporate Governance Principles to Harbor," *National Law Journal* (August 9, 1993):1; John C. Coffee, Jr., "The ALI Corporate Governance Project," *New York Law Journal* (June 9, 1992):1; Kenneth Jost, "Business Lawyers Win Showdown Vote in ALI: Tough Line on Shareholder Suits," *Legal Times,* May 18, 1992.

16. American labor law maintains a strict legal and practical separation of collective bargaining and firm management by limiting "mandatory subjects" of collective bargaining to a highly circumscribed range of economic issues concerning the terms and conditions of employment. *NLRB v. Borg-Warner Corp.,* 356 U.S. 342 (1958); *Fibreboard Paper Prods. Corp. v. NLRB,* 379 U.S. 203 (1964); see also *First National Maintenance Corp. v. NLRB,* 452 U.S. 666 (1981).

17. *Fibreboard Paper Prods. Corp. v. NLRB,* 379 U.S. 203, 223 (1964) (Stewart, J., concurring); see also *Ford Motor Co. v. NLRB,* 441 U.S. 488, 498 (1979) (quoting *Fibreboard,* Stewart, J., concurring).

18. In fact, labor law, as interpreted by the National Labor Relations Board (NLRB) and the federal courts, impedes the formation of *alternative* forms of employee representation under a broad prohibition of employer-dominated labor organizations (or, more prosaically, company unions) that protects employee organization at the expense of organizational experimentation. For example, these restrictions have led the NLRB and courts to hold that workplace committees dealing with safety and productivity issues are illegal. See *Electromation, Inc.,* 309 N.L.R.B. 990 (1992), enforced sub nom, *Electromation, Inc. v. NLRB,* 35 F.3d 1148 (7th Cir. 1994); *E.I. du Pont de Nemours & Co.,* 311 N.L.R.B. 893 (1993). For academic

analyses attentive to the practical repercussions of *Electromation, du Pont*, and other decisions in this line of cases, see Samuel Estreicher, "Labor Law Reform in a World of Competitive Product Markets," *Chicago-Kent Law Review*, 69 (1993):3–46; Alan Hyde, "Employee Caucus: A Key Institution in the Emerging System of Employment Law," *Chicago-Kent Law Review*, 69 (1993):149–93; Clyde W. Summers, "Employee Voice and Employer Choice: A Structured Exception to Section 8(A)(2), in Symposium on the Legal Future of Employee Representation," *Chicago-Kent College of Law* 69 (1993):129–48. These rulings reinforce the sharp distinction between state corporate law, which sets out the basic rules for corporate organization and decisionmaking, and federal labor law, which creates the rules governing collective organization of employees and collective bargaining at the plant and/or firm level.

19. See, e.g., Janet Cooper Alexander, "Do the Merits Matter? A Study of Settlements in Securities Class Actions," *Stanford Law Review*, 43 (1991):497–598; Joel Seligman, "The Private Securities Reform Act of 1995," in "Symposium: Securities Litigation: The Fundamental Issues," supplemental paper, *Arizona Law Review* 38 (1996):717.

20. For an early and classic article comparing the German and American corporate governance regimes and their legal and political histories, see Detlev F. Vagts, "Reforming the 'Modern' Corporation: Perspectives from the German," *Harvard Law Review* 80 (1966):23. For more recent comparative treatments, see, e.g., Mary O'Sullivan, *Contests for Corporate Control: Corporate Governance and Economic Performance in the United States and Germany* (Oxford and New York: Oxford University Press, 2000); Roe 1994, 1993b; Jonathan P. Charkham, *Keeping Good Company: A Study of Corporate Governance in Five Countries* (Oxford: Clarendon Press, 1994).

21. For discussions, see Peter J. Katzenstein, *Policy and Politics in West Germany: The Growth of a Semisovereign State* (Philadelphia: Temple University Press, 1987), chapter 3; Herbert Wiedemann, "Codetermination by Workers in German Enterprises," *American Journal of Comparative Law* 28 (1980):79.

22. Wiedemann 1980, 79. Supervisory board codetermination laws also apply to close corporations (GmbH).

23. The cochair or vice chair of the board is almost always an employee representative. Charkham 1994, 26.

24. Wiedemann 1980, 80. "Montan" codetermination, the third (and original) variant, applies only to firms in the coal, mining, and steel sectors employing more than one thousand workers. Alone among the three forms of board codetermination, it provides for *full parity* of shareholder and employee representation. Since the 1970s, the mining and steel sectors have been in decline in Germany, and this trend has reduced the importance of Montan codetermination.

25. Board codetermination has become enormously important as a symbol of the country's neocorporatist and social democratic consensus-driven "social market economy." It does so, however, at the expense of well-defined fiduciary duties. Company law specifies the *corporation's* interests as protected by fiduciary law, rather than the interests of shareholders alone. The "interests of the corporation" implicitly acknowledge the interests of multiple stakeholder groups, and codetermination institutionalizes this recognition on labor's behalf.

26. The Works Constitution Act of 1972 provides for the election of works councils in "all establishments or plants of business organizations with five or more permanent employees." Wiedemann 1980, 80. The works council must be consulted on "social matters" regarding the "formal conditions of work" such as daily working hours, manner of compensation, job security, and workplace safety; and "personnel matters" such as prior notification of any layoff or dismissal. Wiedemann 1980, 81–82. In enterprises with more than twenty

employees, the works council also must be given an opportunity to pass on any "business modifications" that may substantially prejudice the rights of a substantial portion of employees (e.g., reduction of operations, transfer of departments, closure of departments, important changes in organization or purpose of the enterprise or plant within it). Wiedemann 1980. For general accounts of the political origins, structure, impact of codetermination, see, e.g., Vagts 1966, 64–78; Wolfgang Streeck, "Co-determination: The Fourth Decade," in *International Perspectives on Organizational Democracy, Volume 2,* ed. Bernhard Wilpert and Arndt Sorge (Chichester, NY: Wiley, 1984); Katzenstein 1987, chapter 3; Walthier Muller-Jentsch, "Germany: From Collective Voice to Co-Management," in *Works Councils: Consultation, Representation, and Cooperation in Industrial Relations,* ed. Joel Rogers and Wolfgang Streeck (Chicago: University of Chicago Press, 1995); see also Kathleen A. Thelen, *Union of Parts: Labor Politics in Postwar Germany* (Ithaca, NY: Cornell University Press, 1991); *cf.* Lowell Turner, *Democracy at Work: Changing World Markets and the Future of Labor Unions* (Ithaca, NY: Cornell University Press, 1991). For a review of the legal aspects of codetermination by a leading German legal authority, see Wiedemann 1980.

27. Wiedemann 1980 (discussing works council claims under the Social Compensation Law).

28. *Cf.* Heinz-Dieter Assmann, "Microcorporatist Structures in German Law on Groups of Companies," in *Regulating Corporate Groups in Europe,* ed. David Sugarman and Gunther Teubner (Baden-Baden: Nomos Verlagsgesellschaft, 1990); Streeck 1984 (use of the term "microcorporatism" in theoretical discussions of firm structure and organization).

29. In contrast, American proxy rules give *management* control over proxy votes. See Friedrich Kubler, "Juridification of Corporate Structures," in *Juridification of Social Spheres: A Comparative Analysis in the Areas of Labor, Corporate, Antitrust and Social Welfare Law,* ed. Gunther Teubner (Berlin and New York: Walter de Gruyter, 1987), 215. Thus, in addition to their own equity holdings, the banks wield disproportionate voting strength and substantial leverage when it comes to board nominations or influencing key strategic decisions. Charkham 1994, 37–38; Vagts 1966, 53–58. Even where German management attempts to maintain autonomy by diversifying sources of bank debt, see Richard Deeg and Sophia Perez, *International Capital Mobility and Domestic Institutions: Corporate Finance and Governance in Four European Cases* (paper presented at the Conference on the Political Economy of Corporate Governance in Europe and Japan, Robert Schulman Center, Europe University Institute, June 10–11, 1999), 208; banks have adopted a practice of designating a "lead bank" to monitor the corporation, vote their aggregate voting rights of deposited shares, and maintain supervisory board representation. Sigurt Vitols, "Corporate Governance versus Economic Governance: Banks and Industrial Restructuring in the U.S. and Germany," discussion paper FS I 95-310 (Berlin: Wissenschaftszentrum Berlin für Sozialforschung, November 1995), 6.

30. By the end of the Mitterrand nationalization program of the early 1980s, the state owned 100 percent of thirteen of the twenty largest industrial firms and of most of the country's leading banks, including Suez, Paribas, Crédit Lyonnais, Société Générale, and BNP. It also owned controlling stakes in numerous other firms and minority stakes and substantial debt positions in many others. See Mary O'Sullivan, "Change and Continuity in the French System of Corporate Governance," INSEAD working paper, European Institute of Business Administration (February 2001), 4–8.

31. See generally, John Zysman, *Political Strategies for Industrial Order: State, Market, and Industry in France* (Berkeley: University of California Press, 1977); Zysman 1983, ch. 3.

32. See James A. Fanto, "The Role of Corporate Law in French Corporate Governance," *Cornell International Law Journal* 31(1998):31–91; James A. Fanto, "The Role of Corporate Law in the Adaptation of French Enterprises," *Columbia Business Law Review*, special symposium issue (1998):97–120.

33. Code des Sociétés, Ordonnance NE 67-833, September 1967 (as amended), arts. 6, 7 (Fr.). Prior to this law, equity finance was so alien to mainstream policy thinking in France that securities law was not even a recognized area of law and legislation. France has seven separate stock exchanges (six regional centers and Paris as the national financial center). However, in keeping with the long tradition of state centralization in France, there was no delegation of regulatory power over regional stock markets to subordinate levels of government, as was the case in Germany prior to 1994. For discussions of French securities law reforms, see Fanto 1998, 111–12; James A. Fanto, "The Transformation of French Corporate Governance and United States Institutional Investors," in "Symposium: Comparative Models of Privatization: Paradigms and Politics," *Brooklyn Journal of International Law* 21 (1995):41–44.

34. See Code des Sociétés, Ordonnance NE 67-833, September 1967 (as amended), arts. 6, 7 (Fr.); Fanto 1998, 111.

35. The rules requiring the appointment of an official auditor and defining its independent role are set out in Code des Sociétés, Law NE 66-537, July 24, 1966, arts. 218–35 (Fr.).

36. *Insider Trading Scandals: Parisians React with a Smirk and a Yawn,* Int'l Sec. Reg. Rep., October 11, 1989.

37. However, SAs may adopt one of two board structures. First, a corporation may choose the *unitary board* described above. Code des Sociétés, Law NE 66-537, July 24, 1966, arts. 89–117. The board may remove the PDG at any time, with or without cause. Second, a firm may choose a *dual structure* that imposes a strict formal separation between the PDG and executive management and the board of directors (the *conseil de surveillance*, or supervisory board). Code des Sociétés, arts. 118–50. This structure, copied from the German dual-board form, ensures a more independent body overseeing the management, but limits the board's power and entrenches management by granting exclusive power to remove the PDG to poorly organized *shareholders*. Firms cannot mix and match the attributes of the two board models; they must choose one or the other.

38. See Fanto 1995, text accompanying notes 115–17. Large nonstate-owned publicly traded companies also have strong antitakeover protection, by law or through the corporate charter. French law requires disclosure by purchasers (singly or those acting in concert) of acquisitions of listed shares at the following thresholds: 5 percent, 10 percent, 20 percent, 33 1/3 percent, 50 percent, and 66 2/3 percent. Failure to disclose purchases may result in loss of voting rights of the shares exceeding the legal thresholds for a minimum of two years. Fanto 1995 (citing Keith D. Nunes et al., "French & SEC Securities Regulation: The Search for Transparency and Openness in Decisionmaking," *Vanderbilt Journal of Transnational Law* 26 (1993):242). Corporate charters can reduce these thresholds still further. Nunes 1993.

39. See Fanto 1998, 106–7 ("Families rank significantly among the concentrated shareholders, which is not surprising since family ownership of major French firms has been almost as important a feature of French business as State ownership. . . . [F]amily ownership did not give way in France, as it did in other countries, to specialized management and market capitalism[.]") (footnotes omitted).

40. More precisely, they have served as conduits of control. See Fanto 1998, 107–8 ("rather, they have served as proxies for the State or as financial advisors to a controlling shareholder, be it the State or a family").

41. See generally Zysman 1977.

42. This pervasive effect of the activist state truncating the development of autonomous social and economic structures and relationships is analyzed at length in Jonah D. Levy, *Tocqueville's Revenge: State, Society, and Economy in Contemporary France* (Cambridge, MA: Harvard University Press, 1999). For analyses focusing specifically on corporate governance, see, e.g., Fanto 1995, 38; Charkham 1994, 130–31; Oxford Analytica, *Board Directors and Corporate Governance: Trends in the G7 Countries Over the Next Ten Years: Executive Report* (Oxford: Oxford Analytica, 1992), 96.

43. See Cioffi 2000.

44. Ibid.

45. See Mark J. Roe, "Takeover Politics," in *The Deal Decade: What Takeovers Mean for Corporate Governance*, ed. Margaret Blair (Washington, DC: Brookings Institution Press, 1993), 321–53.

46. See Matheson and Olson 1991; Adams and Matheson 2000.

47. See Cioffi 2002, chapter 6.

48. Ibid.

49. The SEC's proxy rules required that shareholders collectively owning more than 5 percent of a corporation's stock could not communicate among themselves without filing an expensive and time-consuming proxy statement with the agency. The rule had been adopted to protect minority shareholders from manipulation of firm governance and unfair takeover tactics. However, it effectively discouraged institutional investors from collaborating in pursuing more activist corporate governance strategies.

50. This blunt use of political clout by the accounting industry and its legislative allies ultimately weakened its political position once the size, seriousness, and number of the accounting scandals of 2001–2002 became public.

51. Although institutional investors could continue to apply public pressure on poorly performing and autocratic management (as in the case of the CalPERS blacklist), these were largely disfavored methods of activism. These funds, with tens or hundreds of millions of dollars invested in target firms, did not want to take public actions against management that might diminish the value of their holdings.

52. The law also increased criminal and civil penalties on executives for failing to disclose material financial information to the public and compelled CEOs and chief financial officers to certify the firm's accounts and internal control procedures for collecting and disseminating financial information. These provisions are likely to be of more symbolic than practical importance, however.

53. There has been a pronounced trend toward the appointment of "outside" directors (i.e., individuals not part of management) beginning with a 1978 New York Stock Exchange listing rule requiring an audit committee of outside directors. See Korn/Ferry International, *20th Annual Board of Directors Study* (New York: Korn/Ferry International, 1993), 3, 7, 13; *cf.* Investor Responsibility Research Center 1996, 3–6; *accord* Charkham 1994, 188–89 (in 1990, outside directors accounted for a majority on 86 percent of boards in the manufacturing sector and 91 percent for those in all other sectors). However, managerial control over their nomination casts their independence in doubt.

54. The overhaul of German corporate governance and company law is recounted and analyzed in detail in Cioffi, "Restructuring 'Germany, Inc.'"

55. Second Financial Market Promotion Act (Gesetz über den Wertpapierhandel und zur Änderung börsenrechtlicher und wertpapierrechtlicher Vorschriften, Zweites Finanzmarktförderungsgesetz) of July 26, 1994, *Federal Law Gazette* 1:1749.

56. See Securities Trading Act (Wertpapierhandelsgesetz) of July 26, 1994, sections 3–11, Bundesgesetzblatt 1 (*Federal Law Gazette* 1) 1994, 1749, promulgated as Article I of the Second Financial Promotion Act (Gesetz über den Wertpapierhandel und zur Änderung börsenrechtlicher und wertpapierrechtlicher Vorschriften, Zweites Finanz-marktförderungsgesetz) (enabling legislation for the creation of the BAWe).

57. Amendment to the Securities Trading Act by Article 2 of the Law Implementing EC Directives for the Harmonisation of Regulatory Provisions in the Field of Banking and Securities Supervision (*Gesetz zur Umsetzung von EG-Richtlinien zur Harmonisierung bank-und wertpapieraufsichtsrechtlicher Vorschriften*) of October 22, 1997, Bundesgesetzblatt 1 (BGBl 1, *Federal Law Gazette* 1) 1997, 2518 (effective June 1, 1998); Amendment to the Securities Trading Act by Article 3 of the Third Financial Market Promotion Act (*Gesetz zur weiteren Fortentwicklung des Finanzplatzes Deutschland, Drittes Finanz-marktförderungsgesetz*) of March 24, 1998, BGBl 1 1998, 529; Amendment to the Securities Trading Act by Article 5 of the Act on Corporate Control and Transparency (*Gesetz zur Kontrolle und Transparenz im Unternehmensbereich*, "KonTraG") of April 27, 1998, BGBl 1 1998, 786; Amendment of the Securities Trading Act (*Wertpapierhandelsgesetz*) by Article 2 of the Law Implementing the EC Deposit Guarantee Directive and Investor Compensation Directive of July 16, 1998, BGBl 1 1998, 1842.

58. See Cioffi 2002.

59. *Gesetz über die integrierte Finanzaufsicht* ("FinDAG"), April 22, 2002 (effective May 1, 2002).

60. For an organizational and policy overview of the BAFin, see "The new German Financial Supervisory Authority." www.bafin.de/indexfle.htm.

61. The government explained the creation of the BAFin as a regulatory and policy response to "a growing tendency among banks, financial services institutions and insurance undertakings to form cross-sectoral groups. . . . [I]n the past, banks and insurance companies maintained only loose connections whereas today, powerful financial conglomerates have emerged in Germany which operate at a global level." Ibid.

62. Corporate Control and Transparency Act (*Gesetz zur Kontrolle und Transparenz im Unternehmensbereich*, "KonTraG") of April 27, 1998, Bundesgesetzblatt 1 (*Federal Law Gazette* 1), 786.

63. The act also formally recognizes the primary duty of custodian banks in voting proxies to protect the interests of the shareholder, thus importing a version of shareholder primacy into the normative framework of corporate governance.

64. Banks voting depositors' proxy votes must also name a management board member as responsible for monitoring the voting of proxies. See Stock Corporation Act (*Aktiengesetz*), section 128(2).

65. Stock Corporation Act (*Aktiengesetz*), sections 170.1, 171.1 (superseding Commercial Code, section 318.1).

66. Stock Corporation Act (*Aktiengesetz*), section 93.1.

67. An auditor is precluded from auditing a firm if it has earned more than 30 percent of its revenues from the client over the past five years and must rotate the signatory of

the audit if the same person has signed the report more than six times in ten years. The limitation on auditor liability was raised from 500,000 DM to 8 million DM for listed corporations (2 million DM for unlisted companies).

68. The 25 percent figure is significant in that this represents a blocking minority under German company law with respect to important corporate decisions.

69. Such lawsuits are similar to derivative suits under American corporate law, with the significant difference that the minority shareholders and their counsel do not control the litigation as in the United States. However, the KonTraG did not alter the *substance* of fiduciary duties, nor did it otherwise alter the mechanisms and procedures for enforcing shareholder rights to make them more effective or prevalent in practice.

70. See, e.g., Nigel Holloway, "The End of Germany AG," *Forbes*, June 11, 2001 (interview with international corporate governance consultant Stephen Davis predicting that the 2000 tax reforms will transform German corporate governance and increase takeover activity). The legislation was actually a corporate finance and governance law. It was not concerned with tax revenues—the anticipated effects of the law were tax neutral. In the absence of the reduction in capital gains taxes, firms and financial institutions would simply have left the crossshareholdings in place.

71. Securities Acquisition and Takeover Act (Wertpapierwerbs un Übernahmegesetzvom) of December 20, 2001, Bundesgesetzblatt 1, 2001. For a translation of the Takeover Act, see Ashurst Morris Crisp. www.ashursts.com/pubs/approvedtakeover.htm. For overviews of the legislation, see Markus Strelow and Jan Wildberger, "The New German Takeover Act—A New Opportunity for Private Equity?" *Thompson Venture Economics.* www.ventureeconomics.com/buy/protected/ ZZZ4HGCLBZC.html; Osborne and Clarke, "New German Securities Acquisition and Takeover Act Enacted, www.osborneclarke.com /publications/text/germansecurities.htm; Dirk Rissel, "Overview of the New German Takeover Law," *Eurojuris Law Journal* (March 2002), www.eurojurislawjournal.net/RA/Rissel /Overview-of-the-new-German-Takkeover-Law.html; Ruth Zehetmeier-Mueller and Richard Ufland, "A New Era for Public Takeover Transactions in Germany Has Begun," *Legal Week Global*, April 17–May 14, 2002, www.legalweek.net/ViewItem.asp?id=8571 &Keyword=takeoverZehetmeier-MuelleandUfland.

72. See Jonathan Braude and Victorya Hong, "Takeover Directive Divides Germany," *The Daily Deal*, May 23, 2001; Hans D. Barbier, "Germany's Intricate Web," *Frankfurter Allgemeine Zeitung*, July 9, 2001.

73. Hugh Williamson, "Germany Acts To Limit Hostile Takeovers," *Financial Times*, July 11, 2001; Braude and Hong 2001; BBC, "Germany To Curb Hostile Takeovers," July 11, 2001, http://news.bbc.co.uk/hi/english/business/newsidfl1433000/1433380.stm; Robert W. Wood, "Germans in the News Again," *M&A Tax Report* 10, no. 2 (September 2001):8.

74. "[T]he managing board of the target company may not perform any acts which might result in the success of the offer being prevented." Securities Acquisition and Takeover Act, section 33.1.

75. Management may seek shareholder authorization to use specified defenses. These resolutions are valid for up to eighteen months and require a 75 percent supermajority vote, and the supervisory board must approve any deployment of these defenses. Securities Acquisition and Takeover Act, section 33.2. More important, the duty of neutrality "does not apply to acts that would also have been performed by a prudent manager of a company not affected by a take-over offer, the looking out for a competing offer, *as*

well as acts approved by the supervisory board of the target company." Securities Acquisition and Takeover Act, section 33.1; see also Jonathan Braude, "Germany Seems Ready To Accept Hostile Takeovers," *The Daily Deal*, May 23, 2000.

76. Without activist courts to clarify the complex legal issues and ambiguous statutory rules, the application of the act will be troublesome. In all likelihood, the courts will construe the act's requirement of 75 percent shareholder approval for capital increases relating to takeover defenses to cover poison pills (even though American practice clearly shows that no capital is raised or anticipated from these plans).

77. Securities Acquisition and Takeover Act, sections 4–9.

78. Ibid., sections 11, 14.

79. Ibid., sections 10.5, 11.2.6.2, 27.2, and 27.3. Labor is also entitled to two representatives on the BAWe's (now the BAFin's) thirteen-member "advisory board" on takeovers created pursuant to the Securities Acquisition and Takeover Act, section 5.1.

80. See Deeg and Perez 1999.

81. Of course, this account cannot do justice to the complex, contentious, and ideological politics of French privatization during the 1980s and 1990s. For an excellent account of the reform of the French political economy, see Levy 1999; see also Deeg and Perez 1999.

82. For discussions of French privatization, see O'Sullivan 2001; Francois Morin, "The Transformation of the French Model of Shareholding and Management," *Economy and Society* (February 2000); Vivian Schmidt, *From State to Market? The Transformation of French Business and Government* (Cambridge and New York: Cambridge University Press, 1996); Andrea Goldstein, "Privatizations and Corporate Governance in France," *Banca Nazionale del Lavoro, Quarterly Review* 199 (December 1996):455–88.

83. See, e.g., Victor Mallet, "France Goes on Sale," *Financial Times*, June 17, 2002 (noting the continuation of privatizations under the Socialist government and the likelihood of further acceleration under the new conservative government following the 2002 election).

84. O'Sullivan 2001, 6–7.

85. Ibid., 26–27 (noting that the vast majority of funds generated through privatization went into state coffers, rather than raising capital for the companies).

86. See Deeg and Perez 1999.

87. This did not mean that the French state withdrew into neoliberalism. As Jonah Levy argues, the erosion of *dirigiste* policy was matched through the 1980s and 1990s by an expansion of welfare state programs and expenditures to cushion the blows of the market. See Levy 1999; Jonah D. Levy, "Activation through Thick and Thin: Progressive Strategies for Increasing Labor Force Participation" (chapter 3 of this volume).

88. The development of the national equity market has been limited by the persistence of public pensions and the inability of policymakers to institute a private pension scheme that could invest in, and generate higher demand for, corporate securities in the open market.

89. See Fanto 1998, note 53.

90. Ibid., 112.

91. See Fanto 1995, 42–43; *cf.* Leslie Goldman, "The Modernization of the French Securities Markets: Making the EEC Connection," *Fordham Law Review* 60 (1992):232–33 (reforms beginning in 1985).

92. See Law NE 88-70, January 22, 1988 (the Law on Security and Disclosure in the Financial Markets); Law NE 89531, August 2, 1989 (Security and Disclosure Law).

93. The first scandal involved insider trading involving Pechiney, SA, a state-owned French aluminum company, and a top contributor to Mitterrand's Socialist Party. The second implicated Société Generale, a large bank controlled by political conservatives through a privatization by the former conservative government, and the new Socialist minister of finance, who orchestrated a hostile takeover attempt to diminish his political rivals' power base. See Goldman 1992, 238–40.

94. The CBV is charged with drafting rules governing the stock exchange, subject to the approval of the minister of finance following consultation and advice of the COB. The CBV was renamed the *Conseil des Marches Financiers* in 1996. See Law 96-597, July 2, 1996. The CBV delegated the SBF to supervise and control the securities market's administration, security, development, and promotion. Goldman 1992, 238; see Fanto 1998, 111.

95. See Goldman 1992, 242–43.

96. Id.

97. Id.

98. These developments challenge cultural theories of political–economic behavior. The rapidity with which the formerly closed and mutually supporting French political and economic elite has embraced adversarial relations and tactics obliterates the image of the French political economy as overdetermined by a shared and ingrained culture of elitism.

99. Levy 1999.

100. French Senate, no. 124-1996-1997.

101. Among other proposals, the Marini Report advocated the following company law reforms:

- Boards should be empowered to form committees and name their membership.
- Corporations should have the legal right (but not an obligation) to separate the offices of chief executive and board chair while maintaining a unitary board structure.
- Corporations should be obliged to disclose a list of owners to all shareholders.
- Shareholders should be given one month's notice of a general meeting (up from 15 days).
- Shareholders should have the right to assign their proxy vote to an independent entity rather than management.
- Directors should not serve on more than five boards.

102. Law NE 97-277, March 25, 1997, section 13.

103. See Samer Iskandar, "Three Wiser Men: The French Government and the Business Community Can Learn Important Lessons from the Drawn-out Takeover Battle in the Banking Sector," *Financial Times*, August 30, 1999. The BNP–Paribas, Total-Fina–Elf Aquitaine, and Carrefour–Promodes mergers represent a new breed of nationally based firms shaped more by market forces than state fiat and oriented toward European and international competition rather than national markets and state economic management. This was especially clear in the consolidation of the French petroleum sector as French government officials oversaw the cross-national merger of Total with Belgium's Petrofina and as the entity, Total-Fina, took over the much larger (and traditional "national champion") Elf Aquitaine. Likewise, other large cross-border mergers by French firms have left the French acquirer in the dominant position. However, the failure of the French ministry of finance to negotiate or impose a resolution to the BNP–Paribas–Société General hostile

takeover battle revealed the limits of the state's willingness and/or capacity to guide the consolidation process or to impose acquisitions on private firms.

104. The outcome of the BNP–Paribas–Société General hostile takeover battle, in which BNP won control over Paribas through a hostile bid, exposed Société General to acquisition by a foreign bank. The French state could have blocked any of the bids and imposed a resolution, but *chose* not to. *Cf.* Peter Ford, "Europe Answers Walmart Threat," *Christian Science Monitor*, September 1, 1999. The result was probably the least favorable outcome for all three banks and for economic nationalists.

105. See Tess Read, "Down with Dirigisme," *Worldlink*, September/October 1999. http://backissues.worldlink.co.uk/articles/08091999111756/08.htm.

106. However, networks of government and financial elites may be making a comeback as they retake control from CEOs of France Telecom and Vivendi, whose disastrous forays into American-style corporate capitalism of mergers and acquisitions nearly destroyed each company.

107. Michael Moran argues that scandals drove the process of financial system reform during the 1980s. See generally Michael Moran, *The Politics of the Financial Services Revolution: The USA, UK, and Japan* (New York: St. Martins Press, 1991). The analysis offered here of policy reforms during the 1990s and early 2000s accepts the importance of scandal for the mobilization of political support for legal and structural change in the financial system—as qualified above. One may speculate further that the crisis and erosion of the solidaristic postwar policies and institutional arrangements during the post-1973 period increased the political importance of these scandals by weakening the systemic legitimacy of the entire political economic order.

108. The general contours of this consensus on privatization, financial system reform, and corporate governance reform were essential to the progress of French policy. For this reason, the policy did not change substantially or grind to a halt despite changes in government and "cohabitation" of opposing parties in the presidency and parliament.

109. See Investment Services Directive of May 10, 1993, *Official Journal of the European Community (OJEC)* L 141/27, June 11, 1993; Second Banking Directive of December 15, 1989, *OJEC* L 375/3, December 31, 1989; First Banking Directive of December 12, 1977, *OJEC* L 322/30, December 17, 1977. For an overview see, e.g., Eddy Wymeersch, "Status Report on Corporate Governance Rules and Practices in Some European Countries," in *Comparative Corporate Governance: The State of the Art and Current Research*, ed. Klaus J. Hopt, Hideki Kanda, Mark J. Roe, Eddy Wymeersch, and Stefan Prigge (New York and Oxford: Oxford University Press, 1998). Sweeping securities market liberalization under EU directives and the Maastricht Treaty also impelled the restructuring of regulatory bodies. See Maastricht Treaty, Art. 73 A-H; Directive 88/361/EEC of 24 June 1988, *OJEC* L 178/5, July 8, 1988; see also Investment Services Directive, *op cit.*

110. The Investment Services Directive of 10 May 1993, *OJEC* L 141/27, June 11, 1993, required the member states to extensively harmonize their disclosure rules and market securities regulation and to create national securities regulators to institutionalize this harmonization and facilitate cooperative enforcement efforts across EU borders.

111. A farther-reaching goal of German policymakers was the creation of a shareholding culture and a securities regulation framework to support it that would eventually be able to absorb a greater share of the country's pension liabilities. *Cf.* Ziegler, J. Nicholas, "Corporate Governance and the Politics of Property Rights in Germany," *Politics & Society*

28, no. 2 (June 2000):195–222. This policy goal of greater use of private pensions remains distant at present and mired in political conflict between unions and the left wing of the Social Democratic Party, on the one hand, and employers and financial institutions, on the other.

112. If the analysis of regulatory centralization presented here holds true, this current fragmentation of policymaking and enforcement will likely mobilize opposition in favor of consolidating authority and legal uniformity at the federal level.

CONCLUSION

Politics and Policy: A Transatlantic Perspective

MARTIN SHAPIRO

PUTTING PIECES TOGETHER

IN THE SOCIAL SCIENCES, THERE IS GREAT CONCERN FOR BEING ON THE CUTTING EDGE. The real cutting edge of any given moment, however, only sporadically and spasmodically over time turns into orthodoxy or normal science. There is an intermediate stage that is crucial to whether sooner, or later, or never, the avant garde becomes orthodox or becomes a passing fancy or a continuing minority report. Successful cutting edges at some point turn into avant garde orthodoxies, that is, movements the members of which still pride themselves on being avant garde but that have actually, if only recently, entered the orthodox canon. Much work of repetition, elaboration, and consolidation must occur on both sides of this turning point.

This book is structured by three movements, all essentially integrative and all, we hope, in the process of passing from avant garde to avant garde orthodoxy. One of these movements can be labeled "transatlantic" studies, a second is the unification of political and policy studies. The third concerns the integrated study of the political process. And, from another perspective, the book is an exercise in that wing of the "new institutionalism" that emphasizes the influence of existing rules and institutions on new political developments.

The first, or "transatlantic" movement is a response to a more or less accidental pathology in the organization of political science, the split between American and comparative politics. For a long time "comparative politics" really referred far less to a method of inquiry than to an omnibus catalogue heading under which could be grouped all those who studied the politics of some single nation-state other than the United States. Some political scientists studied the United States, others France, others the United Kingdom. There was no particular reason an Americanist should know about France or a French specialist should know about America. Because there were many courses taught in America about America and few about France, one whole section of the department catalogue was labeled America and the one course about France was thrown into a "comparative" section of the catalogue along with the one course on Germany, etc. But the result of training graduate students and organizing research on the basis of catalogue headings was that Americanists did not and should not know anything about the rest of the world and comparativists nothing about the United States.

Once the word "comparative" in comparative politics came to be taken seriously—that is, as referring to a method of inquiry rather than a fancy way of saying non-U.S. in course catalogues—it became increasingly absurd that comparativists could and did compare any country A with any country B, except the United States, the country we knew most about, and that Americanists might use any methodology they chose except comparison. Whether this increasingly obvious absurdity would have done the trick on its own is not clear. Two other factors, both reflected in this book, contributed to bridging the American comparative gap. One was the move toward policy studies in political science. France, the United States, and the United Kingdom may have very different constitutional arrangements, party and electoral systems, and so on, but they encounter roughly the same policy problems including unemployment, the environment, and risk. Whether trained as Americanists or comparativists, political scientists who became policy specialists were far more likely to look across national boundaries than were students of political parties or legislatures.

Second, no matter how deep the scholarly entrenchments, political science will eventually change in response to changes in real-world politics. All the real-world stuff that is badly captured by the catch word "globalization" makes it harder for political science to divide itself into the United States and the rest. The growing importance of the European Union with its obvious but indeterminate relation to U.S. federalism pushes comparativists to look at the United States. The mushrooming of constitutional judicial review in Europe and the generally increasing "judicialization" of politics in Europe have pushed the public law subfield of political science, which used to be really a subfield of American politics, in comparative directions.

Of course, this closing of the gap between American and comparative politics need not, and is not, limited to transatlantic studies, but such studies are the most obvious and easiest bridge. This volume is far from the first in which U.S.–European comparisons are systematically made. Nor do all of its contributions explicitly employ the United States as one of the entities compared. The volume as a whole, however, seeks to be a step toward consolidating a movement in which a substantial number of political scientists treat the comparison of U.S. and European politics as normal and natural. At that point, a substantial number of graduate students may see themselves as equally responsible for knowledge of the United States and at least Europe rather than treating their required subfield in American politics or comparative politics as a distribution requirement hurdle to be gotten over and forgotten as soon as they pass their Ph.D. qualifying exams. We hope this book will equally infect the curriculums of American and comparative politics.

This book, like the earlier two in the series,[1] is explicitly designed to integrate policy and political-process studies. That integration has been easier from the policy than the politics side. To the extent that policy studies sees itself as policy science, or those with normal political science affiliations become policy specialists, there is a natural tendency to move from studying the policy itself to how it is made and implemented, because if one concentrates exclusively on the substance of the policy itself, some substantive evaluation of the policy, some conclusion about whether it is a good or bad, a right or wrong, policy cannot long be avoided. Turning to the policymaking and implementation process is a way to avoid violating political science's positivistic commitments and descending into the hurly-burly of partisan politics. Moreover, very typically the public announcement of policy, in the form of legislation or executive decree, is so delphic that only a detailed knowledge of the politics that engendered the pronouncement and the subsequent politics of enforcement will allow us to know what the policy really is. Even now, most policy-oriented political scientists began as politics people.

Those political scientists basically concerned with political institutions and behavior have a more difficult time integrating policy, which they see as a series of metorlike objects flashing through the Congress or executive or political party constellation they study. Of the various moves from avant garde to avant garde orthodoxy attempted in this volume, perhaps the most problematic is the attempt to move politics people to see the policy outputs of the institutions, processes, and behaviors they study as an essential piece of data for understanding what they study. In spite of many years of urging by people inside and outside their fields, it is still the rare American Congress specialist who looks at congressional outputs with anything like the care he or she expends on congressional inputs and throughputs. We admit that many or most of the contributors to this volume are more or less policy people incorporating political stories, but we hope that they have exhibited sufficient sophistication about and concentration on politics that the book can illustrate how paying attention to policy outputs can improve our understanding of political dynamics.

There is another integrative aspect to our attempt here to understand politics better by looking at the policies it produces or fails to produce. Just as specialists on political institutions often shortchange their outputs, the advantages of specialization have often driven them to study one aspect of politics such as pressure groups or the committee system to the exclusion or downgrading of others. Precisely because policies are the products and continue to bear the stigmata of long, multistage, multiactor decision-making processes, the policy person who does choose to enter the political thicket is likely to want to see the whole forest and all the trees. To be sure, the policy specialist is thankful for all the insights he can gather about the assorted actors and episodes of the policy story from the work of interest-group or bureaucracy or political executive specialists. But, unlike them, the policy specialist feels the pressure to bring all those insights together into one coherent policymaking story. It is in some policy course that students will be asked to put together what they learned in their legislatures and parties and public opinion courses, if they finally take a policy course.

This problem of putting the pieces together has been particularly acute among law and courts specialists. Typically, they have concerned themselves very heavily with judicial law making and very little with law making by everybody else. They see legislative law making only through the lens of judicial statutory interpretation and administrative law making only from the perspective of judicial review of agency decision making. We hope this book supports the work of Shep Melnick, Bob Katzman, and others who have been trying to tell whole law-making stories as a better way of understanding both judicial review and the whole political process. We also hope the book will contribute to the consolidation of the view that it is as natural and normal for a political scientist to deal with the whole political story of a particular public policy from beginning to end as to cut the other way and focus on a particular locus through which many policy proposals transit.

Guiraudon's analysis of European immigration reform, for instance, provides a dramatic corrective to the tendency of comparativists to leave the courts out and students of courts to leave everything else out. Rights-based politics and activist courts have rendered European policy more proimmigrant in spite of European intentions to the contrary. And in the United States, anti-immigrant sentiment has been funneled toward border controls precisely because, once immigrants are in the country, courts have made it so difficult to get them out. In his review of environmental policies, Kelemen finds that "the overriding trend is for the continuing dominance of an adversarial, legalistic approach to policy in the U.S. and for the growth of such a style in the EU," and he traces the prevalence of this style to "basic constitutional structures." Students of environmental politics necessarily become students of litigation.

The relationship of this volume to the "new institutionalism" is too obvious and has been too often commented on earlier to require much more here. The story is one of common causes or challenges or stimuli bearing down on the United States and the states of Western Europe and differing responses and patterns of response and nonresponse from those states depending on differences in established national political arrangements and existing policy. This is certainly path dependency on a grand scale but with many unanticipated byways and many unfinished or unattempted trails.

Weaver's analysis of public pension programs, for instance, concludes that despite a broad commonality of policy agendas generated by a common set of economic–demographic forces, major differences in pension retrenchment policies have occurred among OECD states, and these differences in recent outcomes were heavily influenced by national differences in preexisting pension regimes. "Wealthy industrialized countries have all built even their restructuring reforms on the foundations of their current systems."

IDEAS AND INTERESTS

The major theme of the first volume in this series was that politics is driven by ideas as well as interests. The conclusion to the second volume was built around the theme that the politics of public policy in the United States in the 1990s was governed by two broad intellectual or ideological persuasions, a guarded preference for the market over government as the dominant economic decision maker and a continuing but limited commitment to the welfare state. The result was a partisan politics focused on just how regulated so-called free markets should be and just how cost constrained welfare programs ought to be.

This conclusion to our second volume, which was devoted exclusively to U.S. politics and policy, also serves as the introduction to this transatlantic volume. Because this faith in regulated markets and concern for the rising costs of welfare are "global" causes operating on both sides of the Atlantic, comparison of the two sides is possible and useful.

The reaction against socialism and continued commitment to welfare are, of course, ideas at the most general level. This volume, like the earlier ones, also shows the influence of many far more specific ideas. Levy's espousal of a "new social liberalism" tracks specific policy ideas that run counter to neoliberalism. His work, as well as that of many others in this volume, shows why the reaction against socialism should be phrased in that negative way, rather than in positive terms of a triumph of neoliberalism. Distrust of government ownership and central economic planning as a substitute for markets is not identical to rejection of either government regulation or positive intervention in those markets.

Similarly, Sheingate tracks the fate of the bundle of ideas labeled "new public management" and shows the linkage of these ideas both to the general, ideological, transatlantic commitment to constrained welfare and particular structures of interests both inside and outside government.

POLICY DRIFT

The central theme of our second volume was that U.S. politics of the 1990s, although marked by high levels of partisan electoral competition, were so dominated by the intellectual consensus on regulated markets and constrained welfare that the policy product of that closely divided politics was not stalemate but a modest flow of moderate and incremental policy innovations. The other side of that "modest," "moderate," "incremental" coin was obviously that little or nothing happened on some policy fronts.

The contributors to this volume often place more emphasis on the half-empty aspects of the policy glass. Vogel addresses himself to the intriguing question of why Europe recently has been so concerned with government risk management while U.S. concern appears to have declined. One of Hacker's major themes is "policy drift," particularly in the United States. Yet, the widespread European failure to successfully address high unemployment and the labor market rigidities that appear to be one of the causes of that unemployment speak to European drift as well. Europe, like the United States, has been going through a period of fierce and closely divided electoral competition, with now nonsocialist socialist parties returning to power after long absence in the United Kingdom, barely retaining power in Germany, and alternating with conservatives in France. Thus, this volume, like the last, pays a good deal of attention to fierce, partisan credit claiming and blame avoidance often in the context of quite meager policy product.

UPWARD AND DOWNWARD FROM THE NATION STATE

Seeking the Center necessarily confronted Clinton's pronounced affection for "positive, small government," but did so largely by treating it as a rhetorical device for adopting the traditional Democratic penchant for government action to the contemporary political climate of distrust of big government. In this volume, more explicit attention is paid to movement "upward, downward, and outward" from national government decision making. While a striking number of the contributions to this volume can continue to treat national capitals as the principal or sole locus of policymaking, it would hardly be possible to examine Western Europe in any breadth or depth without encountering the European Union. Indeed, because this volume concentrates on welfare policies, giving relatively less attention to regulation, it no doubt underemphasizes the European Union because the European Union has become increasingly active in regulation while the member states individually retain the main responsibility for welfare. Thus, Weaver's analysis of public pension reform can proceed exclusively at the national level. Even so, Burke, moving on from the concern for U.S. rights he pursued in *Seeking the Center* to rights in Europe, finds himself quickly moving "upward" from the national to the EU arena. Guiraudon and a number of other contributors to this volume show the proclivities of political actors in the new Europe to engage in the kind of strategic shifts between local and "higher" arenas of government that students of American federal politics have long highlighted. Of course, this kind of strategic play is clearest in Germany, with its formal, federal structure and its sometimes direct relationship between the *länder* and the European Union, but the vigor of the European Union creates at least two levels of action for even the most formally unitary European states. In his study of corporate governance regulation, Cioffi can concentrate almost entirely on national government and national elites in France but must tell a more complicated story of EU and national interactions for Germany. And while he assumes it, rather than explicitly factoring it in, the curiously federal structure of U.S. corporate regulation is at the heart of his American story. I say curious because it is curious that U.S. corporations, so noteworthy for their national, and now global, scope, have remained essentially legal creatures of, and basically subject to, state, not national, law. It is for that reason that the American national model of government regulation of corporations that

Cioffi shows to have had worldwide influence is a model of securities regulation, which is a federal realm, rather than direct regulation of corporate governance itself. The very same diversity of viewpoint among relevant elites that led to American policy drift on securities regulation in the 1990s has led for over a century to the most massive and fundamental American policy drift of all, the failure to enact a general national corporations law.

Guiraudon, Vogel, and Kelemen simply could not deal with their topics without dealing extensively with the European Union. Indeed, at least half of Keleman's story centers on federalism, where he finds that "[f]ormerly weak E.U. regulators substantially increased their control over member state regulation, while powerful federal regulators in the U.S. devolved considerable power to the states."

HIGH- AND LOW-VISIBILITY POLITICS

Both of the two earlier volumes dealt, sometimes explicitly and more often implicitly, with the differing politics of high- and low-visibility policy areas and the strategies of various political actors designed to move issues from low to high visibility. The much-touted Dutch style has relied on low-visibility negotiations between government and the "social partners." Guiraudon makes much of the advantages to certain actors of low-visibility politics. Vogel's European story is largely one of high-visibility events radically altering the policymaking process for what had previously been low-visibility policy areas. The large change without reform in U.S. health care traced by Hacker is, to be sure, policy drift but is also the product of low-visibility decision making, low because it was made by private, decentralized decision makers.

However, the public pension programs studied by Weaver are almost by definition high-visibility policy areas. And Weaver indeed finds that interest groups, "social partners," electoral politics, party structures, and constitutional structures that provide multiple, partisan-controlled veto points do play an important but complex part in specific policy outcomes within a discernable pattern of path dependency. In such a context, it becomes difficult to determine whether various reform ideas play a real part or are simply vehicles for preexisting political interests and interest groups playing high-stakes politics.

TECHNOCRACY

Both the distrust of government and high- versus low-visibility themes sometimes implicate yet another theme of this and the earlier volumes: technocratic versus democratic government. Here again, ideas and interests are deeply entwined. All of the states we examine enjoy democratic political cultures. And all are embedded in a general culture of science and technology in which it is axiomatic that those who know how to do something should do it and those who do not should not. Expertise—and in the contemporary western world, that means highly specialized expertise—is the key to legitimacy except in the voting booth. Yet, part of postmodernism, or postindustrialism, is the widespread understanding that experts, by the very nature of their expertise, constitute special interests. So the very claim that brings legitimacy also brings suspicion. We cannot live with them or without them.

Vogel is most dramatic on this point. Nothing could have fueled the flames of antiexpertise more than the initial government response to mad cow disease. Yet, the response to public suspicion of national regulatory experts was the creation of an EU expert regulator. It appeared that the only possible response to expert failure was more and higher experts. The distrust of national expertise leads to transnational expertise. This response makes some sense, however, in the mad cow disease context where it is precisely the national special interest of national experts rather than the special interest endemic to their expertise that must be guarded against. More generally, as Vogel argues, the "precautionary principle" constitutes a kind of synthesis of our contradictory views of experts. Decisions are to be based on expert evidence but are ultimately to be made by politically responsible officials.

Where governments themselves are staffed largely by experts, it is often impossible and/or unnecessary to distinguish between promarket, antigovernment sentiment and antitechnocratic sentiment. The various contributions to this volume are sprinkled with descriptions of antitechnocratic yet ambivalent sentiment. In a sense, the whole rights movement is an assertion of "human values" against technocratic cost–benefit analysis. If you have a "right," you have a claim to government services no matter what the cost or the technical barriers. Sheingate's study of administrative reform is largely about responses to government-employed technical experts.

TECHNOCRACY, DEMOCRACY, AND THE EUROPEAN UNION

Although most of the chapters in this volume are country studies, the European Union inevitably plays a part particularly in regulation and, as Vogel's paper emphasizes, particularly in the more than decade-long gap between European health and safety enthusiasm and U.S. skepticism or inertia. Undoubtedly, mad cow disease and the French tainted-blood scandal are significant factors. But certain generic or structural features of the European Union should be noted. EU regulatory politics presents a distinct democratic deficit not only in the sense that the regulators are almost unconnected with electoral or party democracy but with pluralist democracy as well. Both EU regulatory statutes and supplementary administrative rules basically are generated by bodies of technically expert civil servants and researchers connected to government-funded research institutions. Not only are these experts detached from any direct electoral connection, but most of the commissioners, permanent representatives, and council members to whom they report are also largely insulated from party and electoral politics. They are linked to democratic politics only by the consideration that the national governments that lie behind them are subject to elections, but elections that typically turn on non-EU issues. There are still only adumbrations of EU-wide political parties. Few top EU officials meet any policy question by asking themselves how their stance on a particular issue will affect "my party in the next election," as national political decision makers must. As to the experts, precisely because most of them work in the public sector and in settings whose very *raison d'être* is regulation, they are bound to see themselves as experts at risk reduction. Their duty is to protect the public, not produce more goods and services. Their assessments almost automatically focus toward risk reduction and away from production gains.

In the United States, pluralist regulatory politics offset—some would say overwhelm—this risk focus because many of the interest groups at play and the experts employed or funded by them are more interested in production (or profit) than in risk abatement. It is true that there has been a blossoming of lobbying organizations in Brussels, but it is also true that antiregulatory ones have not done very well. They have not done well basically for two reasons. Public sector experts dominate EU regulation and, more imbued than their American equivalents with public service esprit, they disesteem their private sector counterparts. Two American physicists—one in the government and one not—remain more fellow physicists and less public servant versus private profit seeker than do two European physicists similarly situated. Second, American pluralist regulatory politics is bolstered by electoral politics. U.S. lobbyists imply campaign contributions and other electoral support for election-oriented politicians who ultimately control experts. U.S. parties may be held electorally accountable for regulatory missteps. The Brussels lobbyist has few electoral carrots or sticks and hardly anyone to wave them at.

Absent strong political risks, the expert regulator, whose business after all is regulating and whose mission is to protect the public, not foster private gain, is likely to focus heavily on long-term diffuse risk reduction to the neglect of short-term concentrated regulatory costs. Although the precautionary principle is many different things to many different people, including some degree of political control over technocrats, one of the things it is most importantly is as a confirmation of this proregulatory inclination of public technocracies.

Brussels' lobbyists are paying increasing attention to parliament, and particularly its specialized legislative committees, precisely because there the electoral connection is closer and the in-house technocracy less than in the commission and councils. But members of the European Parliament are elected mostly by national proportional representation election mechanisms that give real control to national party leaders to whom Brussels lobbyists can promise little in terms of their own primary electoral concerns.

Unlike the United States, Australia, the United Kingdom, and even some continental states, EU regulatory politics has not been marked by much talk of regulatory impact, regulatory cost, or regulatory failure. Deregulation urges must be masked as single-market enthusiasms. So long as a politically insulated, invisible, basically public sector–oriented technocracy largely controls EU regulation, regulatory enthusiasm is likely to run much higher in Europe than in the United States, no matter what real dangers lurk in which farmyard.

POLICY SUCCESS AND FAILURE

Having laid out a dozen or so policymaking processes and products on a transatlantic basis, it is tempting to assess success or failure in these areas on a transatlantic basis as well. That is, leaving aside national variations, how well has the transatlantic community been doing at policymaking. Such a question is worth asking because, given the degree of interaction and interdependence in the community, considerable movement toward the mean is to be anticipated. Any nation far out of line in its welfare and regulatory policies is likely to feel considerable political and economic pressure to conform, particularly now that the European Union and World Trade Organization are such potent forces.

It is, of course, always extremely problematic to ask questions about policy success. Obviously, success cannot be measured simply by whether the observer approves or disapproves the policies observed. Policy "movement," "innovation," "progress," or "reform" would appear to be more neutral measures, counting change as success no matter whether the observer approves the direction of the change. Even such a measure is not entirely satisfactory, because if the initial policy happens to be the optimal one, changes from it are relative failures, not successes. Moreover, changes in policy that may be considered successes when taken alone may count as failures when their full costs are taken into account. Indeed, political controversies over policies are often about whether a policy goal is worth the costs of achieving it.

In the context of democracy, policy success might be measured in terms of whether the majority got what it wanted, no matter our personal views on the merits of what it wanted. Even aside, however, from the notorious difficulty of discovering majority preferences in pluralist states, the problem of rights arises. If majority-preferred policy infringes on what we, or a constitution or a constitutional court, choose to call a right, can the attainment of such a policy be counted as a policy success? These two problems are somewhat eased in transatlantic studies. Because almost all the states and transstate entities involved now have judicially enforced constitutional rights regimes, it is reasonable to assume that new policies that survive constitutional review in those regimes are not failures on rights grounds. And because our own studies have shown that the transatlantic collection of states faces a number of overarching, pressing problems in common, it seems reasonable to assume that national majorities want some response to those problems and that failure to respond ought to count as failure on both "democratic" and "objective" grounds. Tentatively at least, policy changes in response to those problems may be counted successes while bearing in mind all the problems of simplistically equating change with success.

Finally, some new policies may fairly confidently be labeled successful on efficiency grounds alone. If, for instance, "new public management" policies actually achieved the same level of government services at a lower cost, even those who lost their government jobs in the process would be compelled to admit the success of the policies, although they would call for further political action to ameliorate their costs.

In this light, our story is one of success, albeit marginal and spotty success, for the transatlantic community as a whole. Vogel and Kelemen report that in the consumer protection and environmental areas, substantial amounts of new policy have emerged in Europe, whereas the U.S. situation has been relatively static. Whether the various attempts by the Bush administration to achieve a rebalancing of environmental protection and economic development goals by administrative statutory interpretation ought be counted as successes is obscure both substantively and because it is not clear that they will survive the inevitable court tests. If privatization and deregulation are to be counted as part of the "new public management," then, as Sheingate reports, there has been some degree of administrative reform but, more generally, not much. In the area of corporate governance, Cioffi tracks major policy change in France and Germany but not in the United States. Burke begins from a major U.S. change in disability policy and notes a major formal change in the European Union while awaiting further developments both in implementation and in formal rules. Hacker finds little beyond policy drift on pensions in the United States. In this same pension area, but more broadly considered, Weaver finds that there has been significant restructuring of public pension arrangements, although ultimately those nations that began with more generous treatment of the elderly ended with more generous treatment as well. In immigration policy, Guiraudon notes a major U.S. legislative change and a supranationalization of restrictive control policies in Europe, although again without any particularly observable effect on actual migration flows. In the course of illustrating his "new social liberalism," Levy shows us considerable levels of policy success in labor-market activation in some European states.

RETRENCHMENT AND RECREATION

Just as the earlier volumes in this series devoted to the United States were dominated by the budgetary pressures of deficit-reduction politics, this one repeatedly invokes retrenchment as the central transatlantic theme. Whether or not real retrenchment occurs, where retrenchment is a perceived necessity, the politics of public policy is likely to be depressing and marked far more by drift than dramatic innovation, because retrenchment most often involves taking away highly specific benefits from readily identifiable groups in the name of creating some quite general, highly diffuse "public interest" benefit. Even where the economic ideas driving such retrenchment demands are universally accepted not only among elites but as a matter of general ideology, everything we know about pluralistic, democratic politics leads us to anticipate far more failure to change than success. Every one of the policy stories in this volume records more fits and starts than real innovations, and many record formal change without real change or real change without formal change. All this is hardly surprising under the dark cloud of retrenchment. All the more reason, however, to note the many instances reported in which the political process of some nations and/or the European Union have yielded some new policy product.

That retrenchment is such a crucial transatlantic theme leads me to one final problem of policy evaluation that is too vague, general, and perhaps mythical to play a specific part in the careful social science studies of this volume. It is not irrational or perverse, even in the most neoliberal economic view, for the citizenry of a particular state or complex of cooperating states to conclude that they would prefer to work less and enjoy more leisure at the cost of lower personal income or to decide that they would prefer more public expenditure on joint benefits at the cost of lower individual income, or to opt for both. Nor is it irrational to opt for the highest possible level of work and the highest possible levels of personal income. And even assuming what, as Levy indicates, is far from proved, that high levels of incentives to work necessarily imply or require high levels of social inequality, it is not irrational to choose any particular national trade-off between economic efficiency and social equality. Thus, "failures" to retrench need not necessarily be seen as failures of the political process. They may instead be signs that the political process is highly responsive to the popular desire to achieve a certain mix of values different from maximum gross national product or maximum personal income. Whether Continental Europeans in general really prefer a different mix of personal income, leisure, and public goods than do the Anglo-Saxons is not a question we can answer in this volume, but it would be surprising if every transatlantic population preferred exactly the same trade-offs among them.

INTEREST GROUPS AND DELIBERATION

The concrete accounts of particular policy- or decision-making processes in particular political regimes ought to provide some useful data for those seeking to construct empirical political theory. Every one of our studies exhibits a great deal of directly self-interested, particularistic behavior by interest groups of the sort highlighted by conventional pluralist theory. Many, however, most notably Burke's account of disability rights, also invoke ideas, ideologies, and values as dynamic political forces. Above all, now commonly accepted notions of economic efficiency as an objective, if not the sole legitimate, value, dominate the Sheingate, Hacker, Levy, and Cioffi chapters. The now-familiar story of environmental values and general consumer safety concerns constraining and motivating political action conceived by at least some of the players as being above and beyond the mere aggregation of group interests appears in Kelemen's and Vogel's studies. At quite a different level, policy ideas or innovations proposed as instruments for achieving either group interests or the public good—what Levy calls strategies—play important roles not only in his policy area but in health, corporate governance, pensions, and administrative reform.

Yet, for all these ideas and values offsetting the naked preferences of pluralism, these chapters show few signs of the currently fashionable deliberation. The disillusion over pluralist theories of democracy brought in a great yearning to see something in politics above and beyond the mere aggregation of group preferences. Deliberation—that is, an interaction among parties who brought interests to the table but who could in the course of discussion transcend those interests to arrive at a better approximation of the common good than the mere aggregation of their preferences—became the new hope for democracy. At the procedural end, there is little to distinguish deliberation from pluralism. Both seek open access, maximum information, maximum deployment of expertise, and maximum transparency in the decision-making process. If in any given policymaking process we observed ideal participation, transparency, and information, we still would not know whether we were observing pluralist interest aggregation or deliberation. The more we saw the participants espousing commonly held ideas or values, the more hope might arise that we were seeing deliberation, but naked preferences are so skillful at cloaking themselves in good ideas that we still would not be sure. The real key lies on the output, not the input, side. Real deliberation as opposed to idea-cloaked pluralism should produce transformative outcomes, policies better than those that could have been achieved by mere interest-group bargaining and indeed a change in the bargaining parties away from their initial positions toward less selfish ones.

Readers must determine for themselves whether the studies presented here exhibit any such transformations. Surely the studies that emphasize policy drift do not. They mark failures either to aggregate or deliberate. Several, particularly Guiraudon's, show failures even on the procedural side. Those who fondly hope to find deliberation may be most cheered by Burke's contribution, where the recognition of disability "rights" may be seen as a movement beyond interests to higher values. Pluralists, of course, will see Burke's story as yet another saga of an interest group seeking preference for its interests over others. Indeed, European disability rights appear less to be a product of deliberation—that is, the meeting of many initially opposing minds—than of a phenomenon familiar to pluralists, because pluralists know that in a democracy, policies, particularly policies directly servicing particular groups, more often arise from "turns at bat" than from head-to-head group struggle. Rather than two or more groups opposing each other in legislative or administrative arenas, one group at a time steps up to seek what it wants, pushing not against opposing players but against institutional inertia. That inertia is strong, but once in a while somebody gets a hit. Indeed, Burke shows us an instance where, for particular reasons of EU federalism, the group was pushing against a well-oiled swinging door.

"Rights" brings us to two highjackings of deliberation now being undertaken with relatively greater success than the difficult-to-discern mainstream of deliberation. The most successful highjacking is the judicial one, as illustrated by the American end of Burke's disability story but also in the American end of Guiraudon's. Certain aspects of litigation are easily dressed in the colors of deliberation. The two parties have initial self-interested positions but must engage in a reasoned dialogue. The judge may be seen not as seeking an aggregation of the interests of the two parties but as seeking justice or what he or she perceives as best for society or most in accord with higher values. Academic lawyers are, of course, particularly fond of the vision of three lawyers giving reasons as true deliberation. Precisely because so much is invested in the myth of judicial neutrality and independence, it is tempting for anyone to contrast the "deliberation" of courts with the pluralist hurly-burly of legislative and administrative politics. When courts are announcing rights, their deliberative appearance is reinforced, because rights can appear to be precisely that move beyond naked preferences that is the hallmark of deliberation. Particularly where constitutional rights and constitutional courts are involved, as increasingly they are in Europe as well as in the United States, it becomes easy to speak of a "dialogue" between courts and legislatures in which legislatures concentrate on short-term interest aggregation and distributive politics and courts on long-term values arrived at by litigational deliberation.

From another perspective, however, deliberation by litigation appears to be almost a contradiction in terms. The adversary process tends to drive the two advocates into more and more extreme commitments to their initial interest positions. And, in spite of superficial differences, the so-called inquisitorial procedure of continental Europe is actually just as adversarial as the English and American procedure in the kinds of litigation in which major public policy issues are at stake. Thus, claims that litigation is or can be deliberative inevitably must be claims that the lawyers and the judges do not deliberate together, but that the judges deliberate on the basis of the wholly particularistic, interest-dominated arguments of the advocates. It is true on both sides of the Atlantic that most judicial decisions of public policy significance are rendered by multijudge courts. Most European courts do not publish judicial votes or concurring or dissenting opinions, so their decision-making processes are extremely difficult to discern. Nor do most have rotating clerks who will blab to journalists after they have left the court. What we know of American multijudge courts, however, does not suggest that a great deal of deliberation goes on. Some American higher court judges do spend considerable amounts of time either in face-to-face discussion or in marking up and exchanging each other's draft opinions. Many do not, but simply vote to determine who will write the majority opinion and then proceed to write individual opinions. The judges joining the majority opinion will, of course, have to agree on its wording, but that agreement more often appears to come through arms-length bargaining from fixed positions than through truly transformative discussions. The overwhelming finding of quantitative studies of the voting on American multijudge courts is that the judges' votes are very heavily determined by their relatively long-term political or policy attitudes or preferences. This is not to say that their votes are determined by their own particular economic or social interests or their prior interest group affiliations, but it is to say that their votes are heavily influenced by their long-term beliefs that certain interests in society ought to be fostered over others.

Methods of appointment and judicial career patterns in the United States, or rather the lack of them, may mean that American higher court judges come to their positions more firmly entrenched in long-term political commitments than do those of Europe, but there is no evidence and no a priori reason to believe that European judges have less firm identifications to particular social, economic, and political influences than do American judges. European constitutional court judges typically are appointed on roughly the same political considerations as are U.S. federal judges.

If most higher court judges decide on the basis of the hyperinterest regarding arguments and versions of fact presented to them by advocates, to which they bring their own long-term interest preferences, and about which they are not particularly likely to engage in extended discussions among themselves, then why should we guess that much truly transformative deliberation takes place? Is it not far more likely that what goes on in judicial chambers is pluralist bargaining resulting in interest aggregation, particularly when we understand that courts, like other governing institutions in democracies, ultimately depend on the consent of the governed? The straw that advocates of judicial deliberation must cling to is the longer time perspectives of nonelected judges as contrasted with elected legislators and executives. Such longer time perspectives may incline judges toward greater loyalty to the rules of the democratic game and/or to greater defense of rights (interests?) that cannot garner majority votes, but such perspectives do not necessarily or even probably lead to a greater propensity to abandon initial preferences in favor of better preferences generated by discussion. Indeed, longer time frames may lead to even more determined commitments to initial visions of what would be best rather than a propensity to deliberate to a better outcome.

The other hijacking of deliberation puts its faith not in judges but in technical experts and is particularly prevalent today in the European Union. Faith in expert deliberation rests on two foundations, one illusory and the other confused. The first is the assertion that technical experts come to the table free of entrenched special interests and thus are particularly capable of unselfish deliberation. The accounts in this volume of environmental, consumer protection, health care, pension reform, and government and corporate administration are full of expert participation, but they do not offer much of a vision of expert disinterestedness. Indeed, the mad cow disease incident in Europe so central to Vogel's account is an extraordinarily dramatic negative instance. It is silly to pretend that technical experts are interest free. Nor is it only that they share an interest determined by their own shared expertise. Rather, each brings an array of his or her own particular interests and policy preferences to the table that their shared expertise does not wash away.

The second foundation of faith is that expert deliberation confuses deliberation with objectivity. In most of the policy areas examined in this volume, it can be asserted or prescribed that economic efficiency is an agreed or objective policy norm. In almost any regulatory area, for instance, a group of persons expert at the relevant technologies, and agreed that economic efficiency is the dominating goal, should be able to arrive at an agreed and objectively correct policy—indeed, agreed because it is objectively correct. Because such an outcome would transcend the particularistic interests of both the regulated and the beneficiaries of regulation, such an outcome may be labeled deliberative. And such a process can be kept deliberatively pure by assigning economic efficiency as the determining goal of regulation and excluding the amelioration of any untoward distributional effects of efficient regulation, such as job losses, from the regulatory process, instead assigning them to the "political" process.

The prescription of a pure, economic efficiency–seeking policymaking process and its description as deliberation is misguided for a number of reasons. It assumes what is to be proven: that if experts are agreed on economic efficiency as the dominating goal, they will come to identical policy outcomes even in the face of the uncertainties and nonmonitarily quantifiable costs and benefits entailed in most policy decision making. It is far more likely that experts will assess uncertainties in the light of the interests they bring to the table and thus aggregate their varying uncertainty calculations than that they will deliberate to an agreed assessment of uncertainties. More importantly, to exclude all nonefficiency values from expert decision making and assign them to somewhere else, to politics, in order to construct a sphere of expert deliberation is to admit tacitly that policymaking ultimately is nondeliberative. What is being argued is that deliberation is possible when there is an agreed dominant value but that we must go back to politics as usual when we have to move beyond the agreed value of economic efficiency. As Vogel notes in relation to the "precautionary principle," however, policy almost always seeks to balance economic efficiency against other values. Politicians are entitled, even compelled, to choose noneconomically efficient outcomes that save more lives or preserve more old-growth redwoods or family farms than efficient outcomes would. Put another way, they are entitled to assign whatever arbitrary economic weightings they desire to lives, trees, or families in order to make outcomes appear economically efficient. Seeking to assign all this to politics while asserting that expert deliberators can employ objective, economic efficiency analysis not only buys deliberation at the cost of simply postponing all hard decisions to some other decisional realm, but also pretends that experts are better at assigning essentially arbitrary economic weightings than are nonexperts. There is no reason to believe they are. Instead, assertions of expert deliberation simply privilege expert assignments of economic values over those of nonexpert "politicians" cast in the role of engaging in pluralist, distributive policymaking that messes up expert deliberation.

More fundamentally, deliberation is supposed to occur when initial value positions clash and an agreement is reached on a better value position than mere aggregation would achieve. To set aside a sphere of policy decision making in which one value, economic efficiency, is agreed in advance as dominant is not even to create an isolated sphere of deliberation but rather to construct a sphere in which, by magic or fiat, an agreed value position has already been reached even before deliberation starts.

I do not see much evidence in this volume that either judges or technical experts are more prone to deliberation than the rest of us.

INCREMENTALISM AKA PATH DEPENDENCY

Along another fashionable front, however, this volume is full of evidence. Most of the policymaking presented is incremental or, in the newer jargon, path dependent. Such path dependency is the central theme of the Hacker study. Weaver concludes his study of pension reform by noting that "the wealthy industrialized countries have all built their restructuring reforms on the foundations of their current systems." Cioffi sees some recent convergence in national reforms of corporate governance regulation but also stresses continuing national differences based on differing national starting points. Although Guiraudon believes that global causes may ultimately triumph over institutional differences is her sphere of study, she does chart widely differing responses to those causes in the United States and the European Union. Indeed, the model set out in Levin's introduction is essentially one of path dependency with similar transatlantic causes fed through differing national policymaking processes and policy starting points to arrive at somewhat convergent but distinctly differing effects.

The so-called new institutionalism has two wings, rational choice on the one hand and those who stress the centrality of particular institutional arrangements on the other. They are united in their assertion that rules of the game importantly constrain policy making. Both wings in turn have optimistic cohorts who wish to see rule-bound, path-dependent play leading, ultimately at least, to better public policy. Ultimately, however, as the saying goes, we will all be dead. In the shorter run described in this volume, do policy decisions constrained by the paths of earlier policy and the rules of the present policymaking game produce better policy outcomes? Vogel's chapter notes a certain environmental policy hiatus in the United States, although, as Keleman notes, some of this can be characterized as better second thoughts. Cioffi notes a similar U.S. sluggishness in corporate governance regulation. Hacker emphasizes policy drift. Sheingate notes some marked successes in UK administrative reform, but also French failure. Guiraudon notes mixes of pro- and anti-immigration policy change on both sides of the Atlantic, mixes that would be hard to characterize as advances or failures. As noted earlier, the overall picture seems to be one of scattered and very incomplete successes along with much drift and some failure. It is not so much a matter of the glass being half full or half empty as of somewhat befuddled bartenders.

Nor do the studies in this volume lead to clear-cut, general conclusions about the influence of partisan electoral competition on public policy. Nearly all the contributions note the kinds of credit claiming and blame avoidance characteristic of electoral competition for the marginal voter. Much of the drift encountered may well be the result of the difficulty of finding policy outcomes that effectively respond to the real-world situation without offending crucial segments of the electorate. Moreover, when the voters themselves are aware that something must be done but shy away from the costs of doing it, elections can hardly dictate particular policies to elected politicians, although their fear of elections may be a significant motivator of their behavior. I, at least, cannot see in these studies any general propensity of left party–dominated governments to do either better or worse than rightist governments at retrenchment or de- or reregulation. Delicately balanced cabinet coalitions or cohabitation may account for some of the drift encountered, but there was also drift under governments firmly in the saddle.

What is clear, however, is that if we are to reach conclusions about whether policymaking in the transatlantic democracies is pluralist or deliberative, or rationally, institutionally, electorally, or globally driven, those conclusions will have to be based on the accumulation of relatively detailed, relatively short-term comparative studies of the politics of policymaking such as those presented here. This is the data against which our positive and normative theories of political decision making will have to be tested.

In both this volume and its predecessor, *Seeking the Center*, the move toward markets has been a leitmotif composed of such notes as privatization, deregulation, free trade, and even the dominance of private-sector decision making through the drift or default of public decision making. Yet, as was noted in *Seeking the Center*, the move toward markets was inspired less by a love of capitalism than by universal acknowledgment of the failures of socialism. And the attraction of markets was tempered by acute concerns about fairness to and rights of individuals and about equality. The newest transatlantic phenomenon is corporate corruption on a grand scale, a corruption that links the nations of Eastern Europe dismantling socialism, the privatizing states of Western Europe, and the United States pursuing deregulation. Trust in markets erodes as trust in the corporate players in those markets erodes. At the same time, persisting problems of unemployment in the developed states and of poverty in the developing—often not developing—ones has eroded what was, for a time, a remarkable consensus on the glories of global free trade. Hardly anyone denies the benefits of such trade, but its costs increasingly are claiming center stage.

And while all this is going on transatlantically, there has come to be an increasing suspicion, at least in the United States, that seeking the policy center and wooing the marginal, centrist voter may not always be the route to electoral success. With notably low U.S. voter turnouts, a new prescription is clearly on offer. Look for policies that energize your party's core voters to come out and vote, even at the cost of losing some centrist marginal voters. This new prescription is asymmetric in the United States in terms of market policies. It suggests that Democrats ought to move toward espousal of policies of economic equality, of more market tempering and tampering. But it tends to suggest that Republicans move along an entirely different vector, to concentrate on social rather than economic issues, the famous family values. Nevertheless, if Democrats react against markets, Republicans must perforce in some way react to that reaction.

The issues surrounding the constrained welfare state are not going to go away either in the United States or in Europe. To some degree, of course, as we have insisted in this and the previous volume, those issues are closely intertwined with marketization because welfare is both one mode of ameliorating market-generated costs and inequalities and a factor determining market efficiency. If in the United States there is a return to traditional liberal Democratic Party appeals, that return will combine calls for welfare enhancement and for greater public regulation of markets. Yet, even apart from welfare questions, American politics over the next decade is likely to involve a significant critical reexamination of the gospels of the market. A similar exercise will no doubt go on in Europe as well, but in the markedly different context of the accession of the new, economically weaker, members.

NOTE

1. Marc Landy and Martin Levin, eds., *The New Politics of Public Policy* (Baltimore: Johns Hopkins University Press, 1996); Martin A. Levin, Mark K. Landy, and Martin Shapiro, eds., *Seeking the Center: Politics and Policymaking at the New Century* (Washington, DC: Georgetown University Press, 2001).

CONTRIBUTORS

THOMAS F. BURKE is associate professor of political science at Wellesley College. His book, *Lawyers, Lawsuits and Legal Rights: The Struggle over Litigation in American Society* (University of California Press, 2002), is based on his dissertation, which won the Edwin S. Corwin award for best dissertation in public law and the Western Political Science Association's award for best dissertation in political science. Burke has published articles on campaign finance law, the Americans with Disabilities Act, and the politics of rights. He is the coauthor, with Lief Carter, of *Reason in Law,* 7th ed. (Longman, 2004), a textbook on legal reasoning.

JOHN W. CIOFFI is an assistant professor of political science at the University of California, Riverside. He teaches public law and writes on the relationships between comparative law, regulation, and political economy. His ongoing research studies the politics of corporate governance reform in the United States, Germany, and other advanced industrial countries to describe and explain the continued expansion and changing role of the regulatory state in contemporary capitalist societies. His work has been published in a number of journals and edited volumes. Prior to receiving his doctorate in political science from the University of California, Berkeley, he was a law clerk to a federal judge and a practicing attorney.

VIRGINIE GUIRAUDON is a permanent research fellow at the National Center for Scientific Research (CNRS) in Lille, France. She holds a Ph.D. in government from Harvard University, where she focused on explaining the evolution of the rights granted to foreigners in France, Germany, and The Netherlands since 1974. She has been a Jean Monnet Fellow at the European University Institute in Florence, a visiting fellow at the Center for International Studies at Princeton University, and a recipient of the Descartes-Huygens Prize. She was also awarded the CNRS bronze medal and the European Union Studies Association best paper prize. Her current research analyzes the shifting of policy competence in the area of migration, asylum, and antidiscrimination to the European Union–level and the delegation of migration control to local, private, and transnational actors. Her articles on these themes have appeared in a number of volumes and journals. She recently coedited *Controlling a New Migration World* (Routledge, 2001).

JACOB S. HACKER is Peter Strauss Family Assistant Professor of Political Science at Yale University and a faculty associate of Yale's Institution for Social and Policy Studies. He is also a fellow at the New America Foundation and was previously a junior fellow of the Harvard Society of Fellows and a guest scholar and research fellow at the Brookings Institution. A political scientist who studies health and social policy, he is the author of numerous articles and two books: *The Road to Nowhere: The Genesis of President Clinton's Plan for Health Security* (Princeton University Press, 1997), which was cowinner of the 1997 Louis Brownlow Book Award of the National Academy of Public Administration; and *The Divided Welfare State: The Battle over Public and Private Social Benefits in the United States* (Cambridge University Press, 2002), which, as a dissertation, received prizes from the American Political Science Association, the Association of Public Policy Analysis and Management, and the National Academy of Social Insurance. He is currently writing a book with Paul Pierson about the Bush tax cuts and American democracy, as well as a book on the politics of economic insecurity in the United States.

R. DANIEL KELEMEN is university lecturer in the Department of Politics and International Relations, and politics fellow at Lincoln College, University of Oxford. His research focuses on European Union politics, comparative political economy, and environmental policy. He is author of *The Rules of Federalism: Institutions and Regulatory Politics in the EU and Beyond* (Harvard University Press, 2004) and recent articles in *International Organization, Comparative Political Studies, West European Politics,* and the *Journal of Public Policy.*

MARTIN A. LEVIN is professor of political science at Brandeis University. He is the author of *The Political Hand: Policy Implementation and Youth Employment Programs* (Pergamon Press, 1985), *Urban Politics and the Criminal Courts* (University of Chicago Press, 1977); coauthor of *After the Cure: Managing AIDS and Other Health Public Health Crises* (University Press of Kansas, 2000), and *Making Government Work* (Jossey-Bass, 1994); and coeditor of *The New Politics of Public Policy* (Johns Hopkins University Press, 1995), and *Seeking the Center: Politics and Policymaking at the New Century* (Georgetown University Press, 2001).

JONAH D. LEVY is an associate professor of political science at the University of California, Berkeley. He teaches courses in political economy, social policy, and European politics. Levy is the author of *Tocqueville's Revenge: State, Society, and Economy in Contemporary France* (Harvard University Press 1999) and "Vice into Virtue? Progressive Politics and Welfare Reform in Continental Europe" (*Politics and Society* 1999). Levy's current book projects include *Toward a New Social Liberalism: Combining Compassion and Competitiveness in Western Europe,* and, as editor, *The State after Statism: New State Activities in the Age of Globalization and Liberalization.*

MARTIN SHAPIRO is Coffroth Professor of Law at the University of California and teaches in the Jurisprudence and Social Policy Program. He is a political scientist who has taught at Harvard, U.C. Berkeley, and U.C. San Diego. He is the author of numerous books and articles on law and politics in the United States and Europe. His most recent book, with Alec Stone Sweet, is *On Law, Politics, and Judicialization* (Oxford University Press, 2002).

ADAM D. SHEINGATE is an assistant professor of political science at The Johns Hopkins University, where he teaches American politics and comparative public policy. From 2002 to 2004, he was a Robert Wood Johnson Foundation Scholar in Health Policy Research at the University of California, Berkeley. He is the author of *The Rise of the Agricultural Welfare State: Institutions and Interest Group Power in the United States, France, and Japan* (Princeton University Press, 2001).

DAVID VOGEL is a professor in the Haas School of Business and the Department of Political Science at the University of California, Berkeley. He has written extensively on comparative business–government relations and environmental politics and policy. Vogel's books include *National Styles of Regulation: Environmental Policy in Great Britain and the United States*

(Cornell University Press, 1986), *Fluctuating Fortunes: The Political Power of Business in America* (Beard Books, 2003), *Kindred Strangers: The Uneasy Relationship between Politics and Business* (Princeton University Press, 1996), and *Trading Up: Consumer and Environmental Regulation in a Global Economy* (Harvard University Press, 1995).

R. KENT WEAVER is professor of public policy and government at Georgetown University and a senior fellow in the Governance Studies Program at the Brookings Institution. His major fields of research are American and comparative social policy and comparative political institutions. He is the author of *Ending Welfare as We Know It* (Brookings, 2000), *Automatic Government: The Politics of Indexation* (Brookings, 1988), and *The Politics of Industrial Change* (Brookings, 1985), and of many journal articles and book chapters on social policy. He is coeditor, with Leslie Pal, of *The Government Taketh Away: The Politics of Pain in the United States and Canada* (Georgetown University Press, 2003). He is currently completing a book on what the United States can learn from the experiences of other advanced industrial countries in reforming their public pension systems, and writing another book on implementation of welfare reform in the United States.

INDEX